SHONEN JUMP MANGA EDITION

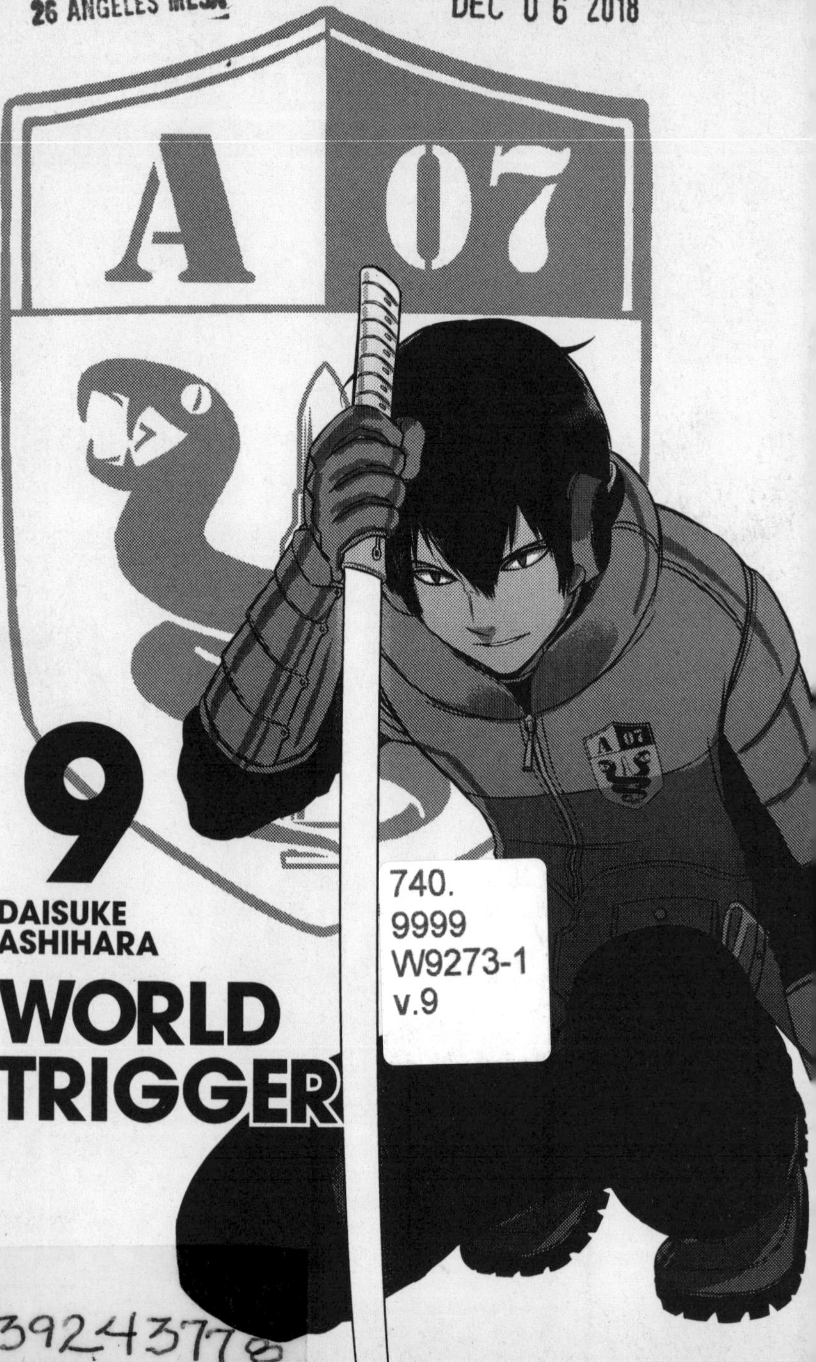
A 07

9

DAISUKE ASHIHARA

WORLD TRIGGER

WORLD TRIGGER DATA BASE

on NEIGHBOR

nvaders from another dimension that enter Mikado City through Gates. Most "Neighbors" here are Trion soldiers built for war. The Neighbors who actually live on the other side of the Gates are human, like Yuma.

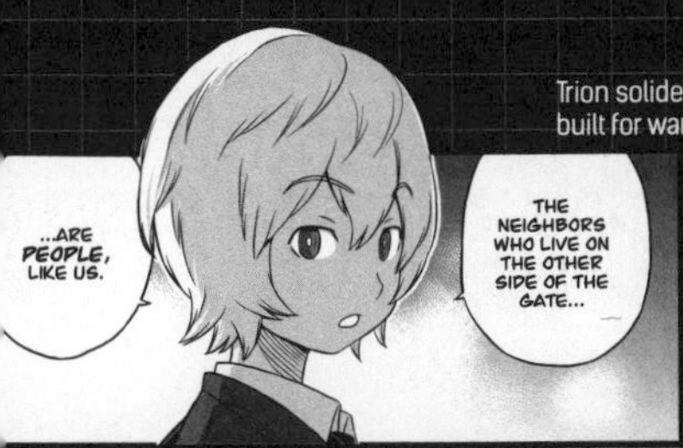
THE NEIGHBORS WHO LIVE ON THE OTHER SIDE OF THE GATE...
...ARE PEOPLE, LIKE US.

Trion solider built for war. ▸

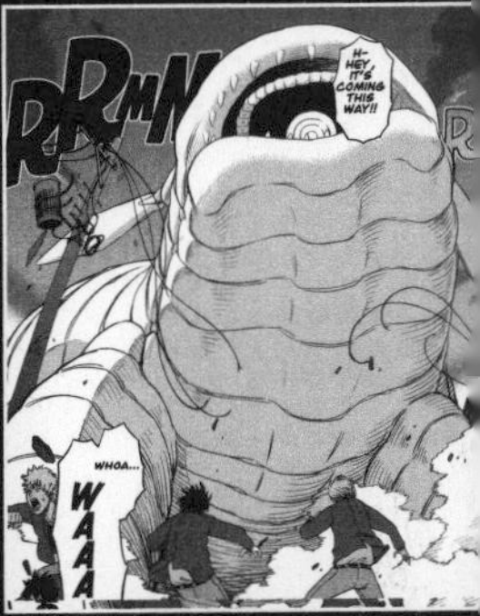
H-HEY, IT'S COMING THIS WAY!!
WHOA...
WAAAA

AFTOKRATOR

he largest military nation in the Neighbor world, eported to have seven Black Triggers 13 years ago. They are invading Earth to kidnap people with Trion abilities.

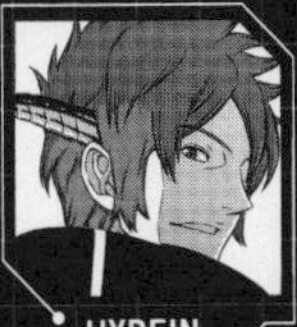

HYREIN

Uses the Black Trigger Alektor that turns people into cubes. Fighting Izumi.

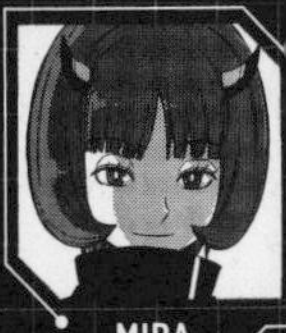

MIRA

Uses a Trigger that makes wormholes. She has black horns so she's likely a Black Trigger user.

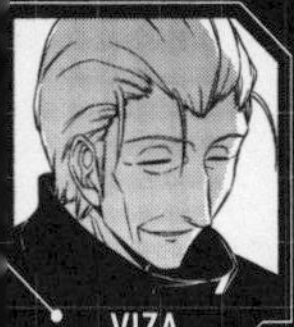

VIZA

Uses Aftokrator's national treasure Organon. Fighting Yuma.

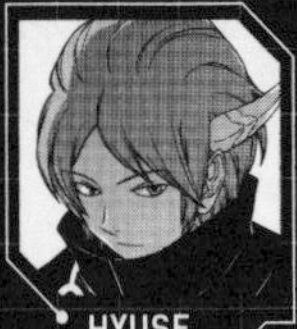

HYUSE

Uses magnetized shards called Lambiris. Fighting Jin.

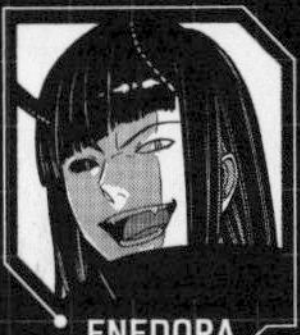

ENEDORA

Uses the Black Trigger Borboros. It liquefies his body. Attacking Border HQ.

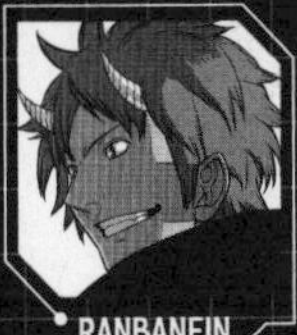

RANBANEIN

Uses the shooting Trigger Keridon. Lost to Izumi, Yoneya and Midorikawa.

Horns

Aftokrator produces humans with exceptional Trion abilities by implanting Trigger-equipped Trion receptors into their heads. A horned person's fighting abilities far exceed those of a normal Trigger user's. Some horns are compatible with Black Triggers, which turns the horns black.

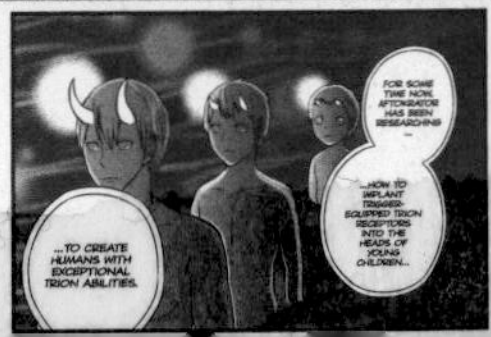
FOR SOME TIME NOW, AFTOKRATOR HAS BEEN RESEARCHING...
...HOW TO IMPLANT TRIGGER-EQUIPPED TRION RECEPTORS INTO THE HEADS OF YOUNG CHILDREN...
...TO CREATE HUMANS WITH EXCEPTIONAL TRION ABILITIES.

BORDER

An agency founded to protect the city's peace from Neighbors. Agents are classified as follows: C-Rank for trainees, B-Rank for main forces, A-Rank for elites and S-Rank for those with Black Triggers. A-Rank squads get to go on away missions to Neighbor worlds.

Resistance

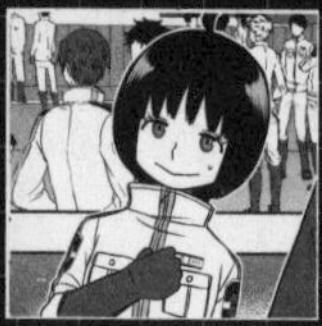

C-Rank: Chika

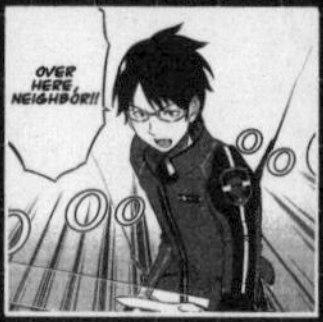
OVER HERE, NEIGHBOR!!

B-Rank: Osamu

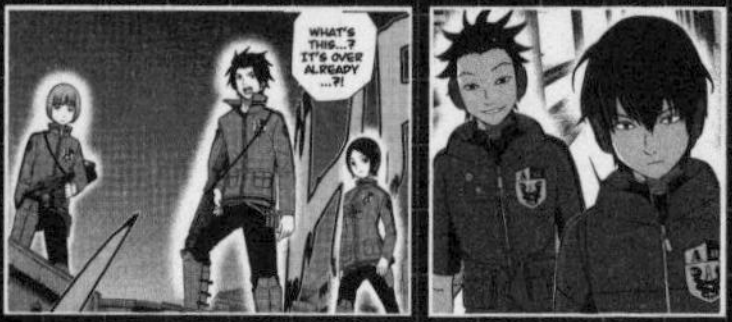
WHAT'S THIS...? IT'S OVER ALREADY...?!

A-Rank: Arashiyama Squad, Miwa Squad

Trigger

A technology created by Neighbors to manipulate Trion. Used mainly as weapons, Triggers come in various types. Border classifies them into three groups: Attacker, Gunner, and Sniper.

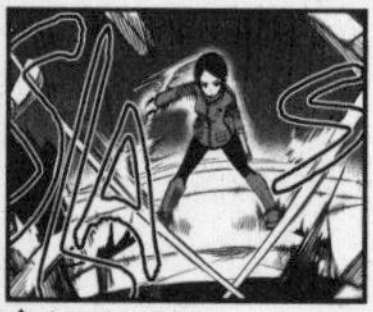

▲ Attacker Trigger

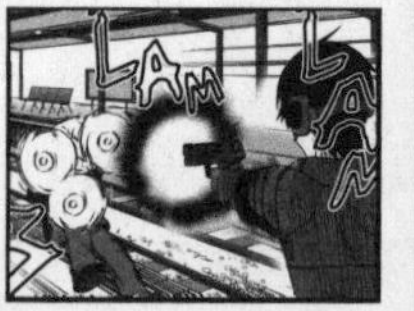

▲ Gunner Trigger

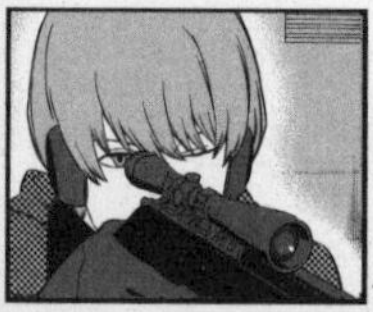

◀ Sniper Trigger

Black Trigger

A special Trigger created when a skilled user pours their entire life force and Trion into a Trigger. Outperforms regular Triggers, but the user must be compatible with the personality of the creator, meaning only a few people can use any given Black Trigger.

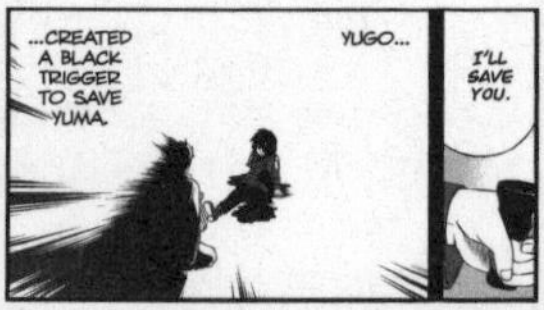
I'LL SAVE YOU.
YUGO...
...CREATED A BLACK TRIGGER TO SAVE YUMA.

▲ Yuma's father Yugo sacrificed his life to create a Black Trigger and save Yuma.

STORY

About four years ago, a Gate connecting to another dimension opened in Mikado City, leading to the appearance of invaders called Neighbors. After the establishment of the Border Defense Agency, people were able to return to their normal lives.

Osamu Mikumo is a junior high student who meets Yuma Kuga, a Neighbor. Yuma is targeted for capture by Border, but Tamakoma branch agent Yuichi Jin steps in to help. He convinces Yuma to join Border instead, then gives his Black Trigger to HQ in exchange for Yuma's enlistment. Now Osamu, Yuma and Osamu's friend Chika work toward making A-Rank together.

Another large-scale Neighbor attack on Mikado City begins and the horned appearance of the Neighbors reveals that they are from Aftokrator, the largest military nation in the Neighborhood. In order to capture Chika, the humanoid Neighbors' captain, Hyrein, cubified her and her powerful Trion. It is up to Osamu to carry her to safety! Meanwhile, Director Shinoda faces off against Enedora at HQ...

WORLD TRIGGER CHARACTERS

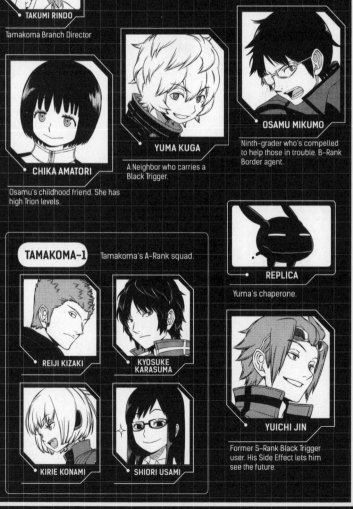

TAMAKOMA BRANCH

Understanding toward Neighbors. Considered divergent from Border's main philosophy.

TAKUMI RINDO

Tamakoma Branch Director

OSAMU MIKUMO

Ninth-grader who's compelled to help those in trouble. B-Rank Border agent.

YUMA KUGA

A Neighbor who carries a Black Trigger.

CHIKA AMATORI

Osamu's childhood friend. She has high Trion levels.

REPLICA

Yuma's chaperone.

YUICHI JIN

Former S-Rank Black Trigger user. His Side Effect lets him see the future.

TAMAKOMA-1

Tamakoma's A-Rank squad.

REIJI KIZAKI

KYOSUKE KARASUMA

KIRIE KONAMI

SHIORI USAMI

BORDER HQ

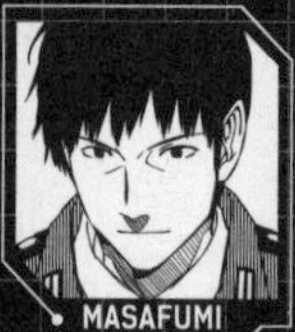

MASAFUMI SHINODA

HQ Director and Defense Force Commander. He is the most powerful among normal Trigger users.

A-RANK AGENTS

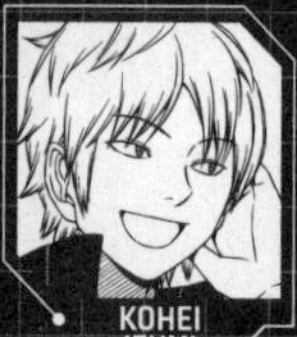

KOHEI IZUMI

A-Rank #1 Tachikawa squad Shooter

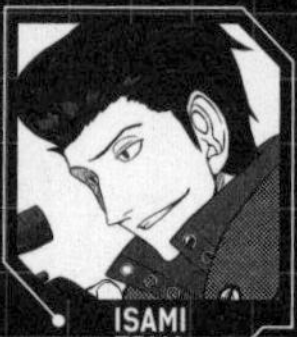

ISAMI TOMA

A-Rank #1 Sniper in A-Rank #2 Fuyushima squad.

MIWA SQUAD

A-Rank #7 squad.
Captain Miwa blames Neighbors for the death of his older sister.

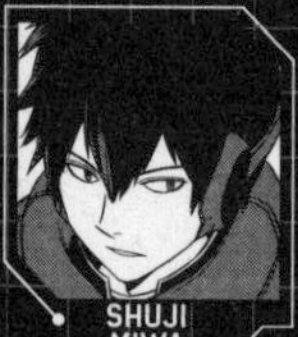

SHUJI MIWA

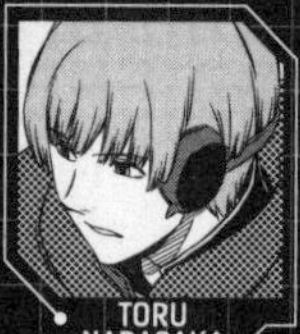

TORU NARASAKA

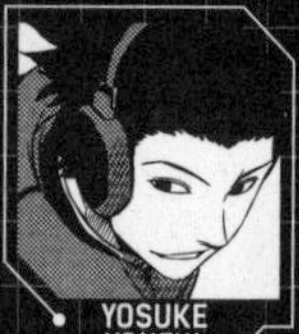

YOSUKE YONEYA

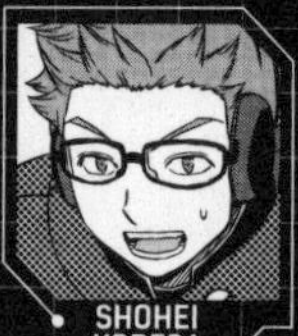

SHOHEI KODERA

KAZAMA SQUAD

A-Rank #3 squad. Captain Kazama bailed out and is unable to fight.

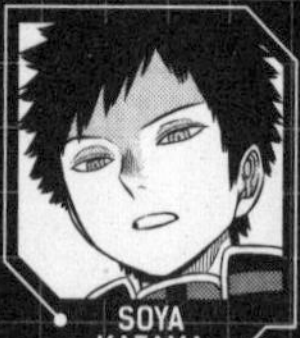

SOYA KAZAMA

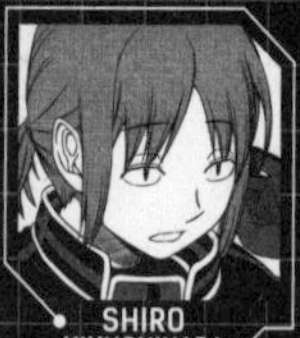

SHIRO KIKUCHIHARA

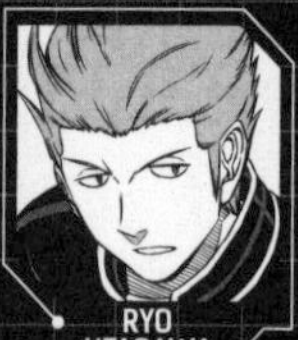

RYO UTAGAWA

B-RANK AGENTS

SUWA SQUAD

B-Rank #10 squad. Fighting Enedora at HQ.

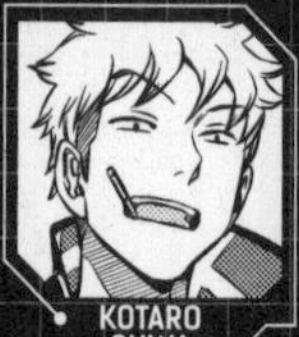

KOTARO SUWA

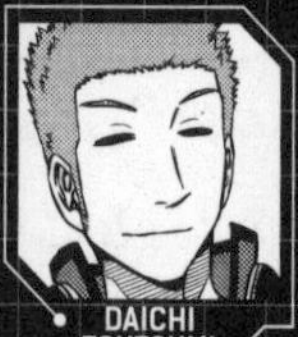

DAICHI TSUTSUMI

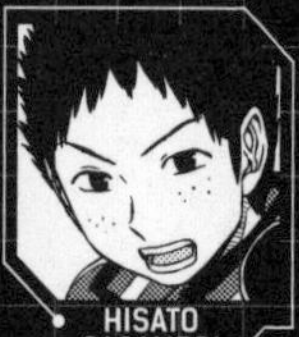

HISATO SASAMORI

WORLD TRIGGER
CONTENTS

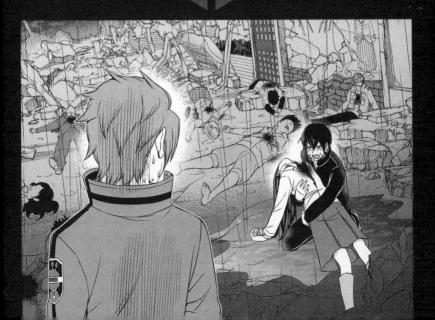

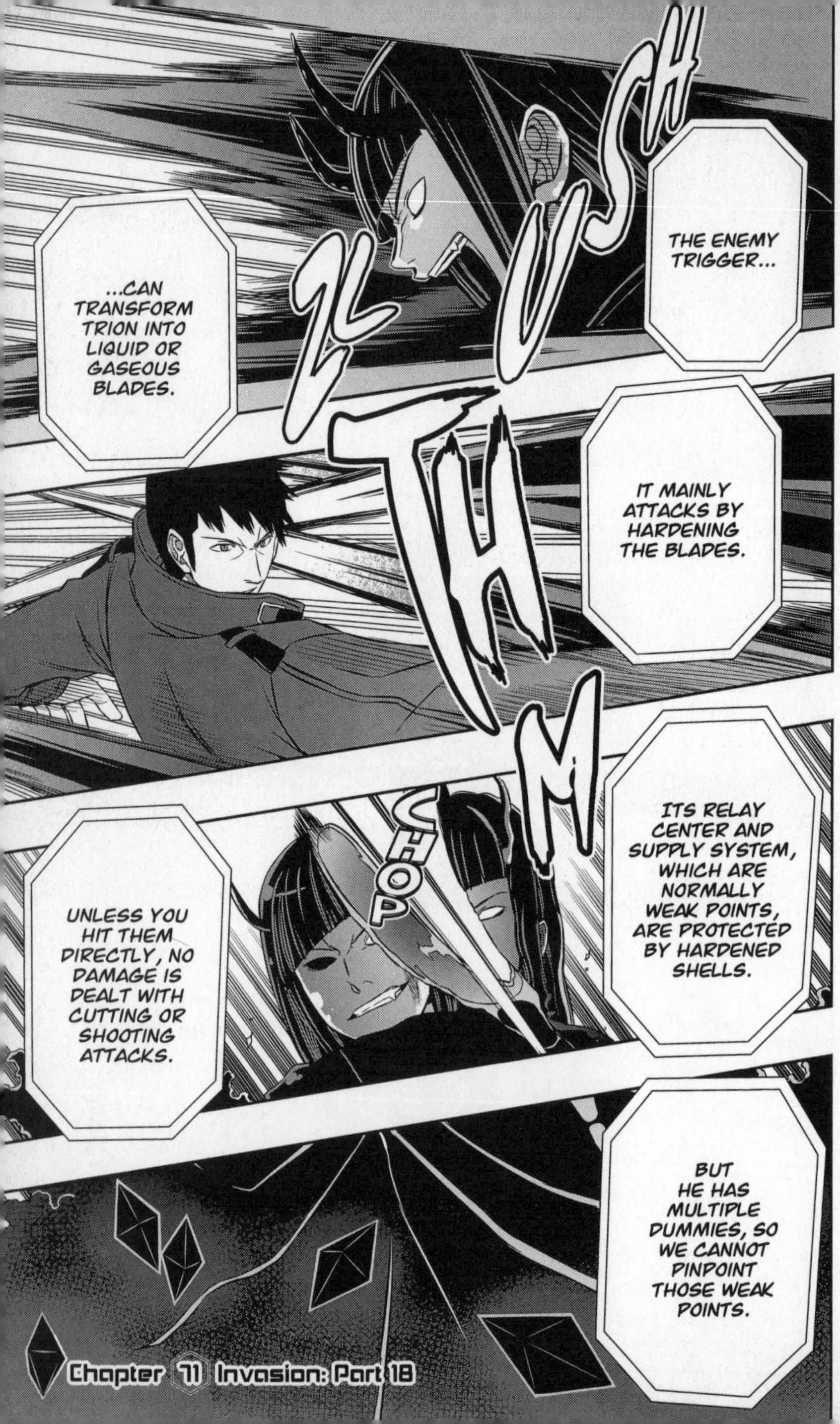
THE ENEMY TRIGGER...
ZUSCH
...CAN TRANSFORM TRION INTO LIQUID OR GASEOUS BLADES.
IT MAINLY ATTACKS BY HARDENING THE BLADES.
THM
ITS RELAY CENTER AND SUPPLY SYSTEM, WHICH ARE NORMALLY WEAK POINTS, ARE PROTECTED BY HARDENED SHELLS.
CHOP
UNLESS YOU HIT THEM DIRECTLY, NO DAMAGE IS DEALT WITH CUTTING OR SHOOTING ATTACKS.
BUT HE HAS MULTIPLE DUMMIES, SO WE CANNOT PINPOINT THOSE WEAK POINTS.
Chapter 71 Invasion: Part 18

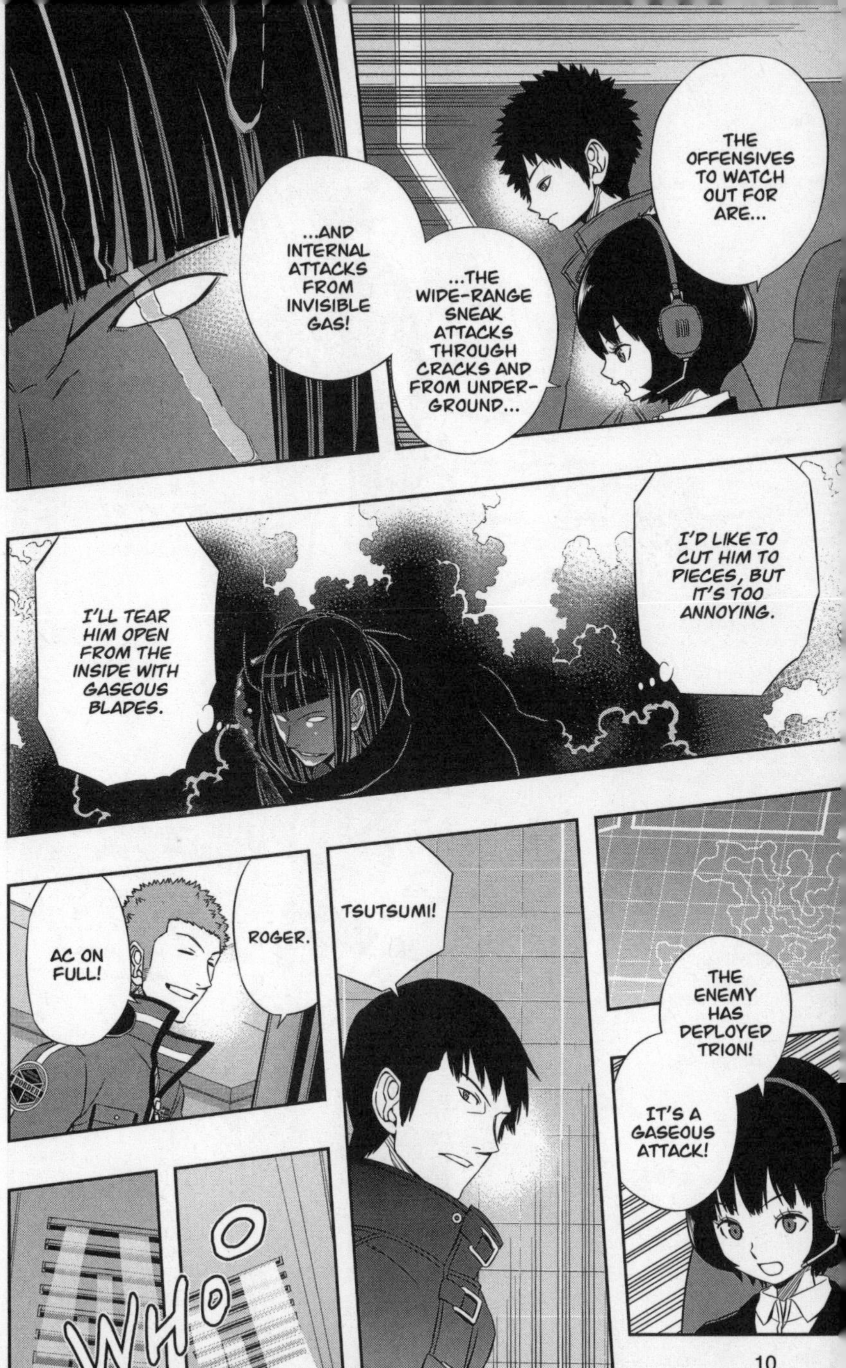
THE OFFENSIVES TO WATCH OUT FOR ARE...
...THE WIDE-RANGE SNEAK ATTACKS THROUGH CRACKS AND FROM UNDER-GROUND...
...AND INTERNAL ATTACKS FROM INVISIBLE GAS!
I'D LIKE TO CUT HIM TO PIECES, BUT IT'S TOO ANNOYING.
I'LL TEAR HIM OPEN FROM THE INSIDE WITH GASEOUS BLADES.
THE ENEMY HAS DEPLOYED TRION!
IT'S A GASEOUS ATTACK!
TSUTSUMI!
ROGER.
AC ON FULL!
WHOO

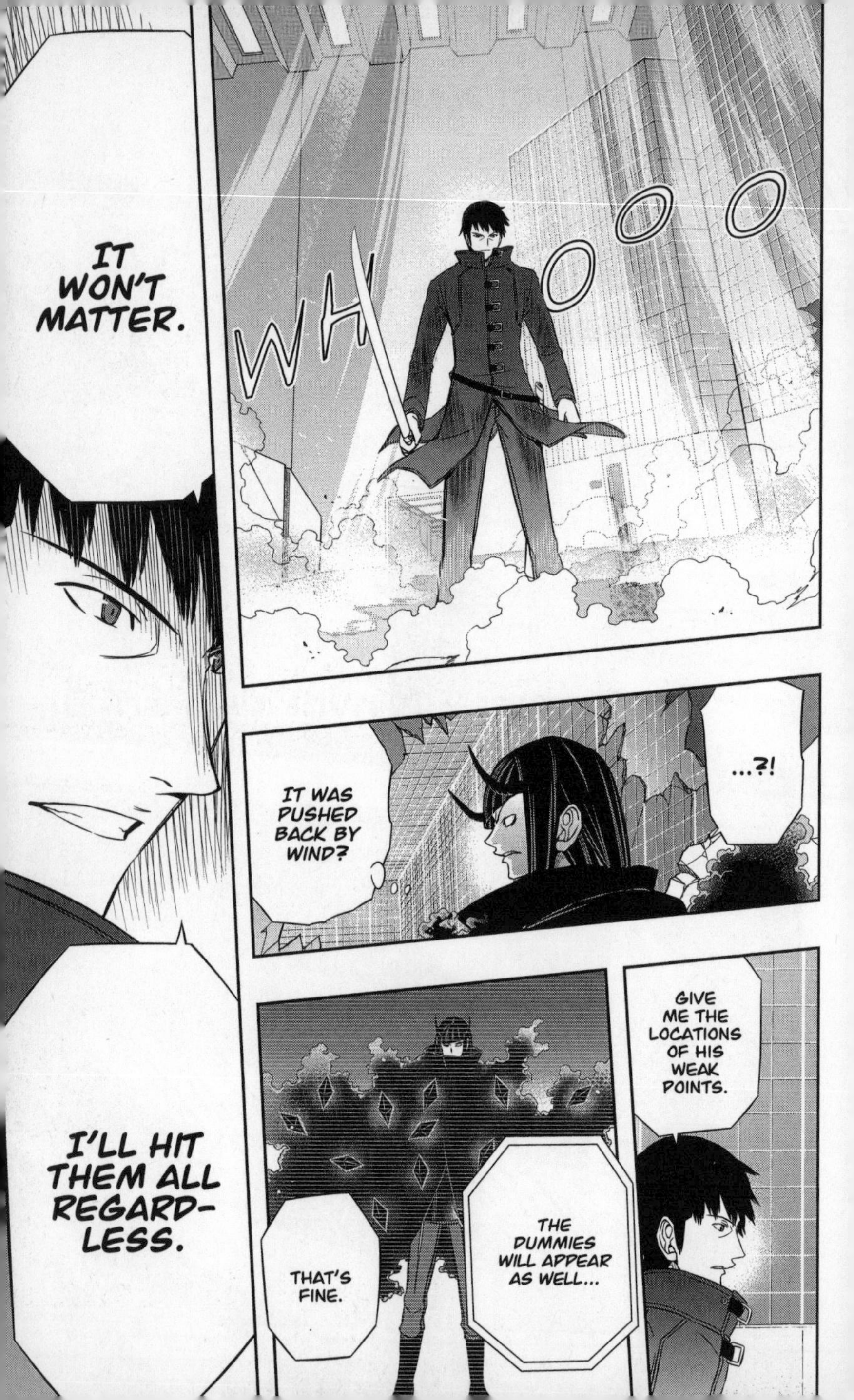
WHOOOO
...?!
IT WAS PUSHED BACK BY WIND?
GIVE ME THE LOCATIONS OF HIS WEAK POINTS.
THE DUMMIES WILL APPEAR AS WELL...
THAT'S FINE.
IT WON'T MATTER.
I'LL HIT THEM ALL REGARD-LESS.

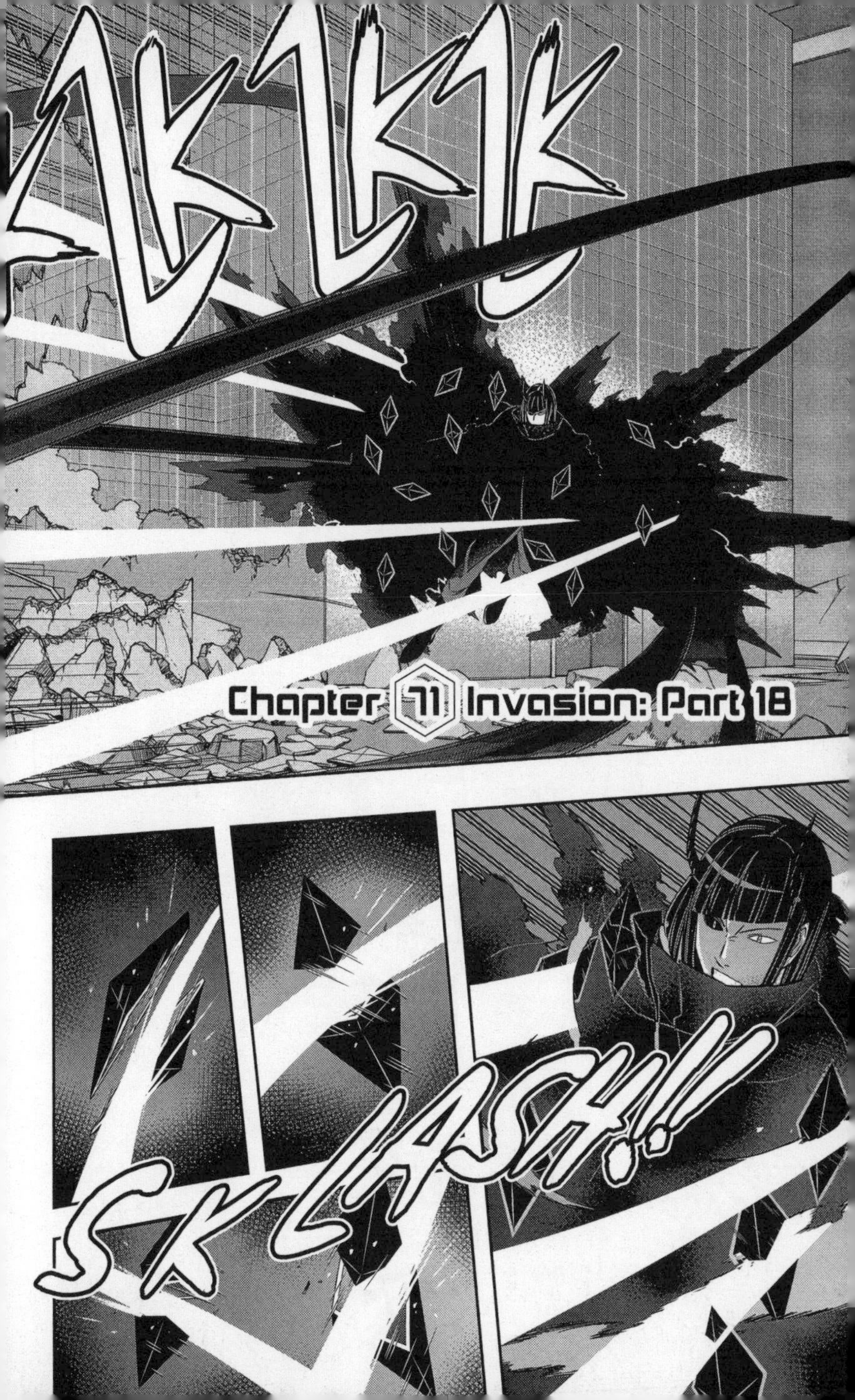
Chapter 71 Invasion: Part 18
SKLASH!!

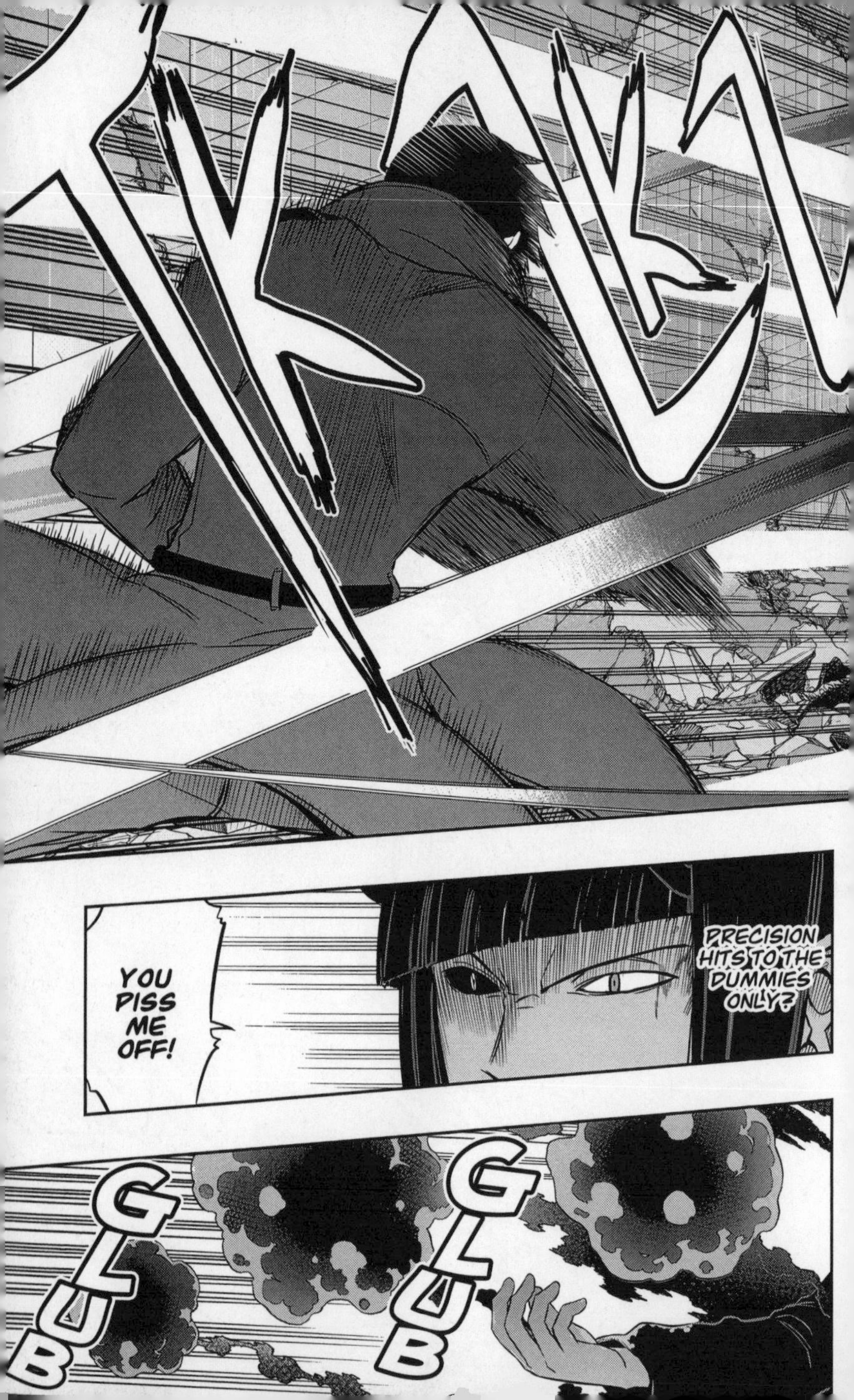
PRECISION HITS TO THE DUMMIES ONLY?
YOU PISS ME OFF!
GLUB
GLUB

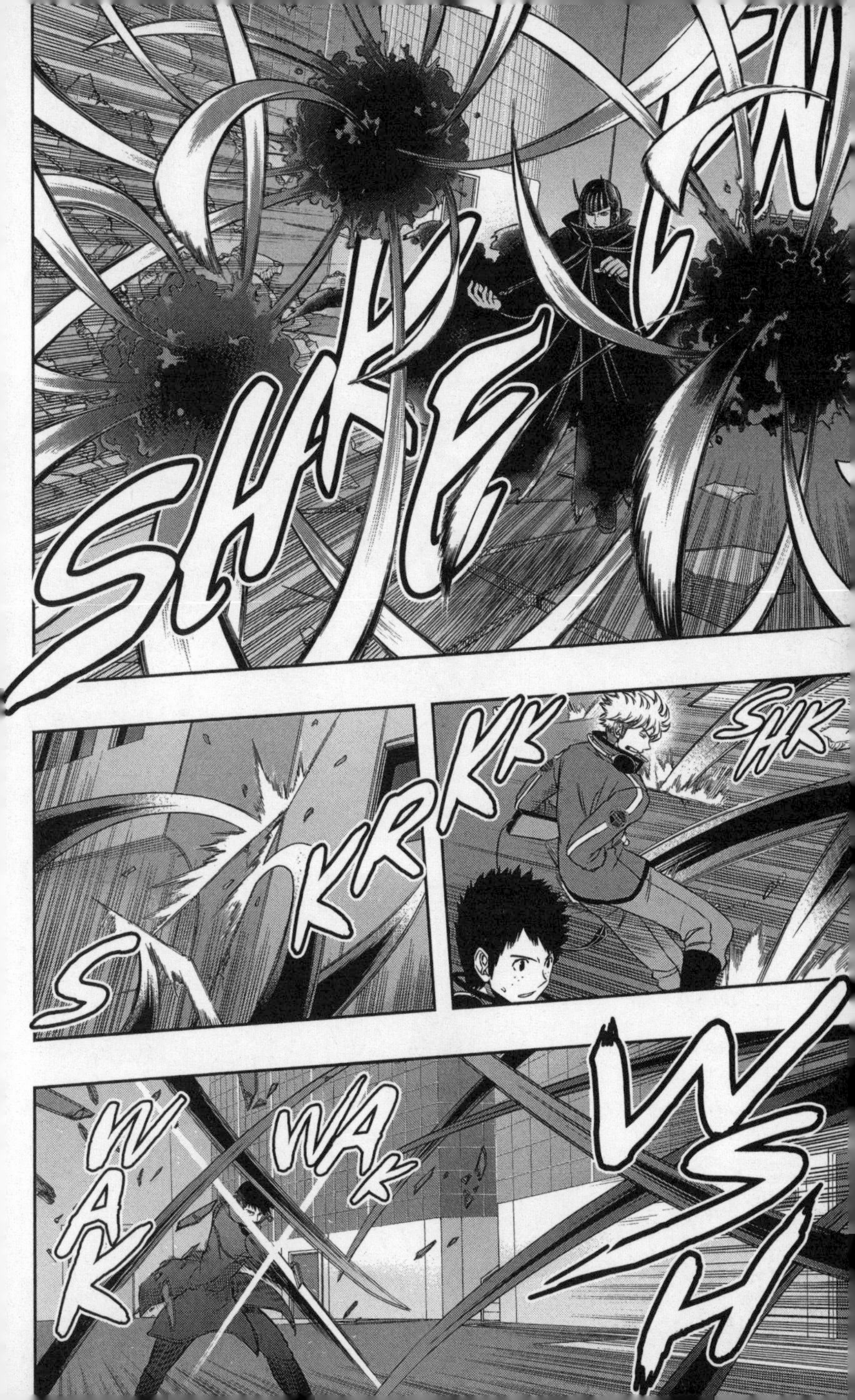
SHK
SKRRKK
WSH
WAK
WAK

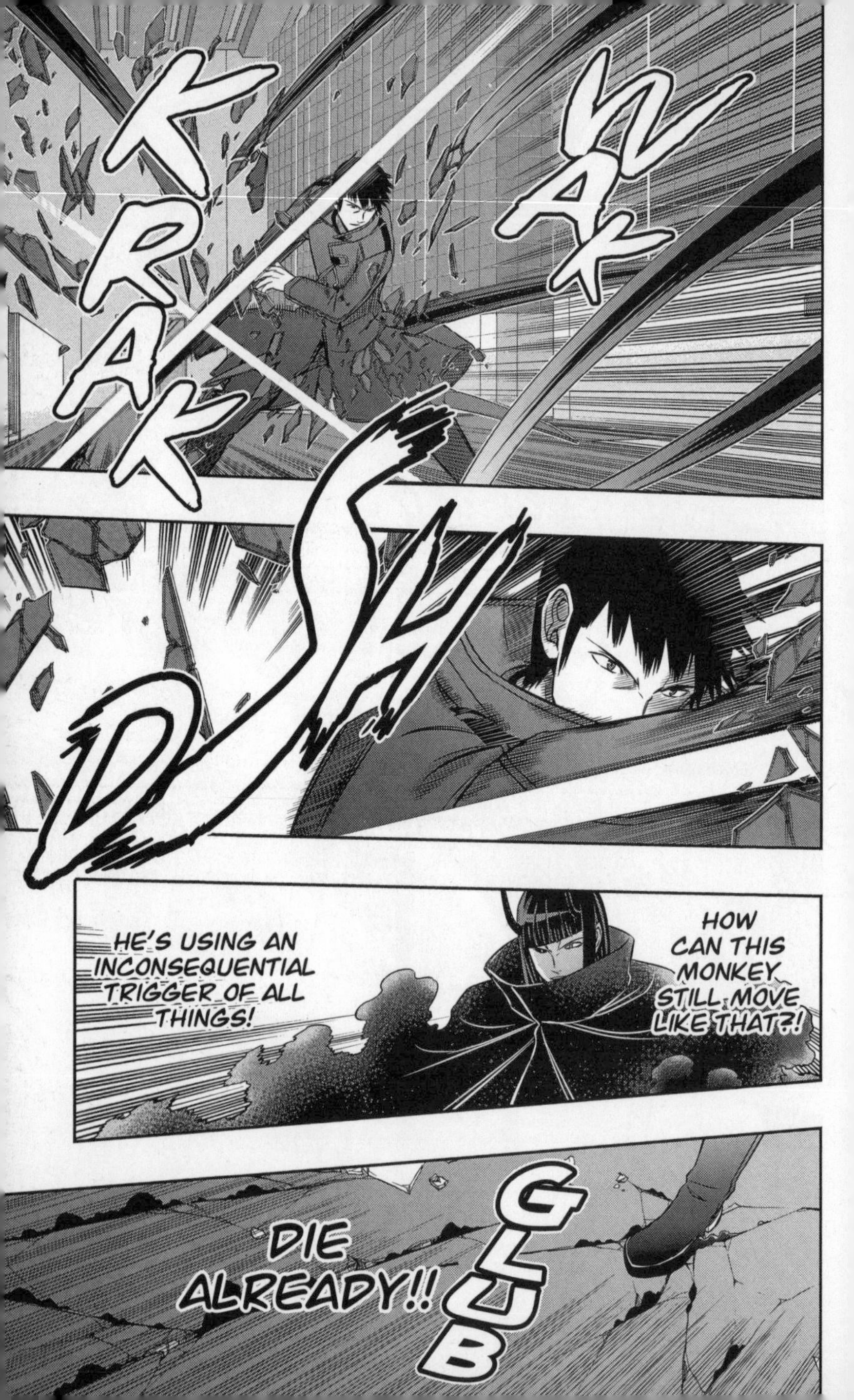
WHAK
KRAK
DSH
HOW CAN THIS MONKEY STILL MOVE LIKE THAT?!
HE'S USING AN INCONSEQUENTIAL TRIGGER OF ALL THINGS!
GLUB
DIE ALREADY!!

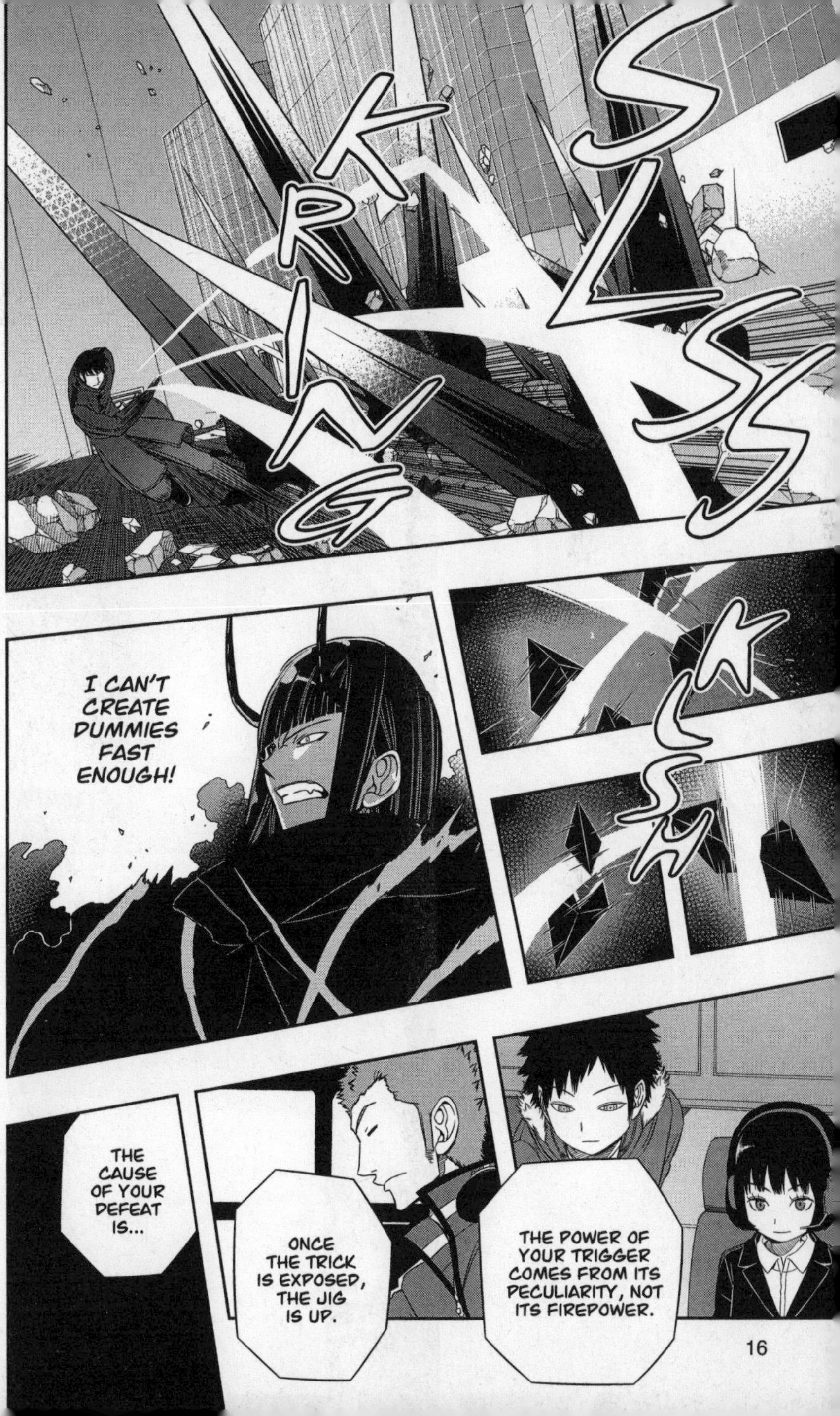
KRING
I CAN'T CREATE DUMMIES FAST ENOUGH!
THE POWER OF YOUR TRIGGER COMES FROM ITS PECULIARITY, NOT ITS FIREPOWER.
ONCE THE TRICK IS EXPOSED, THE JIG IS UP.
THE CAUSE OF YOUR DEFEAT IS...

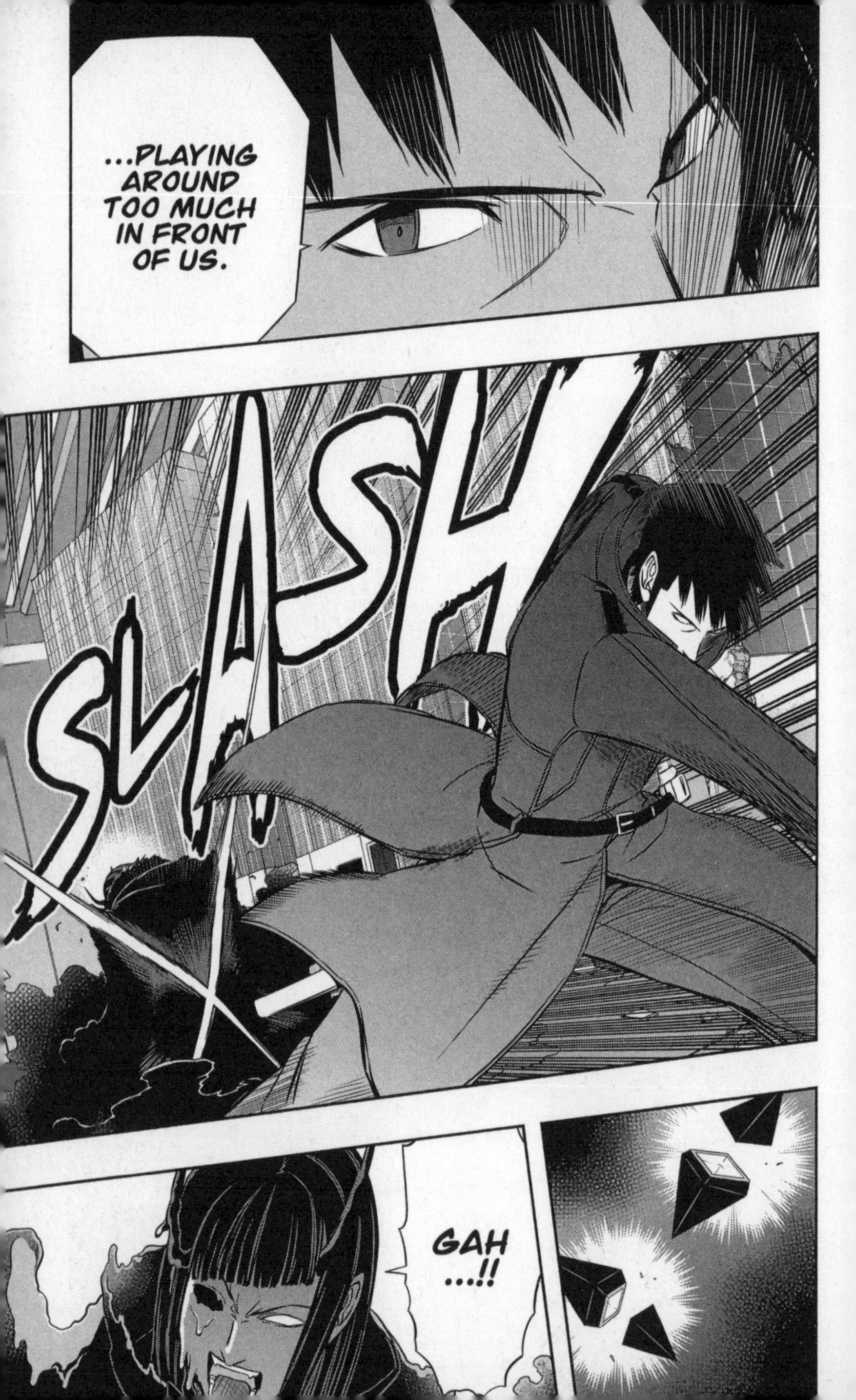
...PLAYING AROUND TOO MUCH IN FRONT OF US.
SLASH
GAH ...!!

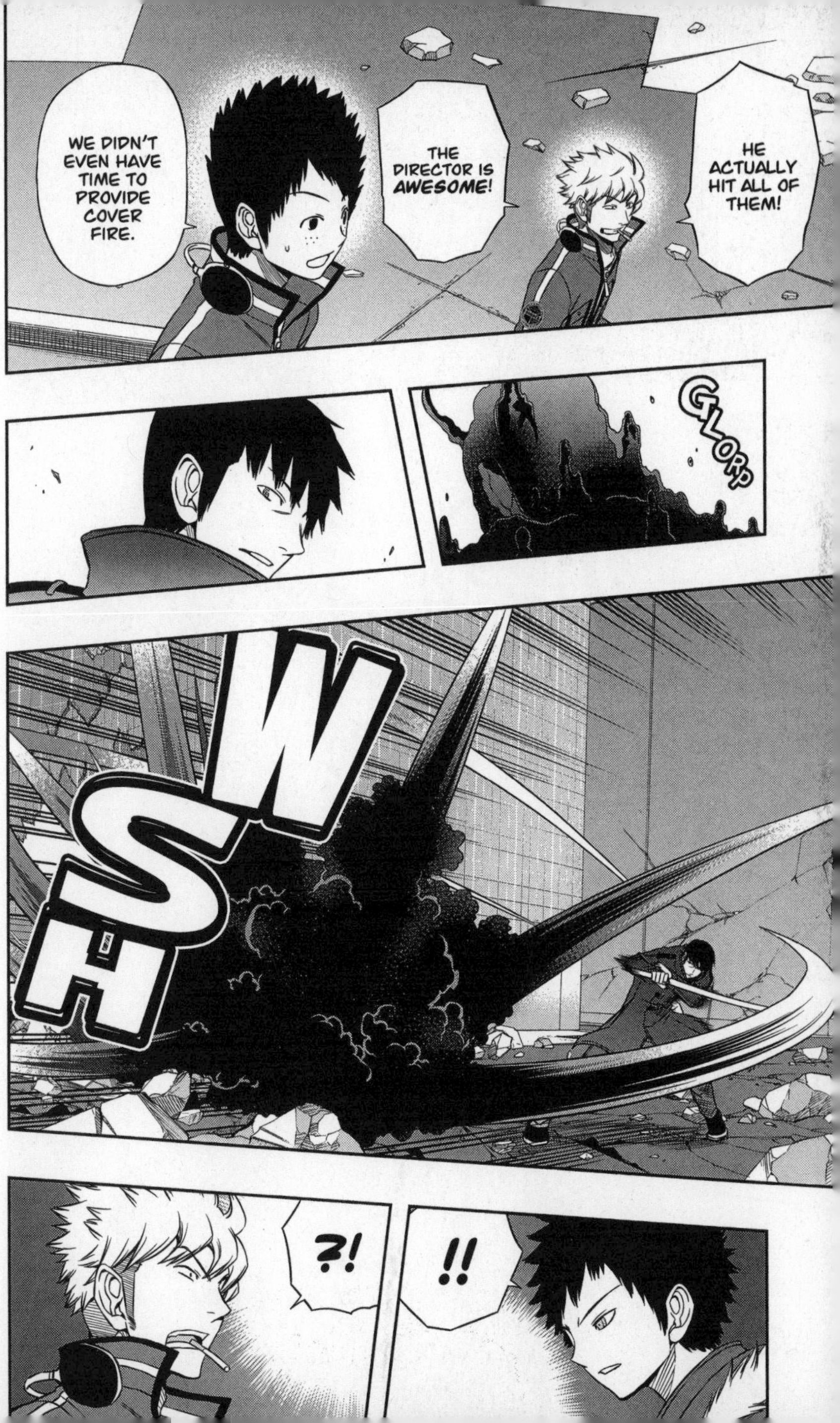
HE ACTUALLY HIT ALL OF THEM!
THE DIRECTOR IS AWESOME!
WE DIDN'T EVEN HAVE TIME TO PROVIDE COVER FIRE.
GLORP
SWSH
!!
?!

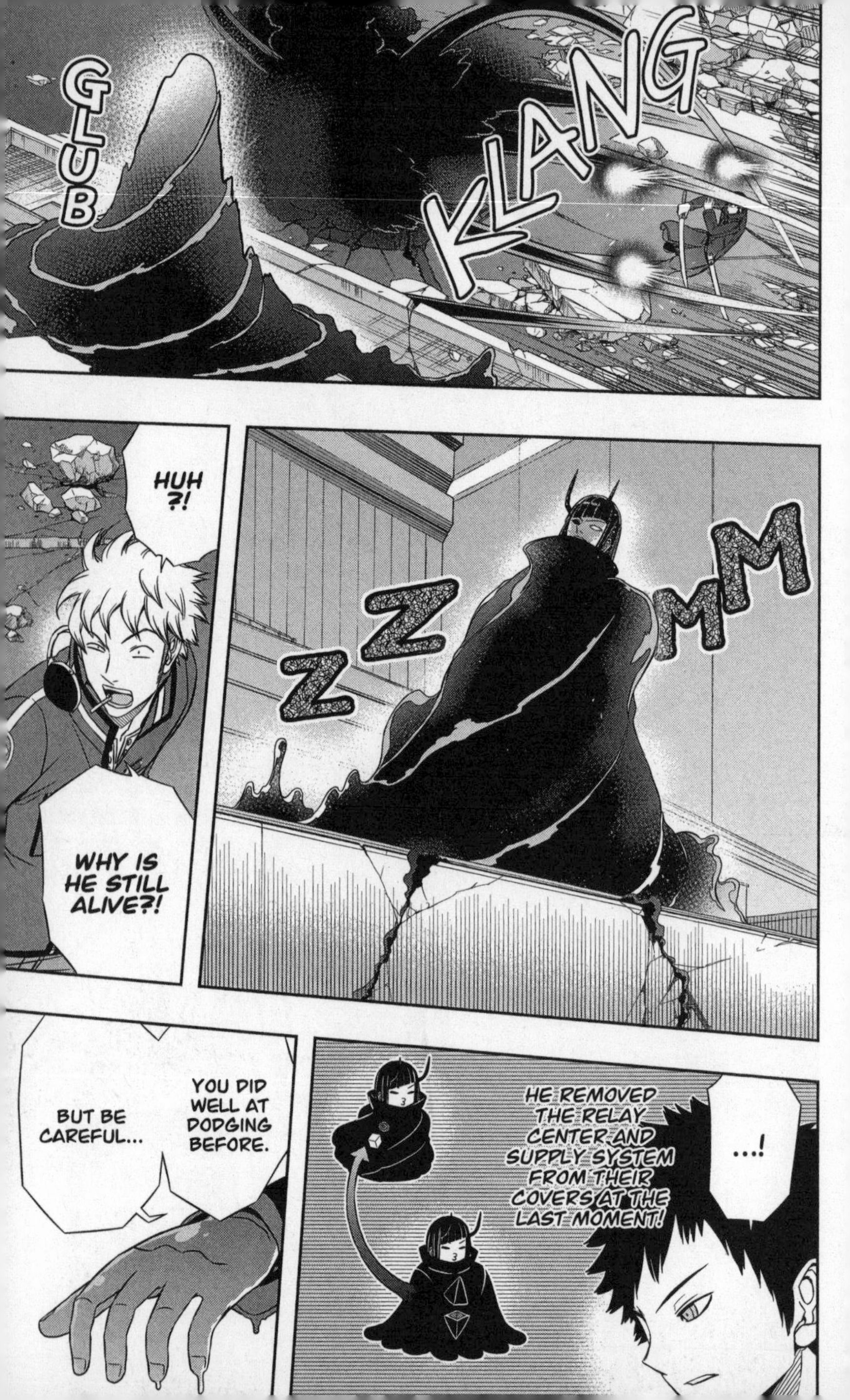
KLANG
GLUB
ZZMMM
HUH?!
WHY IS HE STILL ALIVE?!
...!
HE REMOVED THE RELAY CENTER AND SUPPLY SYSTEM FROM THEIR COVERS AT THE LAST MOMENT!
YOU DID WELL AT DODGING BEFORE.
BUT BE CAREFUL...

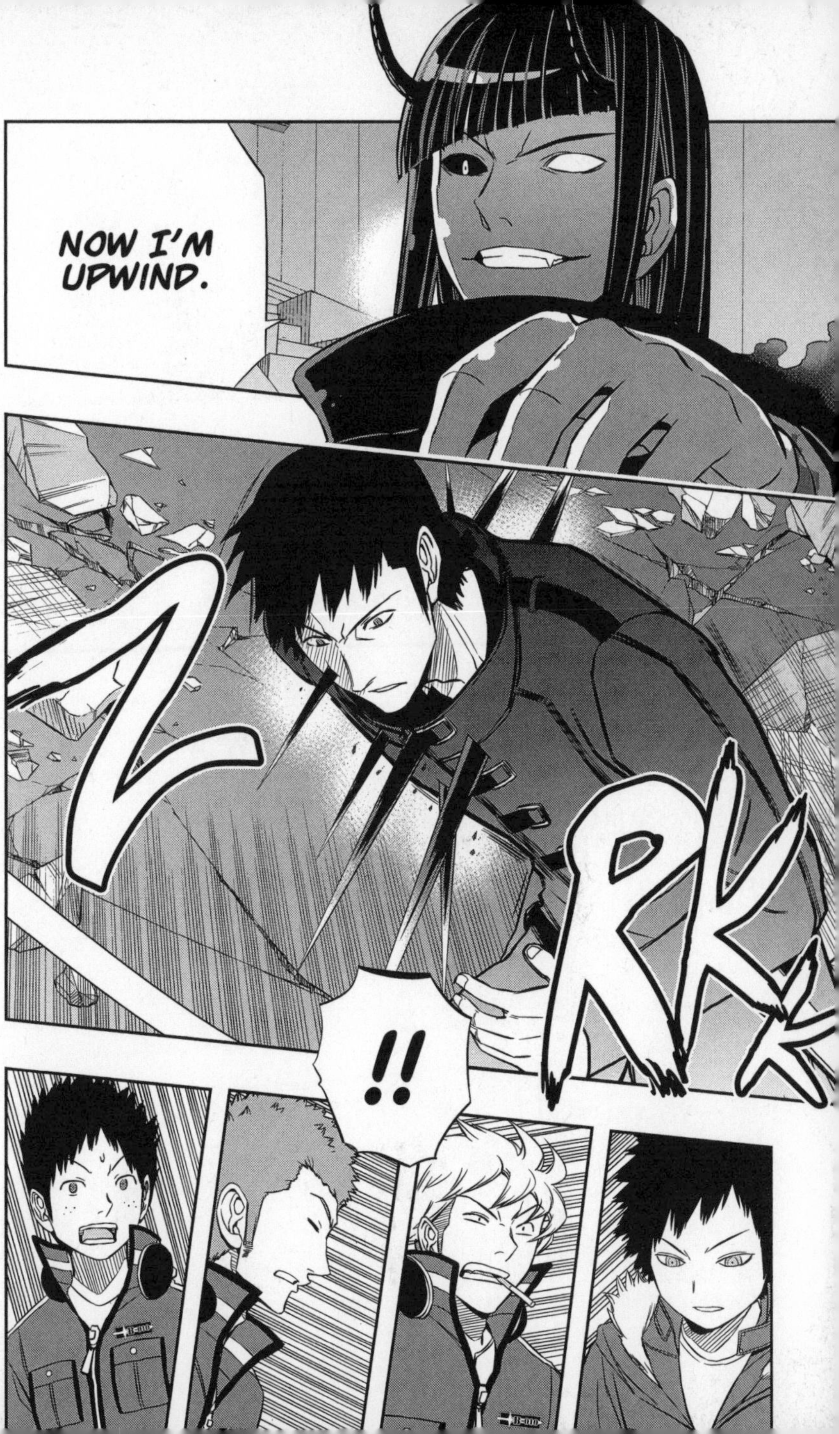
NOW I'M UPWIND.
ZRK
!!

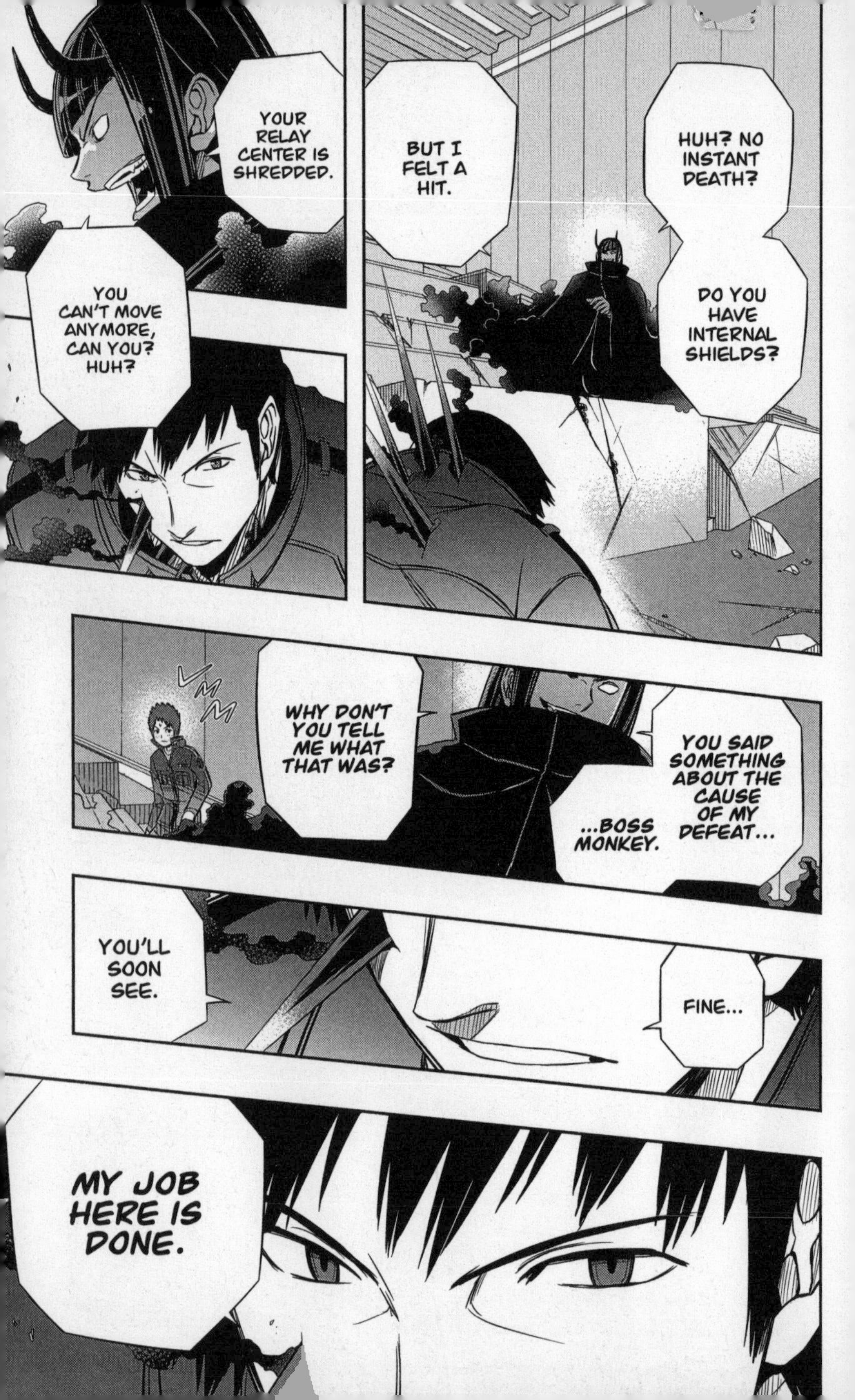
HUH? NO INSTANT DEATH?
DO YOU HAVE INTERNAL SHIELDS?
BUT I FELT A HIT.
YOUR RELAY CENTER IS SHREDDED.
YOU CAN'T MOVE ANYMORE, CAN YOU? HUH?
YOU SAID SOMETHING ABOUT THE CAUSE OF MY DEFEAT...
...BOSS MONKEY.
WHY DON'T YOU TELL ME WHAT THAT WAS?
VMM
FINE...
YOU'LL SOON SEE.
MY JOB HERE IS DONE.

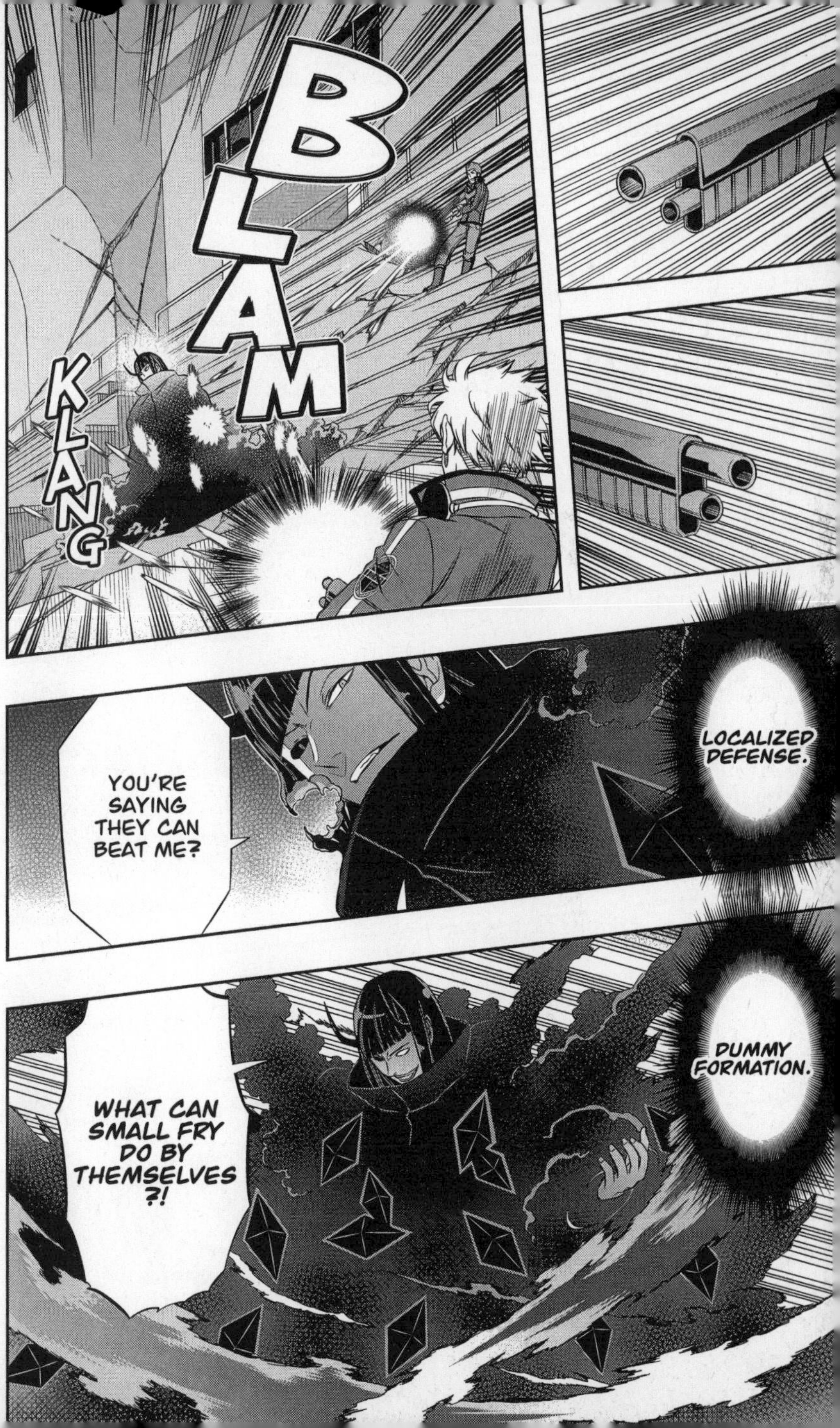
BLAM
KLANG
LOCALIZED DEFENSE.
YOU'RE SAYING THEY CAN BEAT ME?
DUMMY FORMATION.
WHAT CAN SMALL FRY DO BY THEMSELVES ?!

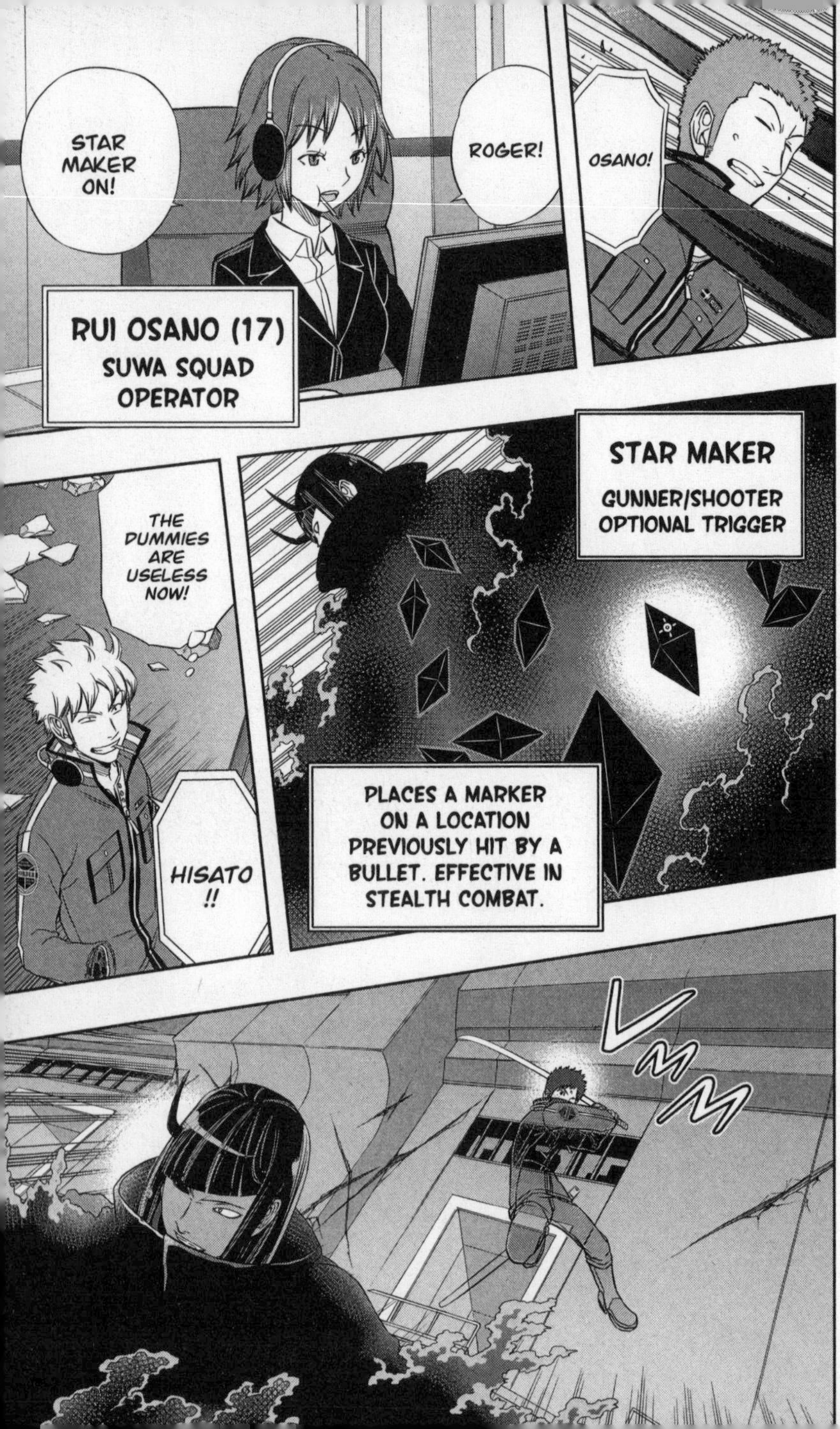
OSANO!
ROGER!
STAR MAKER ON!
RUI OSANO (17) SUWA SQUAD OPERATOR
STAR MAKER
GUNNER/SHOOTER OPTIONAL TRIGGER
PLACES A MARKER ON A LOCATION PREVIOUSLY HIT BY A BULLET. EFFECTIVE IN STEALTH COMBAT.
THE DUMMIES ARE USELESS NOW!
HISATO!!
VMM

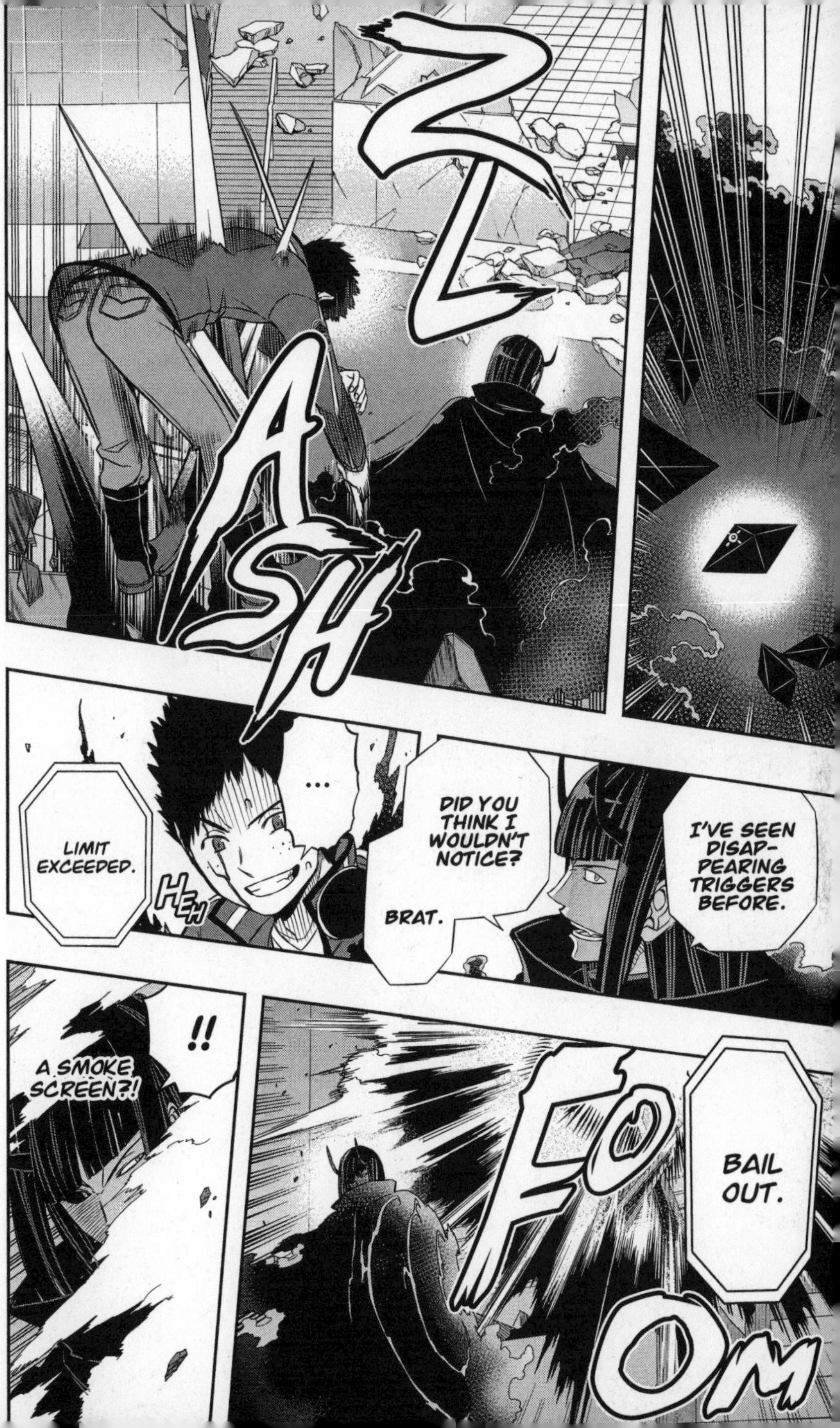
ZZASH
I'VE SEEN DISAP-PEARING TRIGGERS BEFORE.
DID YOU THINK I WOULDN'T NOTICE?
BRAT.
...
LIMIT EXCEEDED.
HEH
BAIL OUT.
FOOM
!!
A SMOKE SCREEN?!

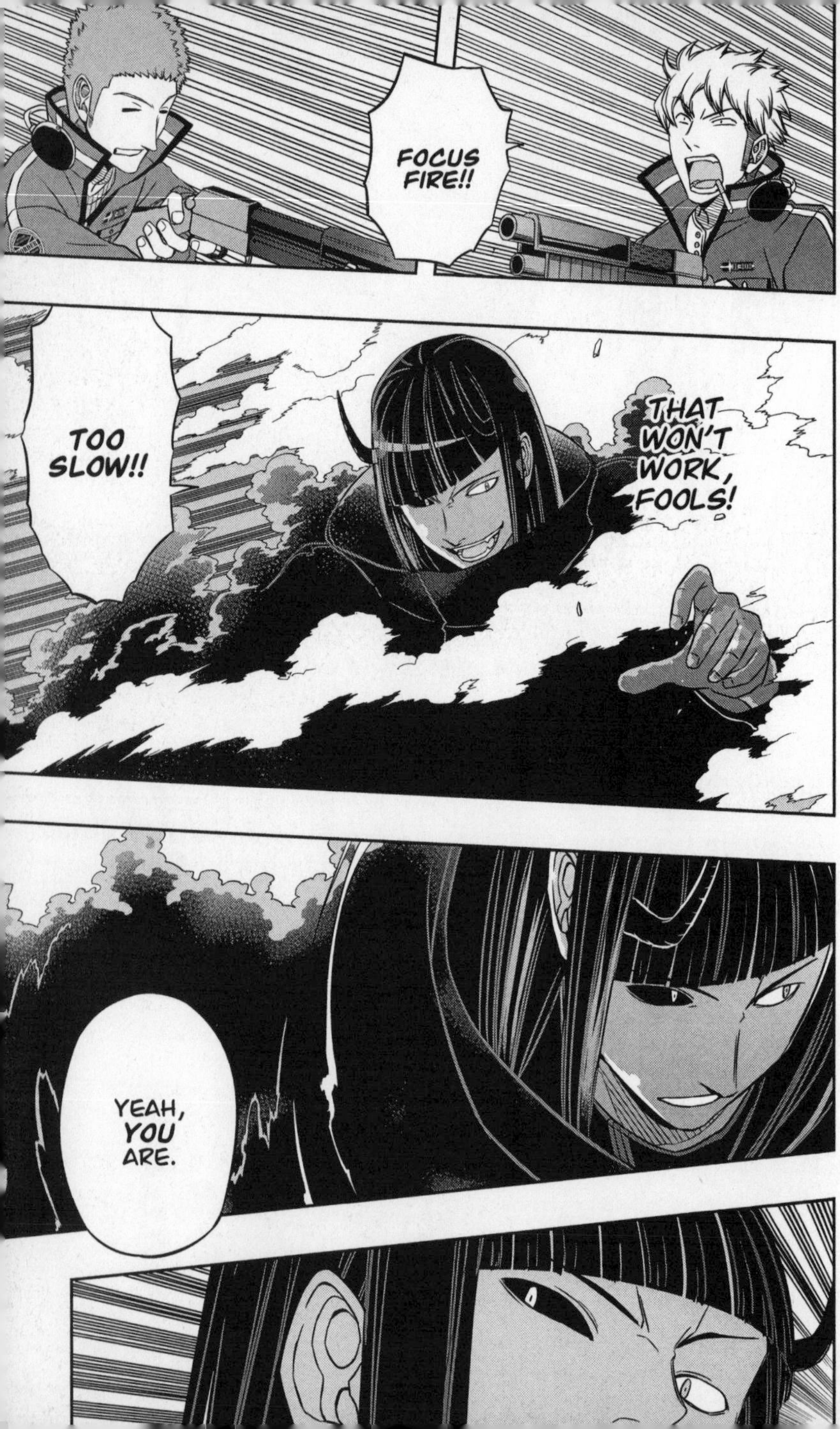
FOCUS FIRE!!
THAT WON'T WORK, FOOLS!
TOO SLOW!!
YEAH, YOU ARE.

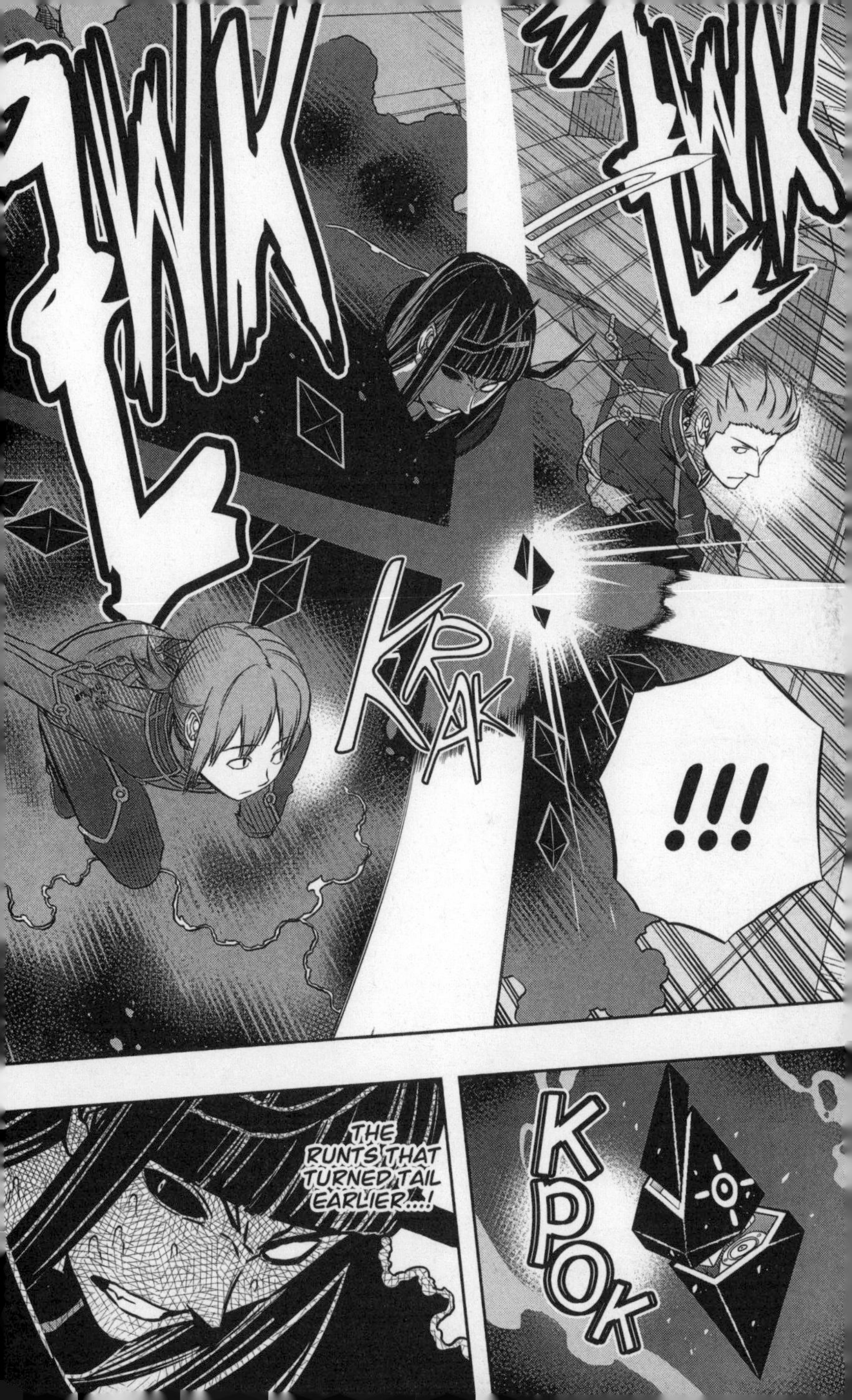
!!!
KRAK
KPOK
THE RUNTS THAT TURNED TAIL EARLIER...!

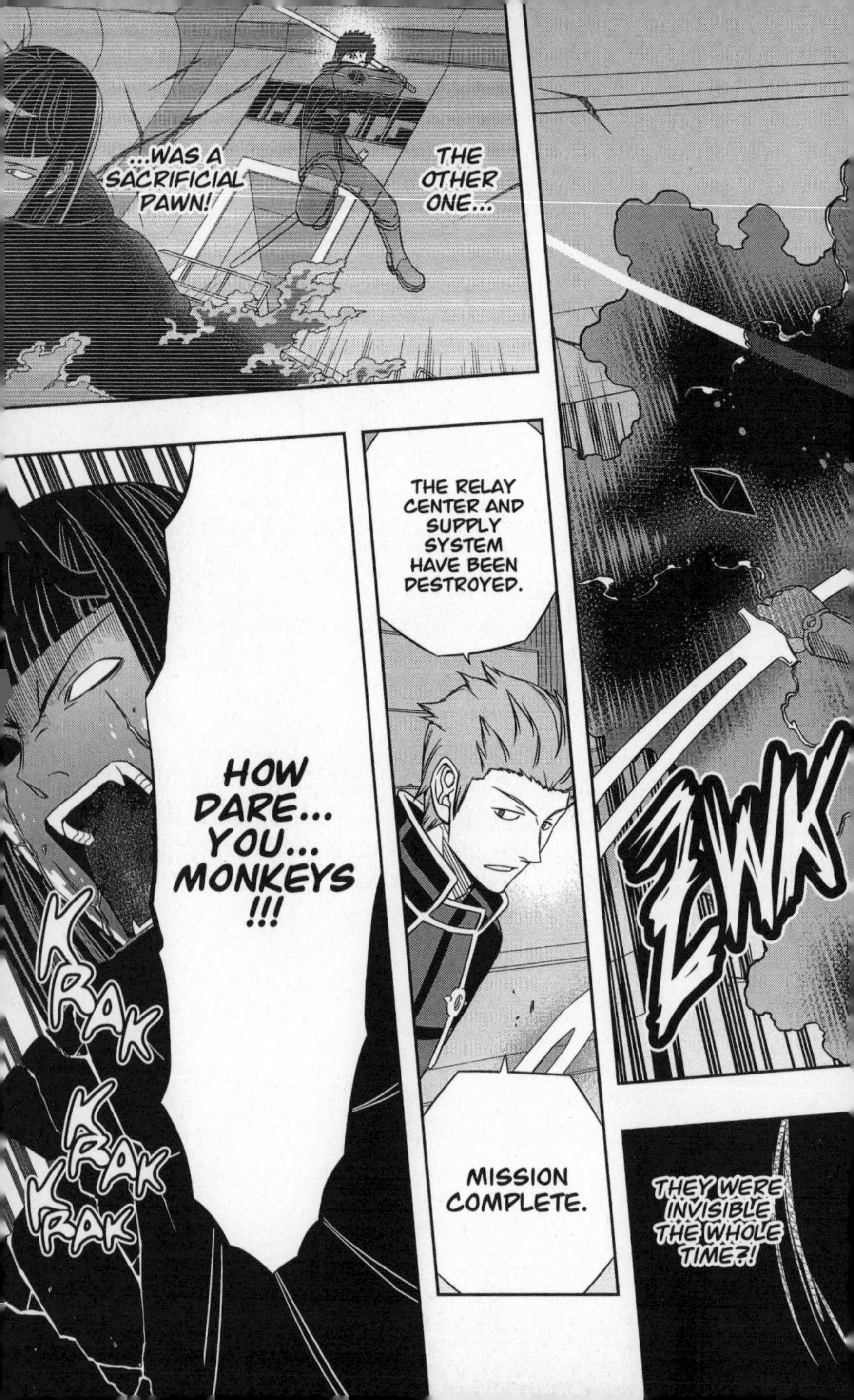
ZWK
THE OTHER ONE...
...WAS A SACRIFICIAL PAWN!
THEY WERE INVISIBLE THE WHOLE TIME?!
THE RELAY CENTER AND SUPPLY SYSTEM HAVE BEEN DESTROYED.
MISSION COMPLETE.
HOW DARE... YOU... MONKEYS !!!
KRAK
KRAK
KRAK

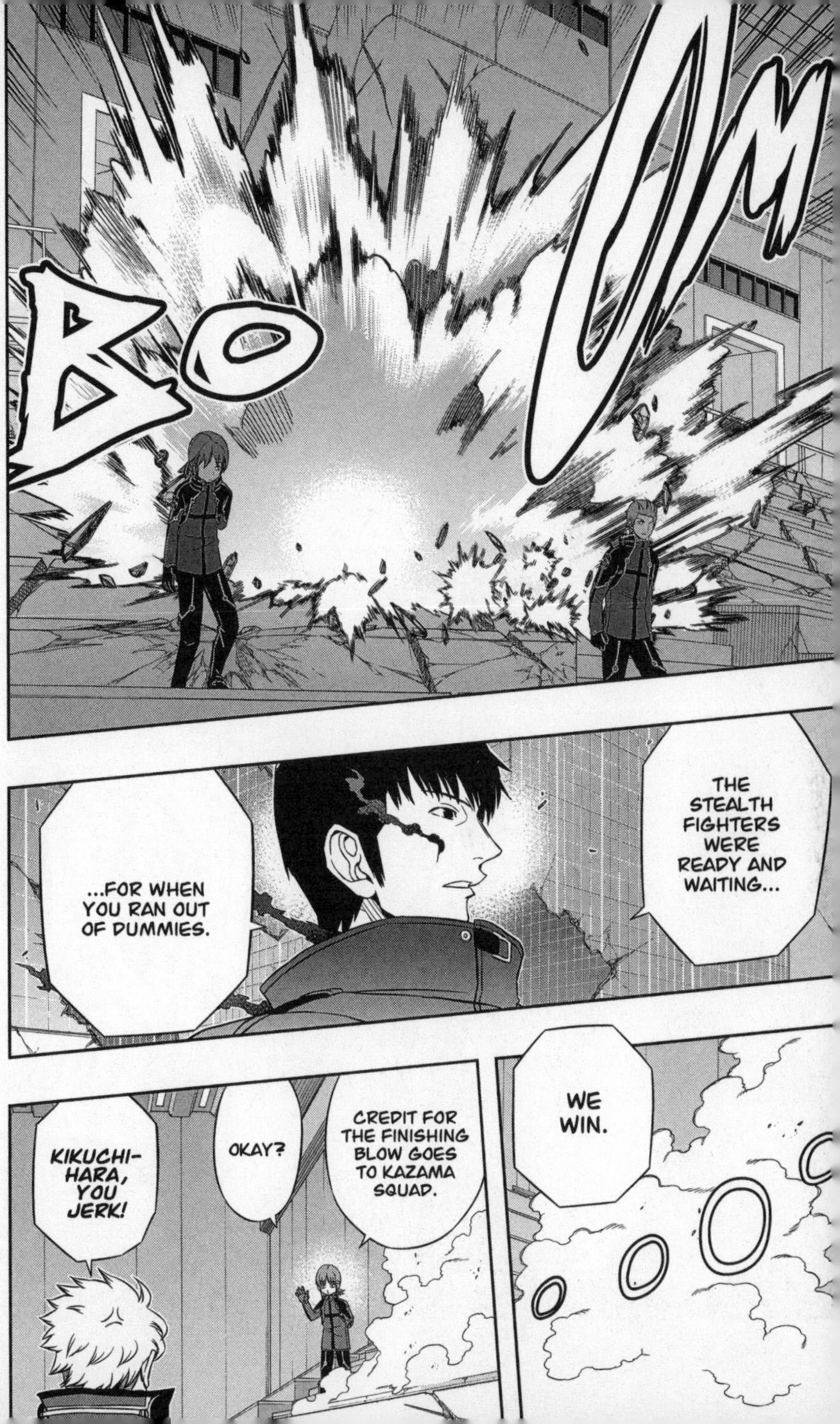
BOOM
THE STEALTH FIGHTERS WERE READY AND WAITING...
...FOR WHEN YOU RAN OUT OF DUMMIES.
WE WIN.
CREDIT FOR THE FINISHING BLOW GOES TO KAZAMA SQUAD.
OKAY?
KIKUCHIHARA, YOU JERK!

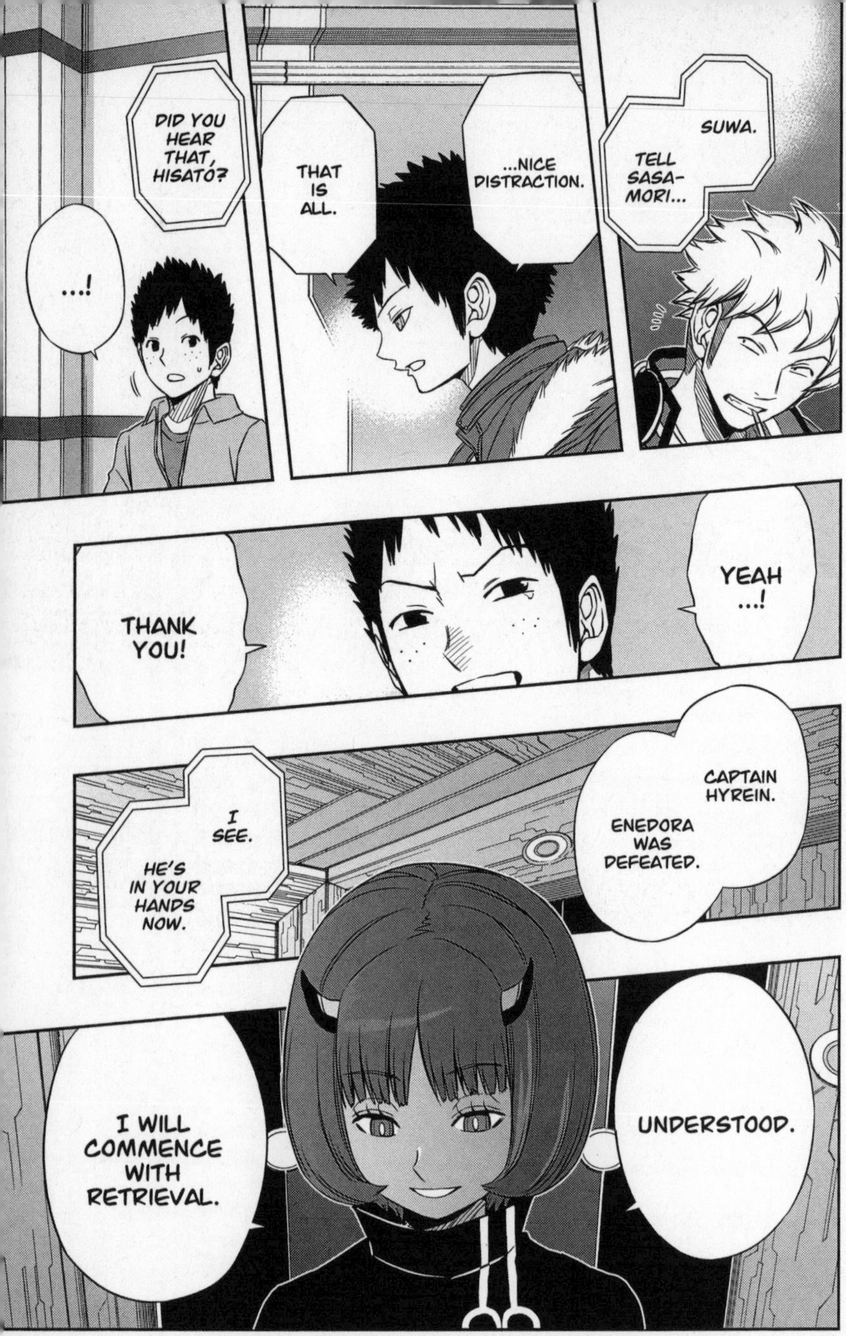
SUWA.
TELL SASAMORI...
...NICE DISTRACTION.
THAT IS ALL.
DID YOU HEAR THAT, HISATO?
...!
YEAH ...!
THANK YOU!
CAPTAIN HYREIN.
ENEDORA WAS DEFEATED.
I SEE.
HE'S IN YOUR HANDS NOW.
UNDERSTOOD.
I WILL COMMENCE WITH RETRIEVAL.

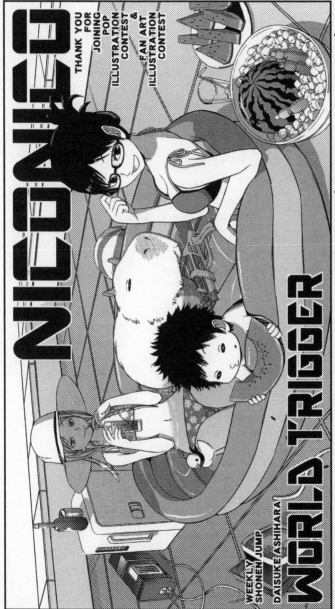

NICONICO

THANK YOU
FOR
JOINING

POP
ILLUSTRATION CONTEST
&
FAN ART
ILLUSTRATION CONTEST

WEEKLY SHONEN JUMP
DAISUKE ASHIHARA
WORLD TRIGGER

■ 2014 Niconico POP & Fan Art Contest Participation Award Illustration (actual image was in color)

I'm sorry that it's sideways. The contest was in the summer so I drew everyone in swimsuits, but then the results weren't announced until the fall. They look like they're having fun. My editor added a pattern to Konami's swimsuit when the image was grayscaled. That wasn't my doing.

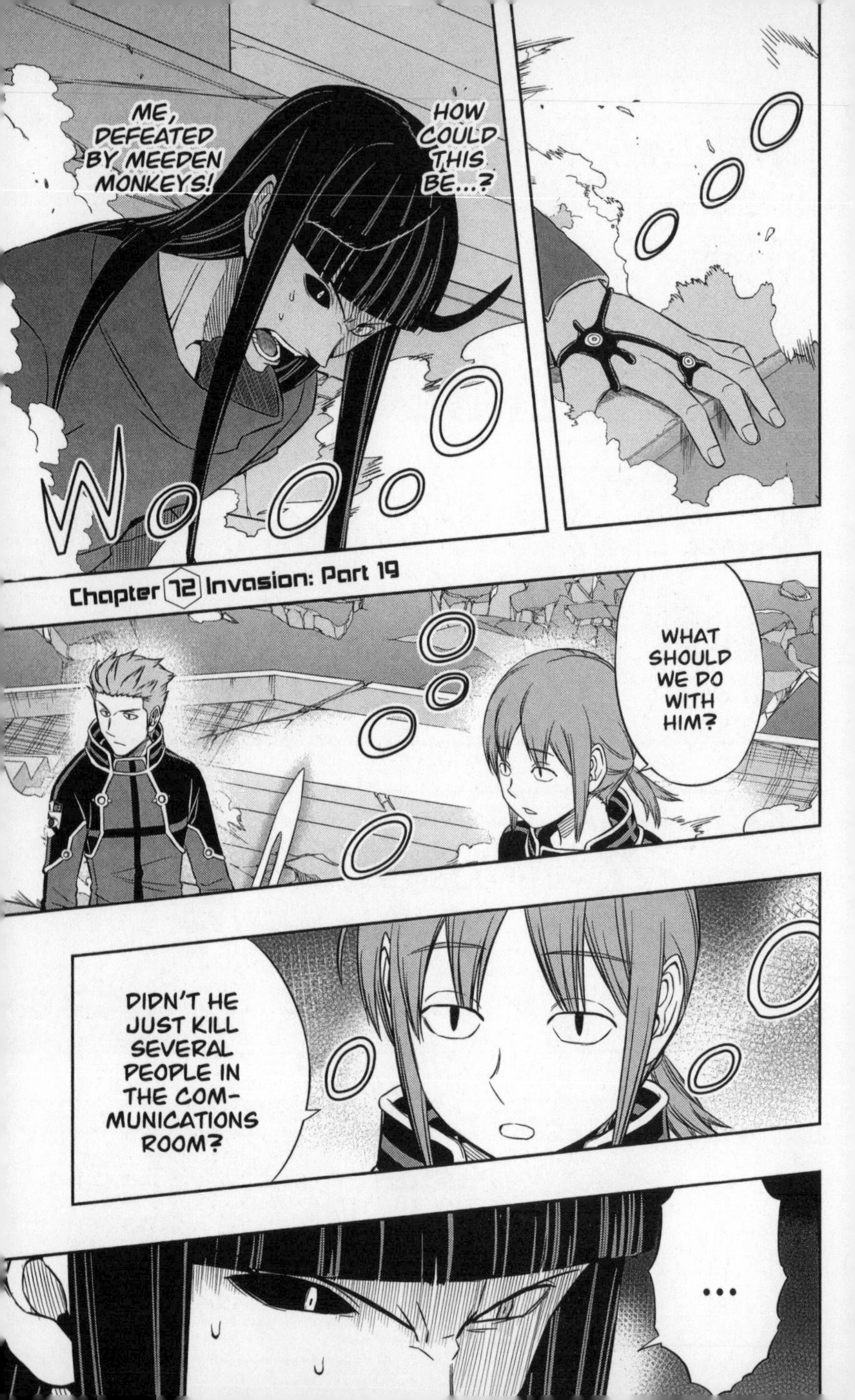
HOW COULD THIS BE...?
ME, DEFEATED BY MEEDEN MONKEYS!
WoOoo
Chapter 72 Invasion: Part 19
WHAT SHOULD WE DO WITH HIM?
DIDN'T HE JUST KILL SEVERAL PEOPLE IN THE COM-MUNICATIONS ROOM?
...

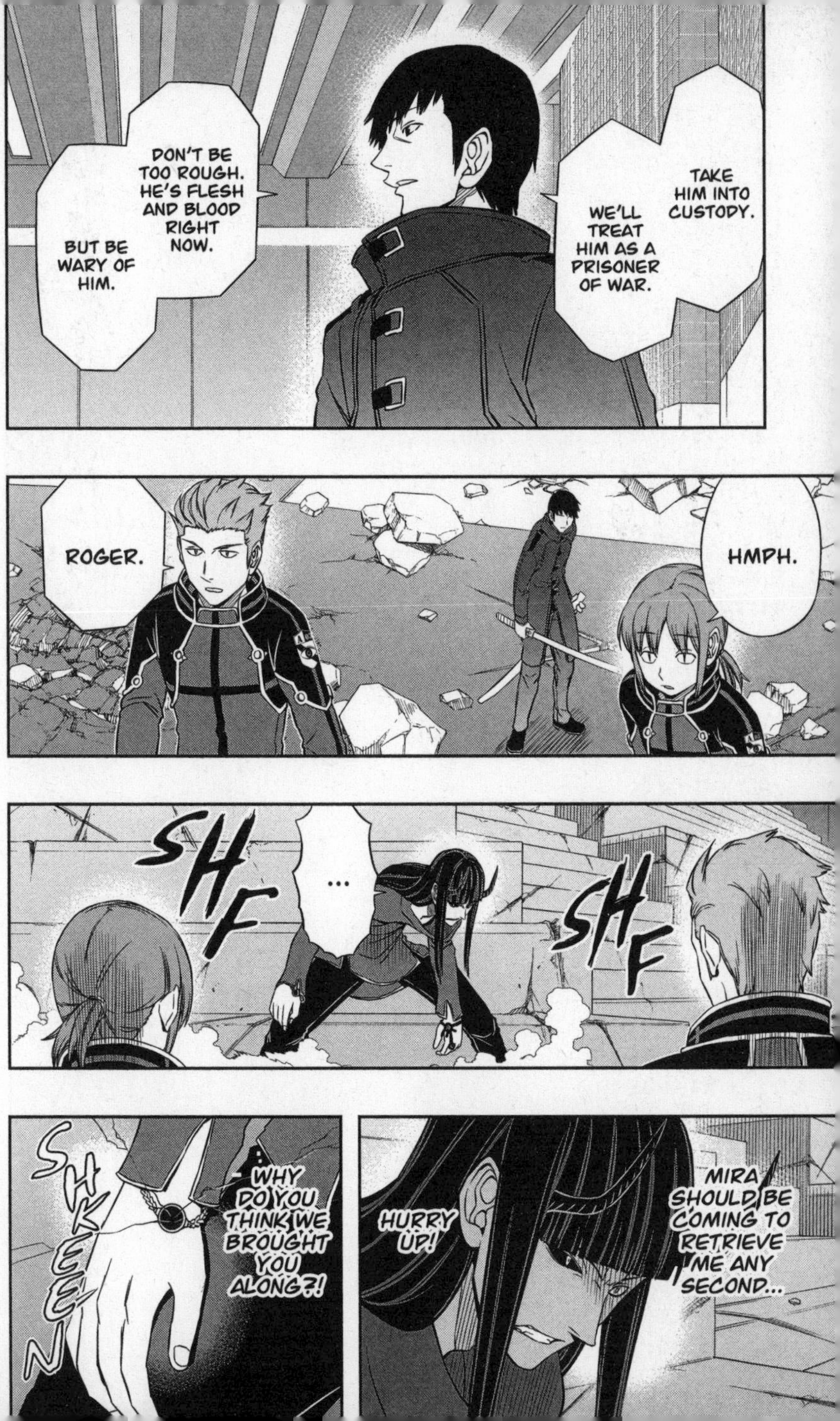
TAKE HIM INTO CUSTODY.
WE'LL TREAT HIM AS A PRISONER OF WAR.
DON'T BE TOO ROUGH. HE'S FLESH AND BLOOD RIGHT NOW.
BUT BE WARY OF HIM.
HMPH.
ROGER.
SHF
...
SHF
MIRA SHOULD BE COMING TO RETRIEVE ME ANY SECOND...
HURRY UP!
WHY DO YOU THINK WE BROUGHT YOU ALONG?!
SHKEEEN

Chapter 72 Invasion: Part 19

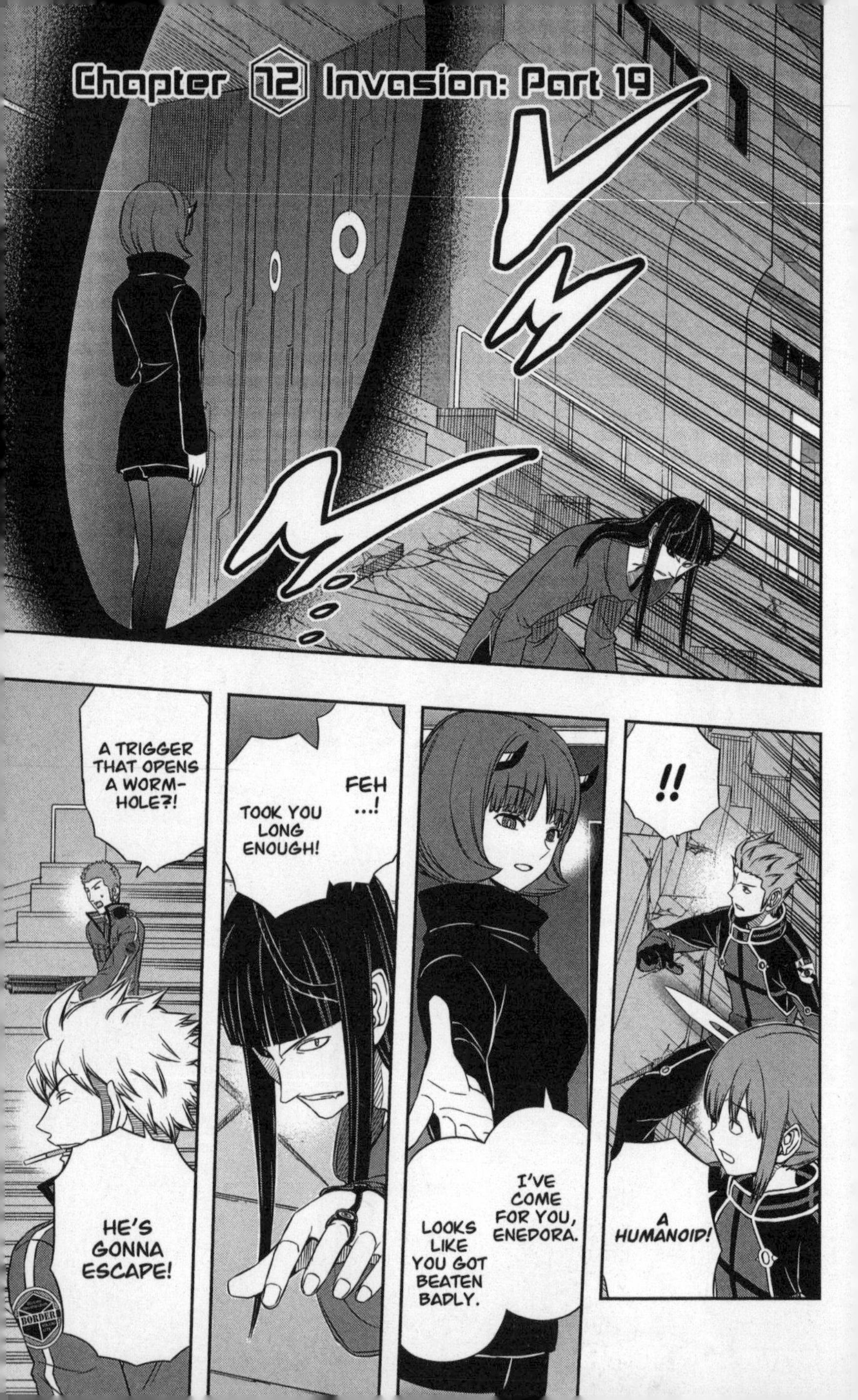
!!
A HUMANOID!
I'VE COME FOR YOU, ENEDORA.
LOOKS LIKE YOU GOT BEATEN BADLY.
FEH ...!
TOOK YOU LONG ENOUGH!
A TRIGGER THAT OPENS A WORM-HOLE?!
HE'S GONNA ESCAPE!

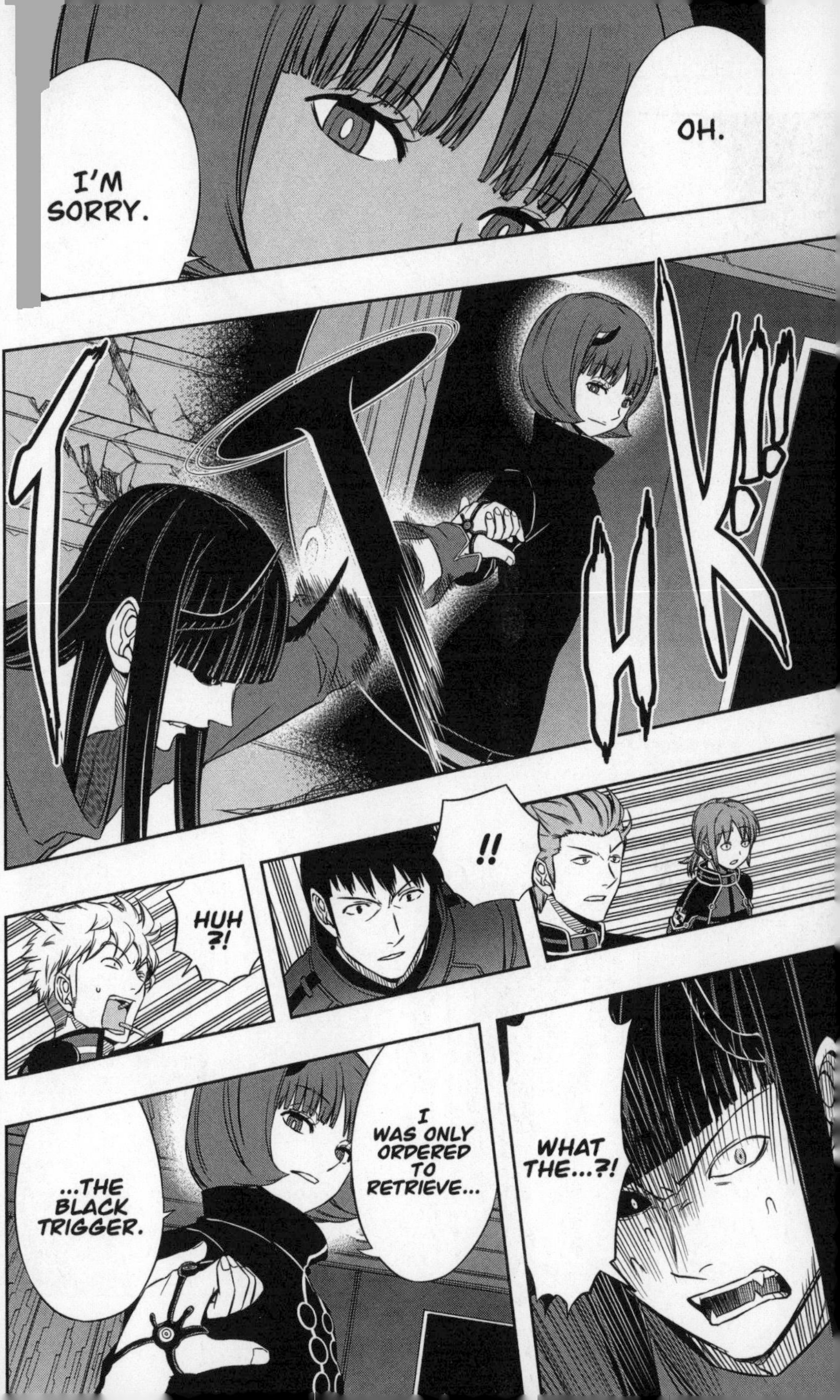

OH.
I'M SORRY.
THK!!
!!
HUH?!
WHAT THE...?!
I WAS ONLY ORDERED TO RETRIEVE...
...THE BLACK TRIGGER.

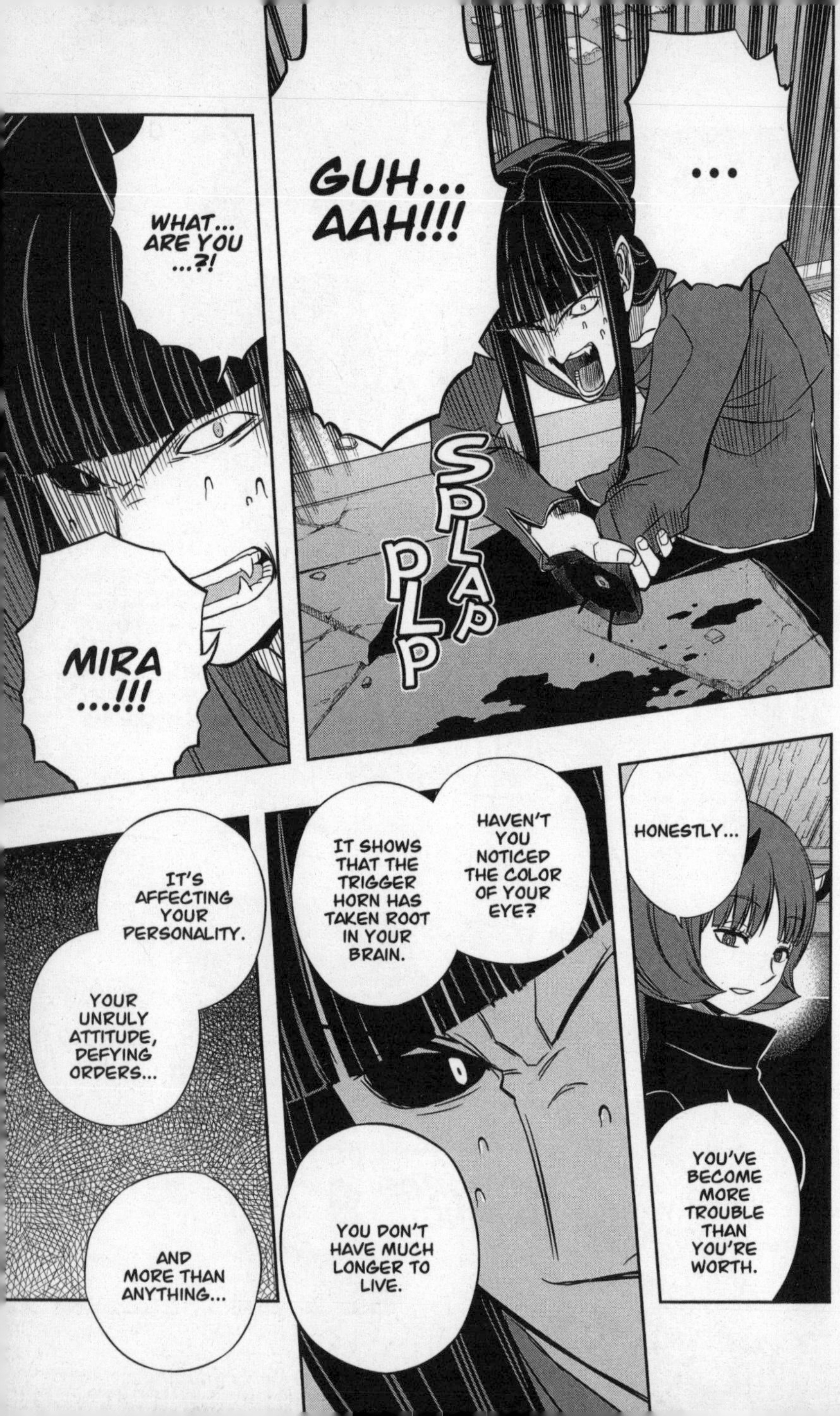
...
GUH... AAH!!!
SPLAP
PLP
WHAT... ARE YOU ...?!
MIRA ...!!!
HONESTLY...
YOU'VE BECOME MORE TROUBLE THAN YOU'RE WORTH.
HAVEN'T YOU NOTICED THE COLOR OF YOUR EYE?
IT SHOWS THAT THE TRIGGER HORN HAS TAKEN ROOT IN YOUR BRAIN.
YOU DON'T HAVE MUCH LONGER TO LIVE.
IT'S AFFECTING YOUR PERSONALITY.
YOUR UNRULY ATTITUDE, DEFYING ORDERS...
AND MORE THAN ANYTHING...

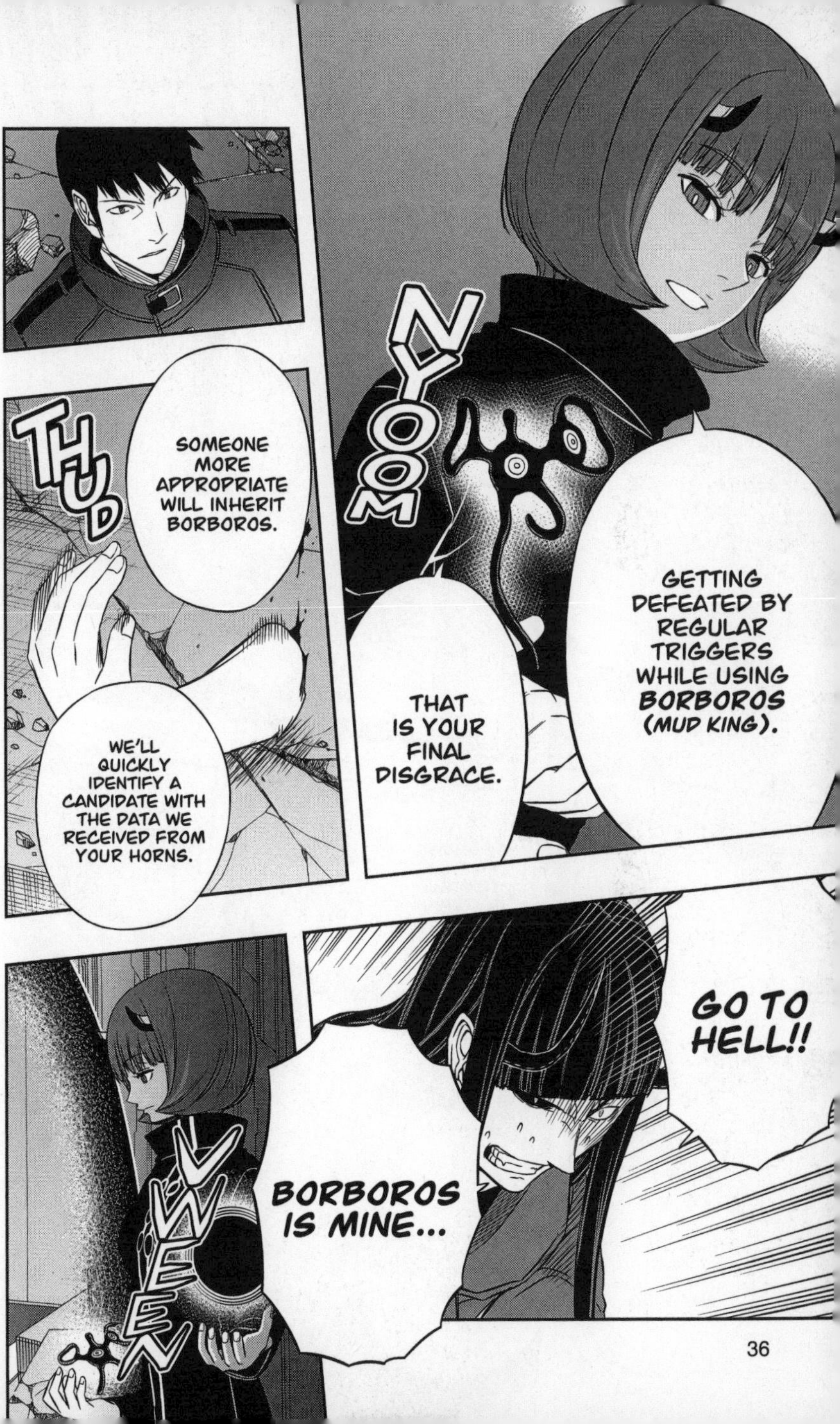
NYOOM
GETTING DEFEATED BY REGULAR TRIGGERS WHILE USING BORBOROS (MUD KING).
THAT IS YOUR FINAL DISGRACE.
SOMEONE MORE APPROPRIATE WILL INHERIT BORBOROS.
THUD
WE'LL QUICKLY IDENTIFY A CANDIDATE WITH THE DATA WE RECEIVED FROM YOUR HORNS.
GO TO HELL!!
BORBOROS IS MINE...
VWEEEN

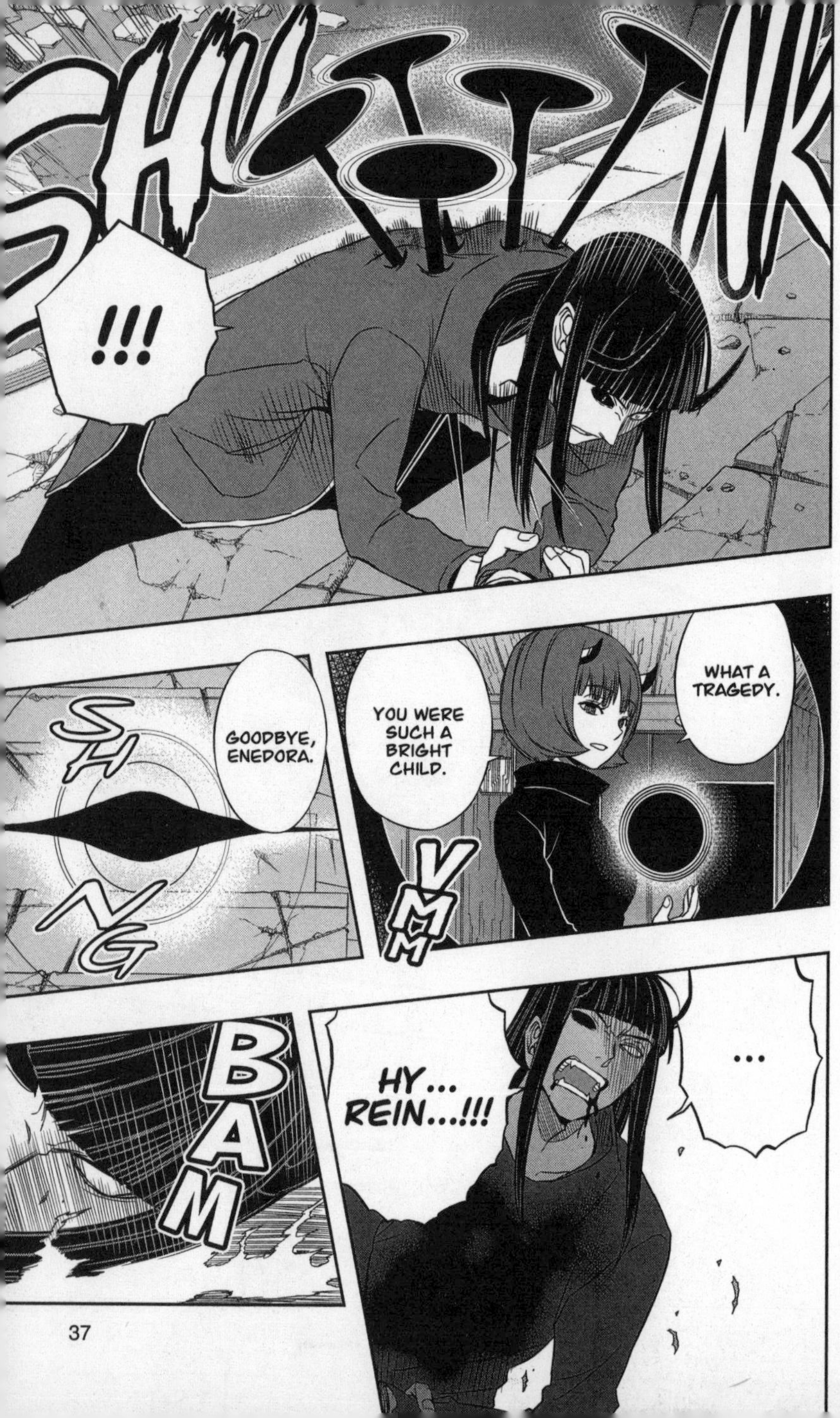
!!!
WHAT A TRAGEDY.
YOU WERE SUCH A BRIGHT CHILD.
VMMM
GOODBYE, ENEDORA.
SHNG
...
HY... REIN...!!!
BAM

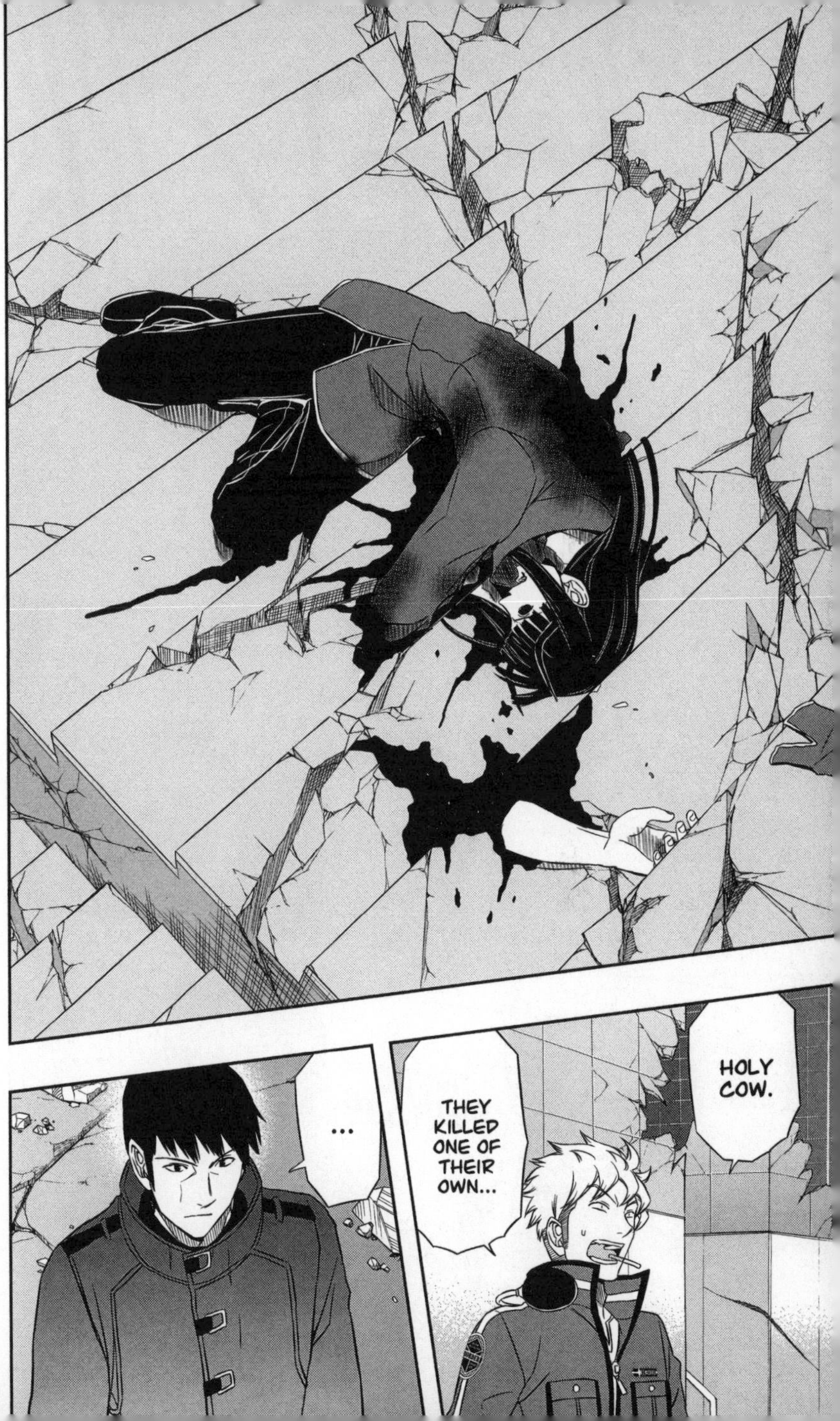
HOLY COW.
THEY KILLED ONE OF THEIR OWN...
...

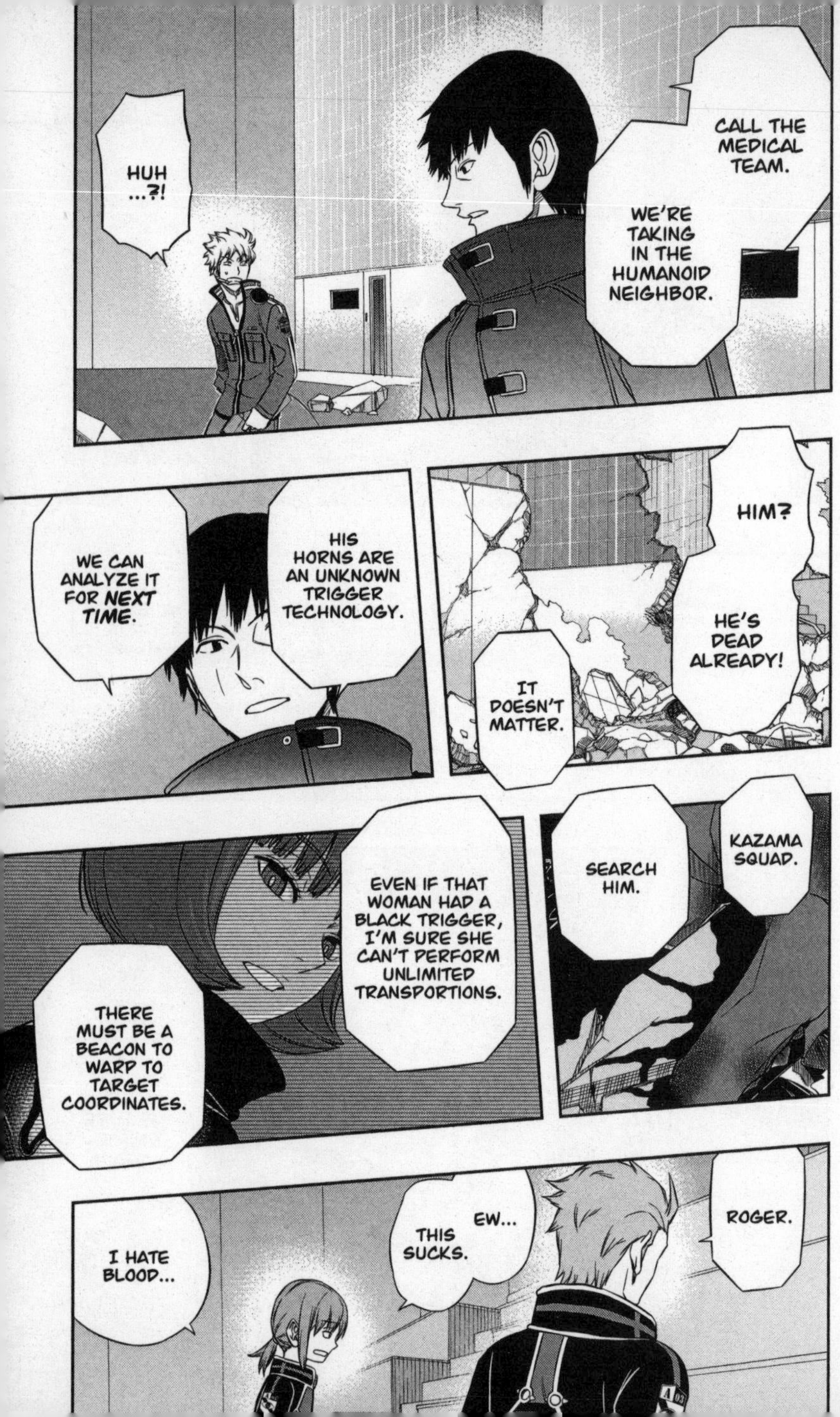
CALL THE MEDICAL TEAM.
WE'RE TAKING IN THE HUMANOID NEIGHBOR.
HUH ...?!
HIM?
HE'S DEAD ALREADY!
IT DOESN'T MATTER.
HIS HORNS ARE AN UNKNOWN TRIGGER TECHNOLOGY.
WE CAN ANALYZE IT FOR NEXT TIME.
KAZAMA SQUAD.
SEARCH HIM.
EVEN IF THAT WOMAN HAD A BLACK TRIGGER, I'M SURE SHE CAN'T PERFORM UNLIMITED TRANSPORTIONS.
THERE MUST BE A BEACON TO WARP TO TARGET COORDINATES.
ROGER.
EW...
THIS SUCKS.
I HATE BLOOD...

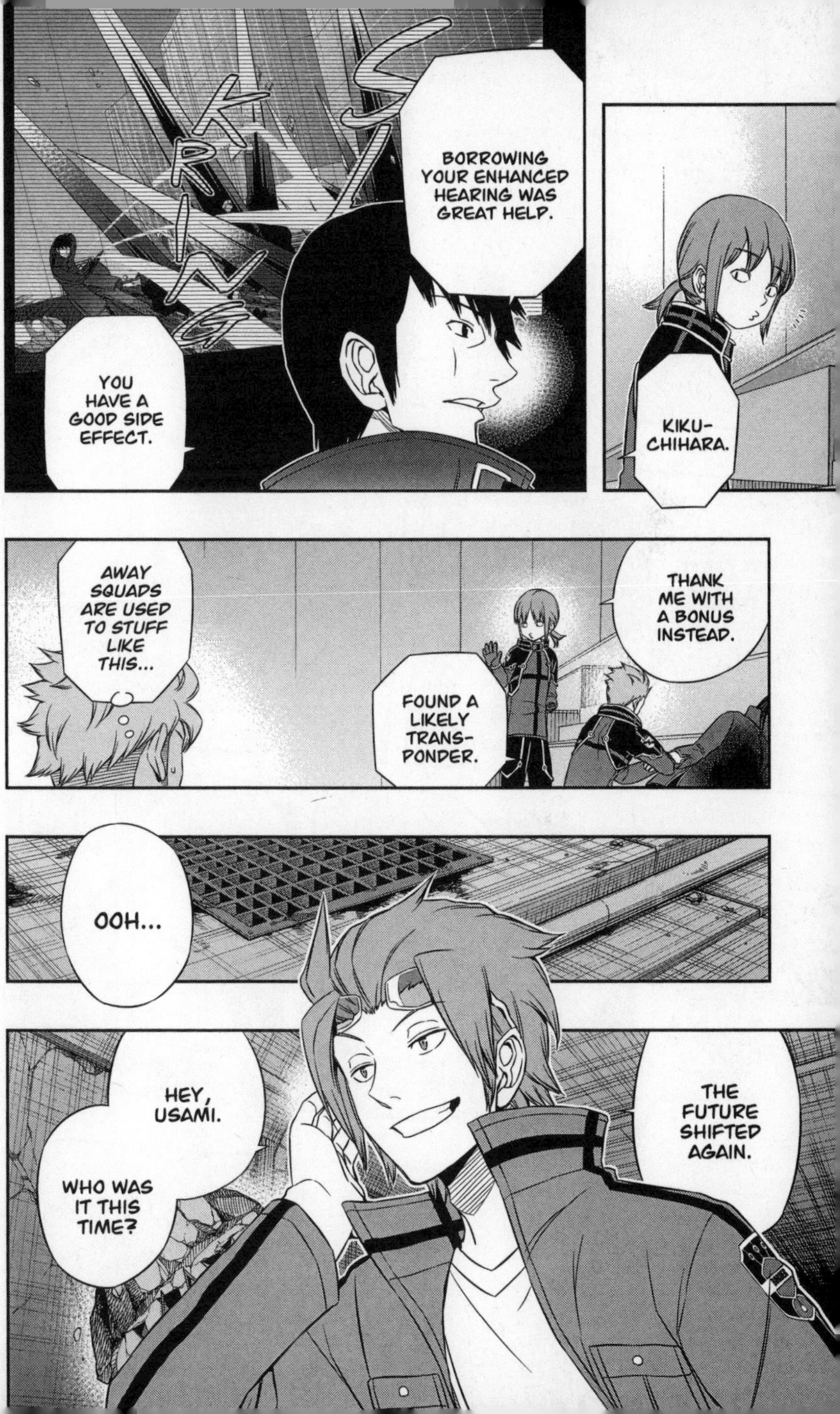
KIKU-
CHIHARA.
BORROWING YOUR ENHANCED HEARING WAS GREAT HELP.
YOU HAVE A GOOD SIDE EFFECT.
THANK ME WITH A BONUS INSTEAD.
FOUND A LIKELY TRANS-
PONDER.
AWAY SQUADS ARE USED TO STUFF LIKE THIS...
OOH...
THE FUTURE SHIFTED AGAIN.
HEY, USAMI.
WHO WAS IT THIS TIME?

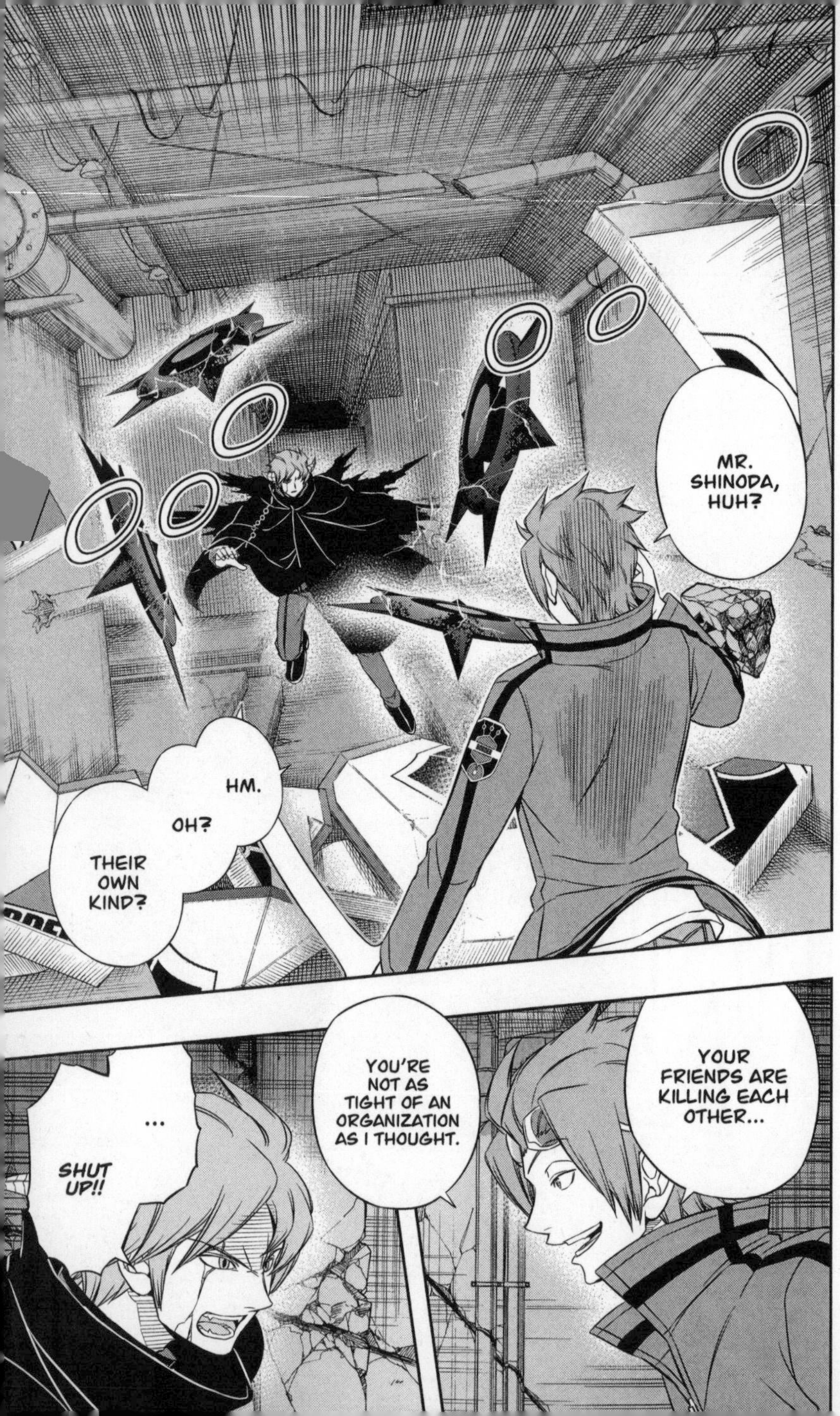
MR. SHINODA, HUH?
HM.
OH?
THEIR OWN KIND?
YOUR FRIENDS ARE KILLING EACH OTHER...
YOU'RE NOT AS TIGHT OF AN ORGANIZATION AS I THOUGHT.
...
SHUT UP!!

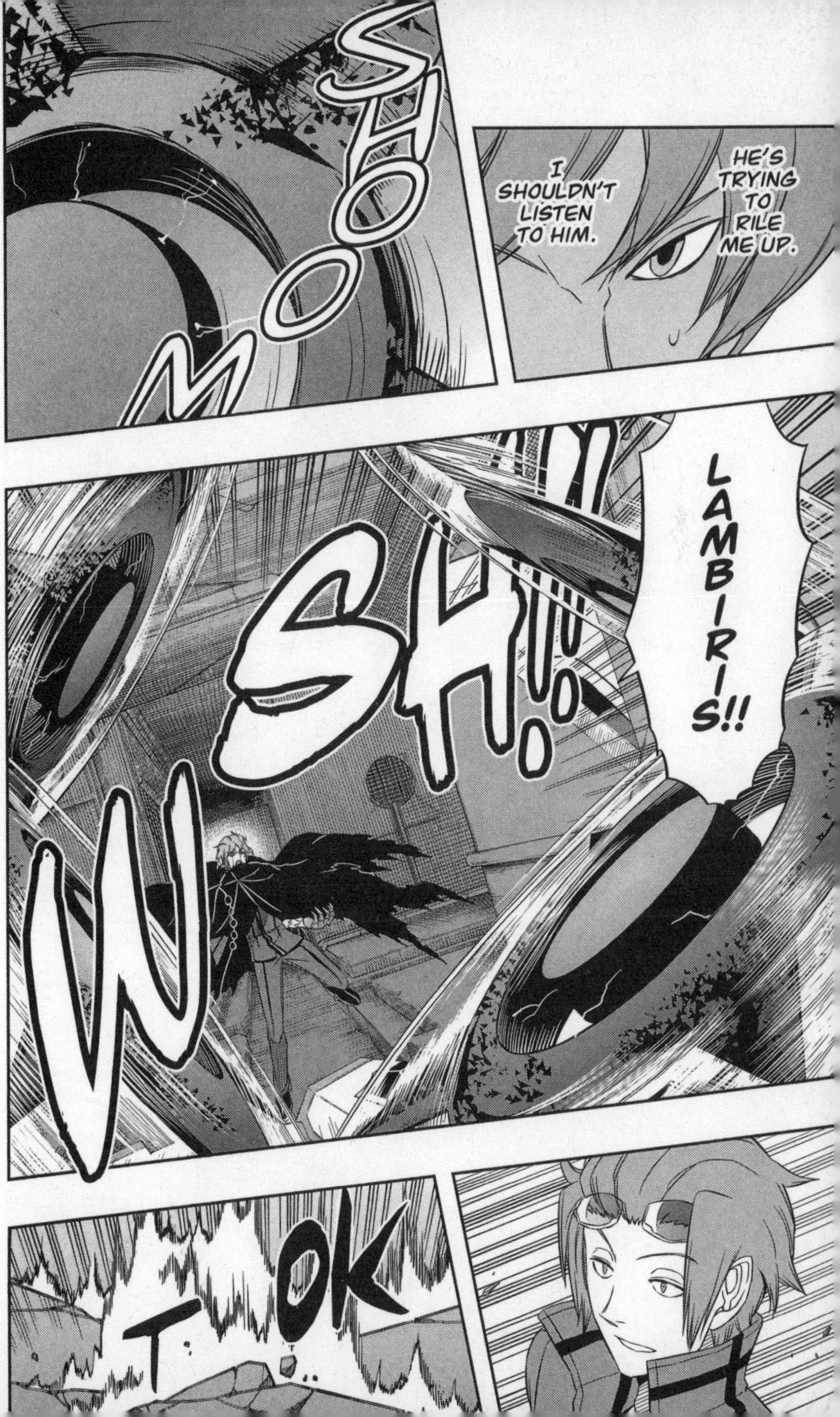
HE'S TRYING TO RILE ME UP.
I SHOULDN'T LISTEN TO HIM.
SHOOOM
LAMBIRIS!!
WSH!!
T OK

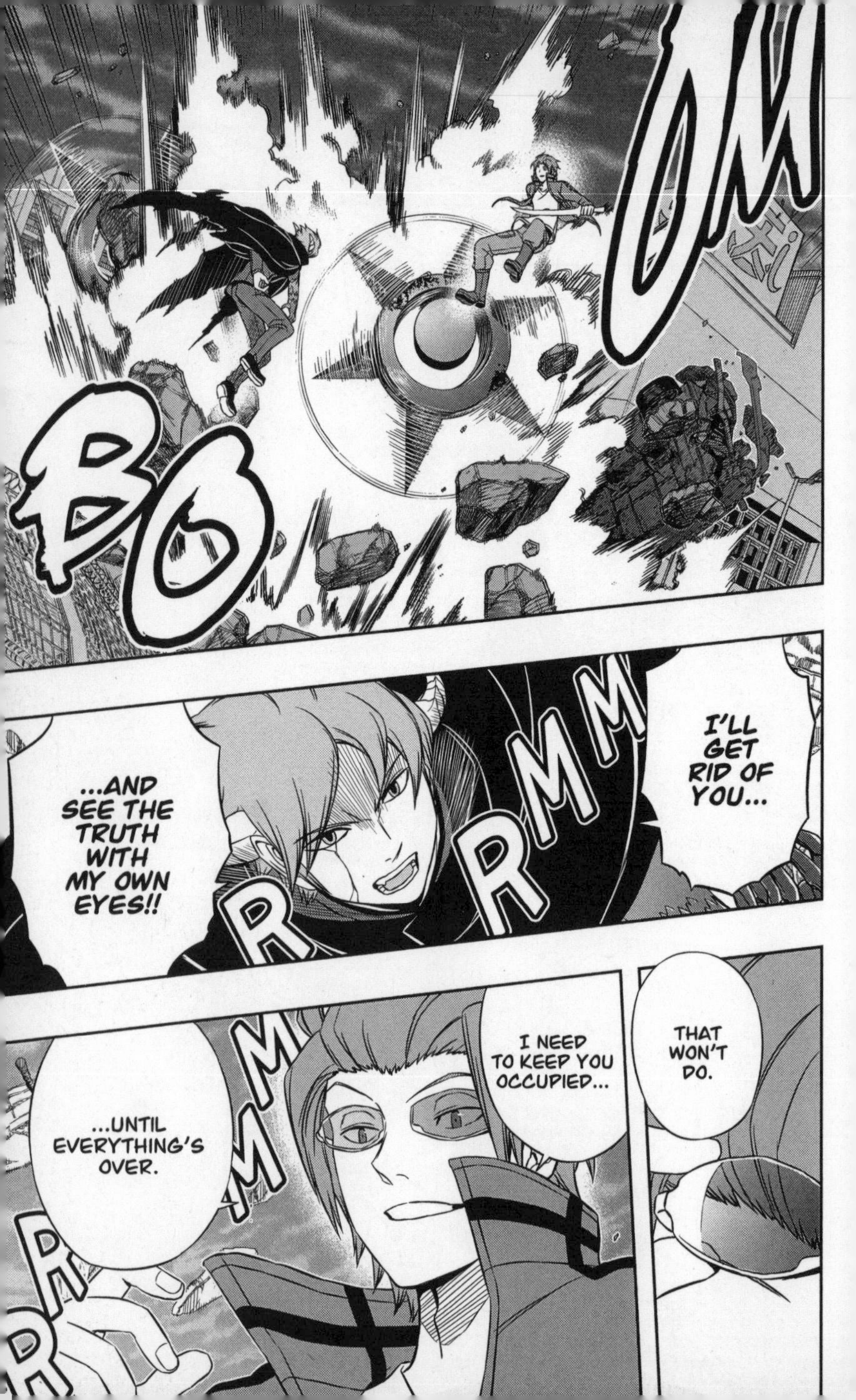
BO
OM
I'LL GET RID OF YOU...
...AND SEE THE TRUTH WITH MY OWN EYES!!
RRMMM
THAT WON'T DO.
I NEED TO KEEP YOU OCCUPIED...
...UNTIL EVERYTHING'S OVER.
RRMMM

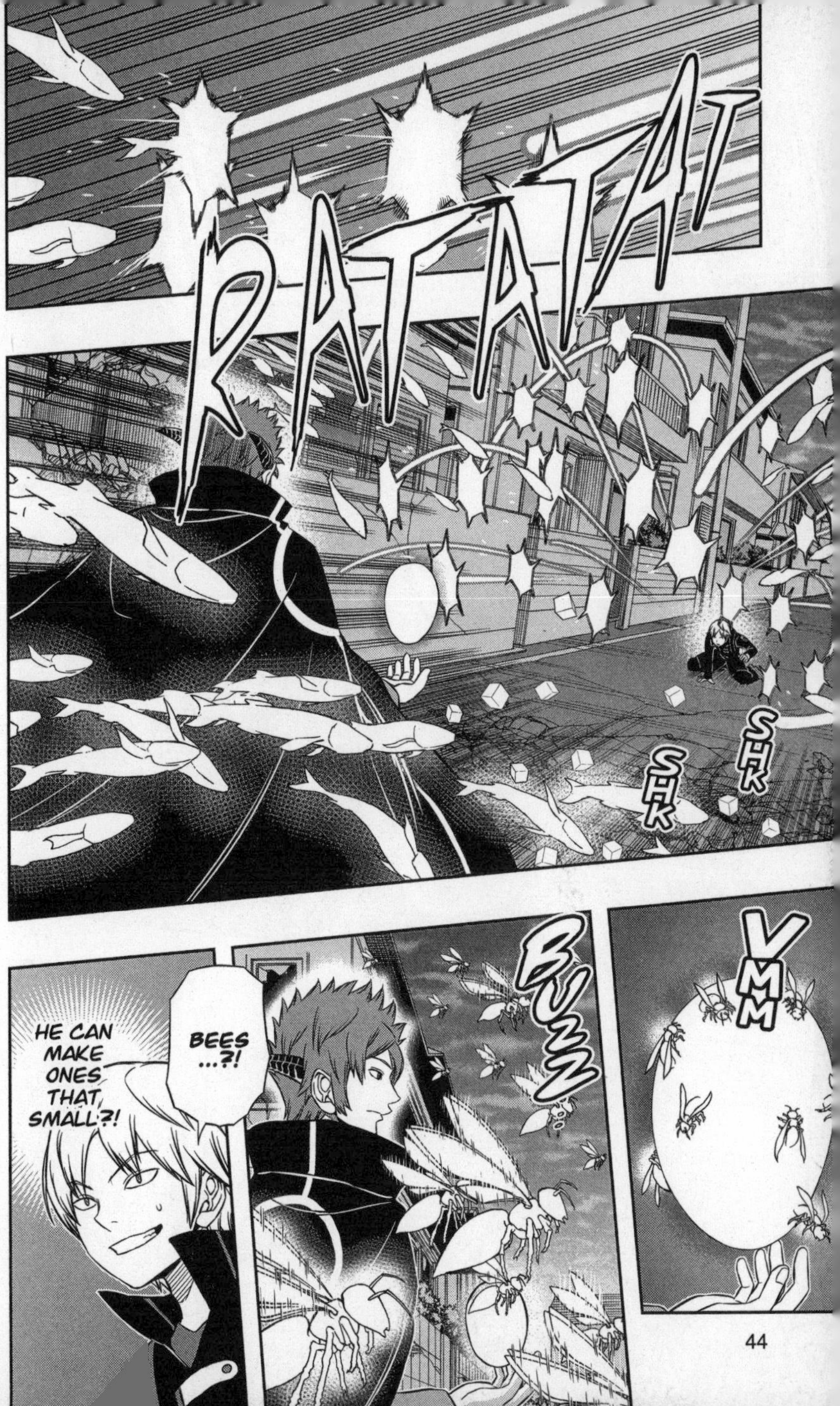

RATATAT
SHK
SHK
VMM
BUZZ
BEES ...?!
HE CAN MAKE ONES THAT SMALL?!

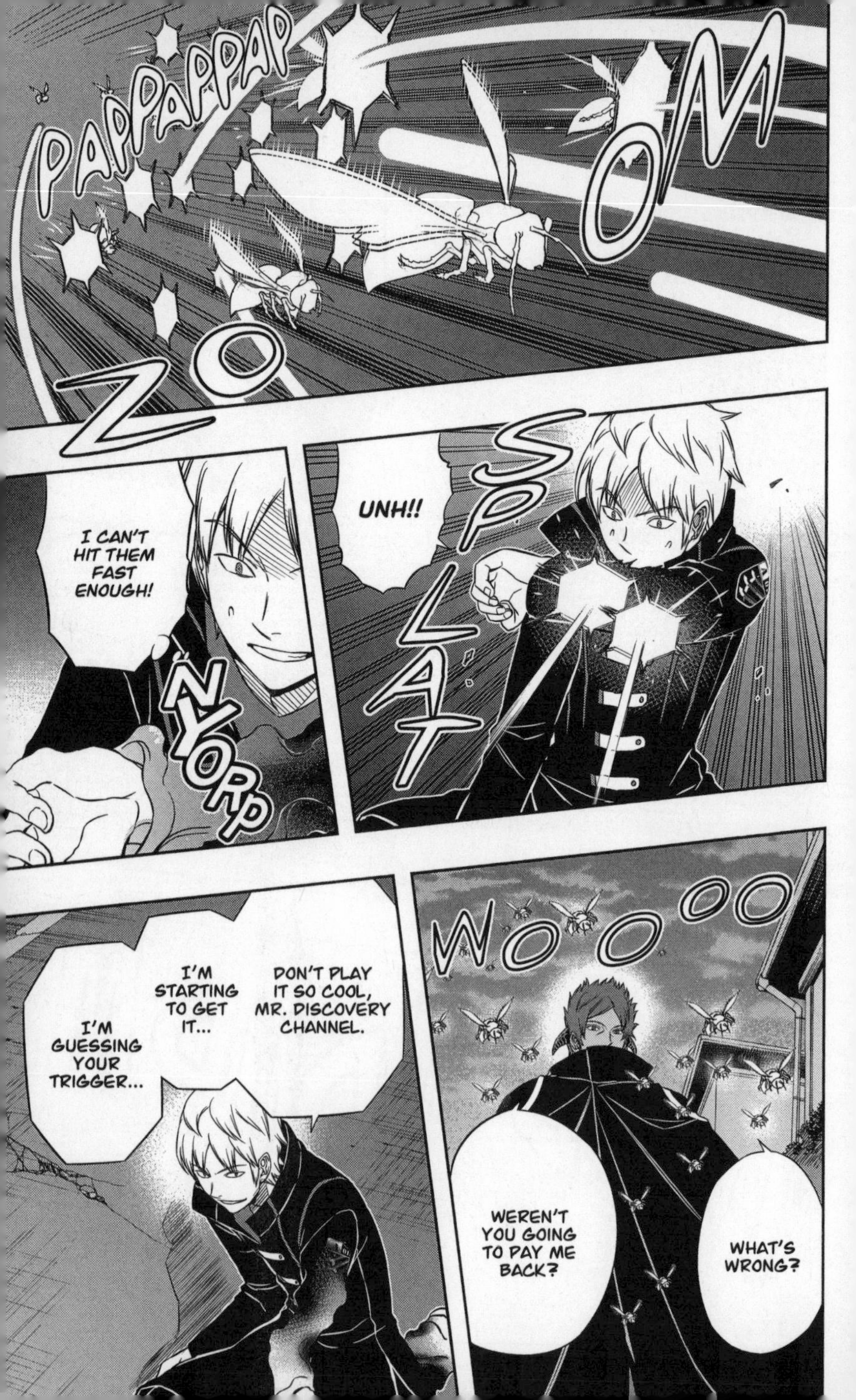
PAPPAPPAP
ZOOM
UNH!!
SPLAT
I CAN'T HIT THEM FAST ENOUGH!
NYORP
WOOOO
WHAT'S WRONG?
WEREN'T YOU GOING TO PAY ME BACK?
DON'T PLAY IT SO COOL, MR. DISCOVERY CHANNEL.
I'M STARTING TO GET IT...
I'M GUESSING YOUR TRIGGER...

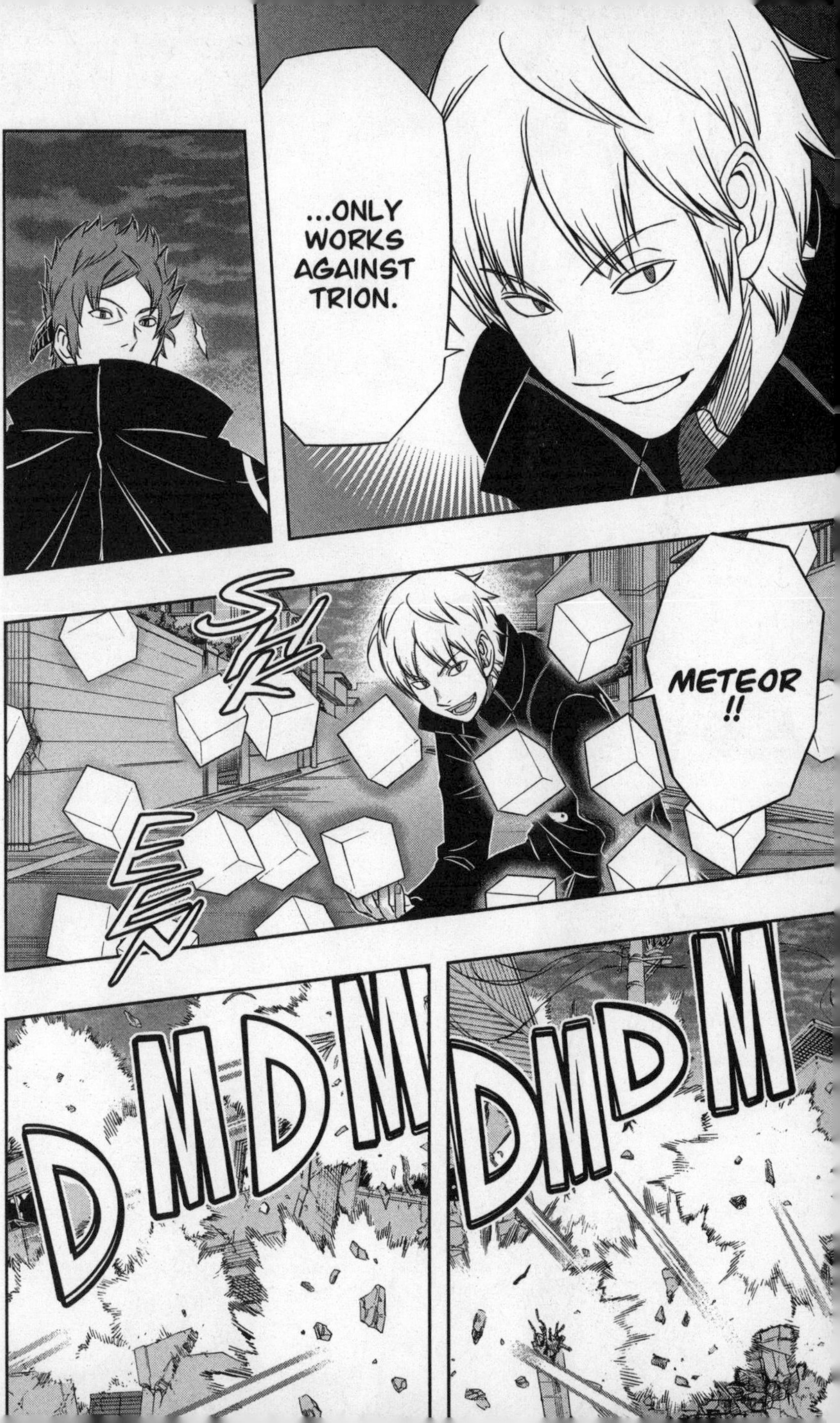
...ONLY WORKS AGAINST TRION.
METEOR !!
SHK
EEN
DMDM
DMDM

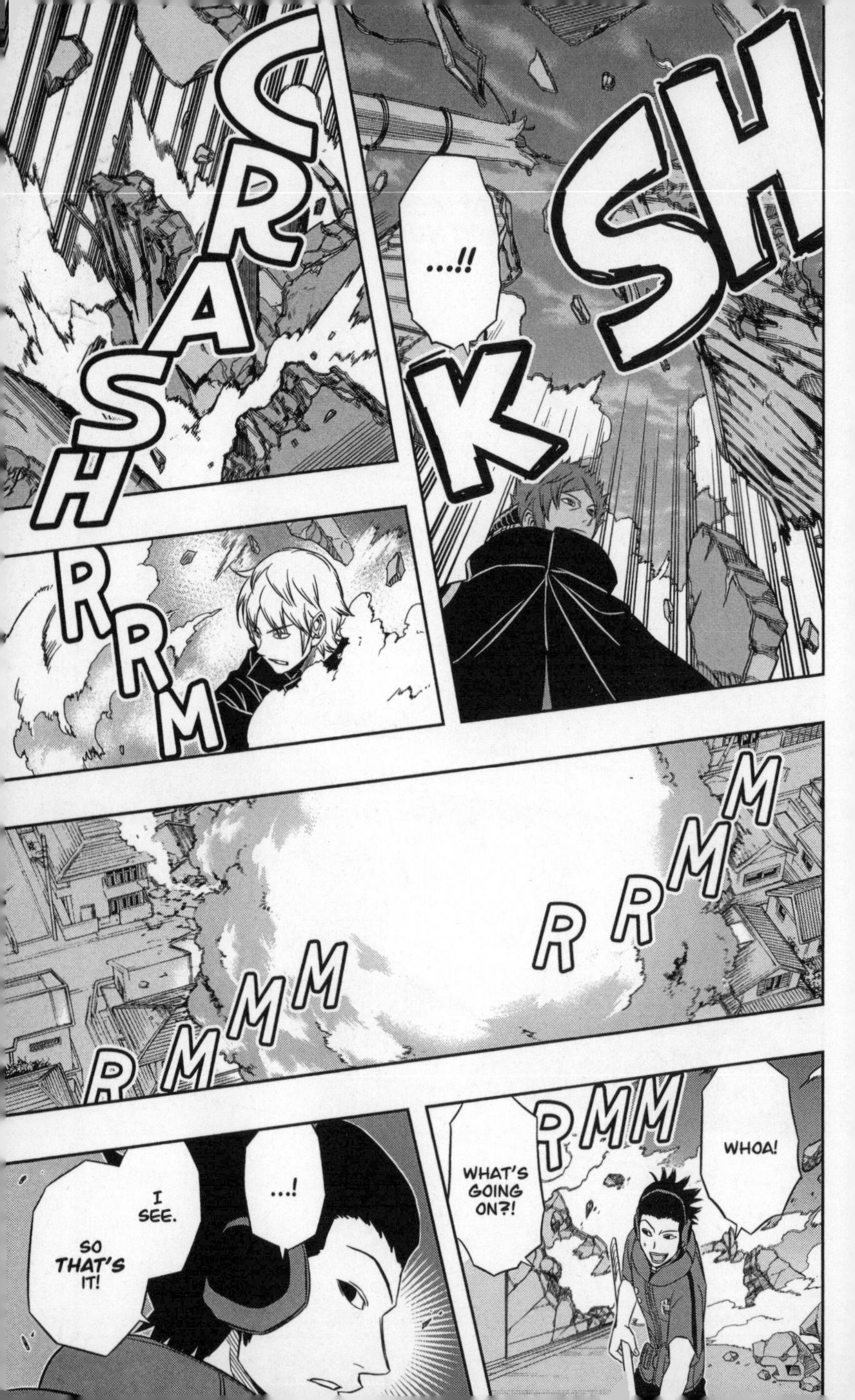
SHK
...!!
CRASH
RRM
RRMM
RMMM
WHOA!
RMM
WHAT'S GOING ON?!
...!
I SEE.
SO THAT'S IT!

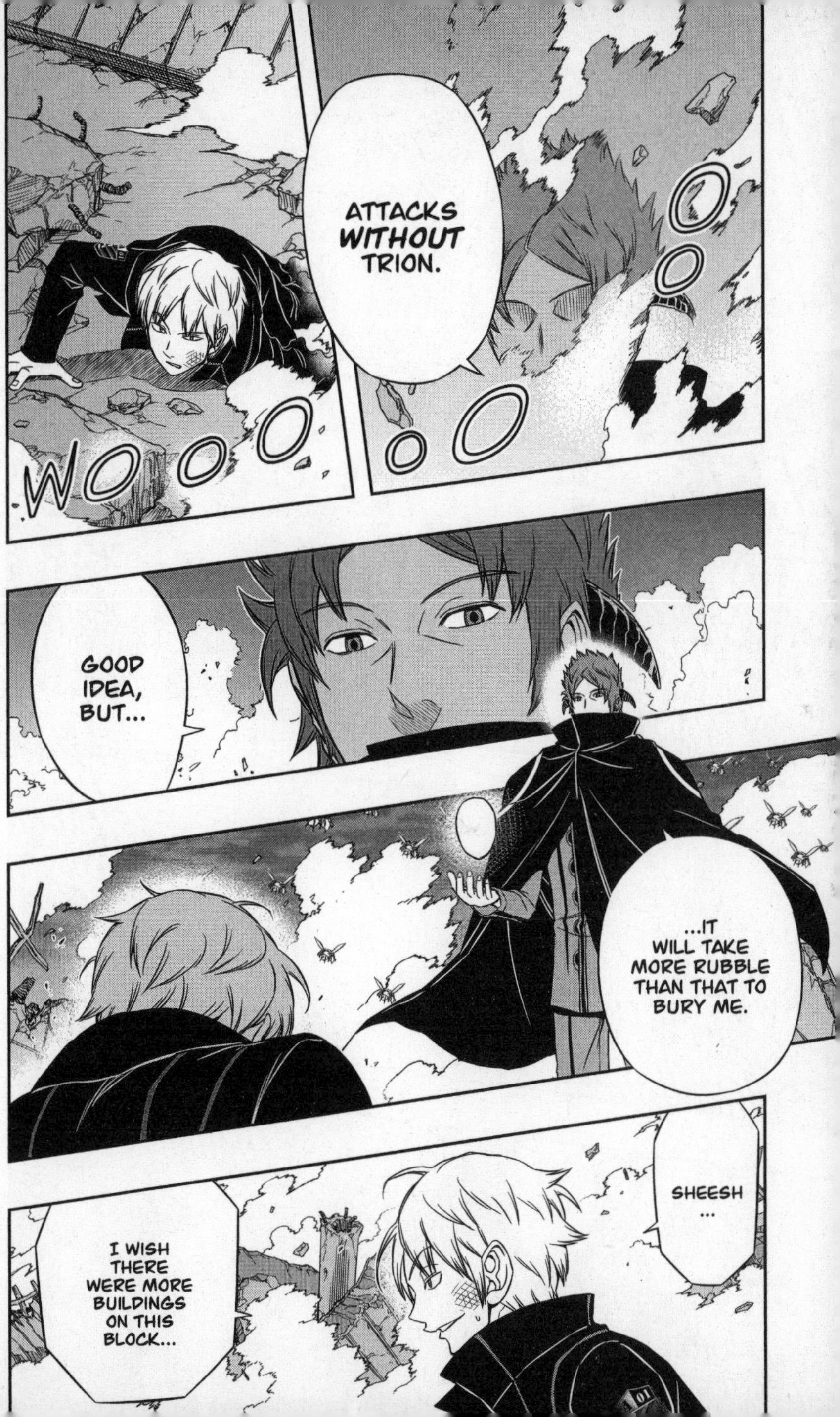
ATTACKS WITHOUT TRION.
OOOO
WOOOO
GOOD IDEA, BUT...
...IT WILL TAKE MORE RUBBLE THAN THAT TO BURY ME.
SHEESH...
I WISH THERE WERE MORE BUILDINGS ON THIS BLOCK...

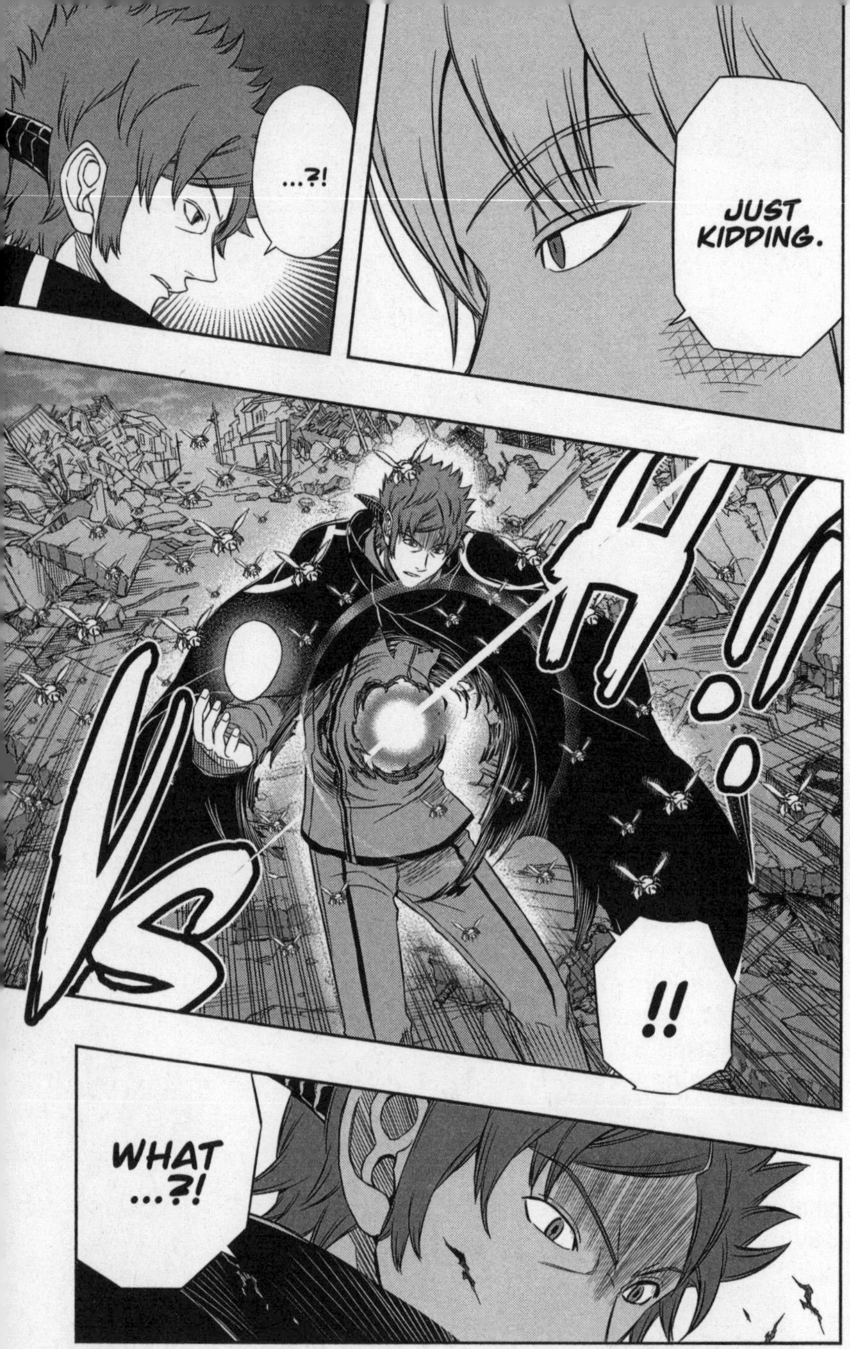
JUST KIDDING.
...?!
!!
WHAT ...?!

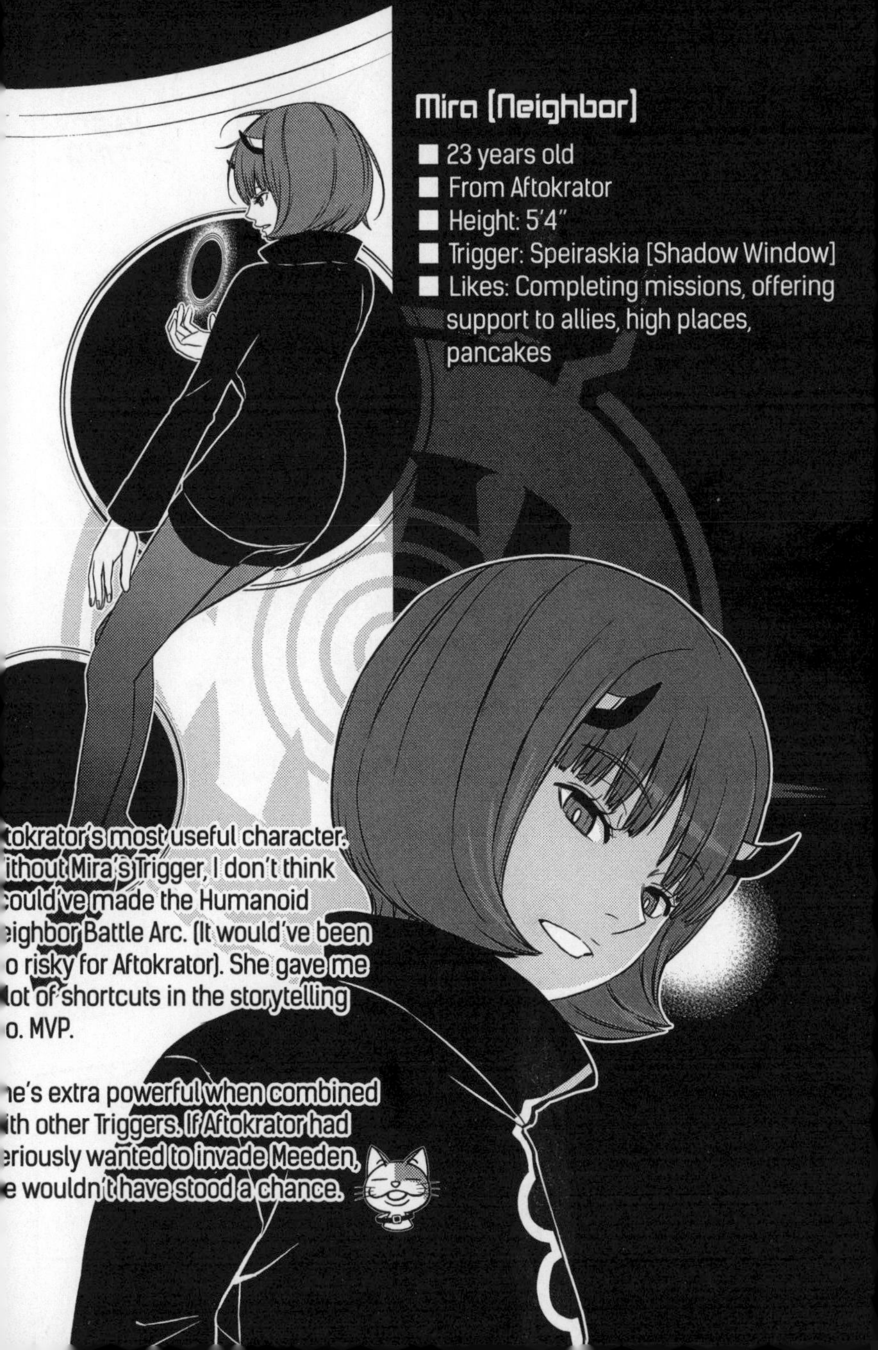

Mira [Neighbor]

- 23 years old
- From Aftokrator
- Height: 5'4"
- Trigger: Speiraskia [Shadow Window]
- Likes: Completing missions, offering support to allies, high places, pancakes

tokrator's most useful character.
ithout Mira's Trigger, I don't think
could've made the Humanoid
eighbor Battle Arc. (It would've been
o risky for Aftokrator). She gave me
lot of shortcuts in the storytelling
o. MVP.

he's extra powerful when combined
ith other Triggers. If Aftokrator had
eriously wanted to invade Meeden,
e wouldn't have stood a chance.

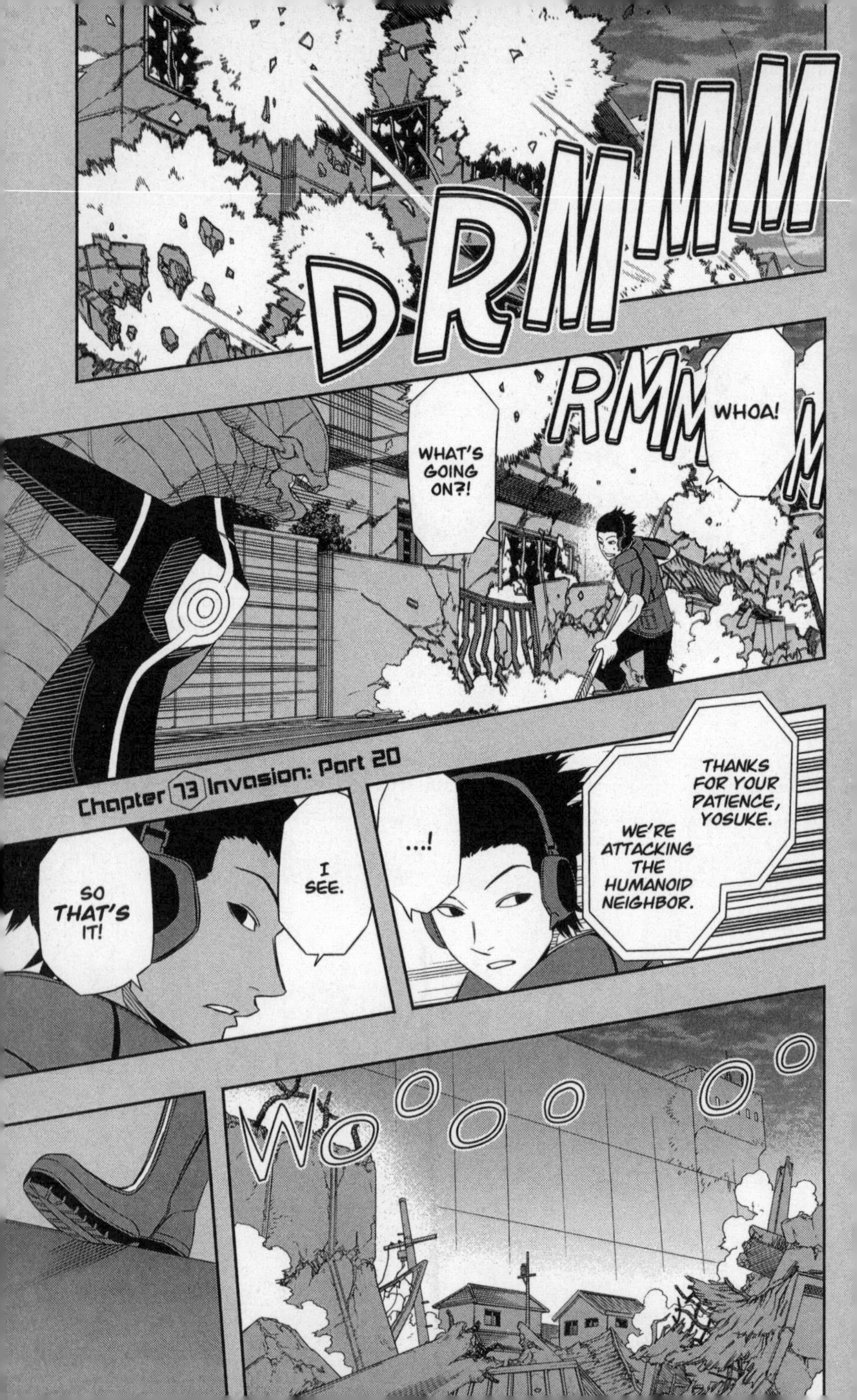
DRMMMMM
RMMMM
WHOA!
WHAT'S GOING ON?!
Chapter 73 Invasion: Part 20
THANKS FOR YOUR PATIENCE, YOSUKE.
WE'RE ATTACKING THE HUMANOID NEIGHBOR.
...!
I SEE.
SO THAT'S IT!
WOOOOOOO

Chapter 73 Invasion: Part 20

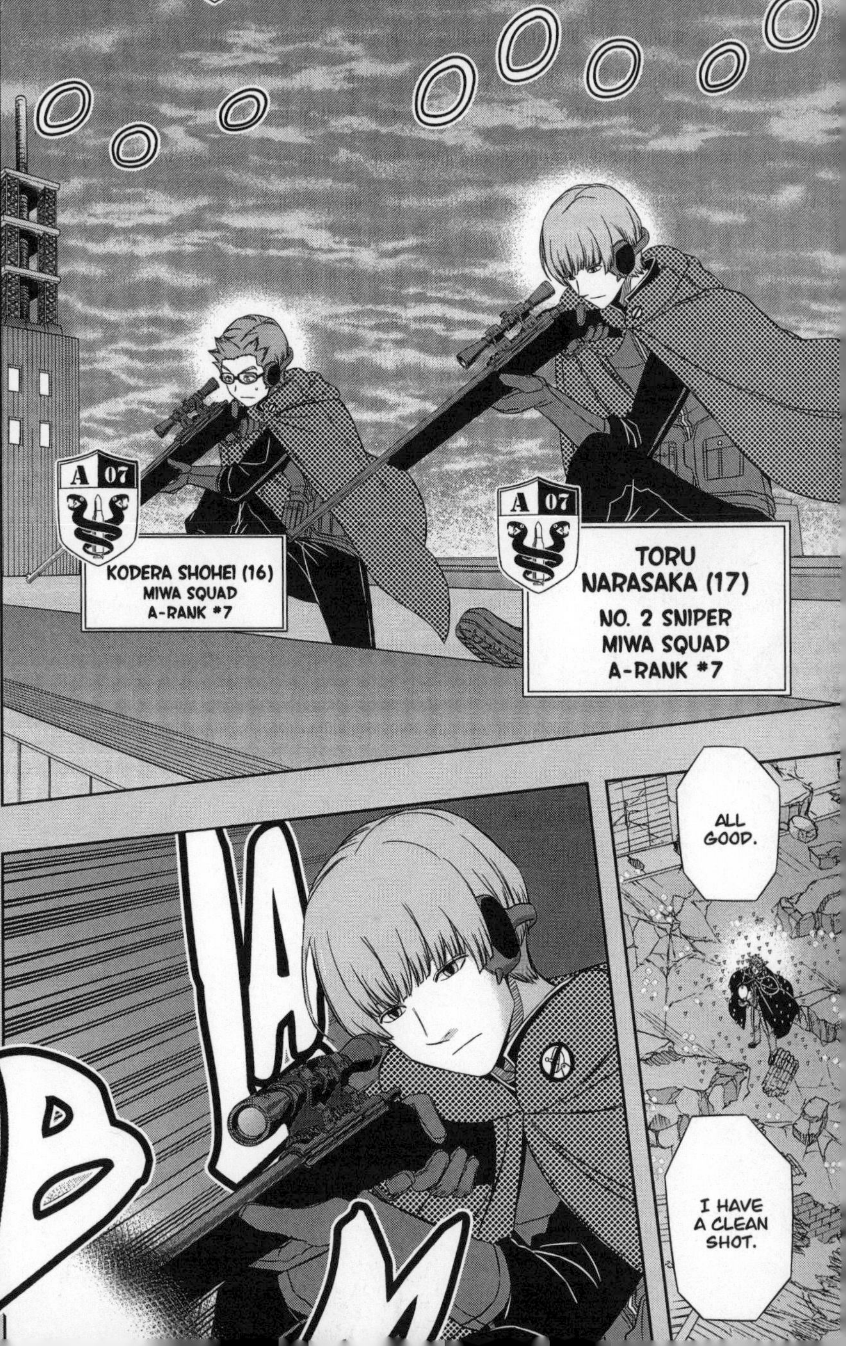
TORU NARASAKA (17)
NO. 2 SNIPER
MIWA SQUAD
A-RANK #7
A 07
KODERA SHOHEI (16)
MIWA SQUAD
A-RANK #7
A 07
ALL GOOD.
I HAVE A CLEAN SHOT.
BLAM

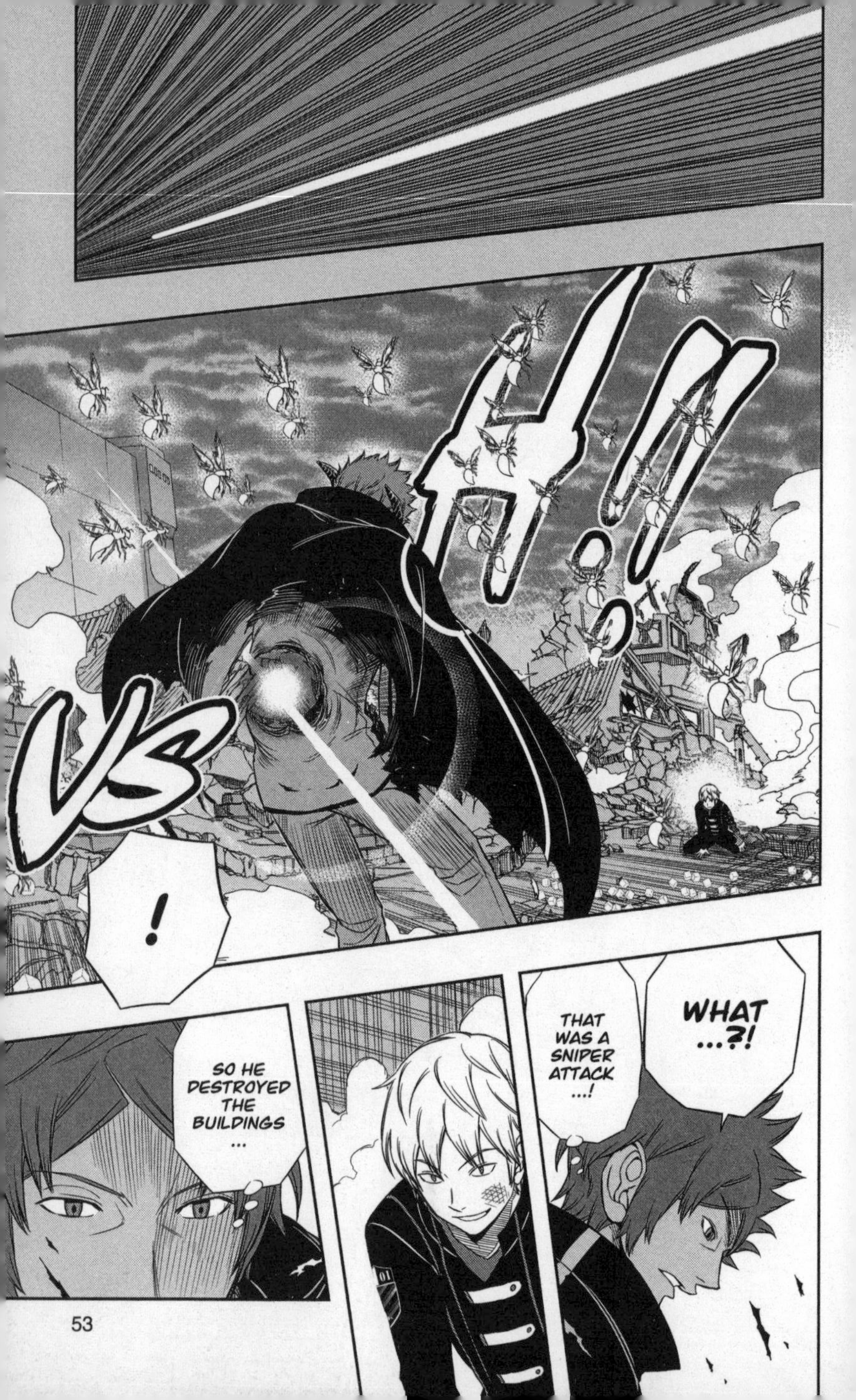
!!
VS
!
WHAT ...?!
THAT WAS A SNIPER ATTACK ...!
SO HE DESTROYED THE BUILDINGS ...

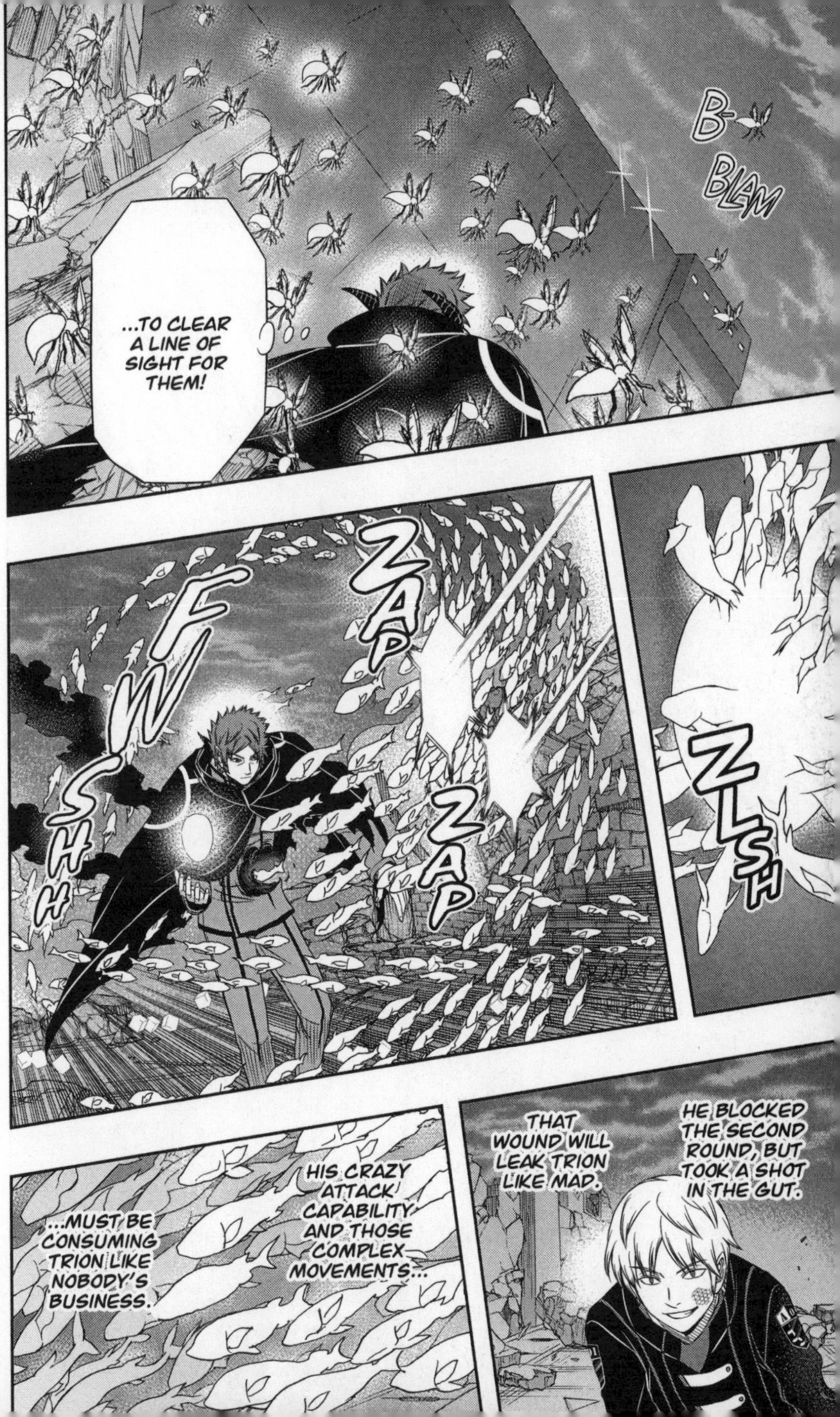
B-BLAM
...TO CLEAR A LINE OF SIGHT FOR THEM!
ZLSH
ZAP
ZAP
FWSHH
HE BLOCKED THE SECOND ROUND, BUT TOOK A SHOT IN THE GUT.
THAT WOUND WILL LEAK TRION LIKE MAD.
HIS CRAZY ATTACK CAPABILITY AND THOSE COMPLEX MOVEMENTS...
...MUST BE CONSUMING TRION LIKE NOBODY'S BUSINESS.

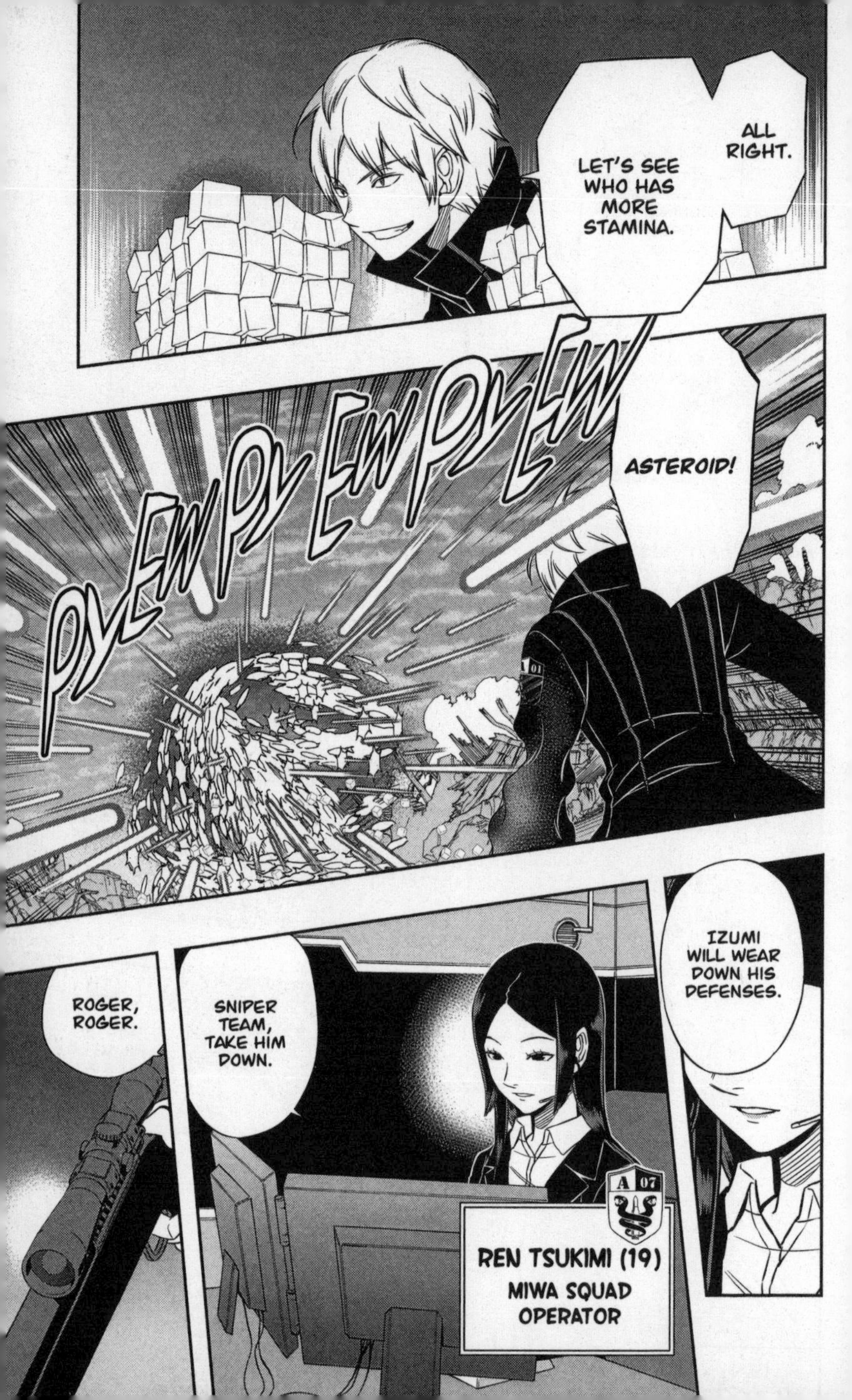
ALL RIGHT.
LET'S SEE WHO HAS MORE STAMINA.
ASTEROID!
PYEW PYEW PYEW PYEW
IZUMI WILL WEAR DOWN HIS DEFENSES.
SNIPER TEAM, TAKE HIM DOWN.
A 07
REN TSUKIMI (19)
MIWA SQUAD OPERATOR
ROGER, ROGER.

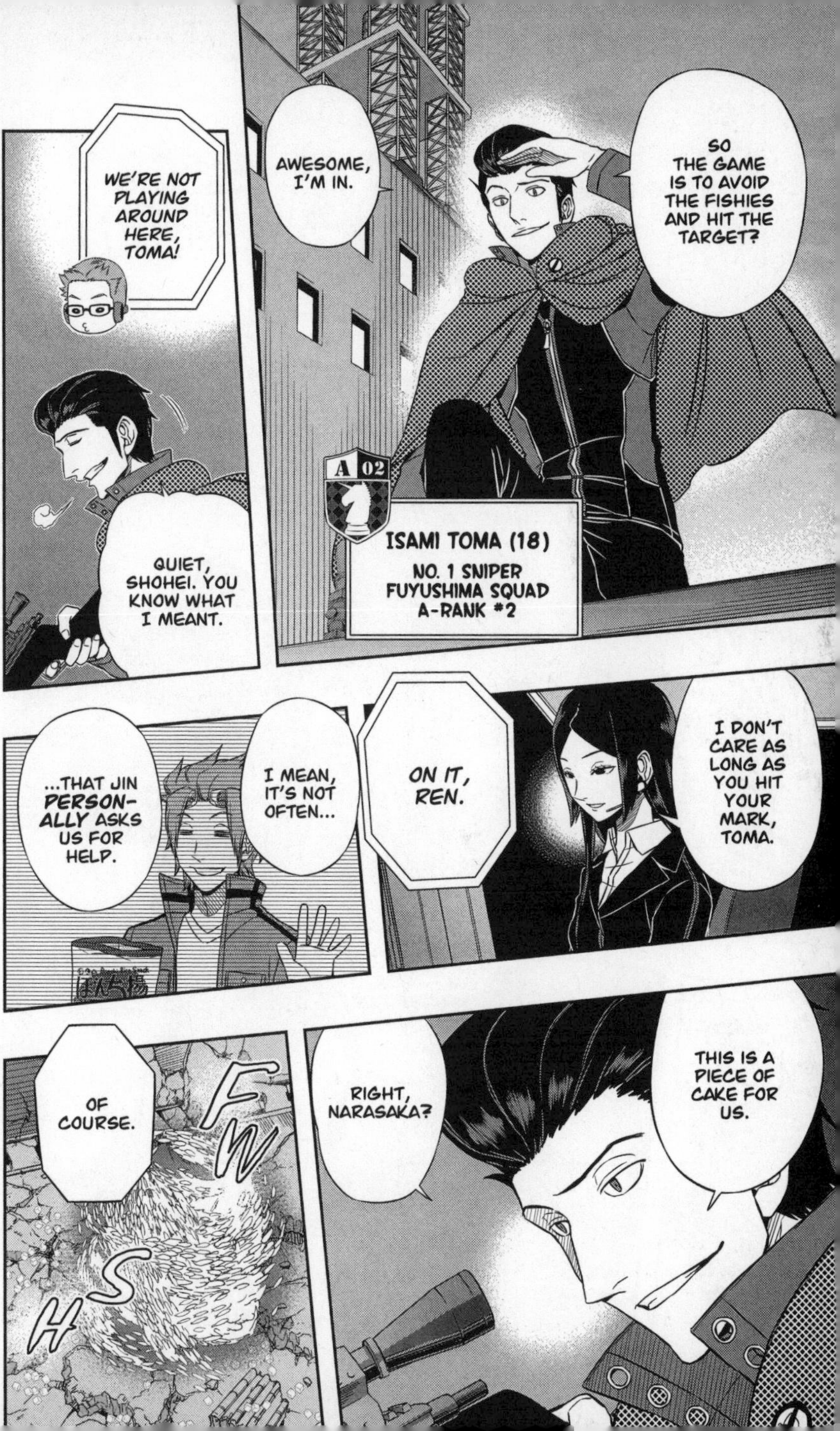
SO THE GAME IS TO AVOID THE FISHIES AND HIT THE TARGET?
AWESOME, I'M IN.
A 02
ISAMI TOMA (18)
NO. 1 SNIPER
FUYUSHIMA SQUAD
A-RANK #2
WE'RE NOT PLAYING AROUND HERE, TOMA!
QUIET, SHOHEI. YOU KNOW WHAT I MEANT.
I DON'T CARE AS LONG AS YOU HIT YOUR MARK, TOMA.
ON IT, REN.
I MEAN, IT'S NOT OFTEN...
...THAT JIN PERSONALLY ASKS US FOR HELP.
THIS IS A PIECE OF CAKE FOR US.
RIGHT, NARASAKA?
OF COURSE.
FWSH

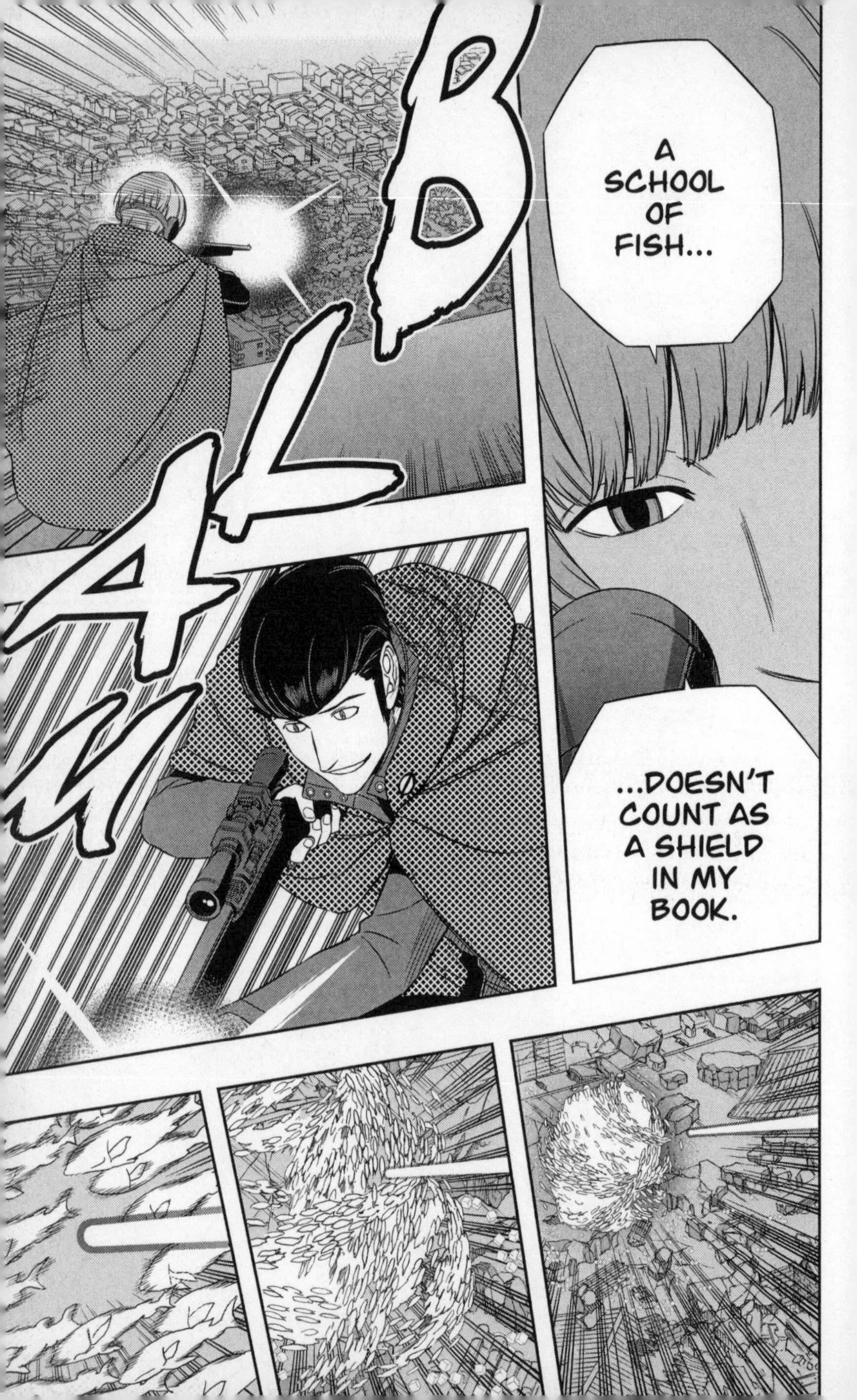
A SCHOOL OF FISH...
...DOESN'T COUNT AS A SHIELD IN MY BOOK.

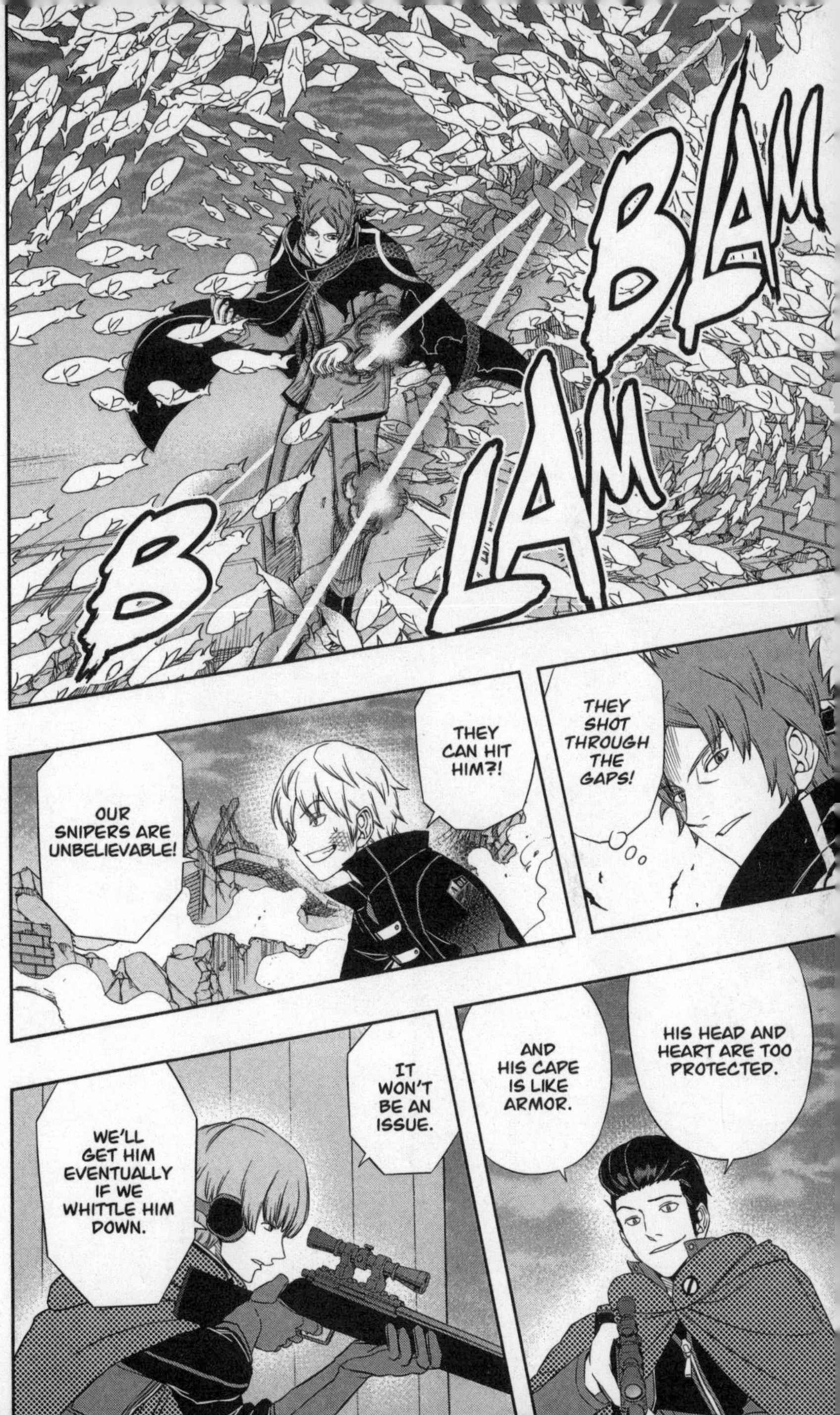
BLAM
BLAM
THEY SHOT THROUGH THE GAPS!
THEY CAN HIT HIM?!
OUR SNIPERS ARE UNBELIEVABLE!
HIS HEAD AND HEART ARE TOO PROTECTED.
AND HIS CAPE IS LIKE ARMOR.
IT WON'T BE AN ISSUE.
WE'LL GET HIM EVENTUALLY IF WE WHITTLE HIM DOWN.

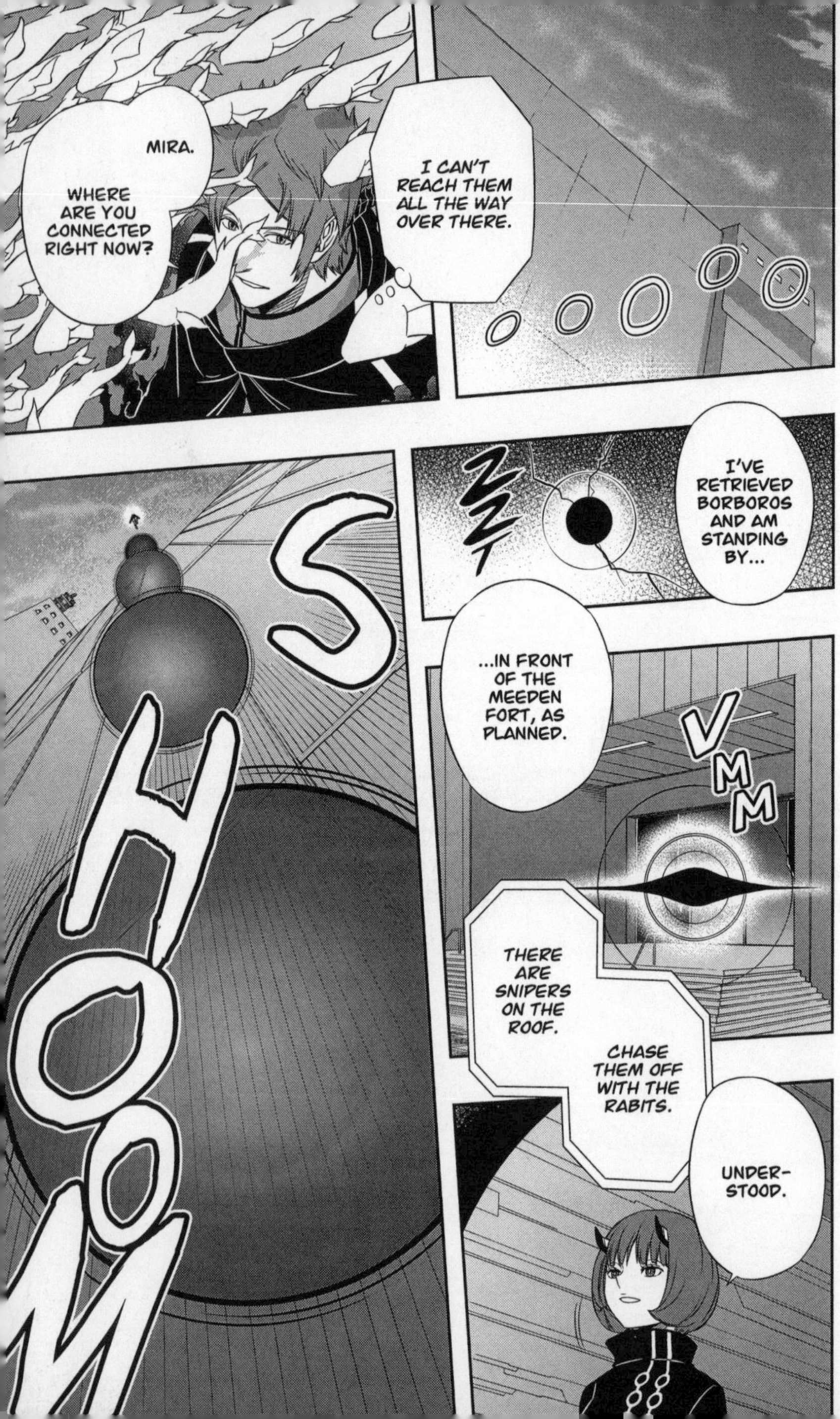
I CAN'T REACH THEM ALL THE WAY OVER THERE.
MIRA.
WHERE ARE YOU CONNECTED RIGHT NOW?
ZZZT
I'VE RETRIEVED BORBOROS AND AM STANDING BY...
...IN FRONT OF THE MEEDEN FORT, AS PLANNED.
VMM
THERE ARE SNIPERS ON THE ROOF.
CHASE THEM OFF WITH THE RABITS.
UNDER-STOOD.
SHOOOM

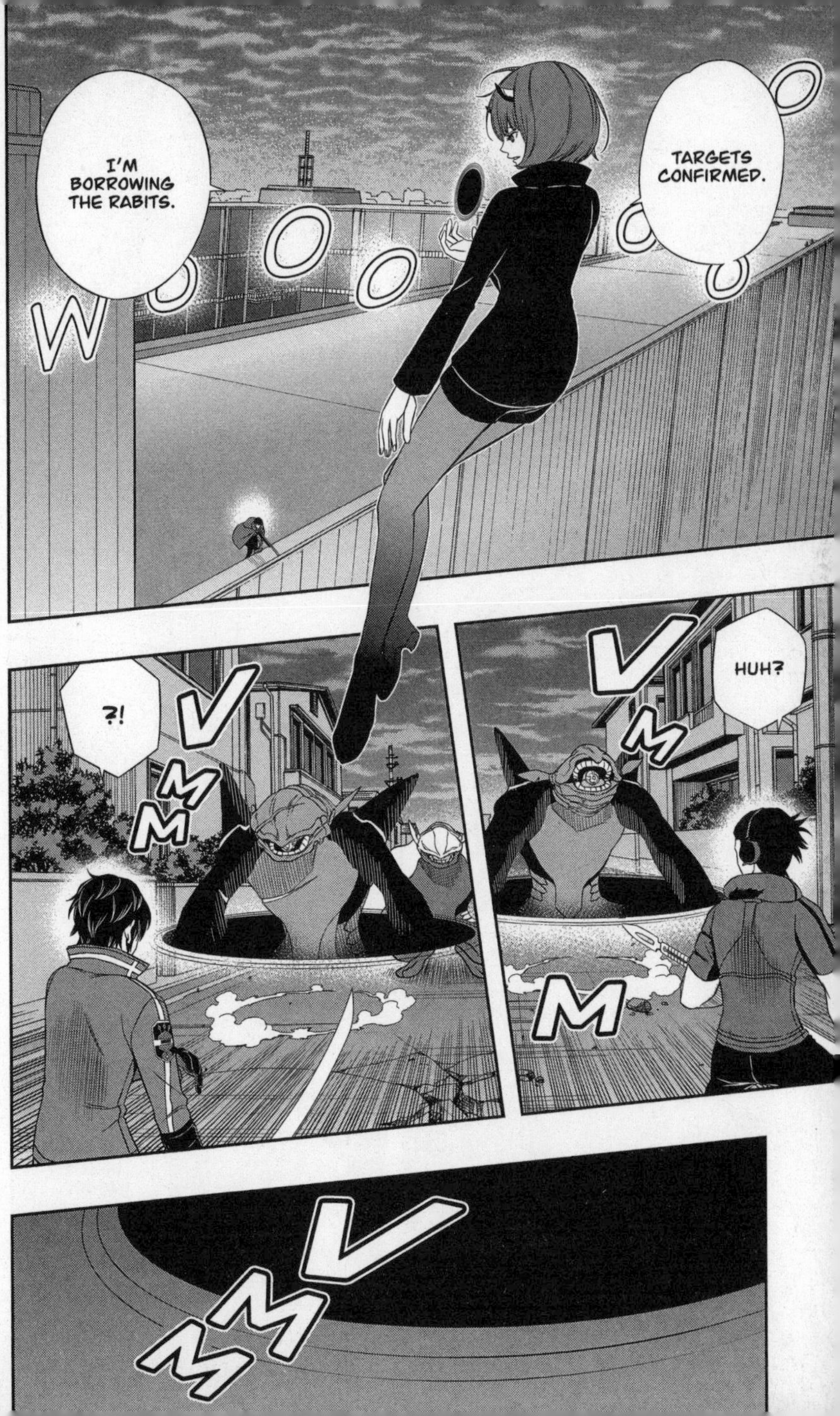
TARGETS CONFIRMED.
I'M BORROWING THE RABITS.
WOOOOOO
HUH?
VMM
?!
VMM
VMMM

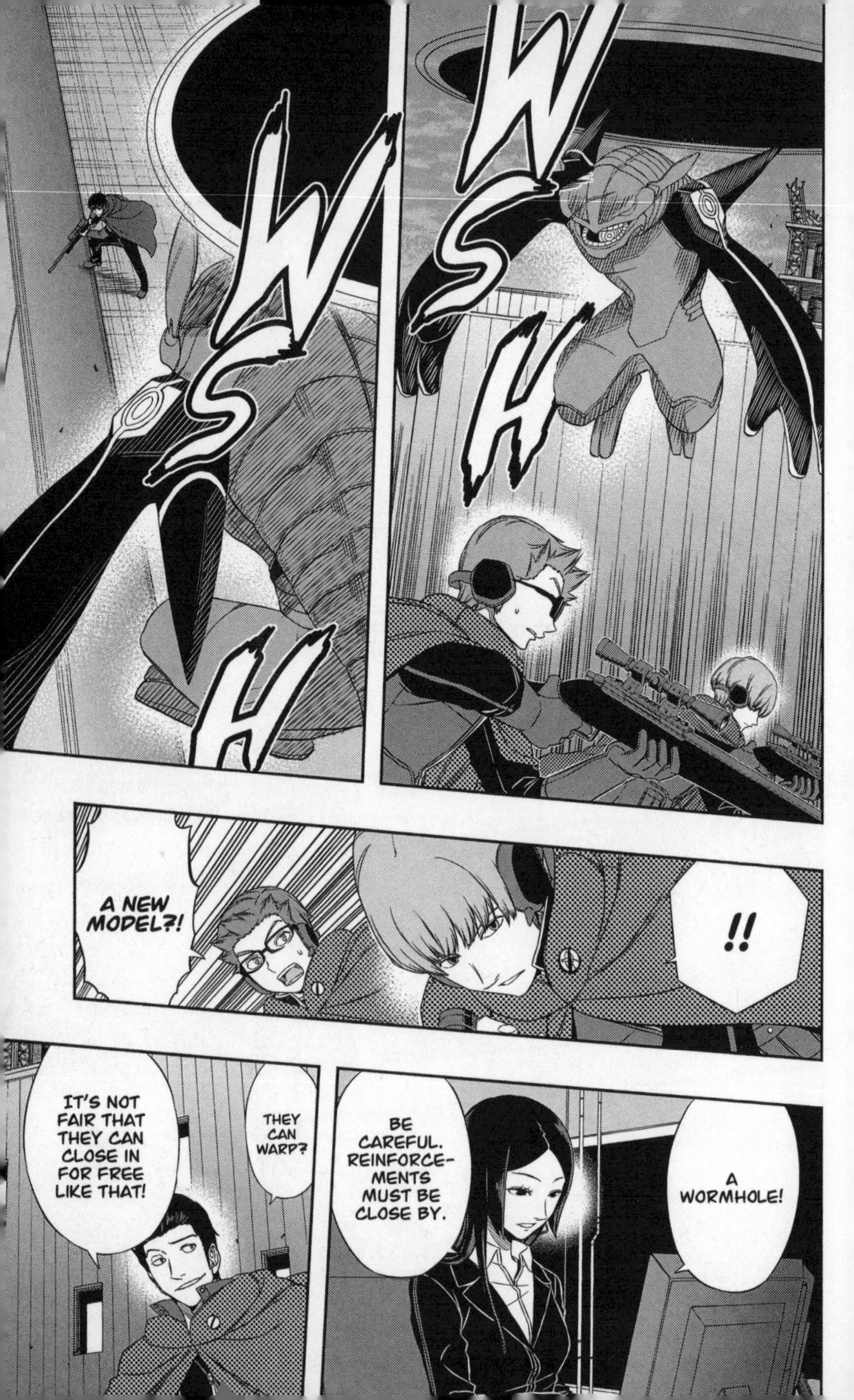
WHSH
WHSH
!!
A NEW MODEL?!
A WORMHOLE!
BE CAREFUL. REINFORCEMENTS MUST BE CLOSE BY.
THEY CAN WARP?
IT'S NOT FAIR THAT THEY CAN CLOSE IN FOR FREE LIKE THAT!

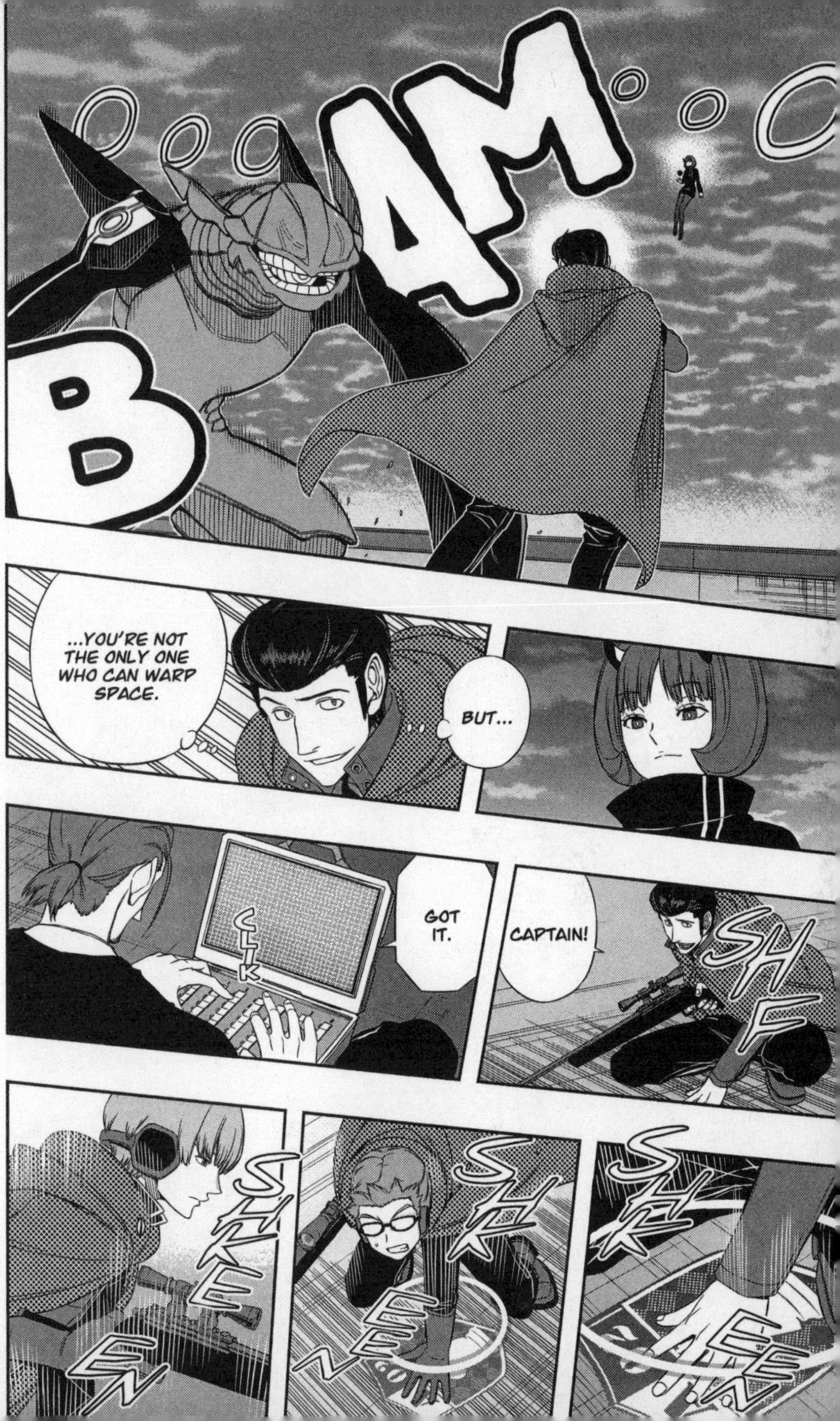
BAM
BUT...
...YOU'RE NOT THE ONLY ONE WHO CAN WARP SPACE.
CAPTAIN!
SHF
GOT IT.
CLIK
SHKEEEN
SHKEEN
SHKEEEN

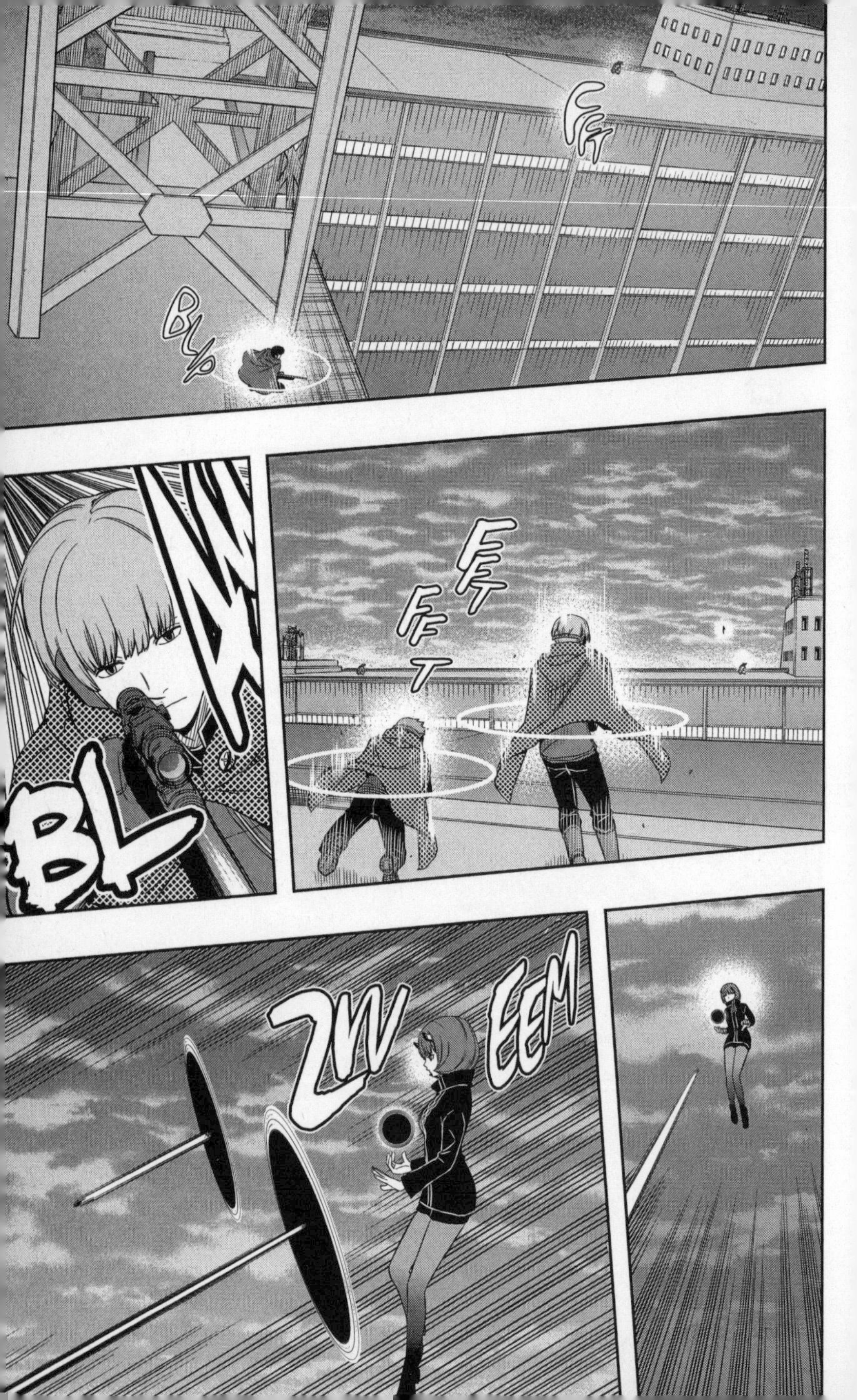

FFT
BLIP
BLAM
FFT
FFT
ZWEEM

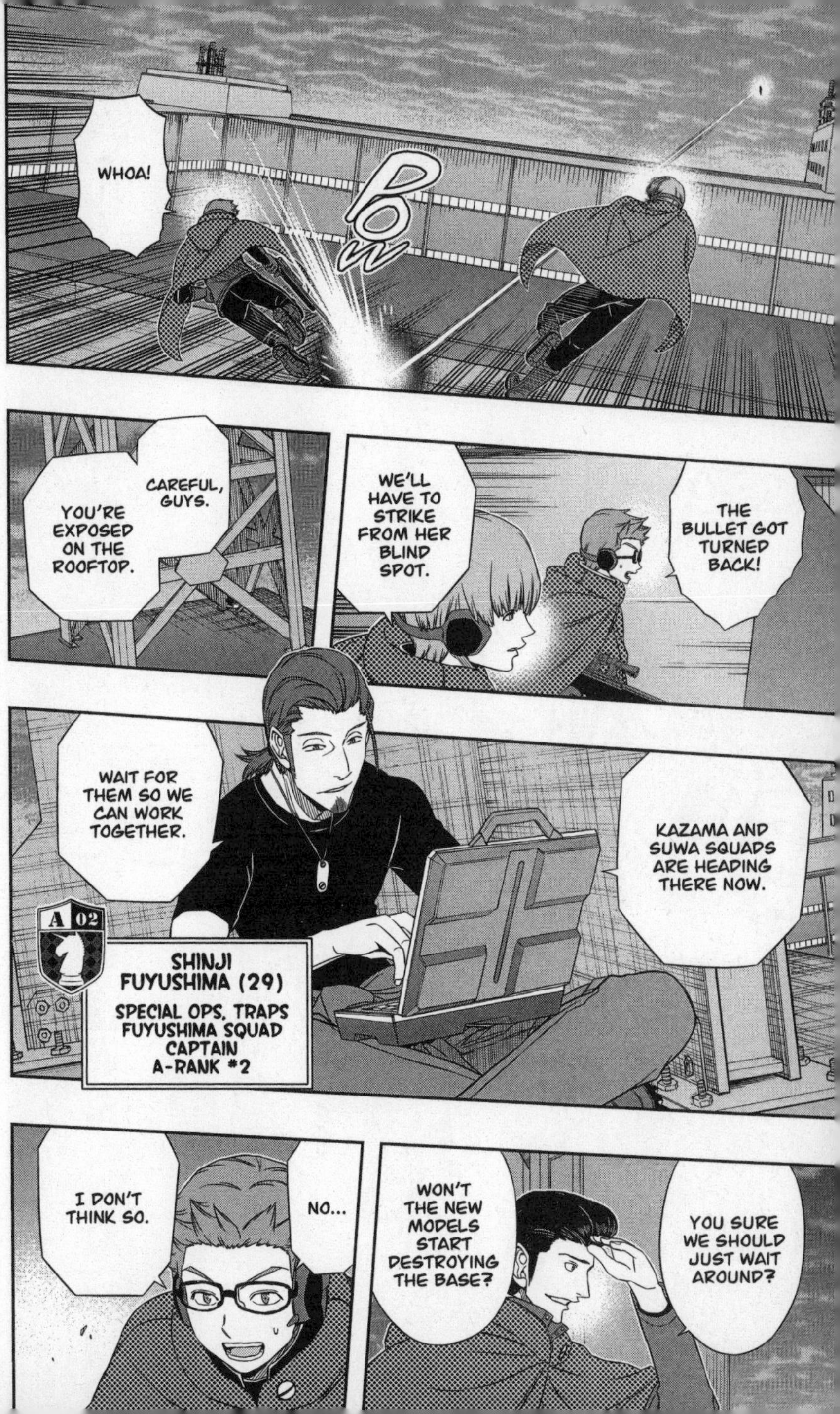
WHOA!
THE BULLET GOT TURNED BACK!
WE'LL HAVE TO STRIKE FROM HER BLIND SPOT.
CAREFUL, GUYS.
YOU'RE EXPOSED ON THE ROOFTOP.
KAZAMA AND SUWA SQUADS ARE HEADING THERE NOW.
WAIT FOR THEM SO WE CAN WORK TOGETHER.
A 02
SHINJI FUYUSHIMA (29)
SPECIAL OPS, TRAPS
FUYUSHIMA SQUAD CAPTAIN
A-RANK #2
YOU SURE WE SHOULD JUST WAIT AROUND?
WON'T THE NEW MODELS START DESTROYING THE BASE?
NO...
I DON'T THINK SO.

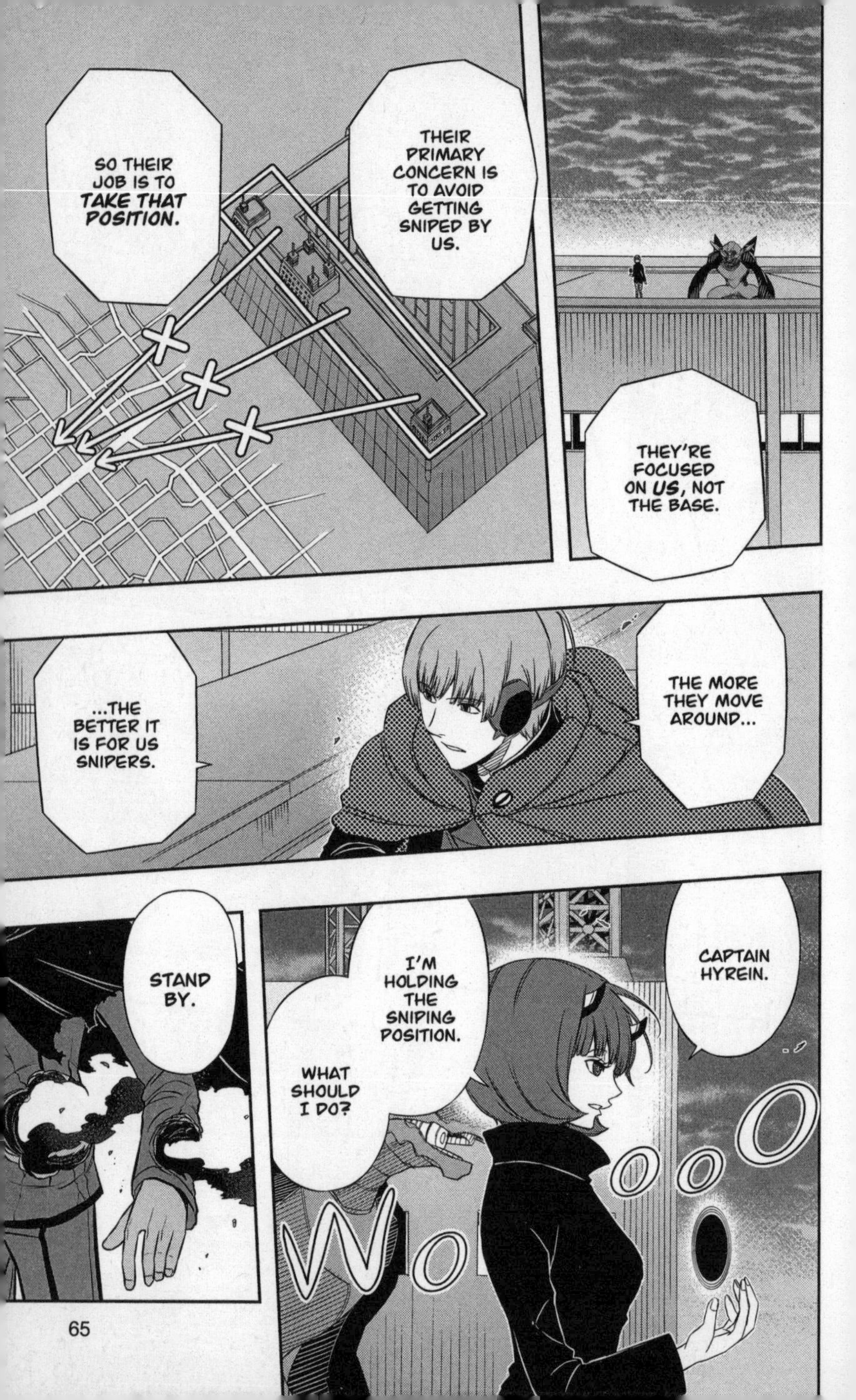
THEY'RE FOCUSED ON US, NOT THE BASE.
THEIR PRIMARY CONCERN IS TO AVOID GETTING SNIPED BY US.
SO THEIR JOB IS TO TAKE THAT POSITION.
THE MORE THEY MOVE AROUND...
...THE BETTER IT IS FOR US SNIPERS.
CAPTAIN HYREIN.
I'M HOLDING THE SNIPING POSITION.
WHAT SHOULD I DO?
WOOOOO
STAND BY.

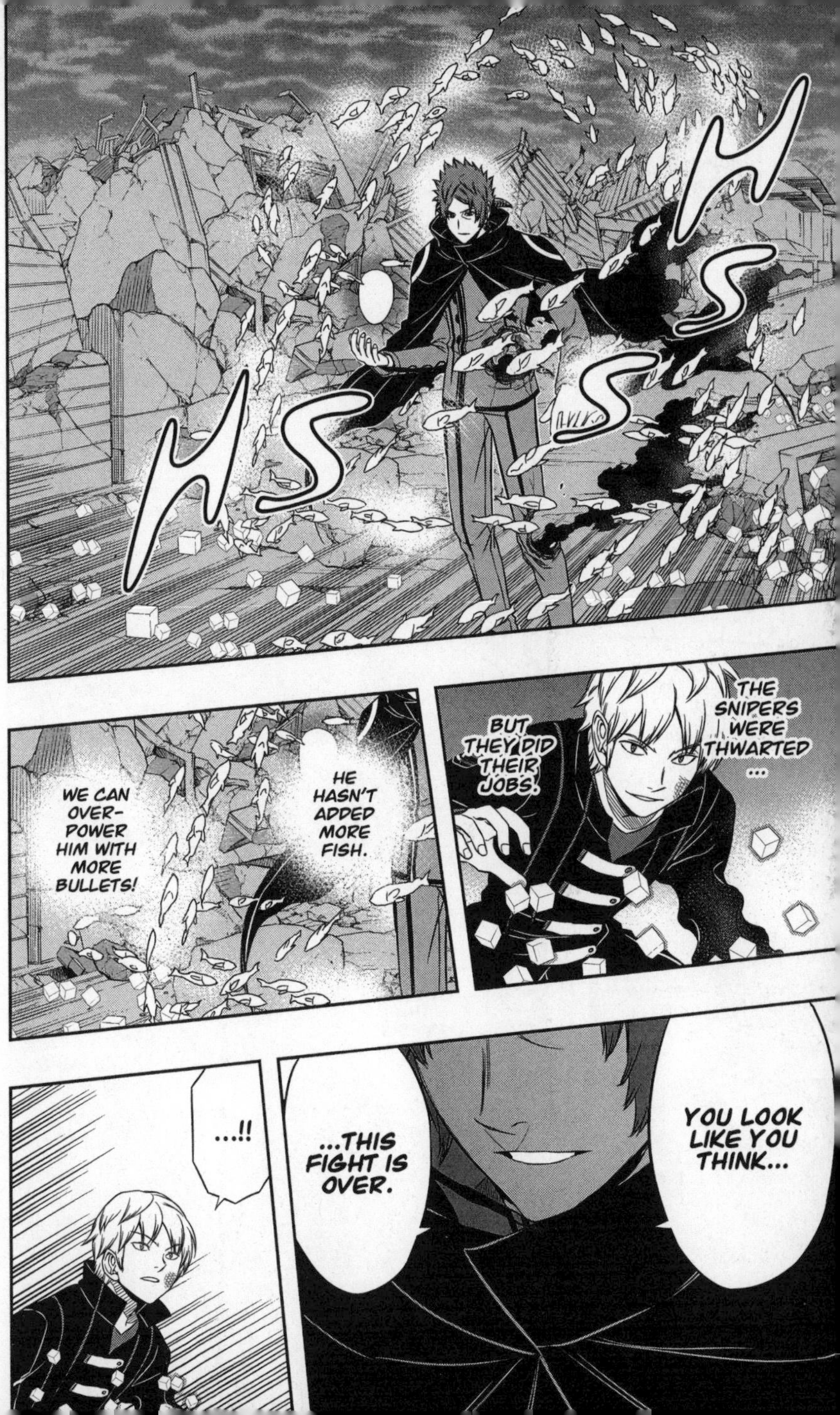
HSSSH
THE SNIPERS WERE THWARTED...
BUT THEY DID THEIR JOBS.
HE HASN'T ADDED MORE FISH.
WE CAN OVER-POWER HIM WITH MORE BULLETS!
YOU LOOK LIKE YOU THINK...
...THIS FIGHT IS OVER.
...!!

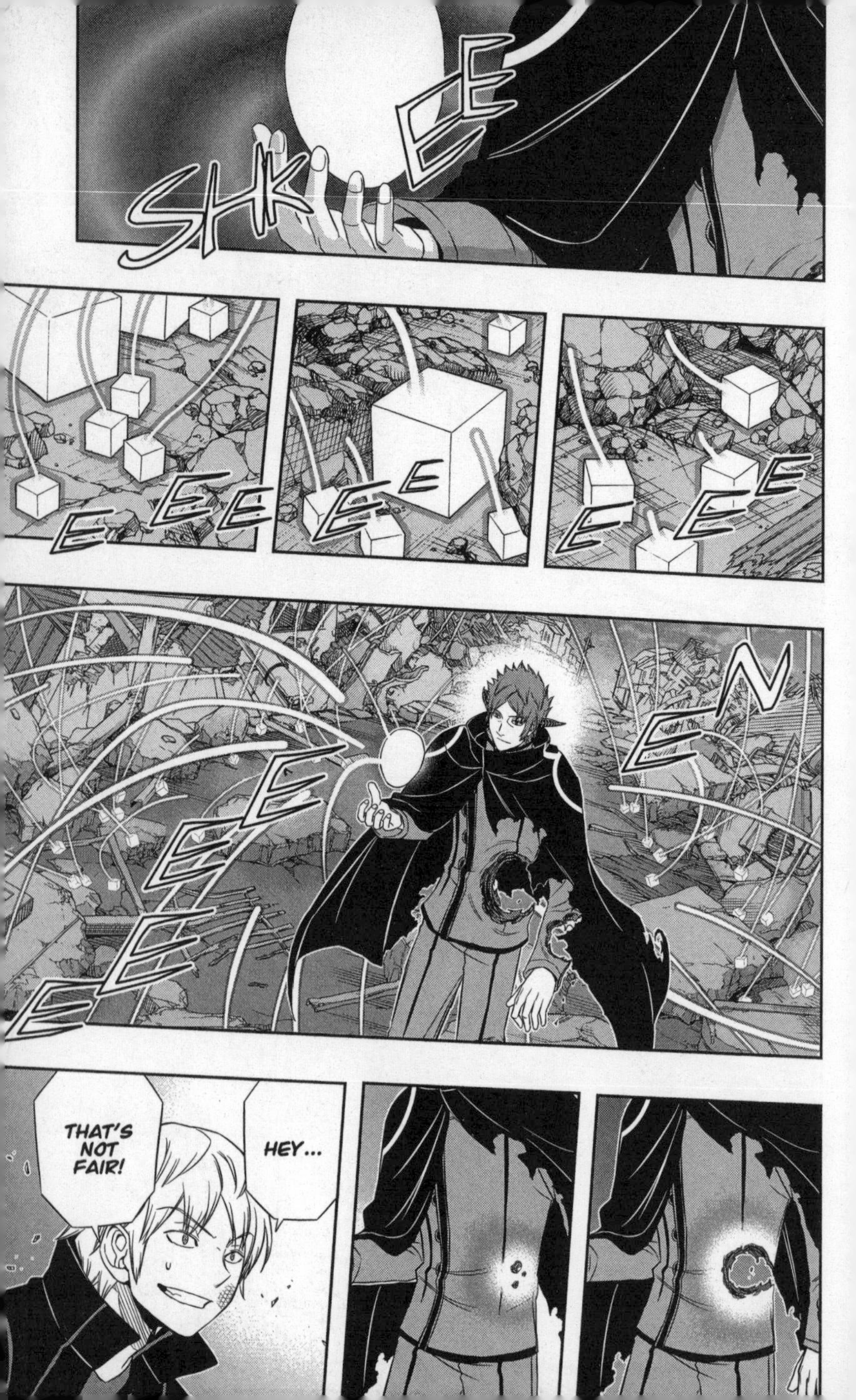
SHKEEE
EEEE
EEEE
EEEE
EEEEEE
EEN
HEY...
THAT'S NOT FAIR!

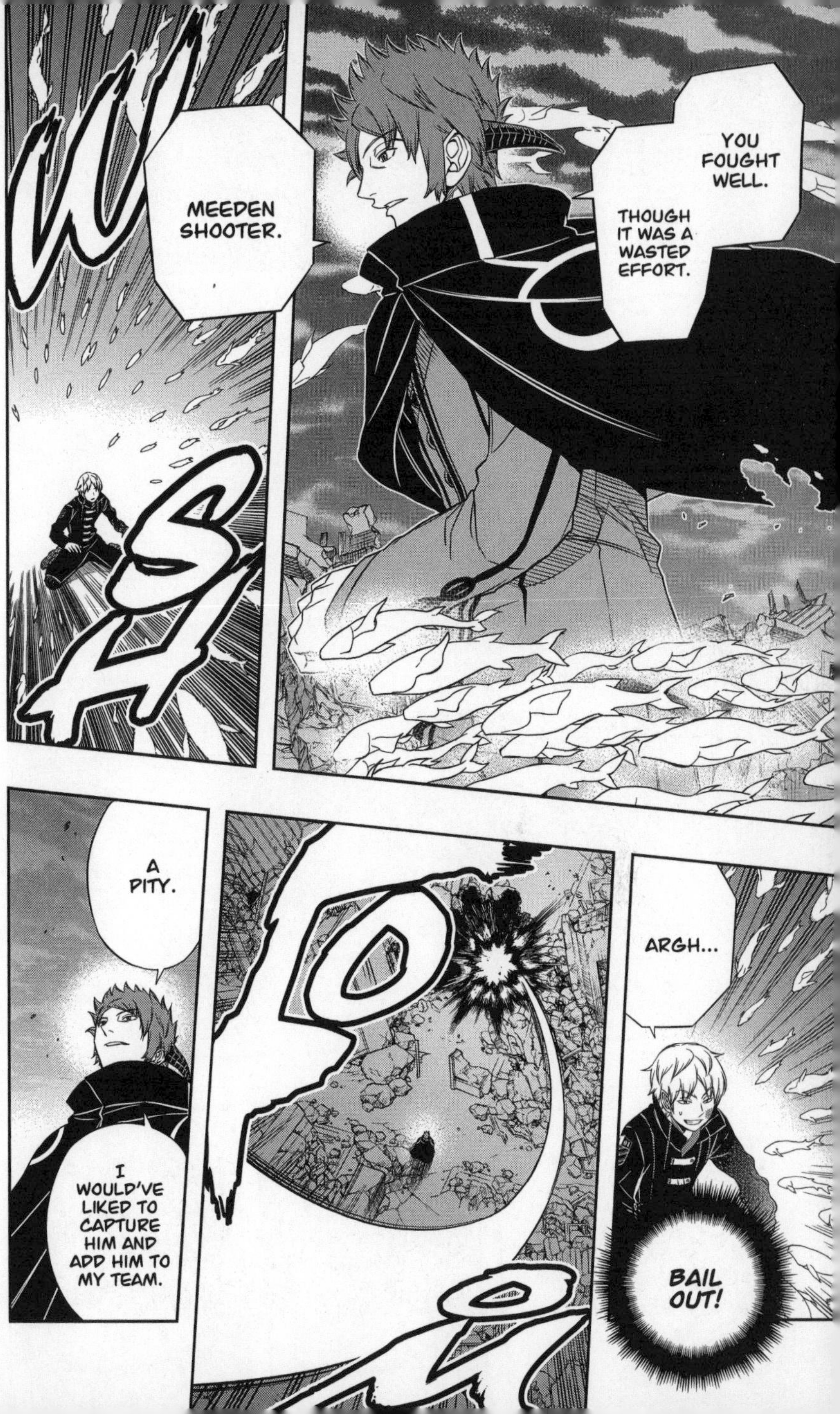
YOU FOUGHT WELL.
THOUGH IT WAS A WASTED EFFORT.
MEEDEN SHOOTER.
ARGH...
BAIL OUT!
A PITY.
I WOULD'VE LIKED TO CAPTURE HIM AND ADD HIM TO MY TEAM.

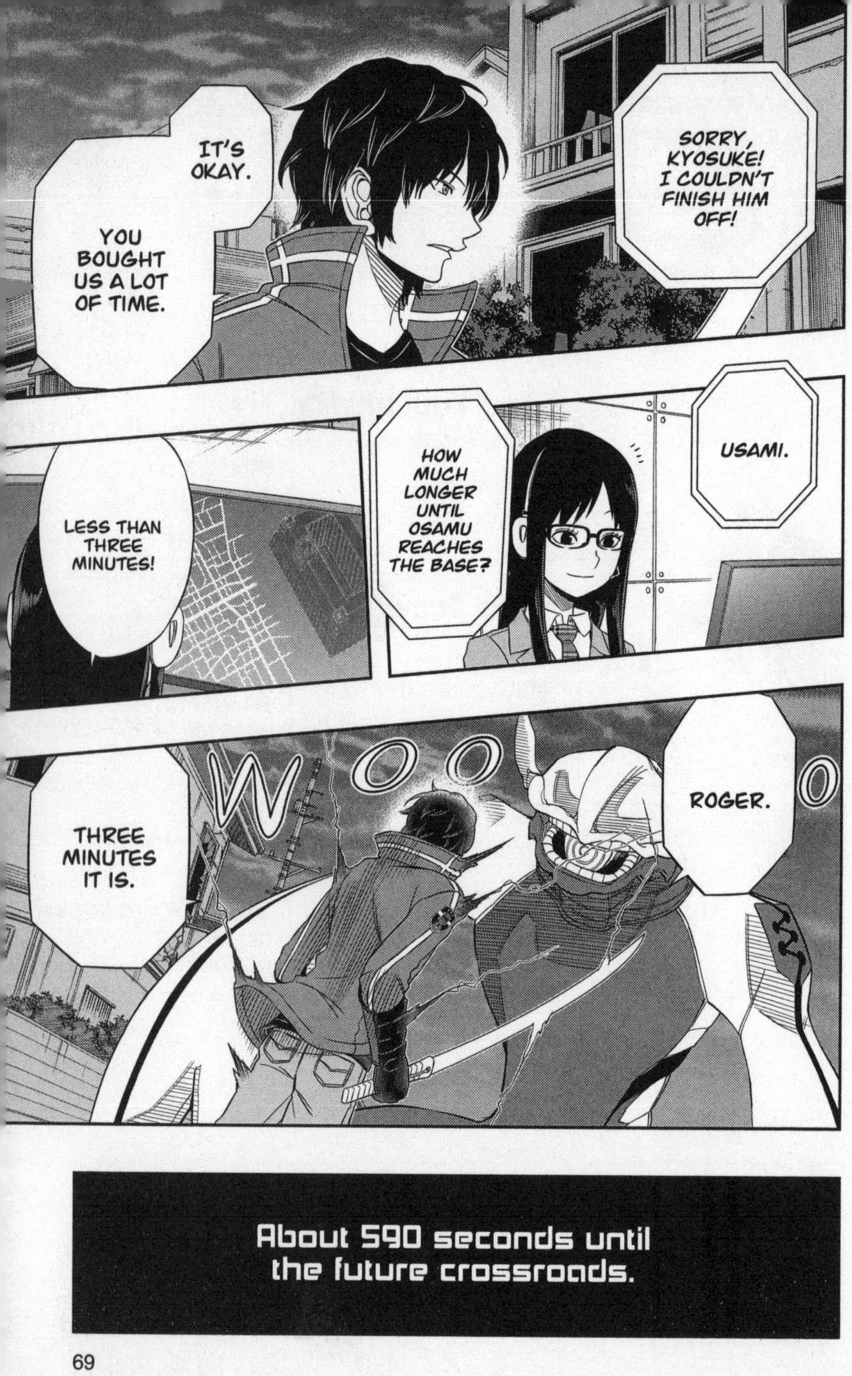
SORRY, KYOSUKE! I COULDN'T FINISH HIM OFF!
IT'S OKAY.
YOU BOUGHT US A LOT OF TIME.
USAMI.
HOW MUCH LONGER UNTIL OSAMU REACHES THE BASE?
LESS THAN THREE MINUTES!
ROGER.
WOOOO
THREE MINUTES IT IS.

About 590 seconds until the future crossroads.

Fuyushima Squad

Border HQ A-Rank #2

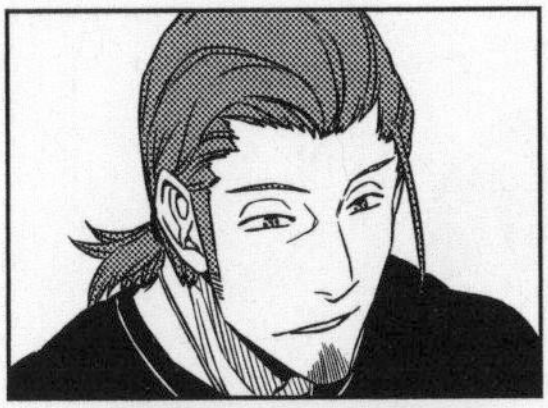

Shinji Fuyushima

Captain, Trapper

■29 years old
■Born Jan. 3

■Clavis, Blood type B
■Height: 6′
■Likes: Games, sukiyaki, Legos

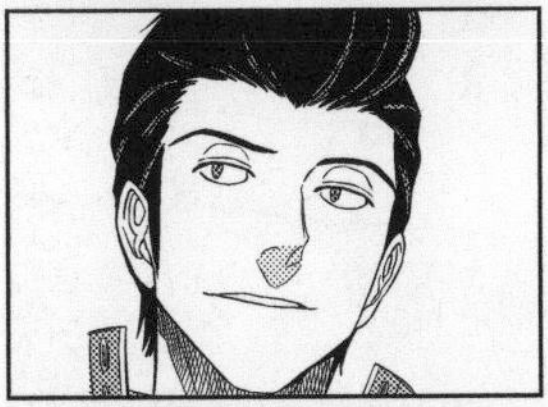

Isami Toma

Sniper

■18 years old (high school student)
■Born July 7

■Gladius, Blood type AB
■Height: 6′
■Likes: Naps, bananas, ramen, cats

NO IMAGE

Risa Maki

Operator

■16 years old (high school student)
■Born March 1

■Apis, Blood type AB
■Height: 5′3″
■Likes: Movies, pickled plums, cleaning and organizing

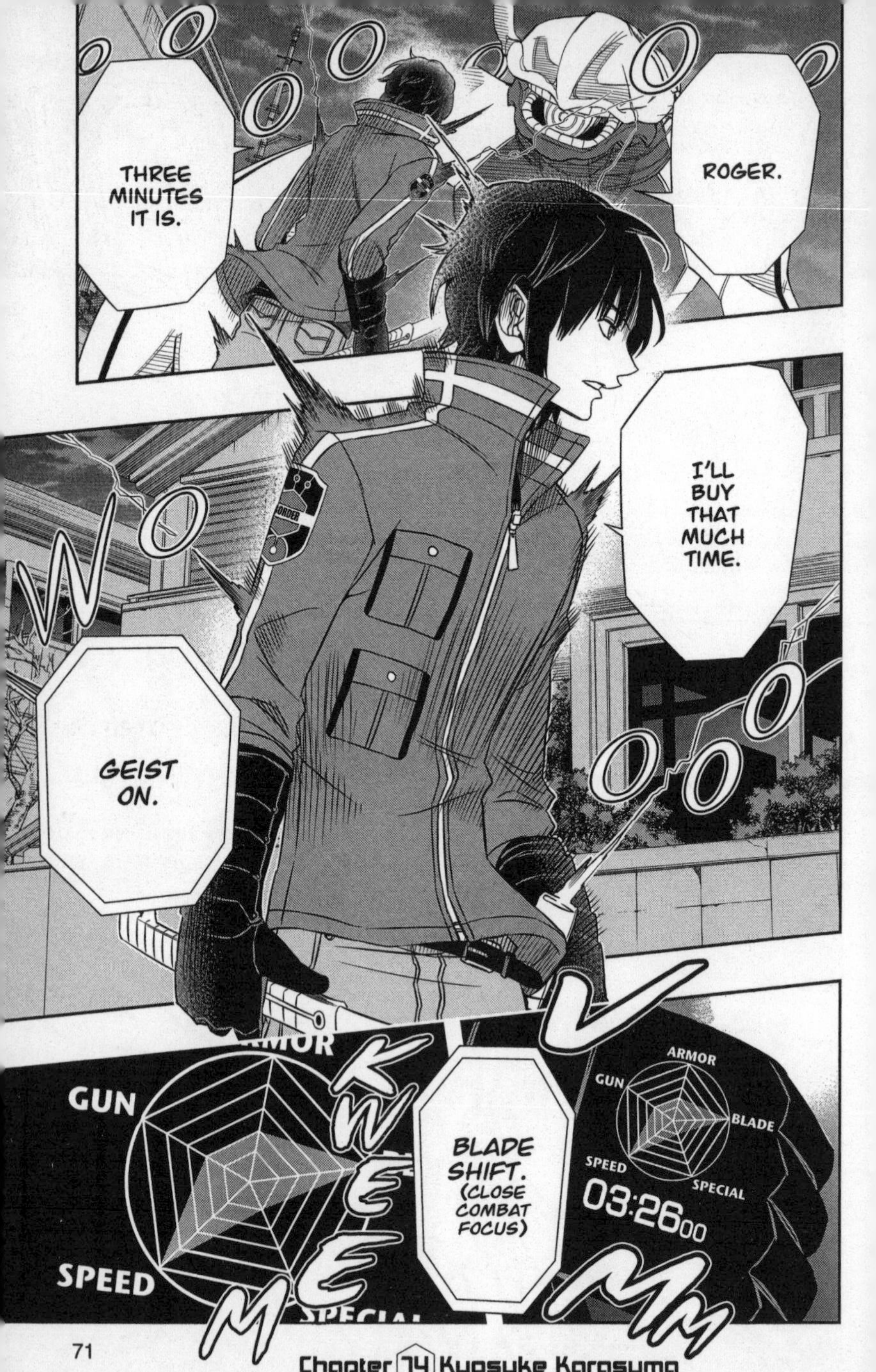
ROGER.
THREE MINUTES IT IS.
I'LL BUY THAT MUCH TIME.
WO
GEIST ON.
KWEEMMM
ARMOR
GUN
BLADE
SPEED
SPECIAL
03:26 00
BLADE SHIFT. (CLOSE COMBAT FOCUS)
GUN
SPEED
SPECIAL

Chapter 74 Kyosuke Karasuma

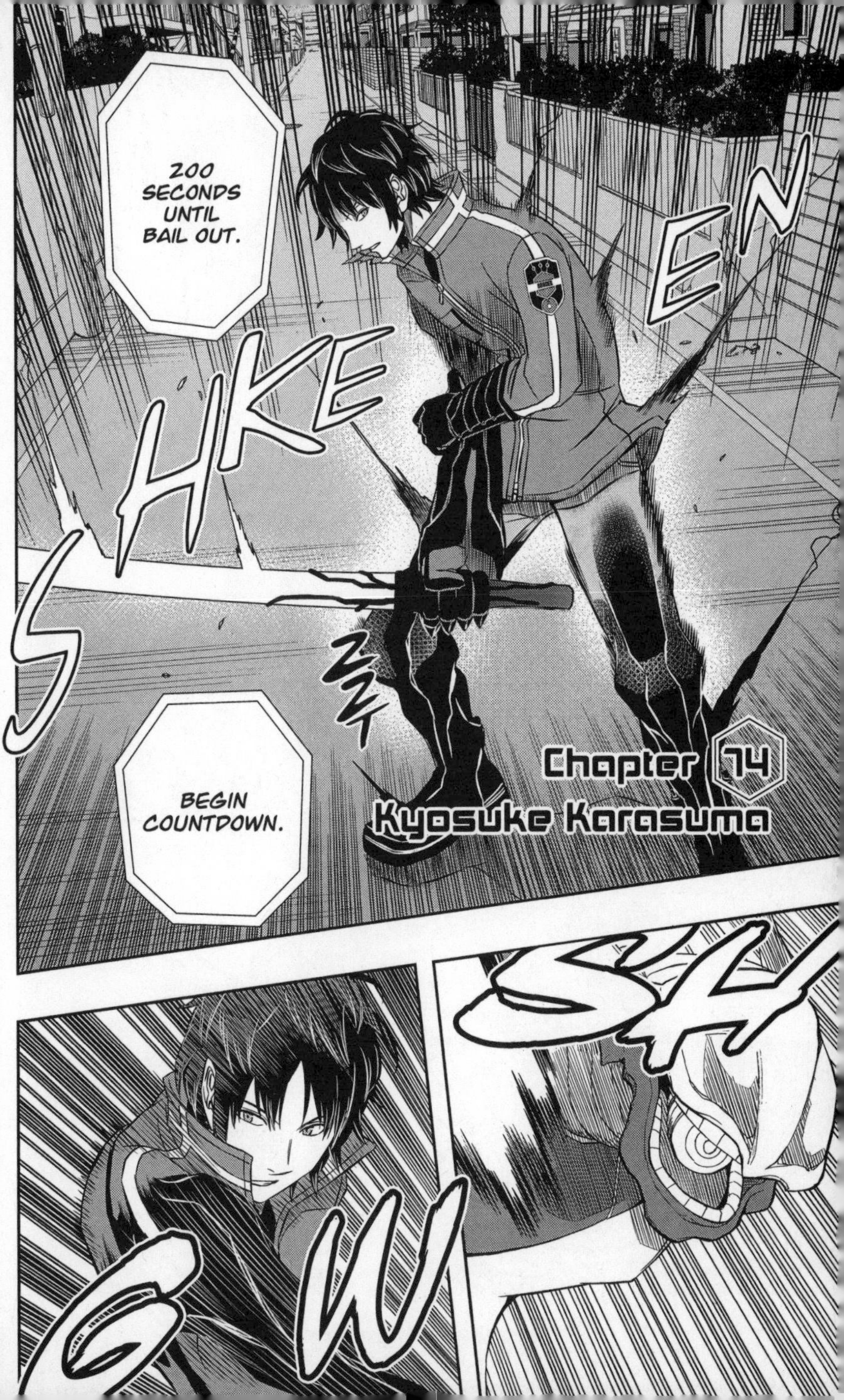
200 SECONDS UNTIL BAIL OUT.
SHKEEN
Chapter 74
Kyosuke Karasuma
ZZZK
BEGIN COUNTDOWN.
SH
SW

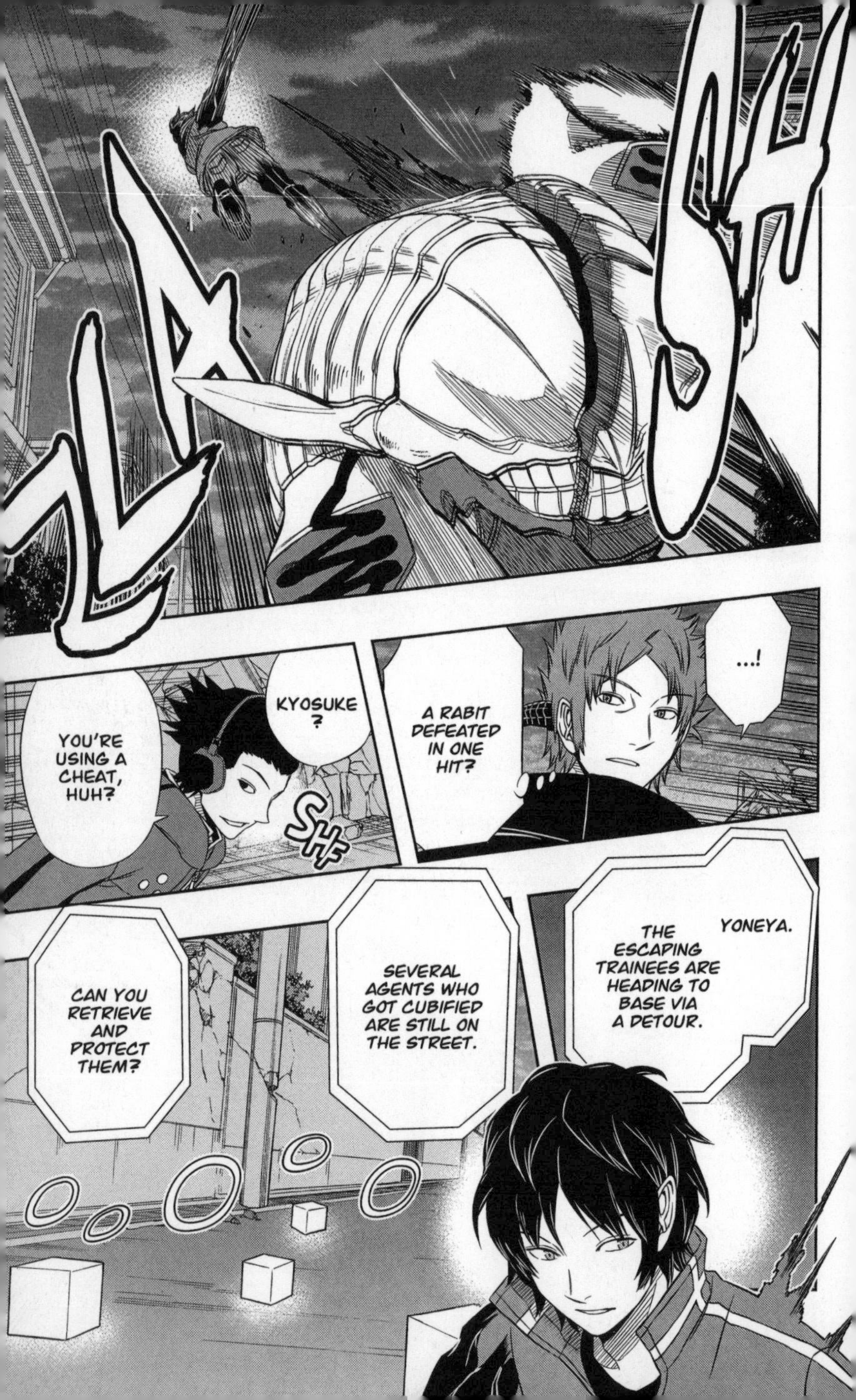
...!
A RABIT DEFEATED IN ONE HIT?
KYOSUKE?
YOU'RE USING A CHEAT, HUH?
SH
YONEYA.
THE ESCAPING TRAINEES ARE HEADING TO BASE VIA A DETOUR.
SEVERAL AGENTS WHO GOT CUBIFIED ARE STILL ON THE STREET.
CAN YOU RETRIEVE AND PROTECT THEM?

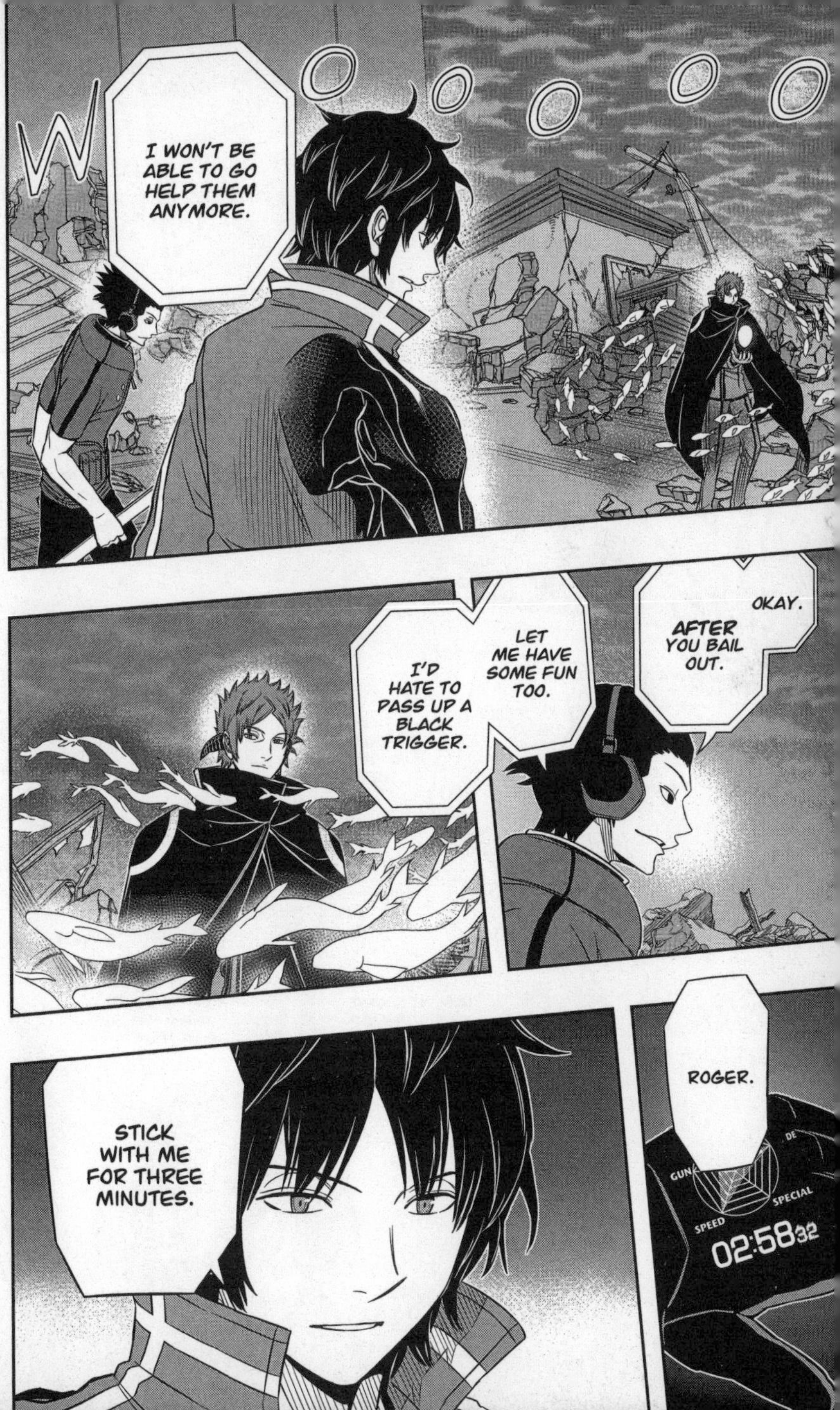
I WON'T BE ABLE TO GO HELP THEM ANYMORE.
OKAY.
AFTER YOU BAIL OUT.
LET ME HAVE SOME FUN TOO.
I'D HATE TO PASS UP A BLACK TRIGGER.
ROGER.
GUN
DE
SPECIAL
SPEED
02:58 32
STICK WITH ME FOR THREE MINUTES.

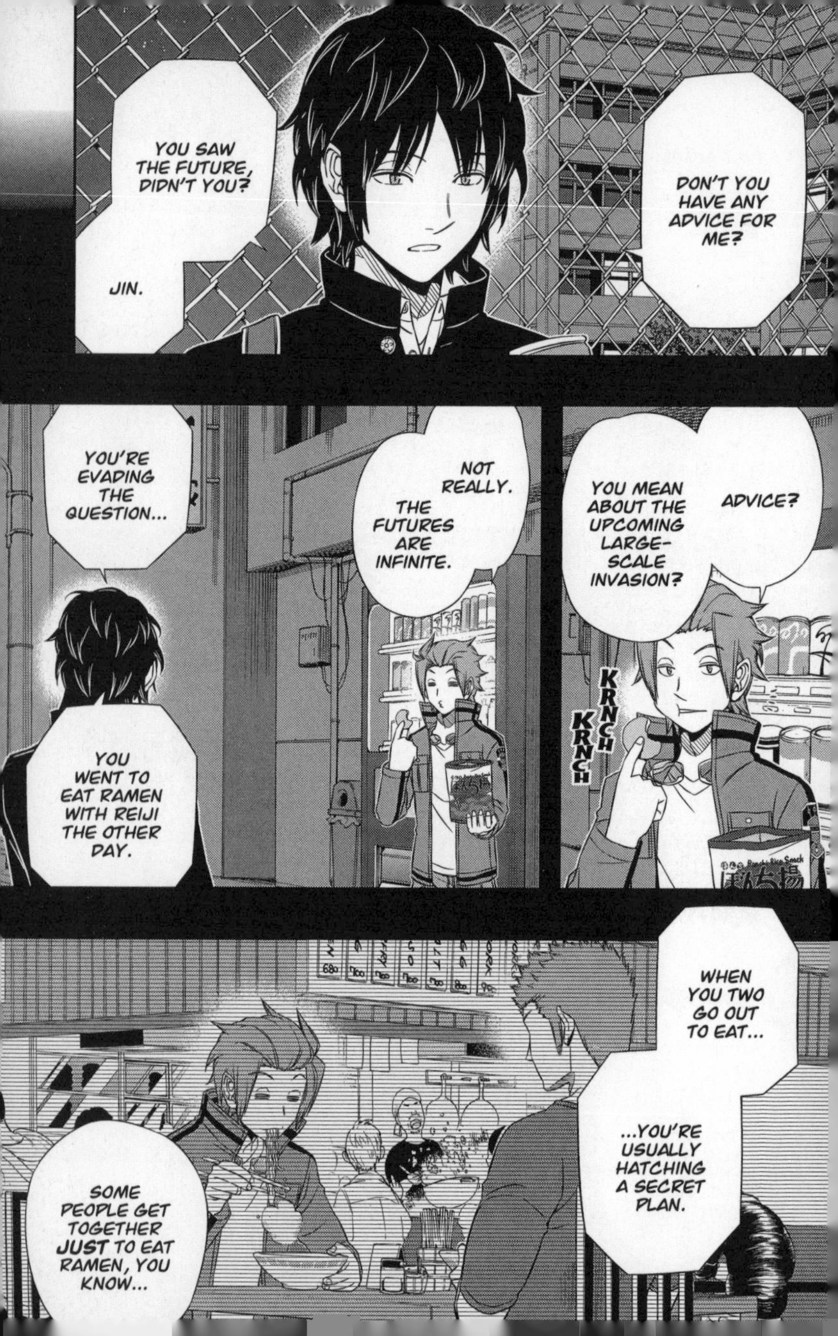
DON'T YOU HAVE ANY ADVICE FOR ME?
YOU SAW THE FUTURE, DIDN'T YOU?
JIN.
ADVICE?
YOU MEAN ABOUT THE UPCOMING LARGE-SCALE INVASION?
KRNCH
KRNCH
NOT REALLY.
THE FUTURES ARE INFINITE.
YOU'RE EVADING THE QUESTION...
YOU WENT TO EAT RAMEN WITH REIJI THE OTHER DAY.
WHEN YOU TWO GO OUT TO EAT...
...YOU'RE USUALLY HATCHING A SECRET PLAN.
SOME PEOPLE GET TOGETHER JUST TO EAT RAMEN, YOU KNOW...

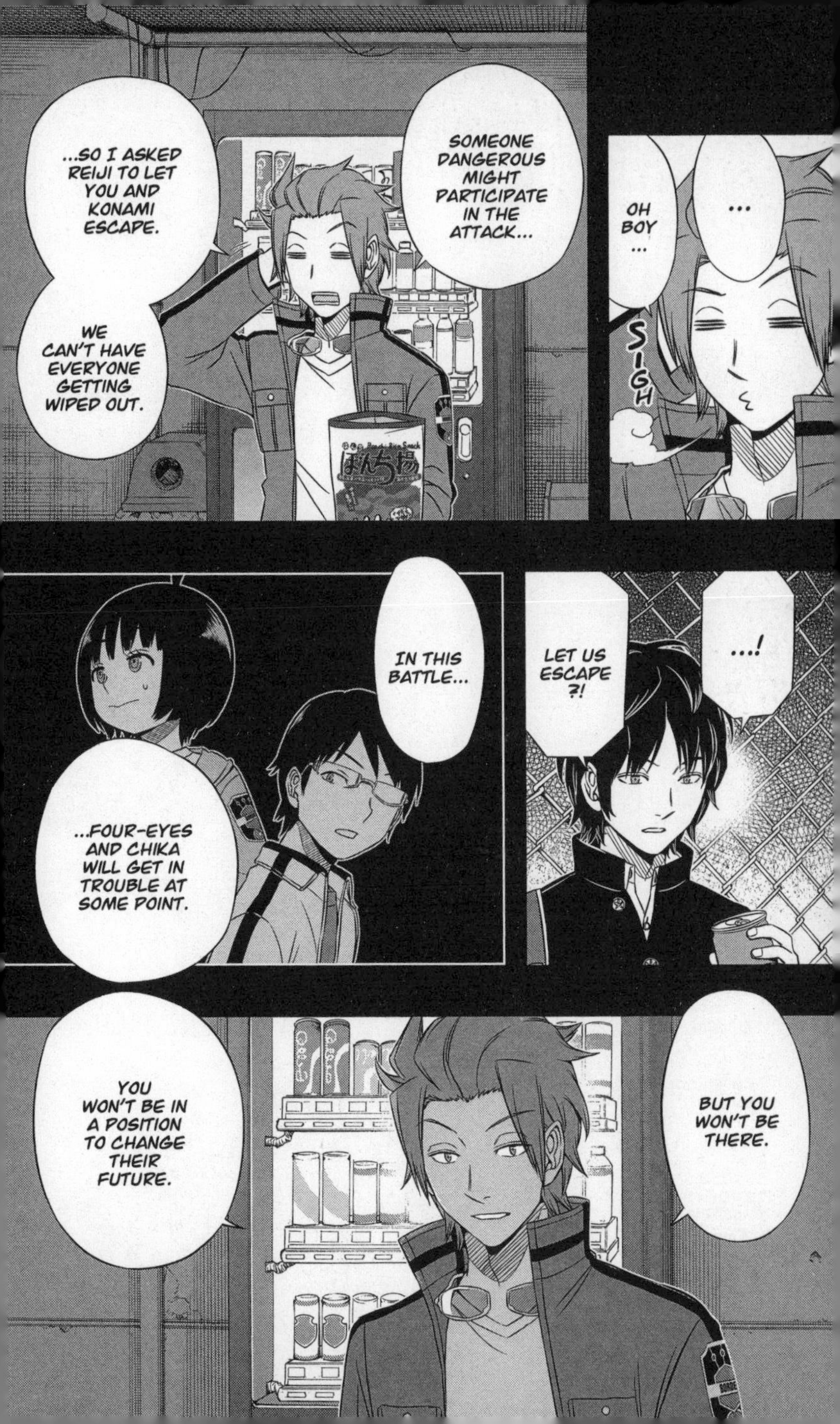
...
OH BOY ...
SIGH
SOMEONE DANGEROUS MIGHT PARTICIPATE IN THE ATTACK...
...SO I ASKED REIJI TO LET YOU AND KONAMI ESCAPE.
WE CAN'T HAVE EVERYONE GETTING WIPED OUT.
...!
LET US ESCAPE ?!
IN THIS BATTLE...
...FOUR-EYES AND CHIKA WILL GET IN TROUBLE AT SOME POINT.
BUT YOU WON'T BE THERE.
YOU WON'T BE IN A POSITION TO CHANGE THEIR FUTURE.

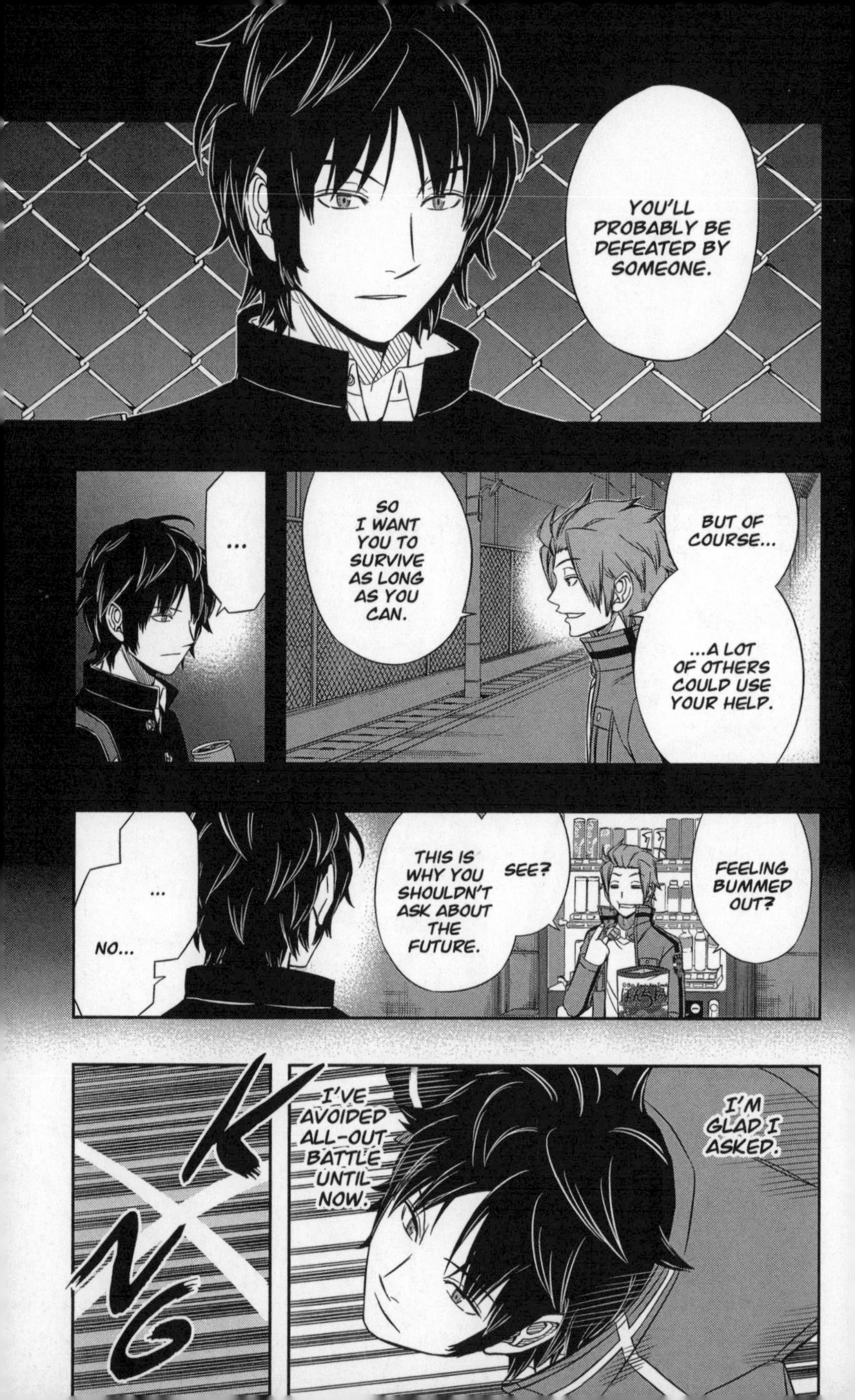
YOU'LL PROBABLY BE DEFEATED BY SOMEONE.
BUT OF COURSE...
...A LOT OF OTHERS COULD USE YOUR HELP.
SO I WANT YOU TO SURVIVE AS LONG AS YOU CAN.
...
FEELING BUMMED OUT?
SEE?
THIS IS WHY YOU SHOULDN'T ASK ABOUT THE FUTURE.
...
NO...
I'M GLAD I ASKED.
I'VE AVOIDED ALL-OUT BATTLE UNTIL NOW.
KNG

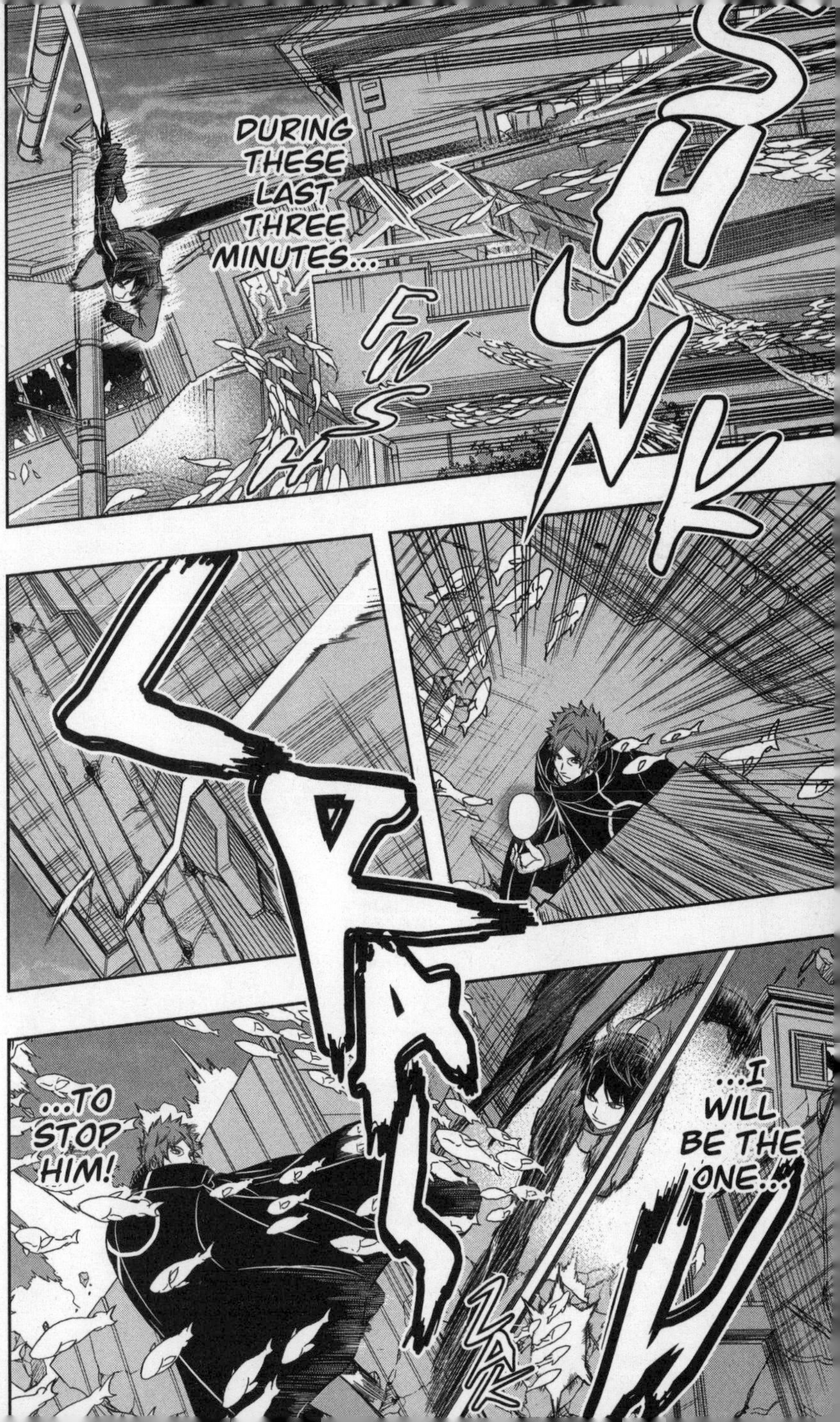
SHUNK
DURING THESE LAST THREE MINUTES...
FWSH
...I WILL BE THE ONE...
ZAK
...TO STOP HIM!

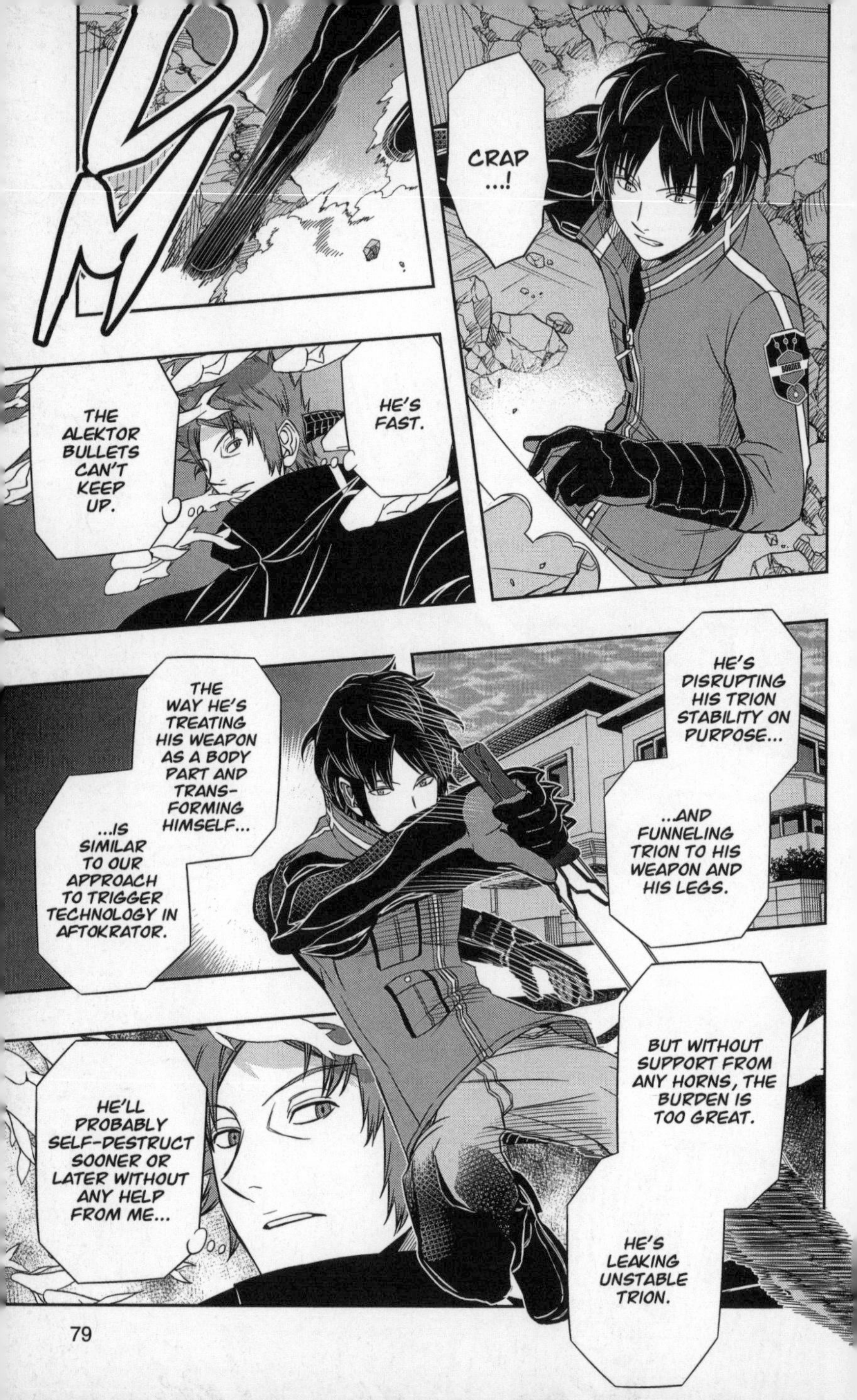
CRAP ...!
HE'S FAST.
THE ALEKTOR BULLETS CAN'T KEEP UP.
HE'S DISRUPTING HIS TRION STABILITY ON PURPOSE...
...AND FUNNELING TRION TO HIS WEAPON AND HIS LEGS.
THE WAY HE'S TREATING HIS WEAPON AS A BODY PART AND TRANS-FORMING HIMSELF...
...IS SIMILAR TO OUR APPROACH TO TRIGGER TECHNOLOGY IN AFTOKRATOR.
BUT WITHOUT SUPPORT FROM ANY HORNS, THE BURDEN IS TOO GREAT.
HE'S LEAKING UNSTABLE TRION.
HE'LL PROBABLY SELF-DESTRUCT SOONER OR LATER WITHOUT ANY HELP FROM ME...

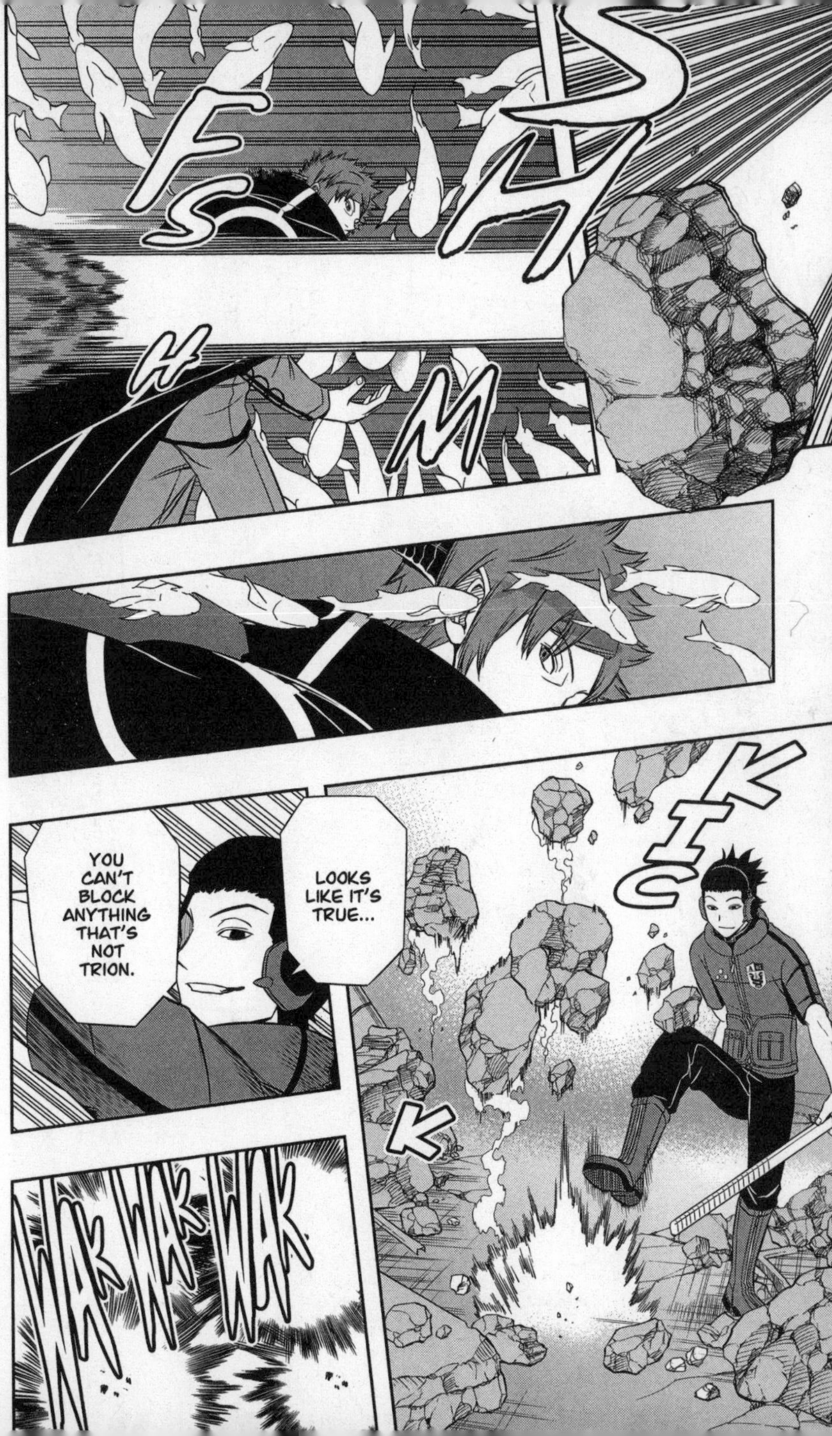

FSSH
HM
KICK
LOOKS LIKE IT'S TRUE...
YOU CAN'T BLOCK ANYTHING THAT'S NOT TRION.
WAK WAK WAK

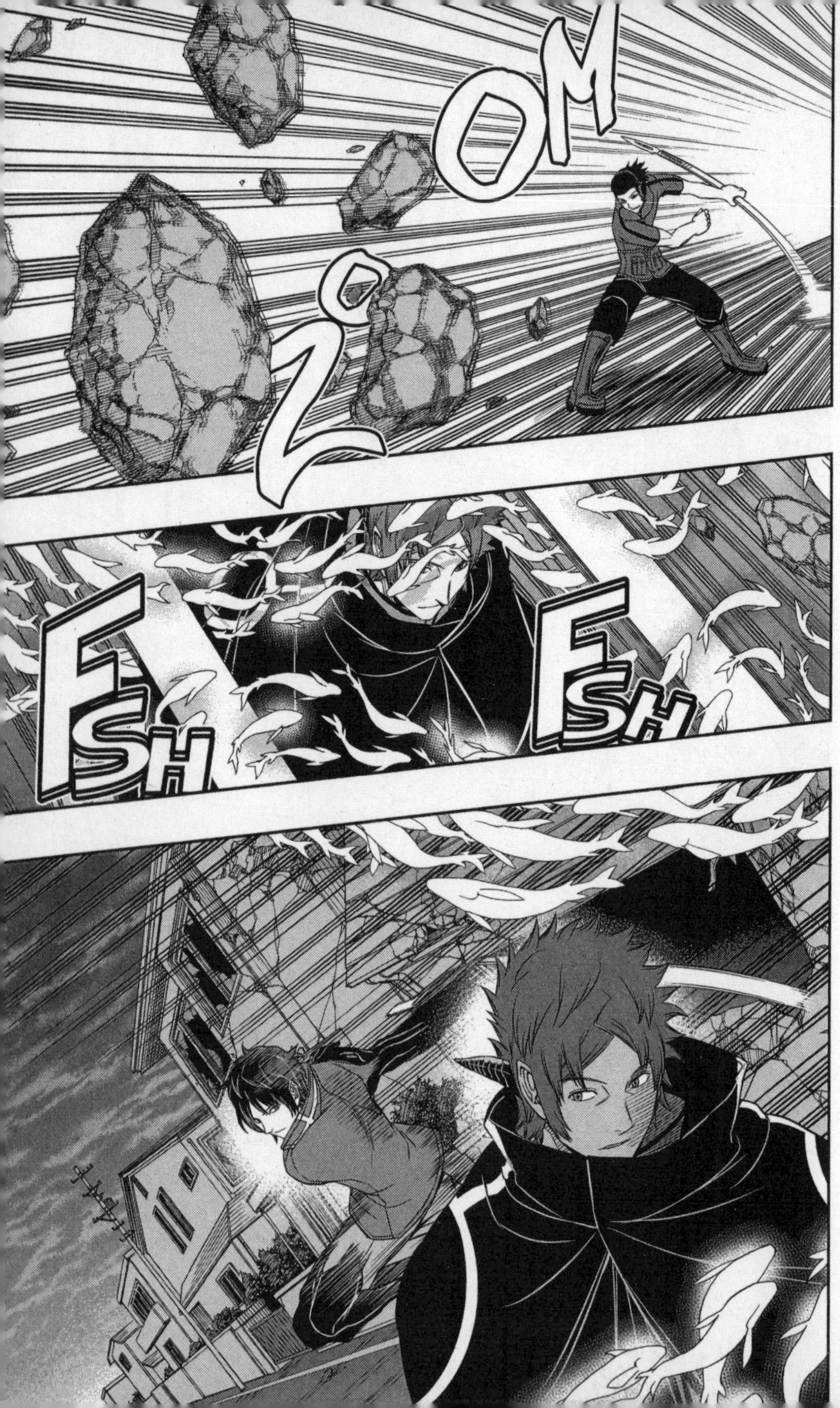
ZOOM
FSH
FSH

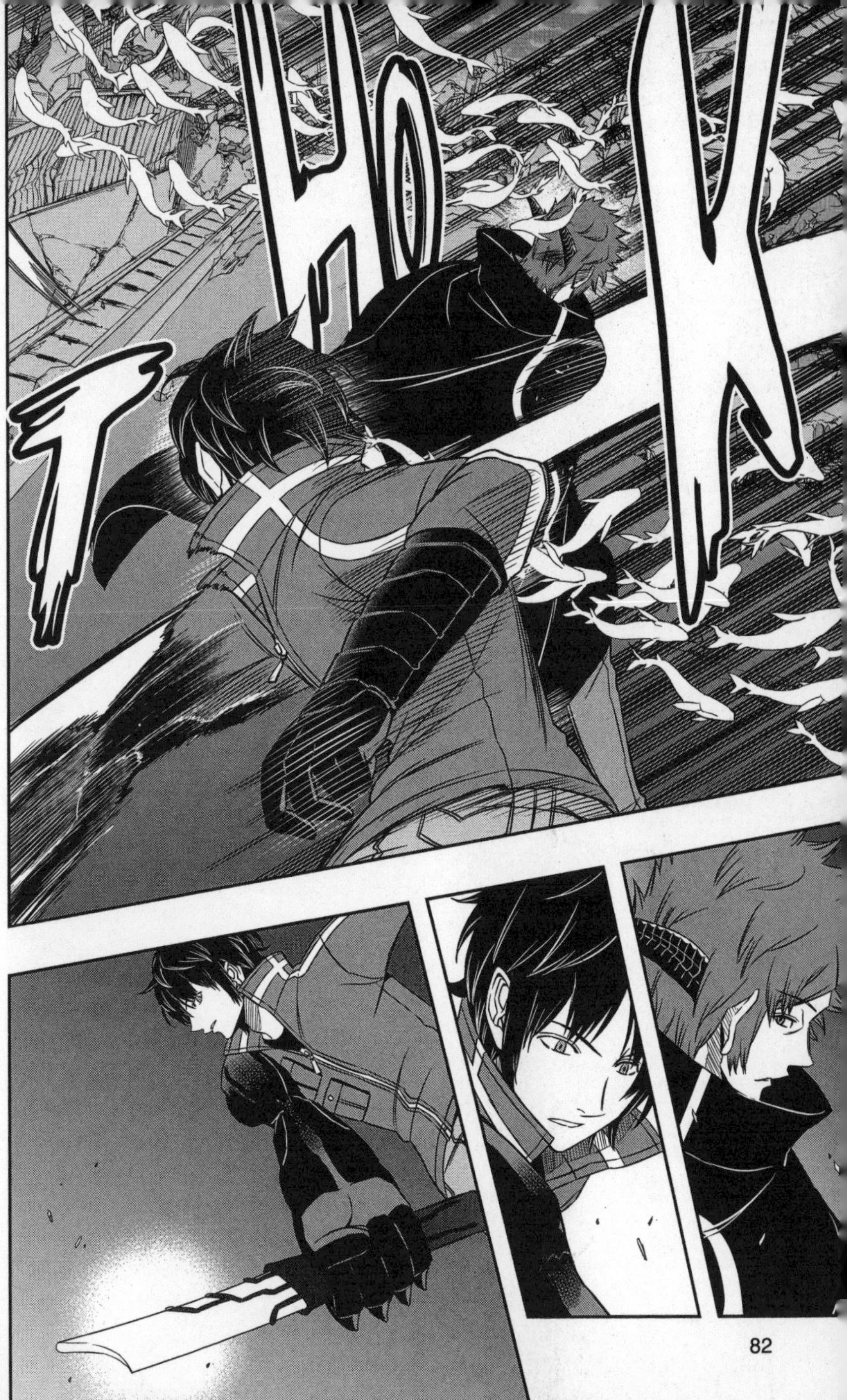

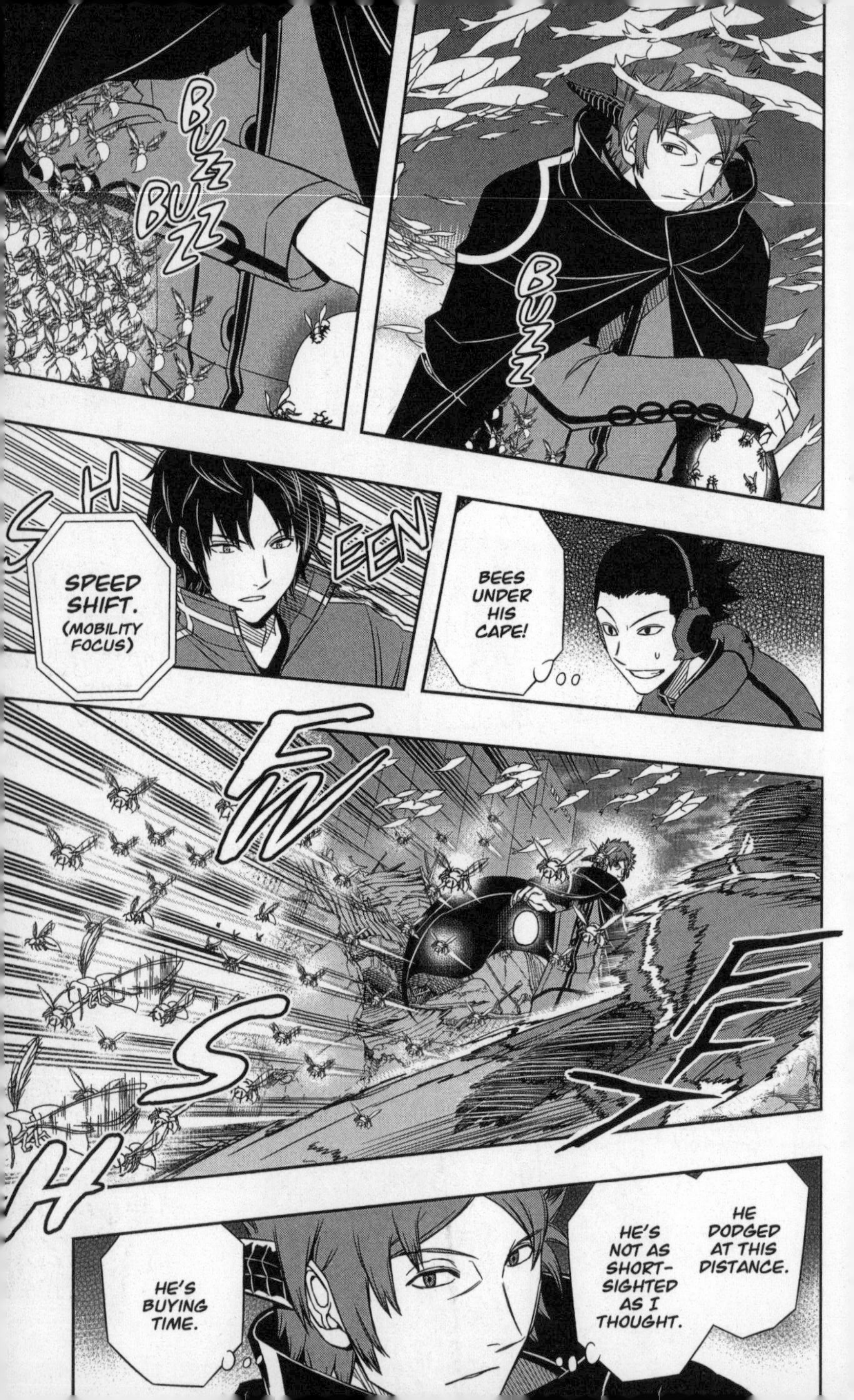

BUZZ
BUZZ BUZZ
BEES UNDER HIS CAPE!
SHEEN
SPEED SHIFT. (MOBILITY FOCUS)
FFT
FWSH
HE DODGED AT THIS DISTANCE.
HE'S NOT AS SHORT-SIGHTED AS I THOUGHT.
HE'S BUYING TIME.

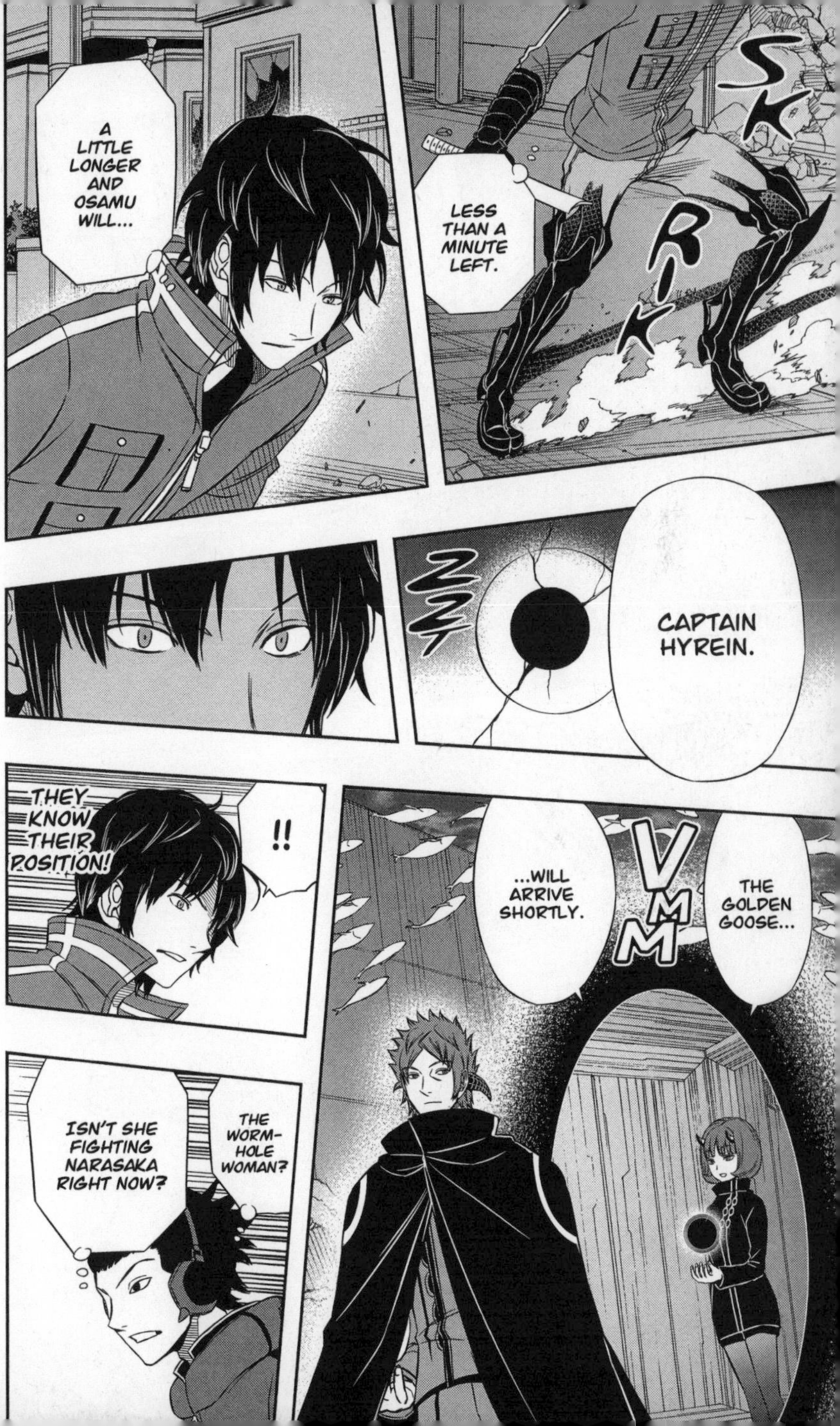
SKRIK
LESS THAN A MINUTE LEFT.
A LITTLE LONGER AND OSAMU WILL...
ZZT
CAPTAIN HYREIN.
THE GOLDEN GOOSE...
VMM
...WILL ARRIVE SHORTLY.
!!
THEY KNOW THEIR POSITION!
THE WORM-HOLE WOMAN?
ISN'T SHE FIGHTING NARASAKA RIGHT NOW?

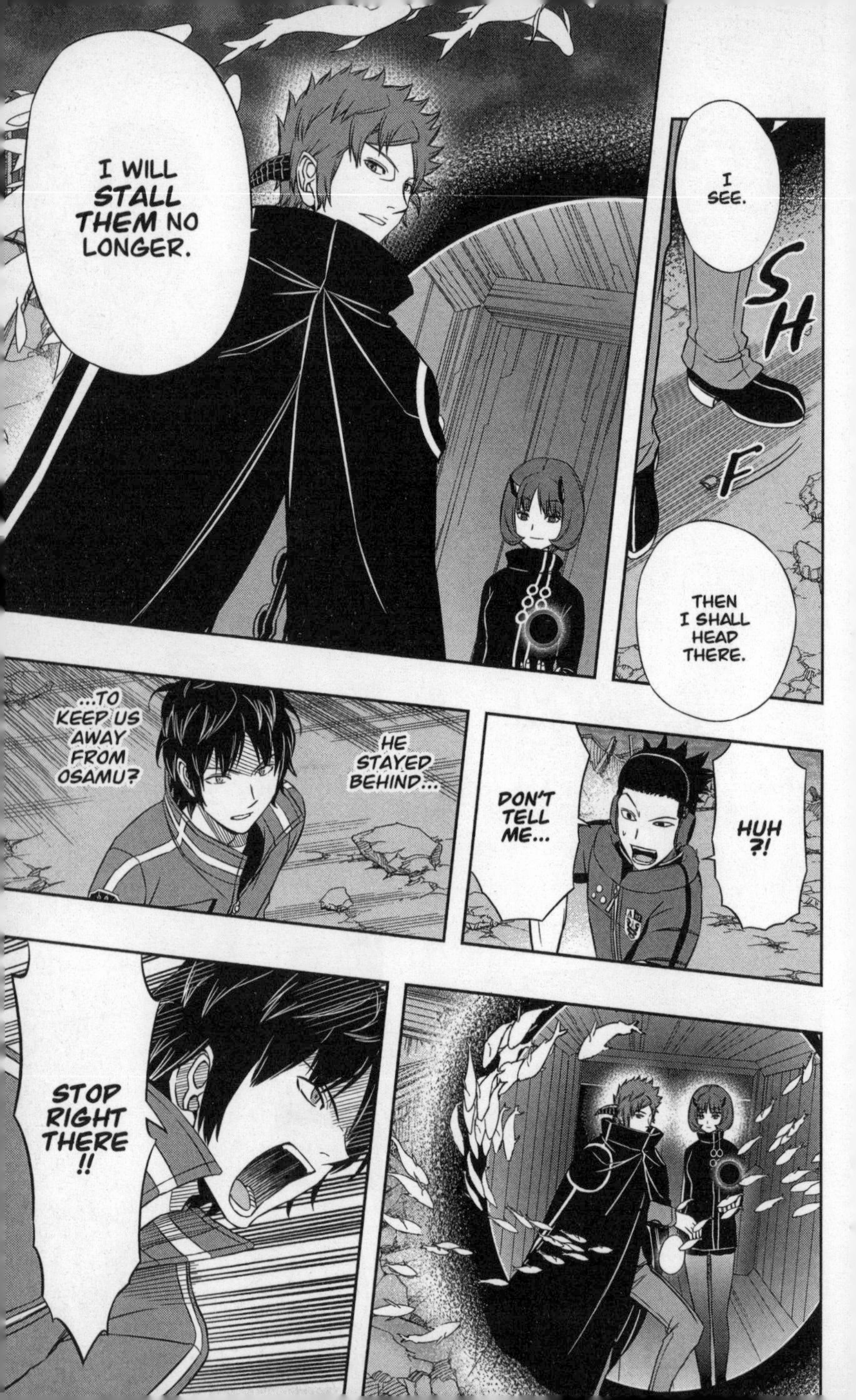
I SEE.
SHF
THEN I SHALL HEAD THERE.
I WILL STALL THEM NO LONGER.
HUH?!
DON'T TELL ME...
HE STAYED BEHIND...
...TO KEEP US AWAY FROM OSAMU?
STOP RIGHT THERE!!

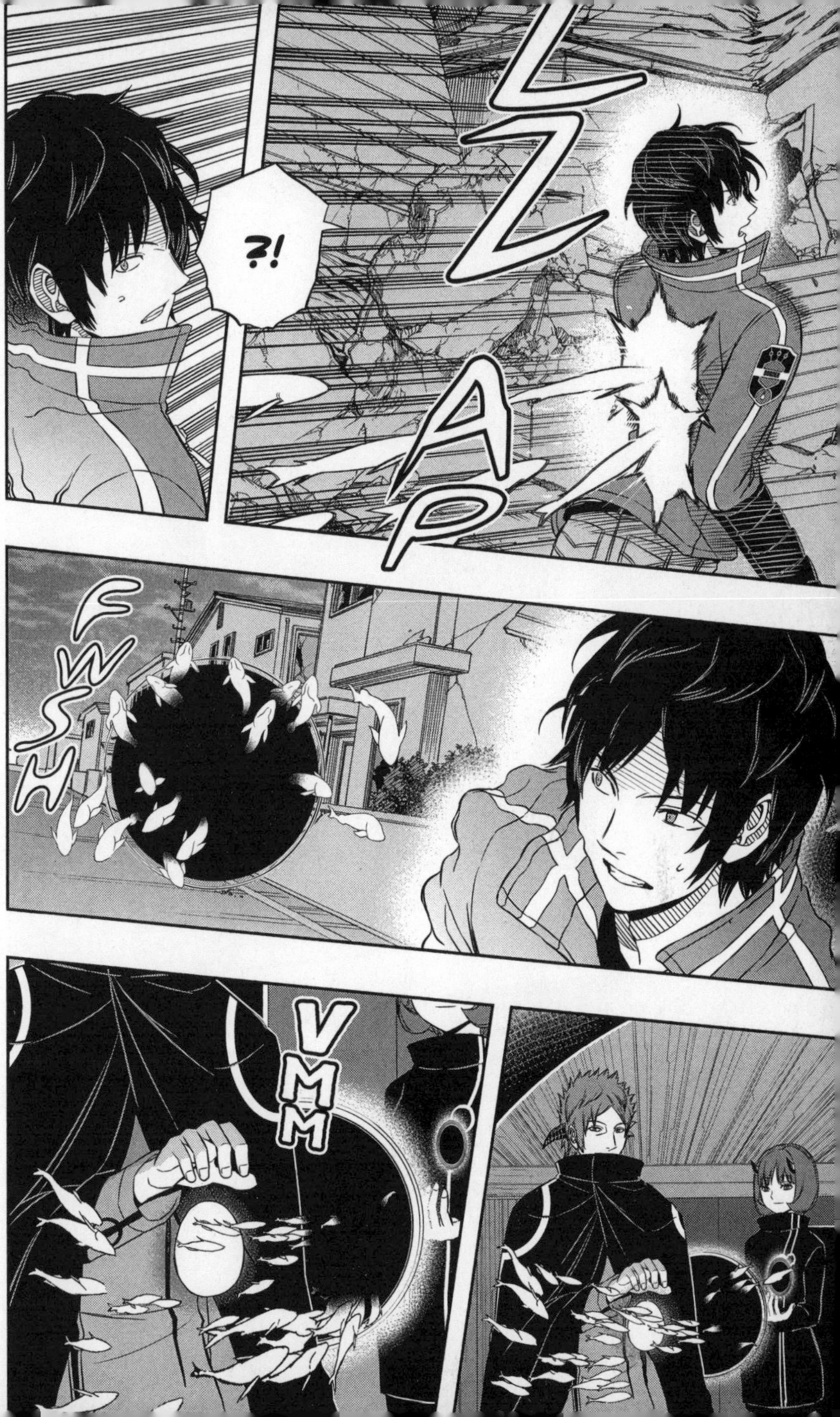
ZZAP
?!
FWSH
VMM

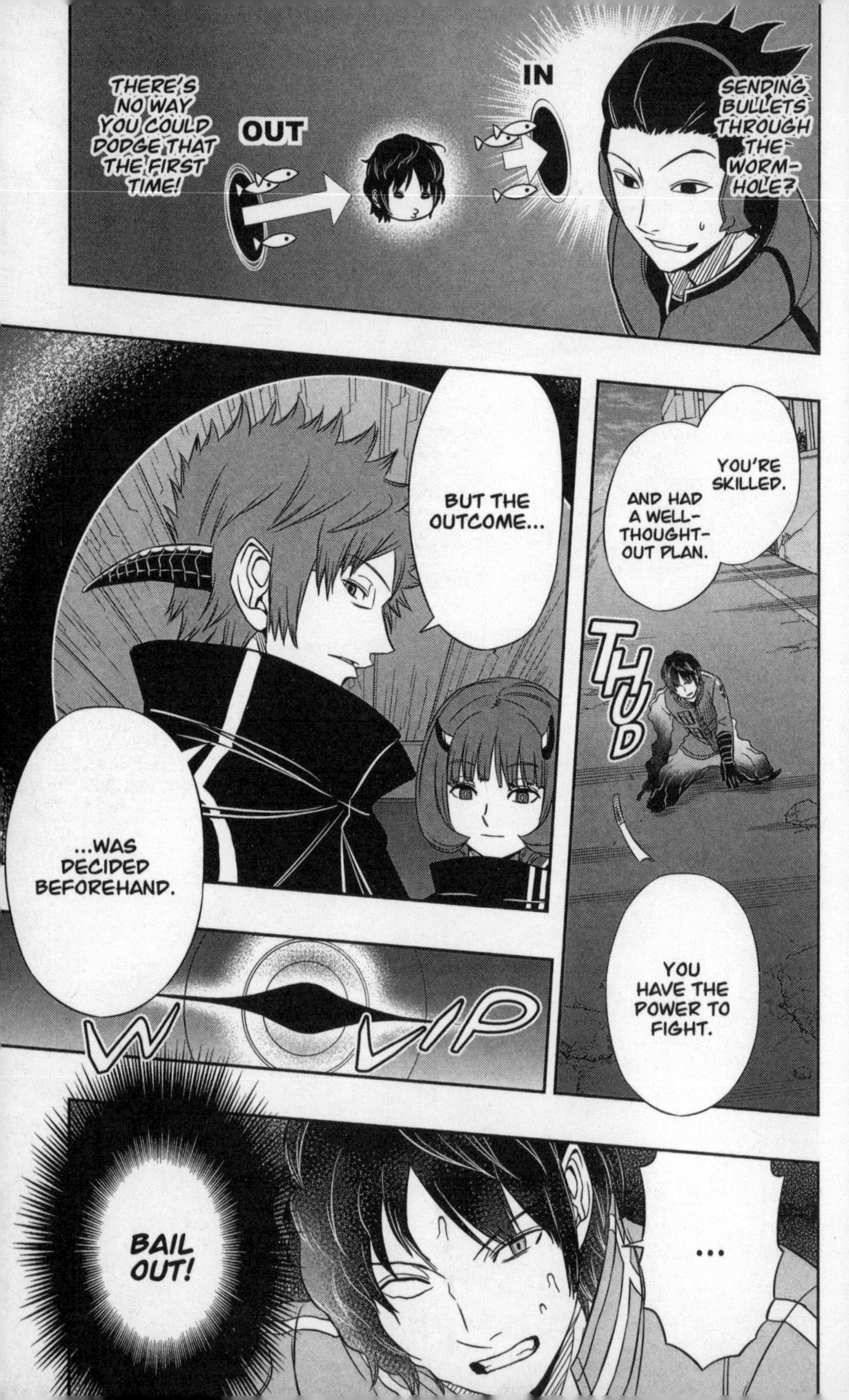
SENDING BULLETS THROUGH THE WORM-HOLE?
IN
OUT
THERE'S NO WAY YOU COULD DODGE THAT THE FIRST TIME!
YOU'RE SKILLED.
AND HAD A WELL-THOUGHT-OUT PLAN.
THUD
YOU HAVE THE POWER TO FIGHT.
BUT THE OUTCOME...
...WAS DECIDED BEFOREHAND.
WVIP
...
BAIL OUT!

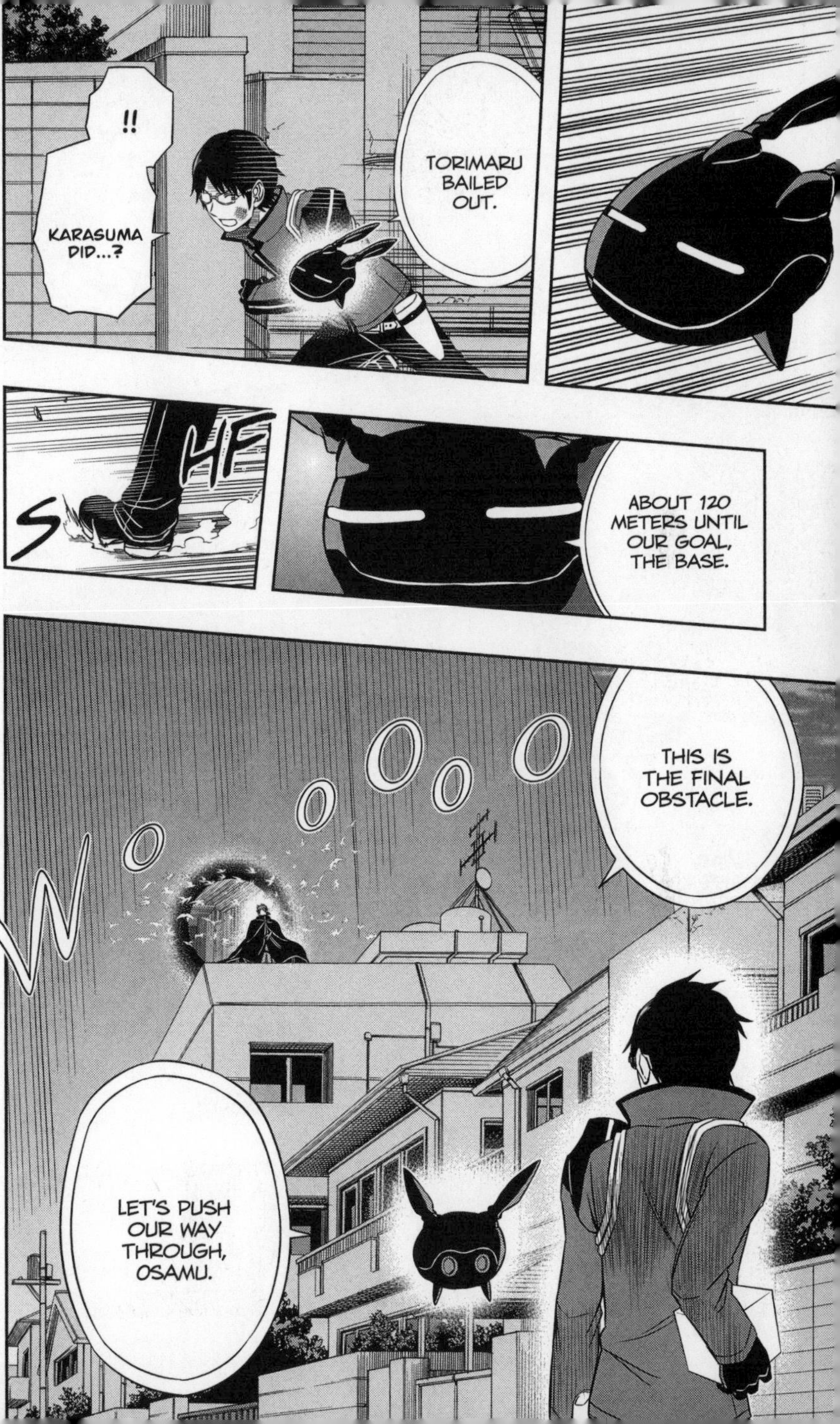
TORIMARU BAILED OUT.
!!
KARASUMA DID...?
ABOUT 120 METERS UNTIL OUR GOAL, THE BASE.
SHF
THIS IS THE FINAL OBSTACLE.
WOOOOO
LET'S PUSH OUR WAY THROUGH, OSAMU.

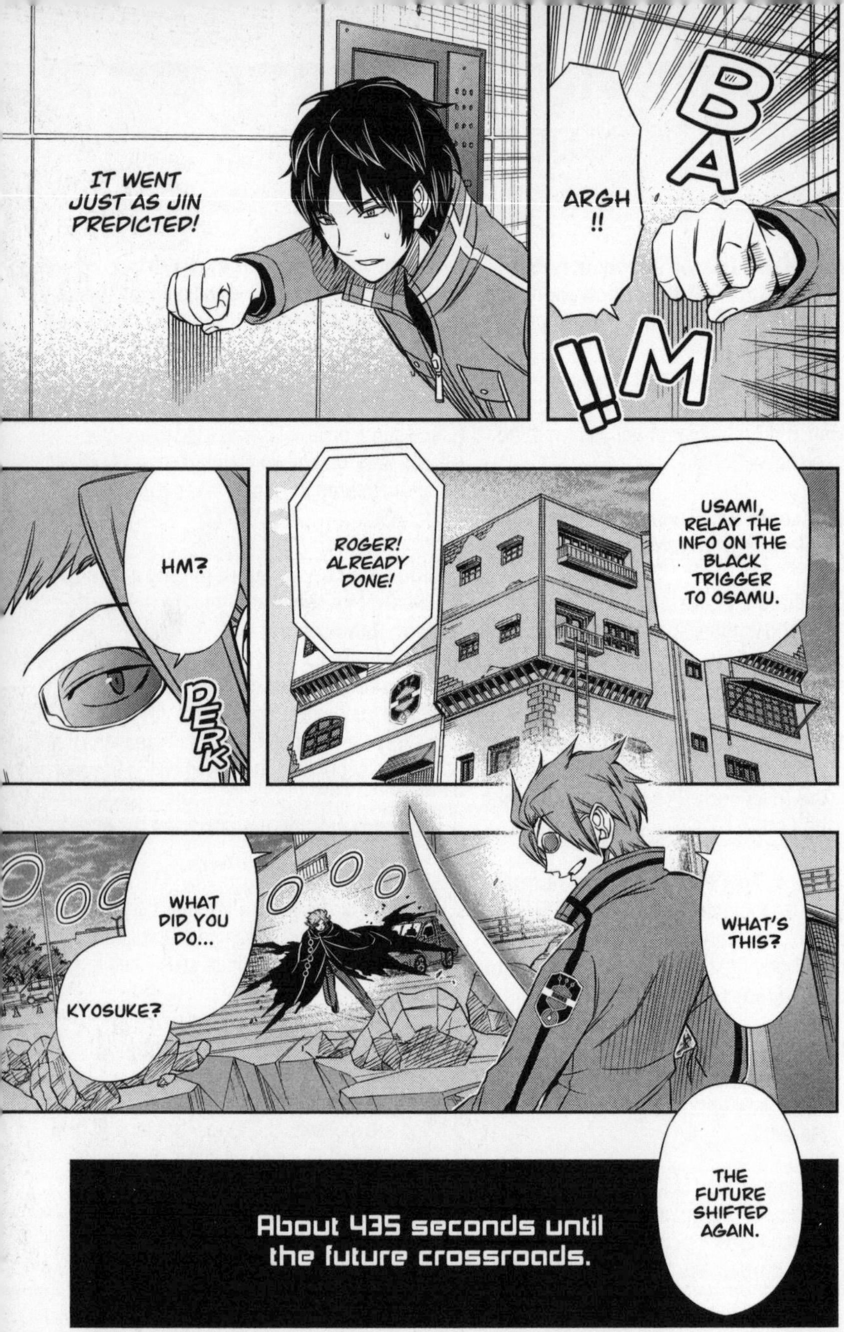
BAM!!
ARGH !!
IT WENT JUST AS JIN PREDICTED!
USAMI, RELAY THE INFO ON THE BLACK TRIGGER TO OSAMU.
ROGER! ALREADY DONE!
HM?
PERK
WHAT'S THIS?
WHAT DID YOU DO...
KYOSUKE?
THE FUTURE SHIFTED AGAIN.
About 435 seconds until the future crossroads.

Q&A: Part 8

There's only one page this time.

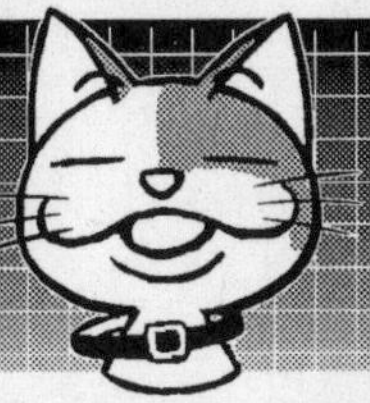

■Rinji was Osamu's mentor, right? So shouldn't Osamu show more respect towards Rinji's sister Chika?

Osamu doesn't act that way towards Chika because he's insensitive. Both Rinji and Chika herself allow him to be informal with her.

■Does the new Three Idiots team have any other formations besides Bird?

They currently have ten formations including Dragon, Snake and Horse. Nine of them are "everyone attack at once," and one is "everyone run for your lives."

■After an agent returns to their normal body, do they have to rebuild the Trion body like they do after they bail out?

When an Agent returns to their normal body on their own, their Trion body is "put away." They can decide to use the same Trion body next time, but the damage to the body won't be repaired.

■Are the wires used in Reiji's traps the same as the ones Kitora uses? Is the box used inside the trap a Meteor?

It's a Trigger called Spider and it's the same as Kitora's. It can do various things depending on which Trigger it's combined with. The box used in the trap was a Meteor (in 27 pieces).

■Izumi synthesized a Tomahawk by combining a Viper and a Meteor. Can he do that because he's a genius or could Osamu do it too with practice?

It's possible to do it with practice, but it would take some time. If Osamu tried to shoot a Tomahawk now, it would take him a whole minute to prepare. It only takes Izumi two seconds.

■How far can an agent deploy a remote shield like the ones used in the battle with Ranbanein?

It depends on individual ability, but they should be able to deploy a Shield up to 25 meters away. This remote defense is one of the reasons that Shield is superior to the shield on the Raygust.

■Do only A-Rank squads have their own emblems?

Once a squad makes A-Rank they can make their own emblem. Even if they are eventually demoted to B-Rank, they can continue to use their emblem until the squad disbands.

■Can you transform without saying "Trigger on" out loud?

If you are touching the Trigger holder and give a clear signal, you can be silent or use a different word. You can even have your own unique transformation phrase.

■ I sometimes answer questions I get in my fan mail on my official Twitter feed. The more followers I get the more my editor will work on it. **World Trigger Official Twitter account: @W_Trigger_off**

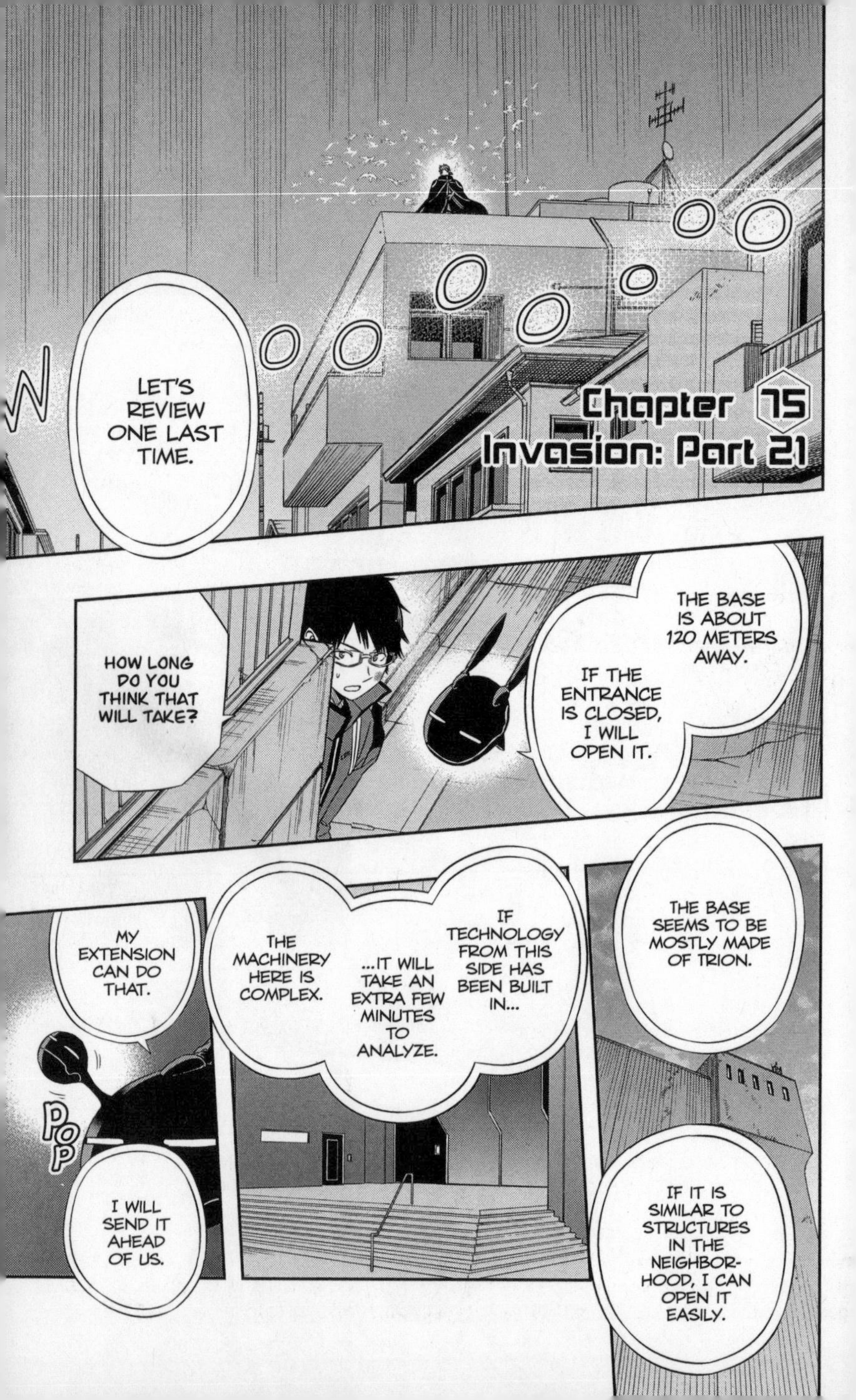
Chapter 75
Invasion: Part 21
WOOOOOOO
LET'S REVIEW ONE LAST TIME.
THE BASE IS ABOUT 120 METERS AWAY.
IF THE ENTRANCE IS CLOSED, I WILL OPEN IT.
HOW LONG DO YOU THINK THAT WILL TAKE?
THE BASE SEEMS TO BE MOSTLY MADE OF TRION.
IF IT IS SIMILAR TO STRUCTURES IN THE NEIGHBOR-HOOD, I CAN OPEN IT EASILY.
IF TECHNOLOGY FROM THIS SIDE HAS BEEN BUILT IN...
...IT WILL TAKE AN EXTRA FEW MINUTES TO ANALYZE.
THE MACHINERY HERE IS COMPLEX.
MY EXTENSION CAN DO THAT.
POP
I WILL SEND IT AHEAD OF US.

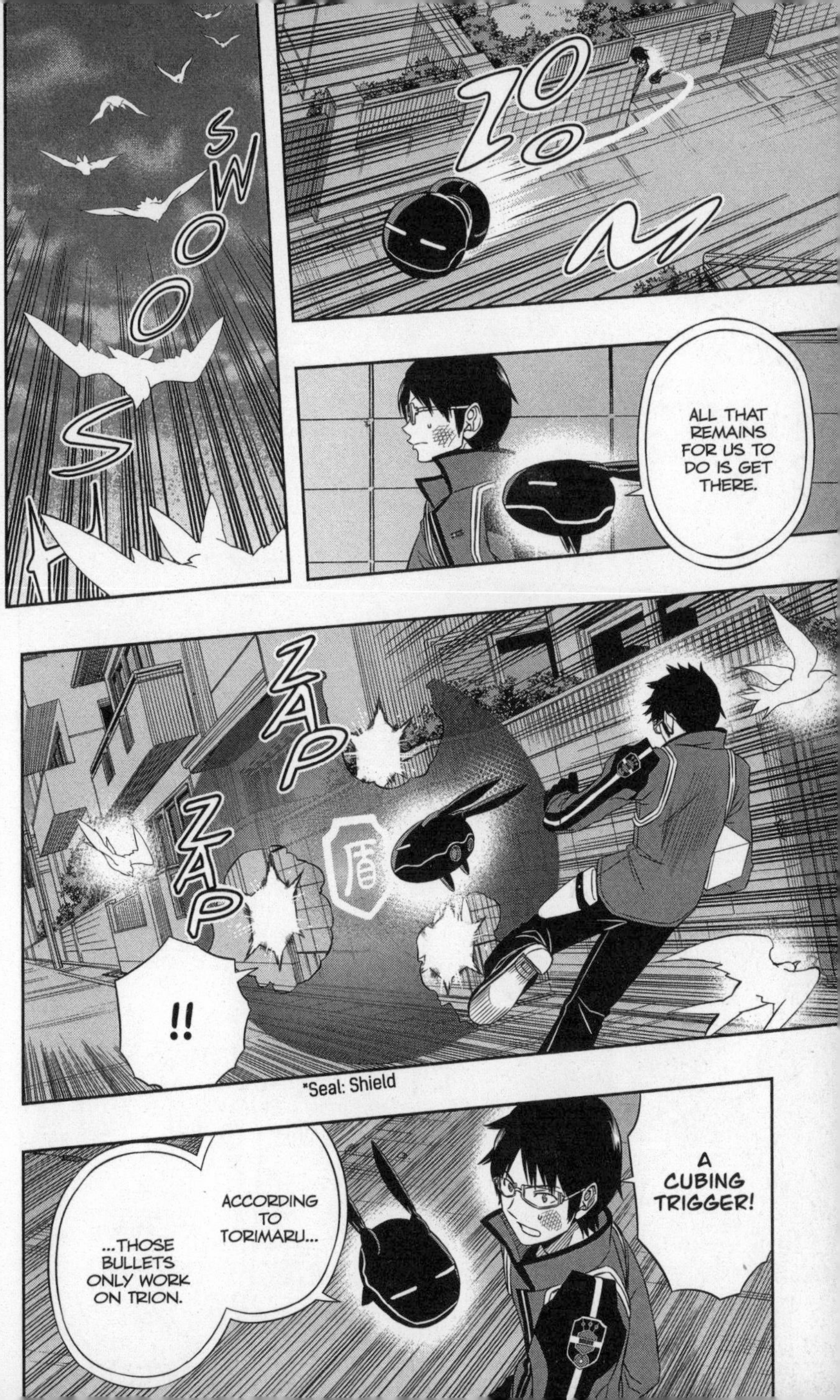
ZOOM
ALL THAT REMAINS FOR US TO DO IS GET THERE.
SWOOOSH
ZAP
ZAP
盾
!!
*Seal: Shield
A CUBING TRIGGER!
ACCORDING TO TORIMARU...
...THOSE BULLETS ONLY WORK ON TRION.

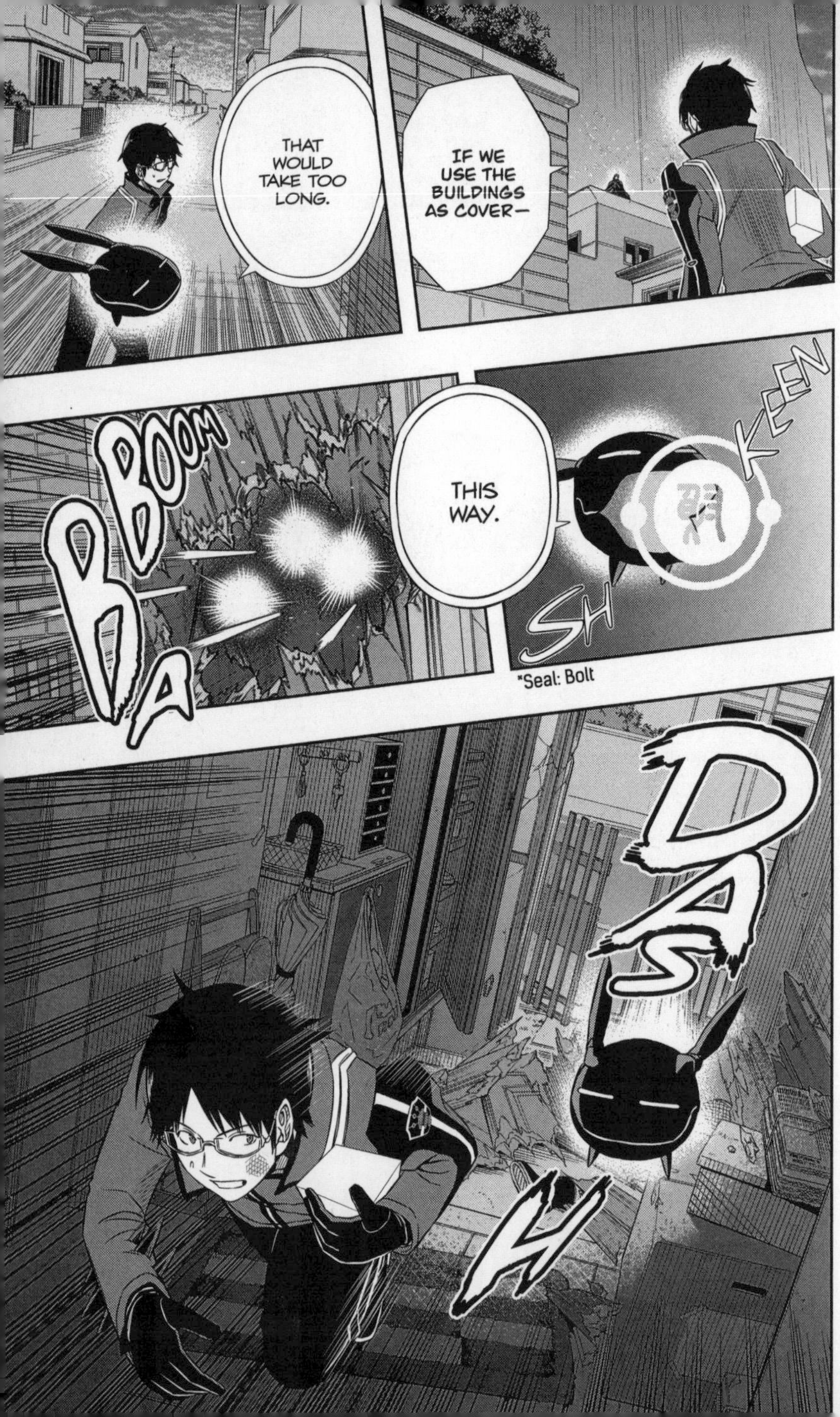
IF WE USE THE BUILDINGS AS COVER—
THAT WOULD TAKE TOO LONG.
THIS WAY.
SH KEEN
BABOOM
DASH
*Seal: Bolt

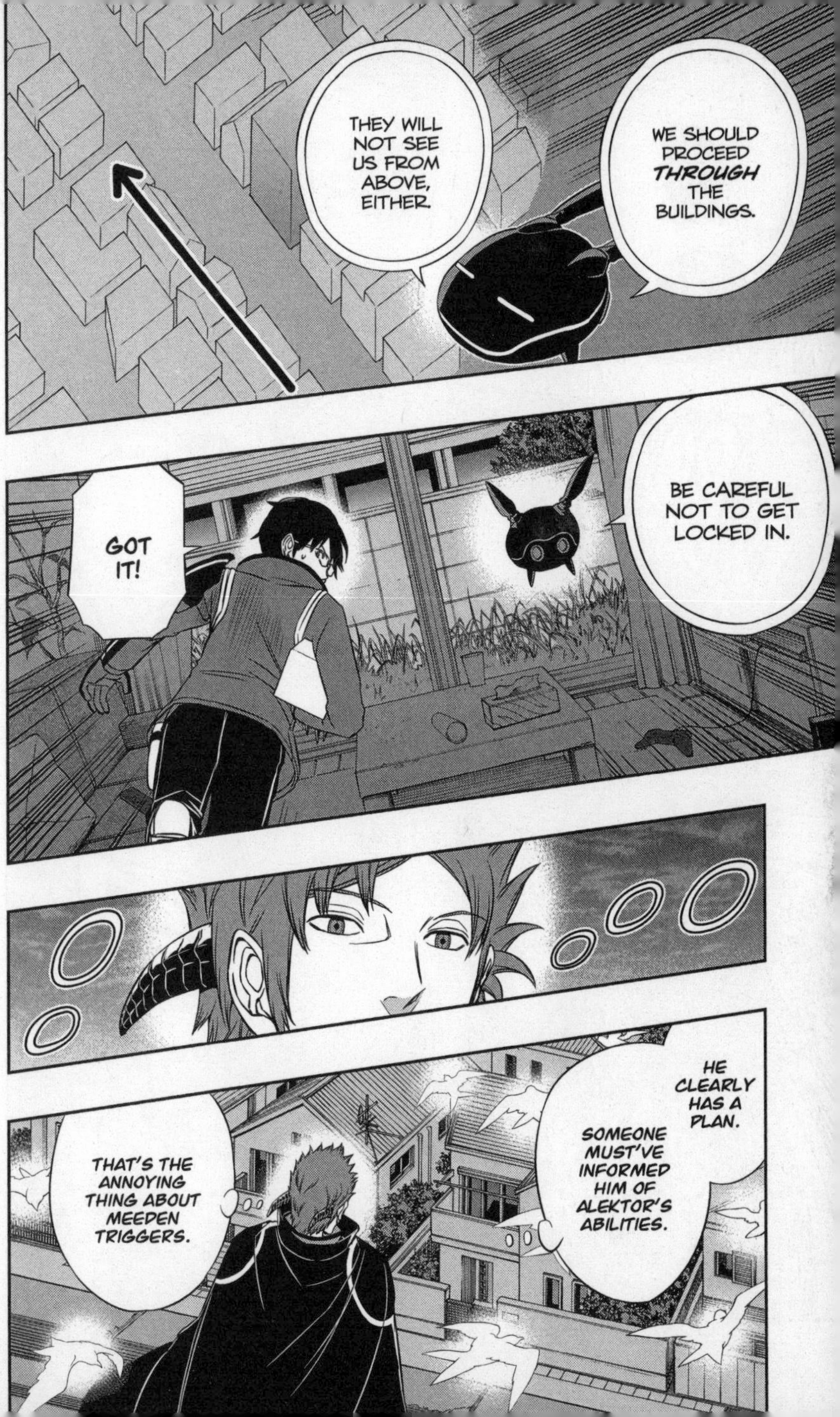
WE SHOULD PROCEED THROUGH THE BUILDINGS.
THEY WILL NOT SEE US FROM ABOVE, EITHER.
BE CAREFUL NOT TO GET LOCKED IN.
GOT IT!
HE CLEARLY HAS A PLAN.
SOMEONE MUST'VE INFORMED HIM OF ALEKTOR'S ABILITIES.
THAT'S THE ANNOYING THING ABOUT MEEDEN TRIGGERS.

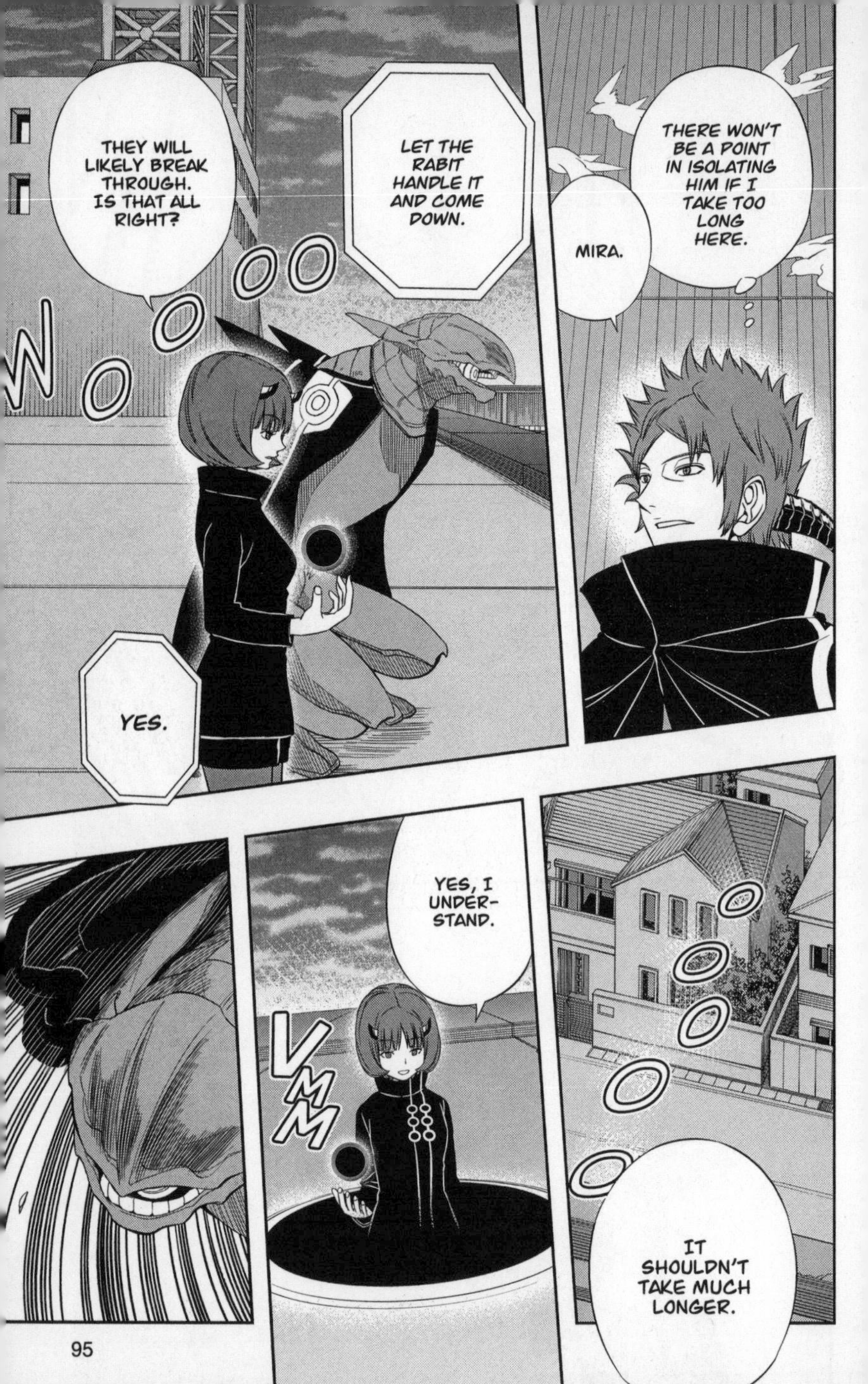

THERE WON'T BE A POINT IN ISOLATING HIM IF I TAKE TOO LONG HERE.
MIRA.
LET THE RABIT HANDLE IT AND COME DOWN.
THEY WILL LIKELY BREAK THROUGH. IS THAT ALL RIGHT?
WOOOOO
YES.
OOOOOO
IT SHOULDN'T TAKE MUCH LONGER.
YES, I UNDER-STAND.
VMM

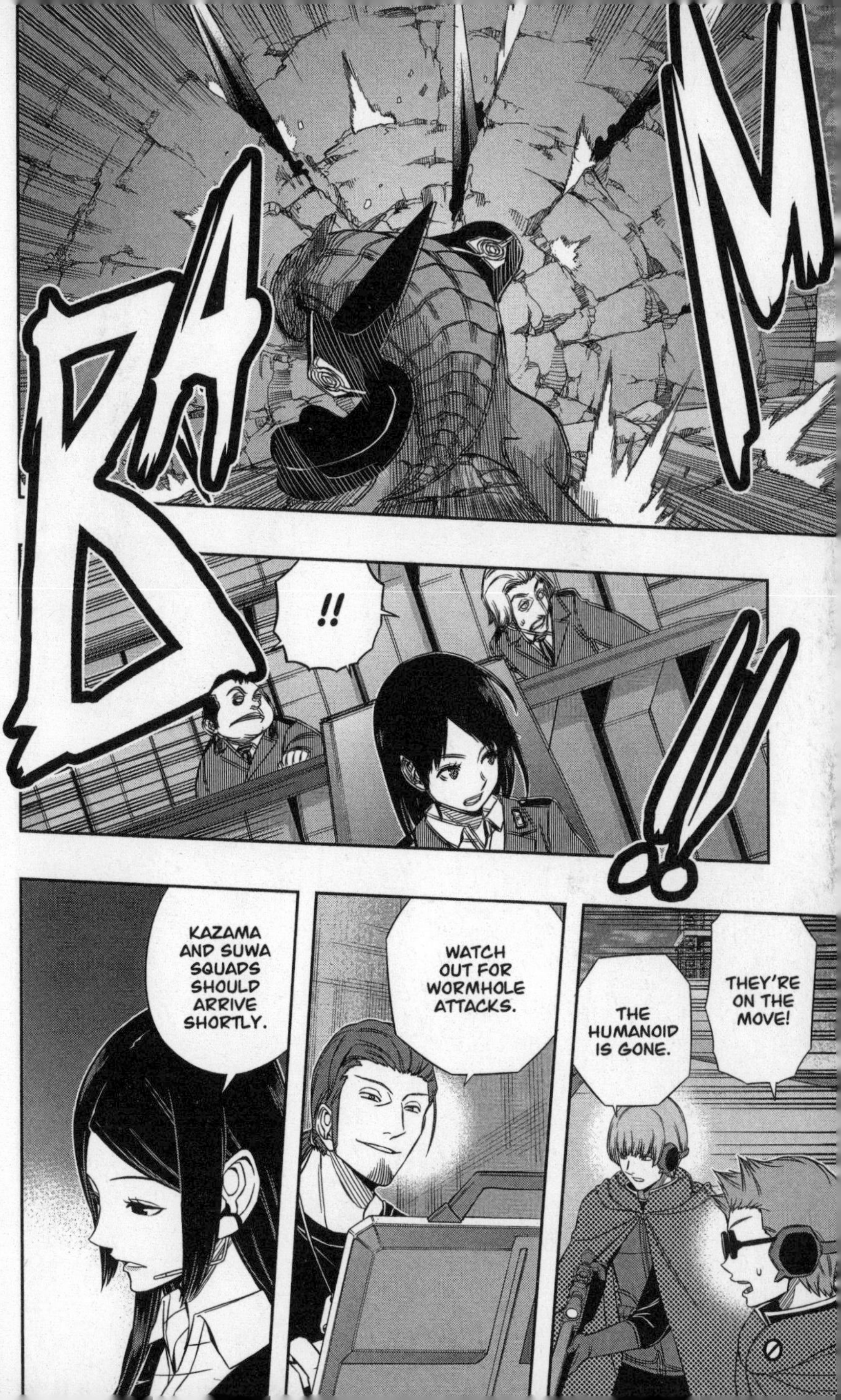
BAM!!
!!
THEY'RE ON THE MOVE!
THE HUMANOID IS GONE.
WATCH OUT FOR WORMHOLE ATTACKS.
KAZAMA AND SUWA SQUADS SHOULD ARRIVE SHORTLY.

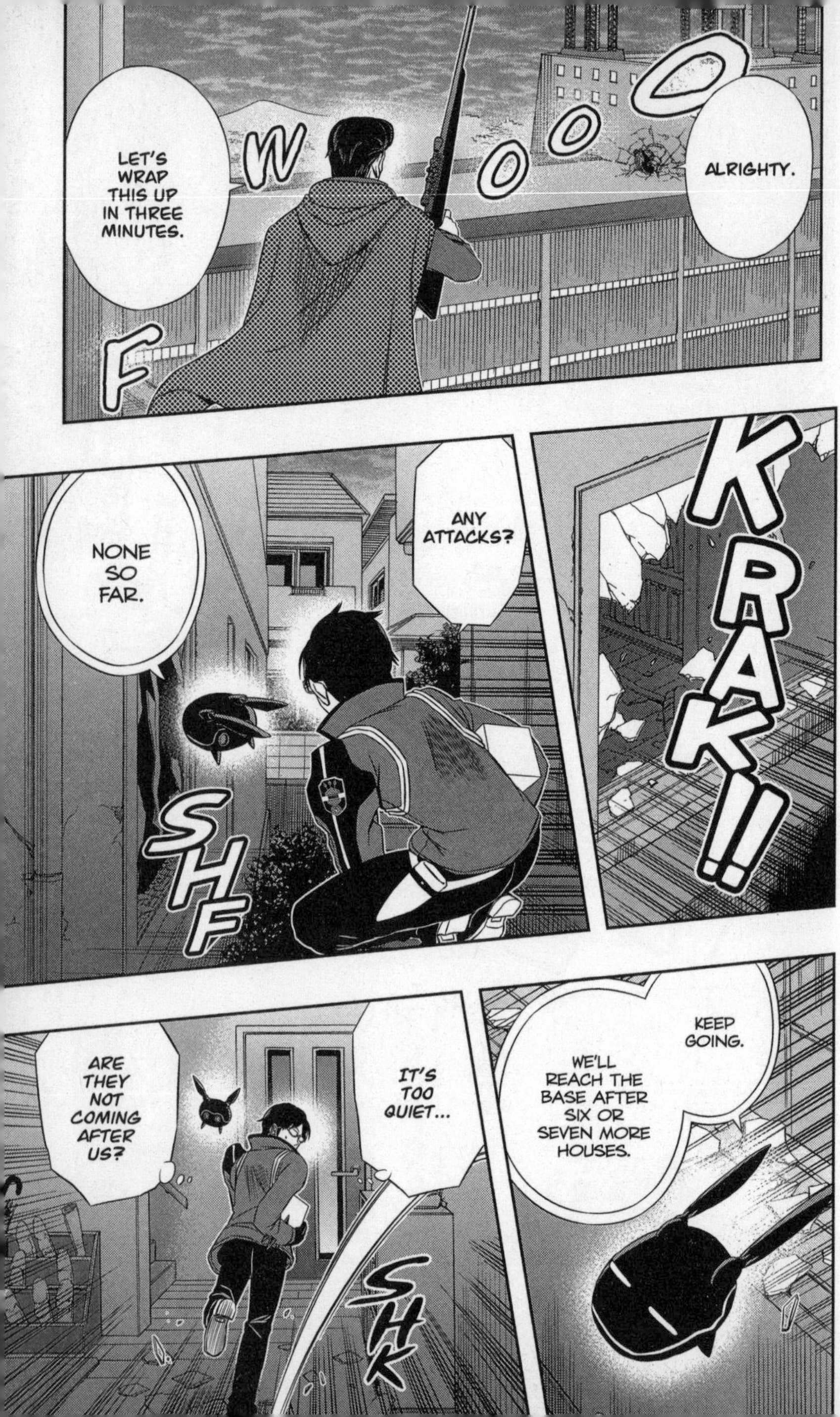
FWOOO
ALRIGHTY.
LET'S WRAP THIS UP IN THREE MINUTES.
KRAK!!
ANY ATTACKS?
NONE SO FAR.
SHF
KEEP GOING.
WE'LL REACH THE BASE AFTER SIX OR SEVEN MORE HOUSES.
IT'S TOO QUIET...
ARE THEY NOT COMING AFTER US?
SHK

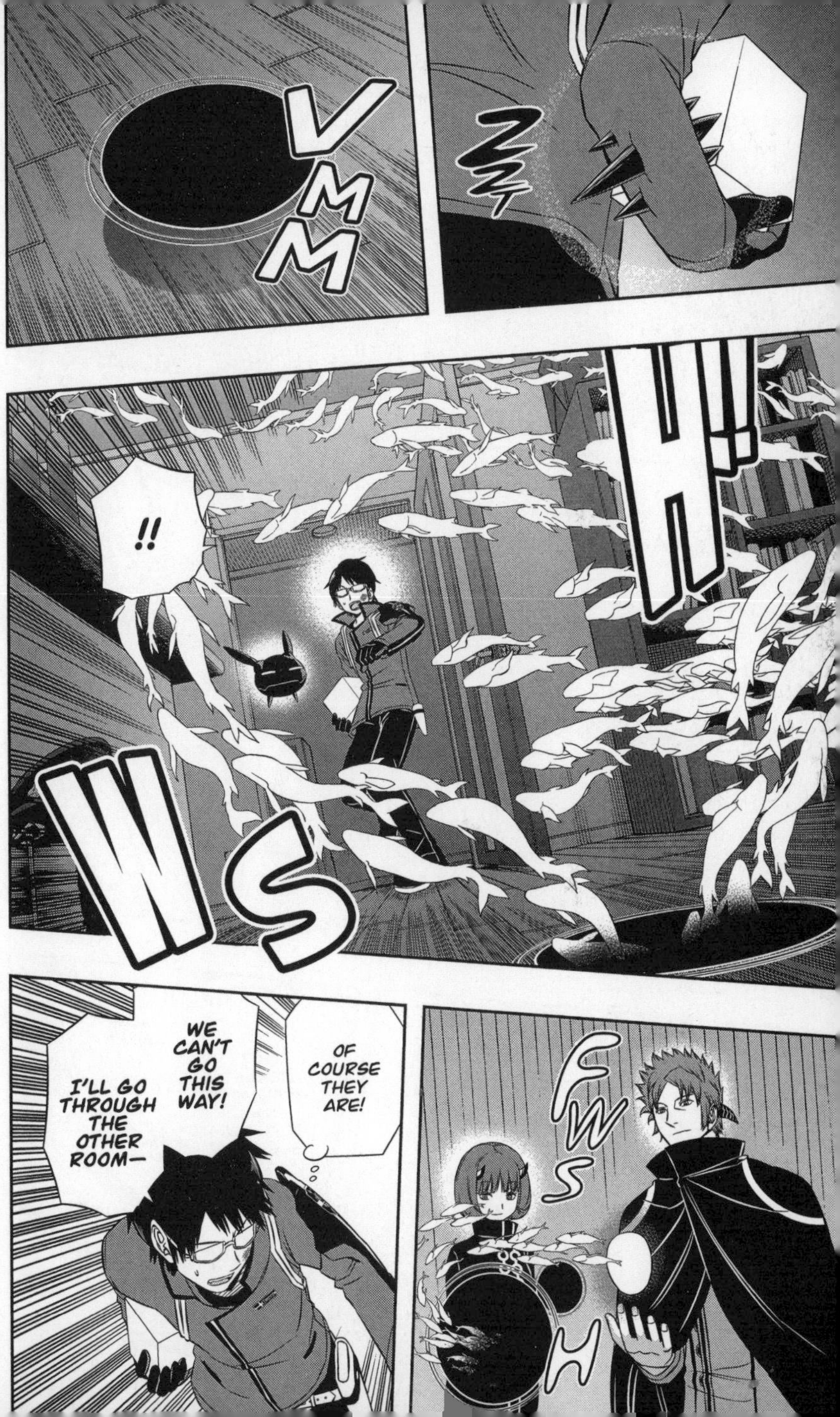
ZZT
VMM
!!
WS
H
FWSH
OF COURSE THEY ARE!
WE CAN'T GO THIS WAY!
I'LL GO THROUGH THE OTHER ROOM—

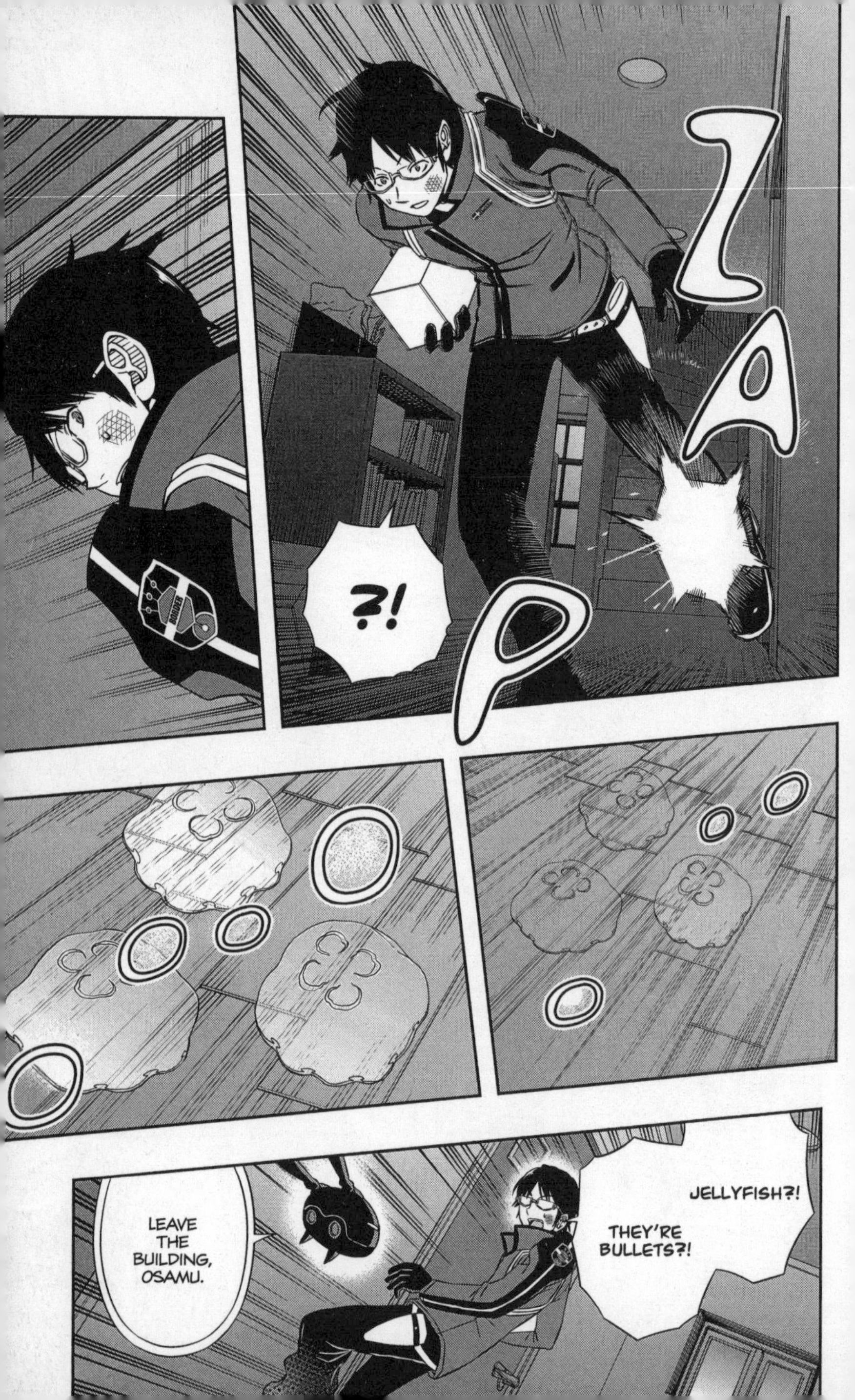
ZAP
?!
JELLYFISH?!
THEY'RE BULLETS?!
LEAVE THE BUILDING, OSAMU.

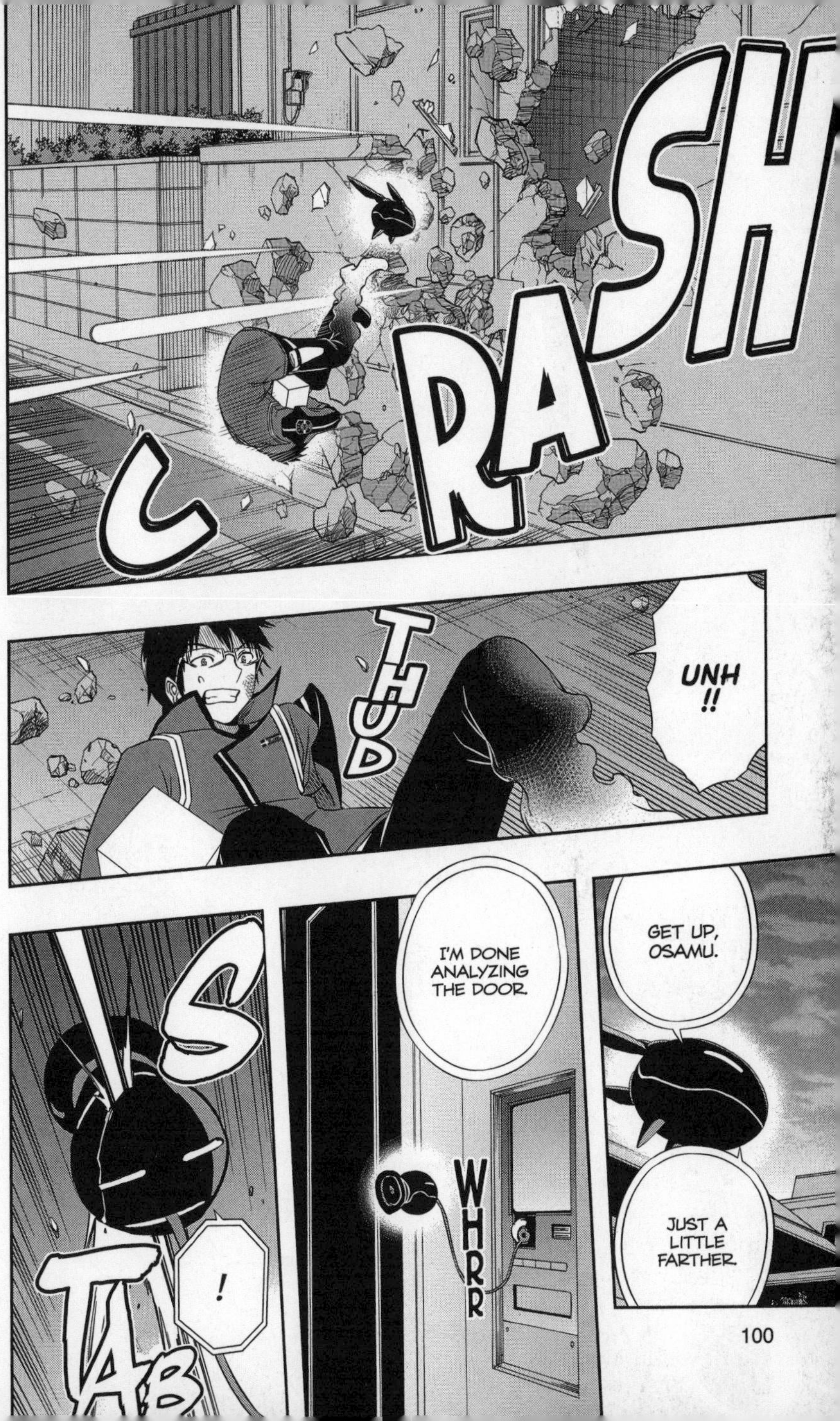
CRASH
UNH !!
THUD
GET UP, OSAMU.
JUST A LITTLE FARTHER.
I'M DONE ANALYZING THE DOOR.
WHRR
S
!
TAB

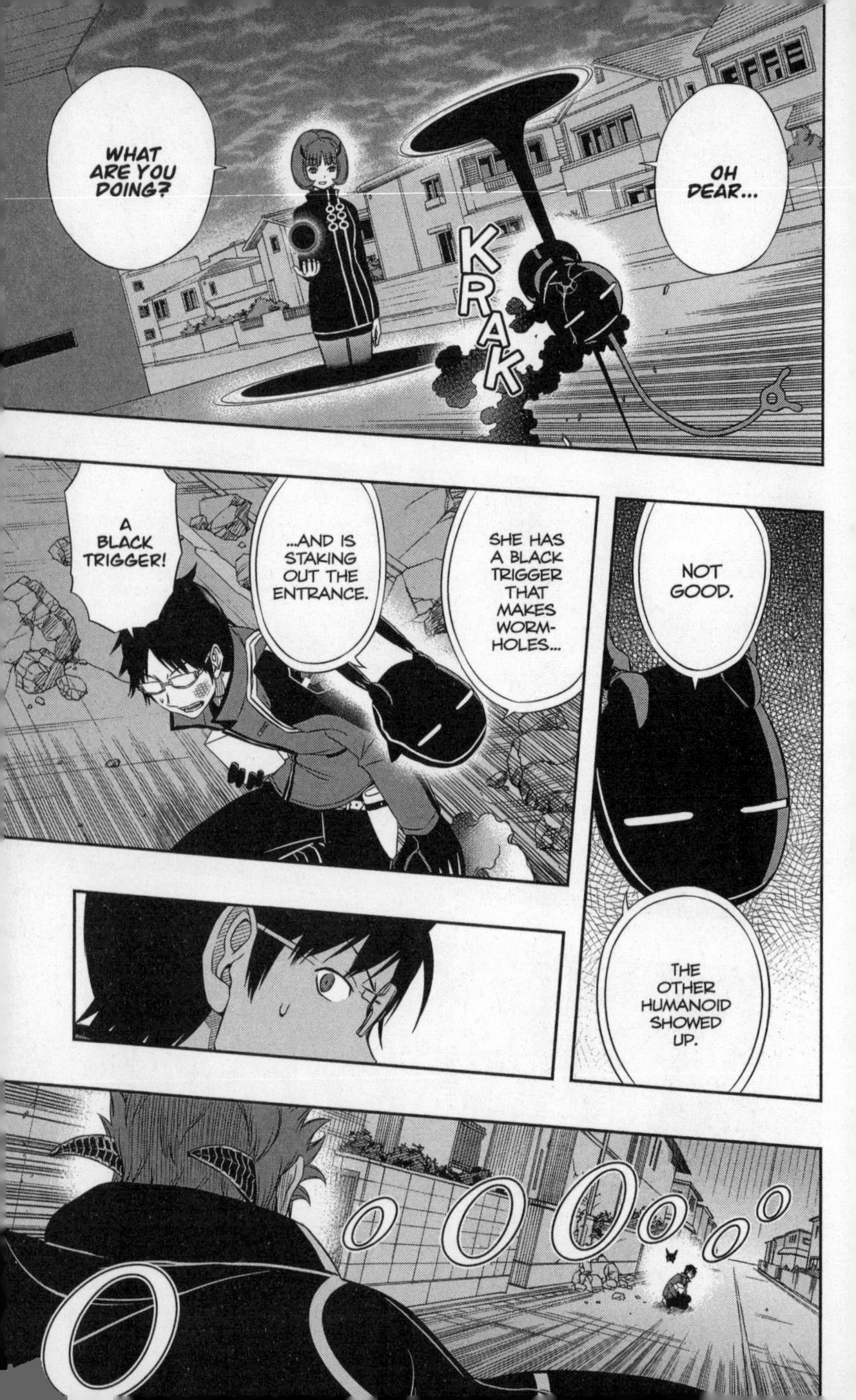
OH DEAR...
KRAK
WHAT ARE YOU DOING?
NOT GOOD.
THE OTHER HUMANOID SHOWED UP.
SHE HAS A BLACK TRIGGER THAT MAKES WORM-HOLES...
...AND IS STAKING OUT THE ENTRANCE.
A BLACK TRIGGER!

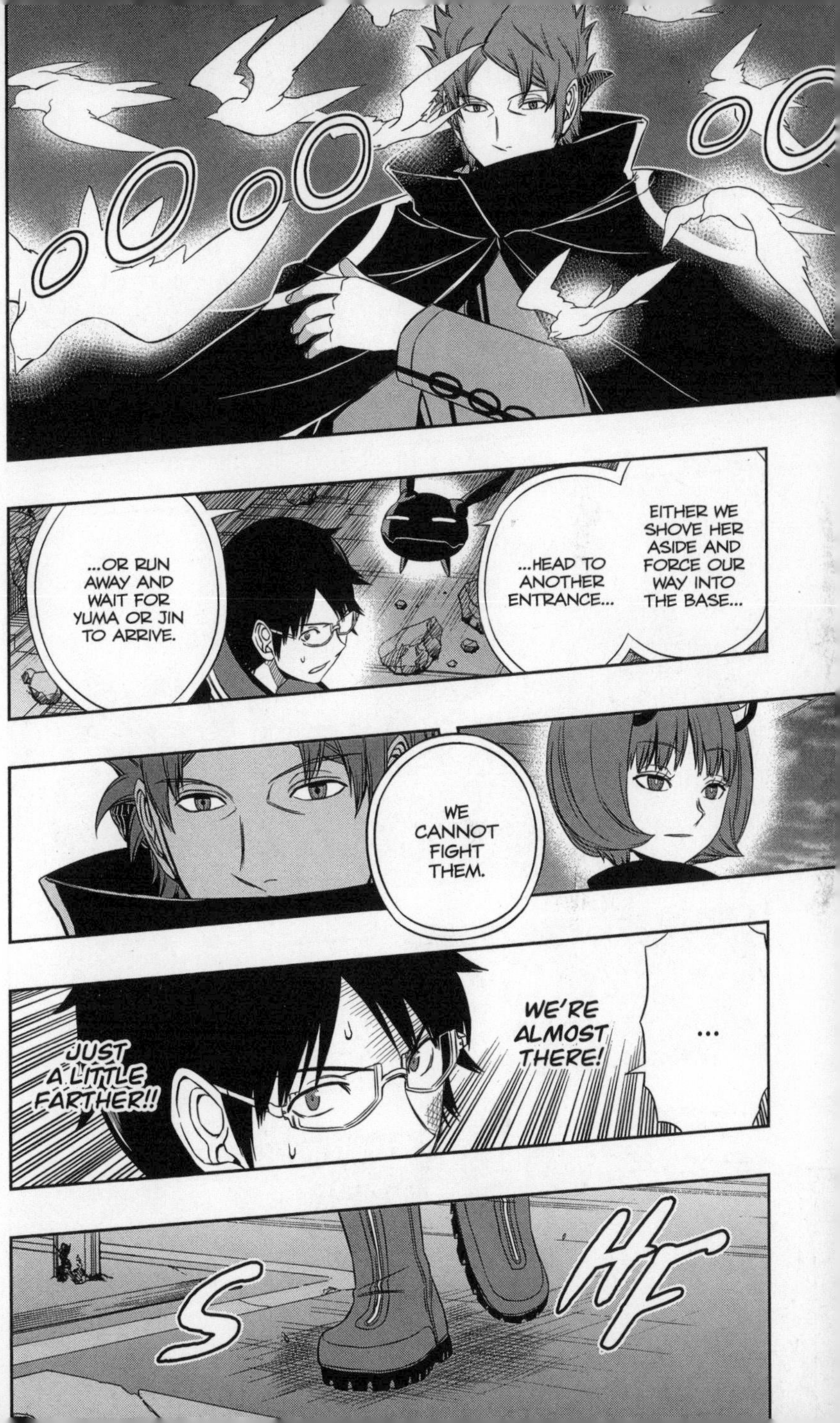
EITHER WE SHOVE HER ASIDE AND FORCE OUR WAY INTO THE BASE...
...HEAD TO ANOTHER ENTRANCE...
...OR RUN AWAY AND WAIT FOR YUMA OR JIN TO ARRIVE.
WE CANNOT FIGHT THEM.
...
WE'RE ALMOST THERE!
JUST A LITTLE FARTHER!!
S Hf

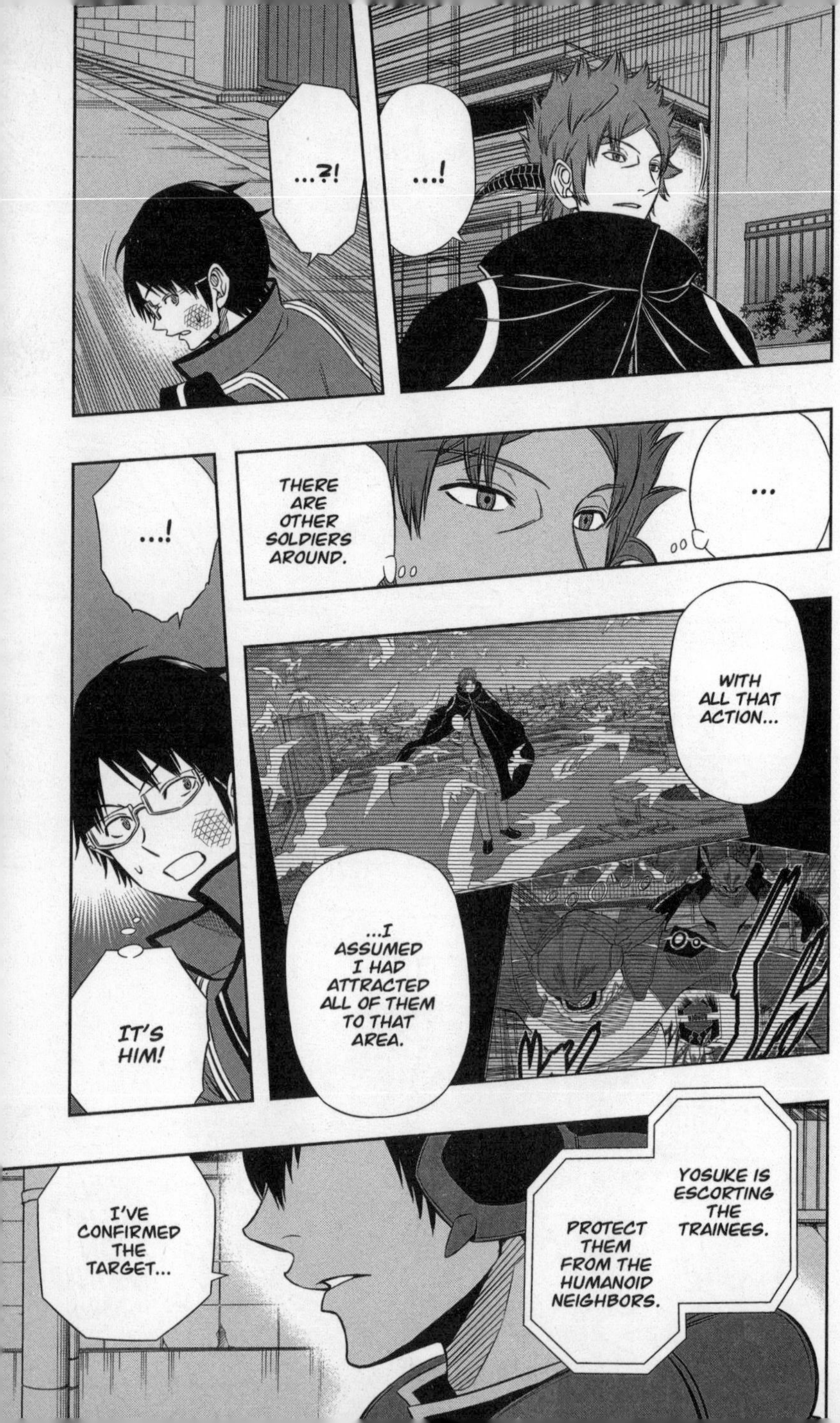
...!
...?!
...
THERE ARE OTHER SOLDIERS AROUND.
WITH ALL THAT ACTION...
...I ASSUMED I HAD ATTRACTED ALL OF THEM TO THAT AREA.
...!
IT'S HIM!
YOSUKE IS ESCORTING THE TRAINEES.
PROTECT THEM FROM THE HUMANOID NEIGHBORS.
I'VE CONFIRMED THE TARGET...

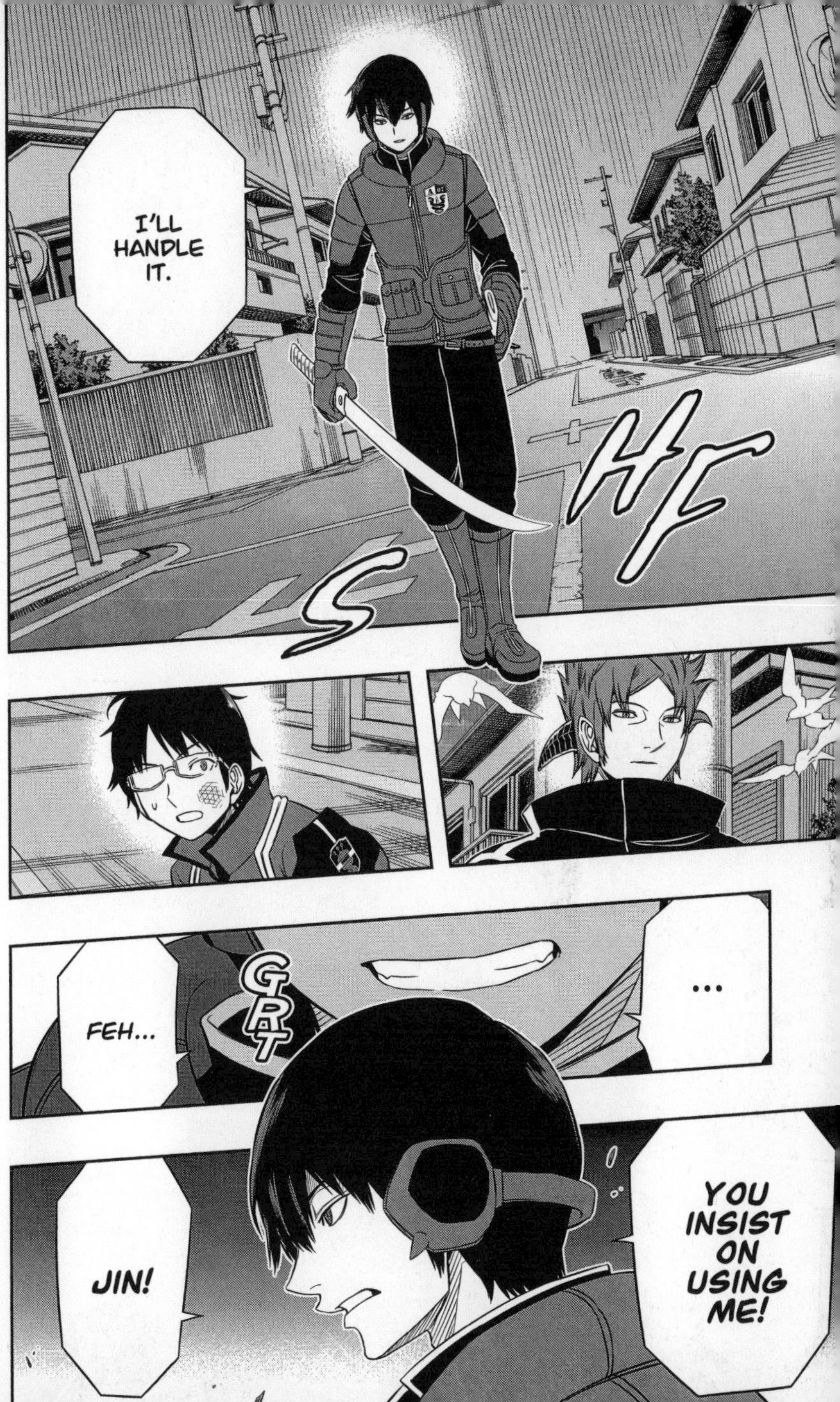
I'LL HANDLE IT.
SHF
...
GRT
FEH...
YOU INSIST ON USING ME!
JIN!

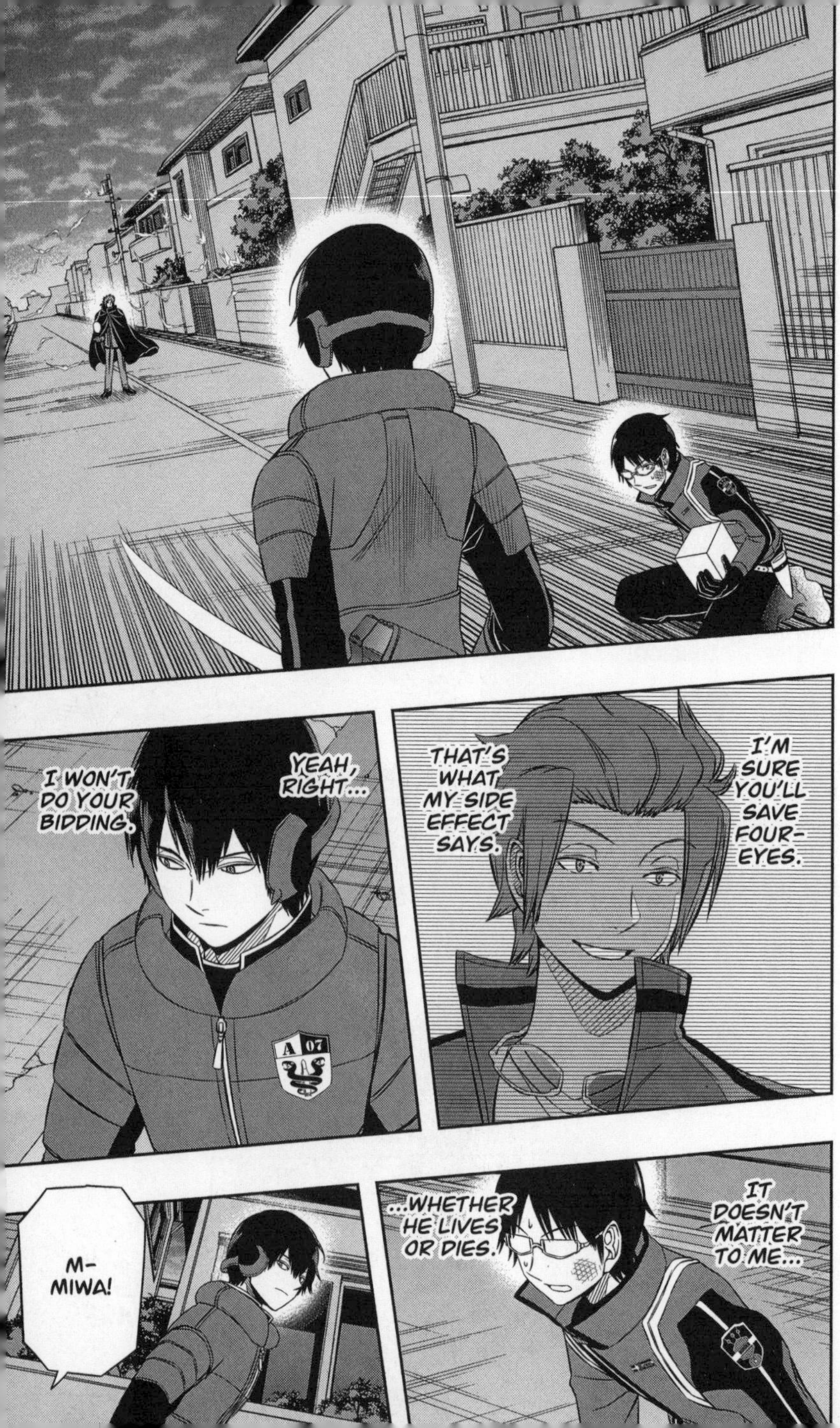
I'M SURE YOU'LL SAVE FOUR-EYES.
THAT'S WHAT MY SIDE EFFECT SAYS.
YEAH, RIGHT...
I WON'T DO YOUR BIDDING.
IT DOESN'T MATTER TO ME...
...WHETHER HE LIVES OR DIES.
M-MIWA!

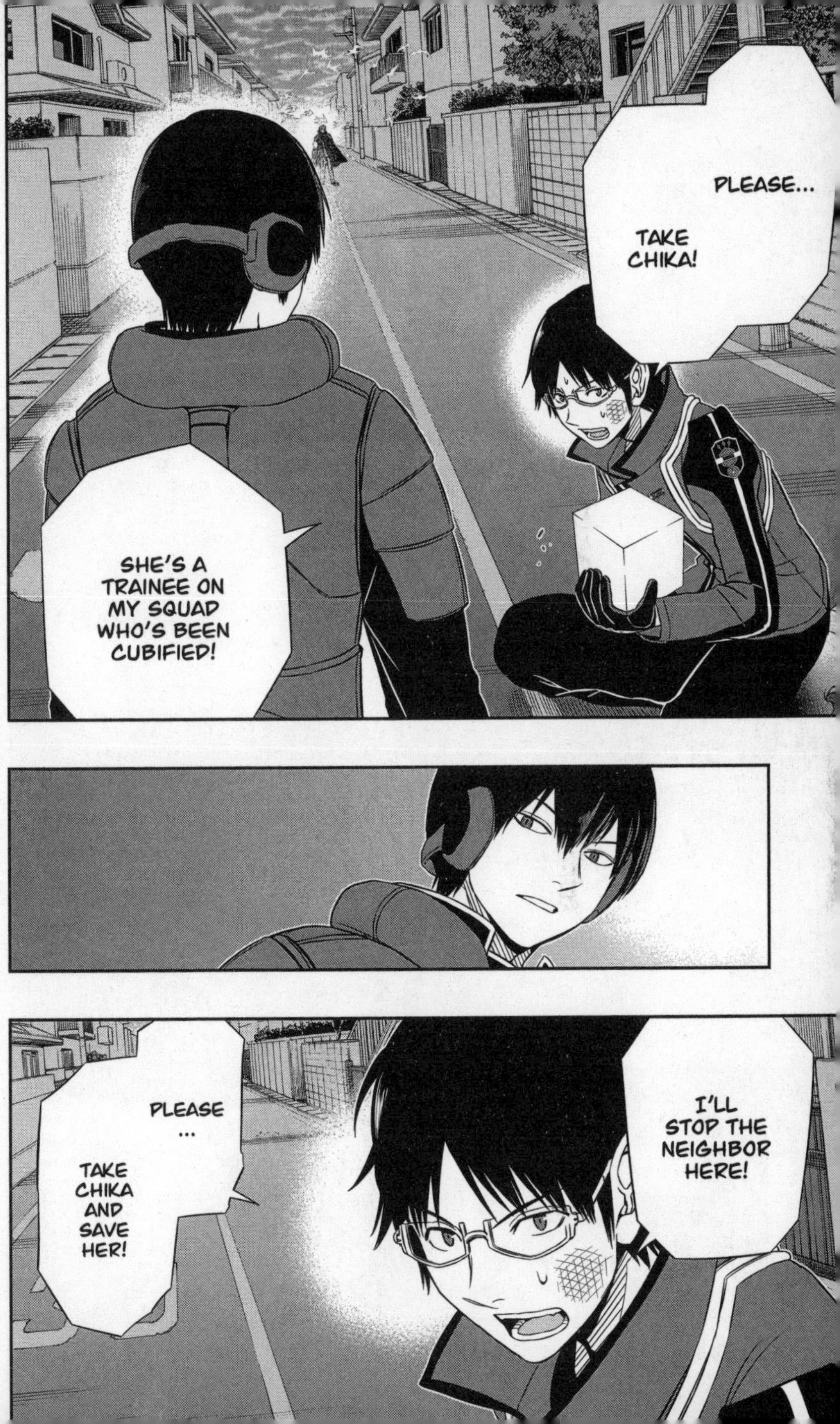
PLEASE... TAKE CHIKA!
SHE'S A TRAINEE ON MY SQUAD WHO'S BEEN CUBIFIED!
I'LL STOP THE NEIGHBOR HERE!
PLEASE ... TAKE CHIKA AND SAVE HER!

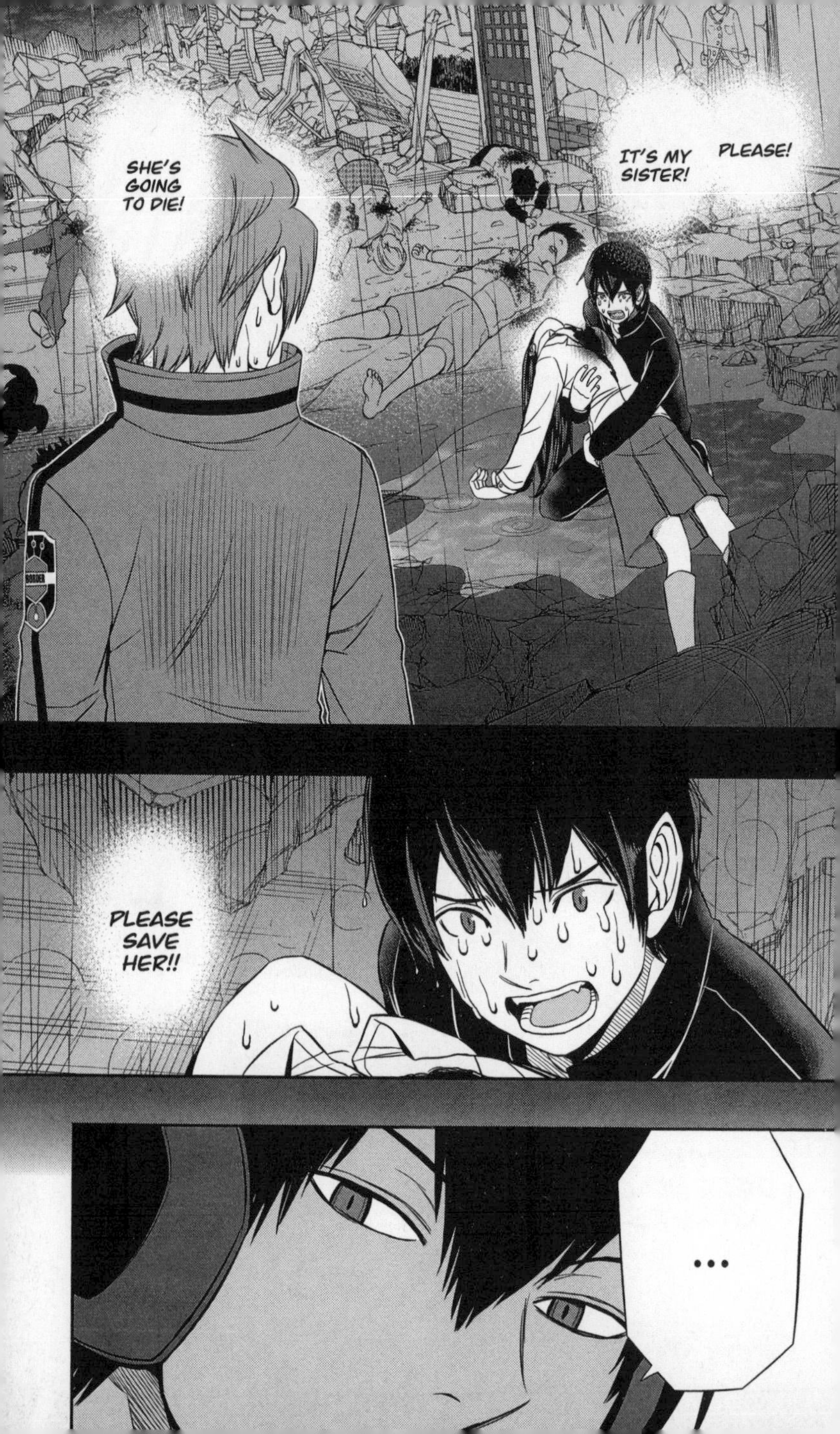
PLEASE!
IT'S MY SISTER!
SHE'S GOING TO DIE!
PLEASE SAVE HER!!
...

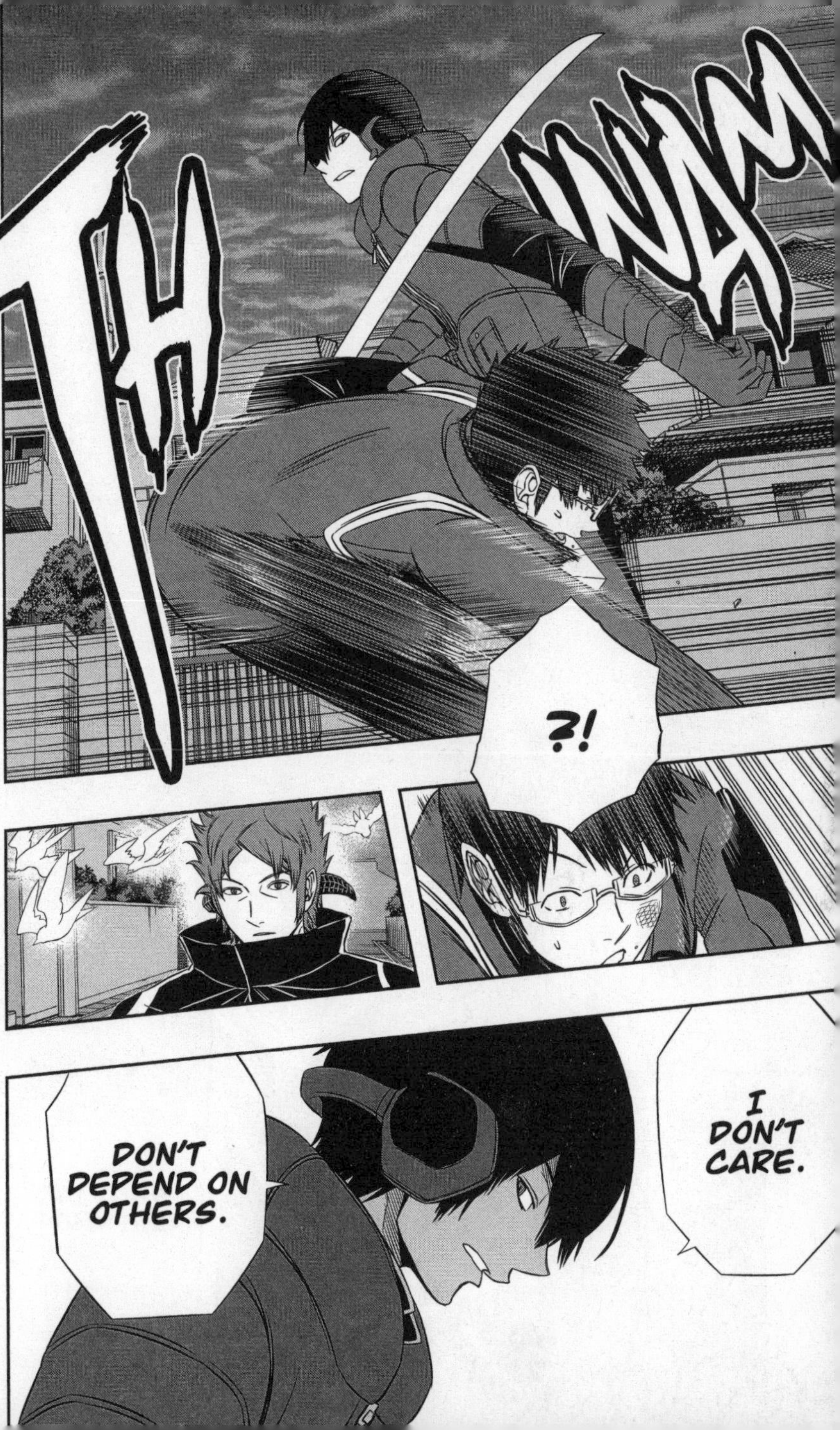
THWAM
?!
I DON'T CARE.
DON'T DEPEND ON OTHERS.

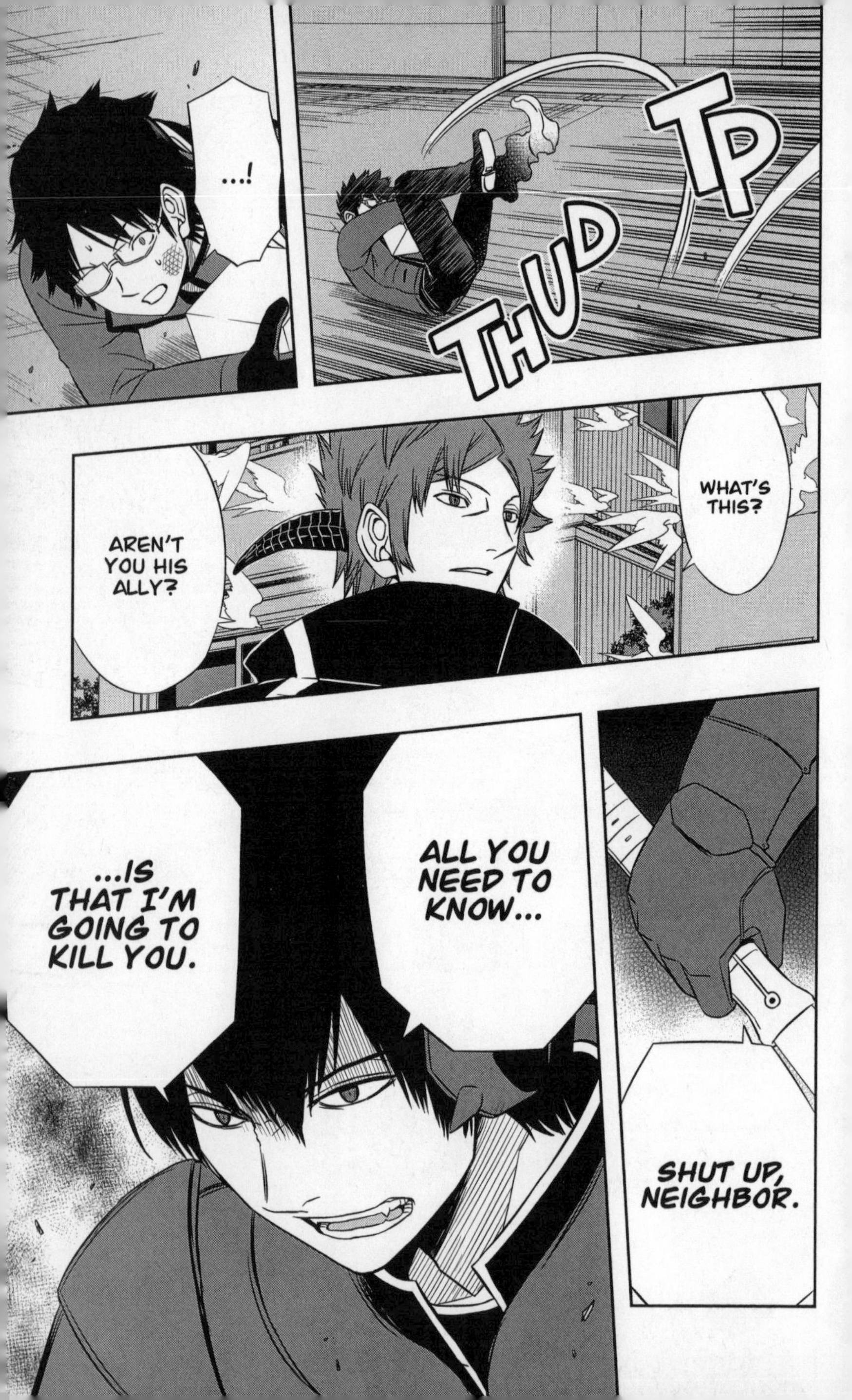
TP
THUD
...!
WHAT'S THIS?
AREN'T YOU HIS ALLY?
SHUT UP, NEIGHBOR.
ALL YOU NEED TO KNOW...
...IS THAT I'M GOING TO KILL YOU.

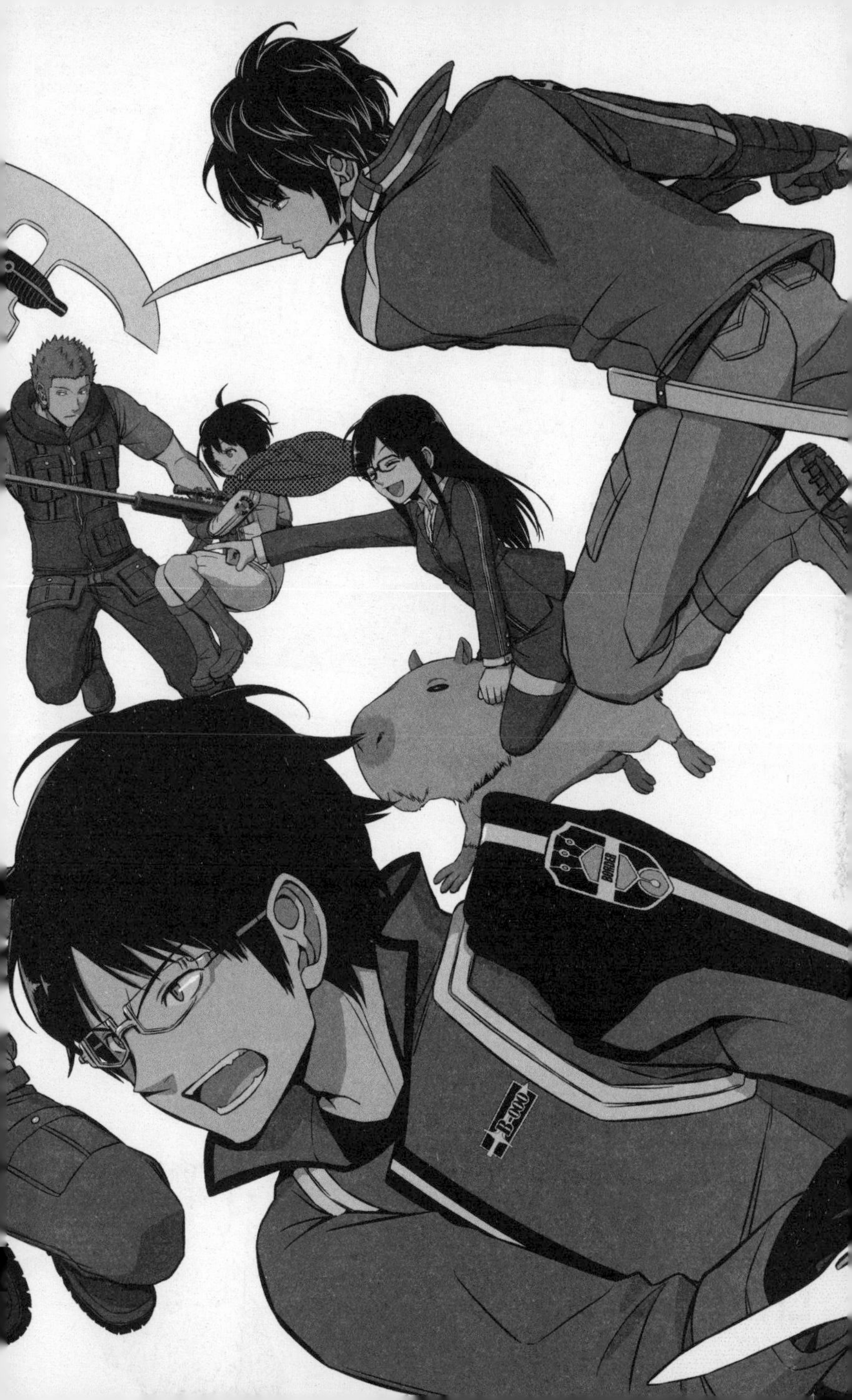

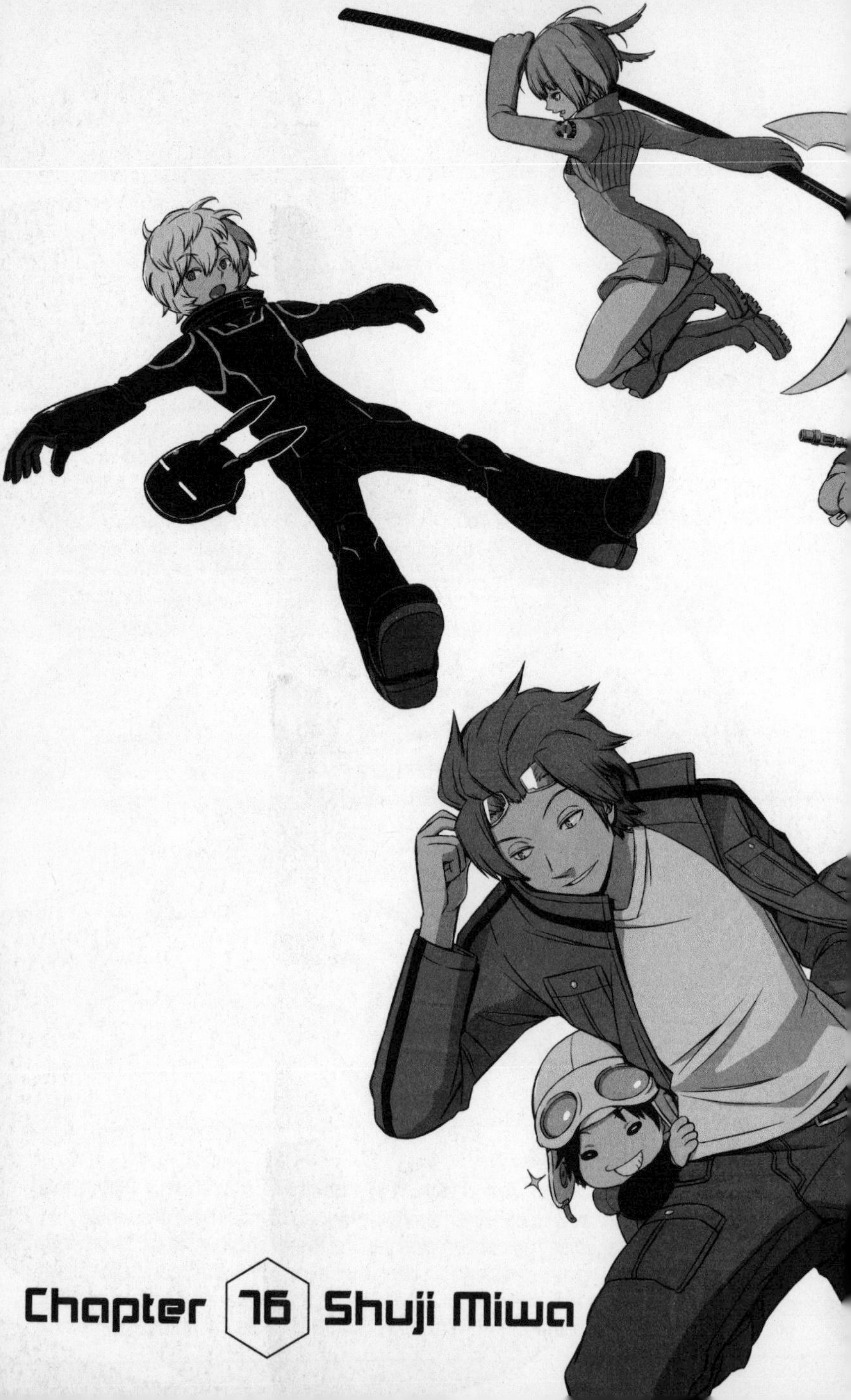

Chapter 76 Shuji Miwa

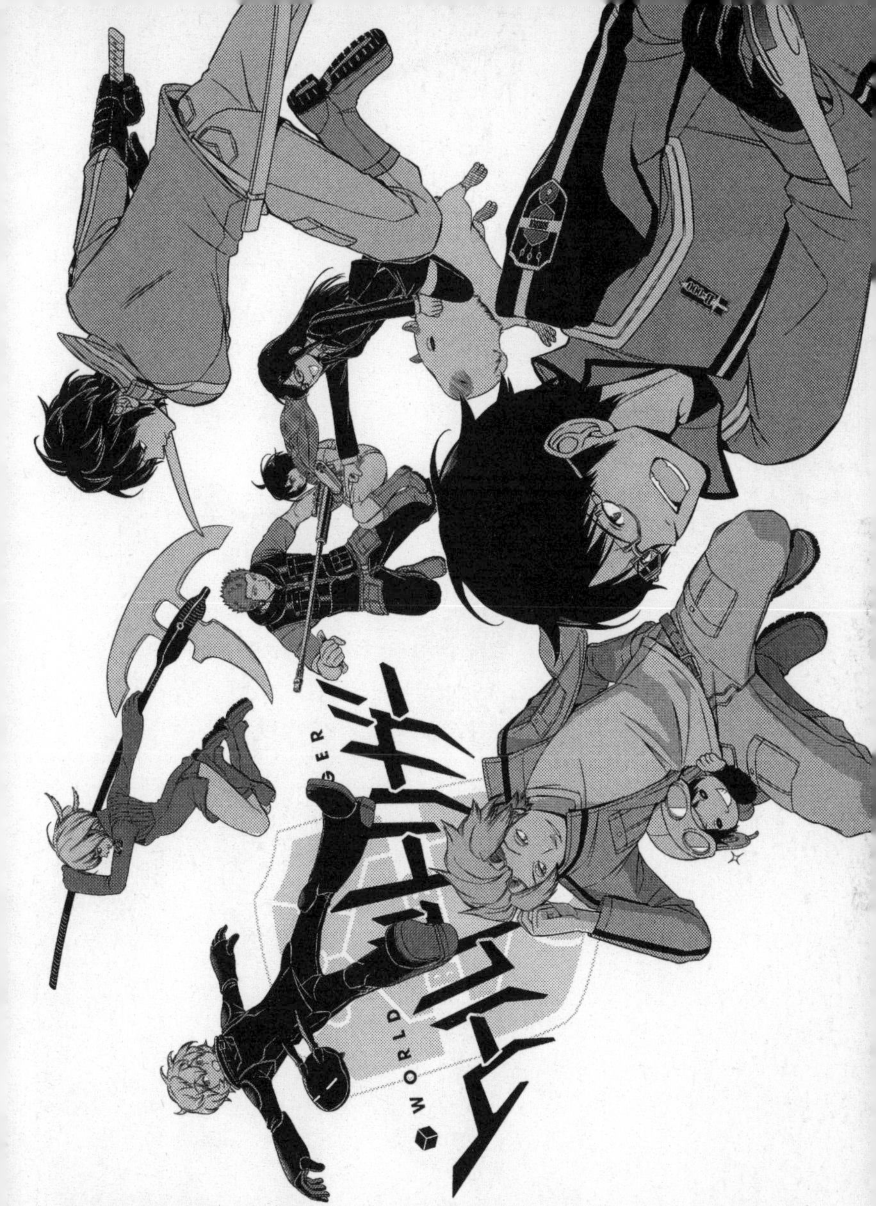

■ 2014 *Weekly Shonen Jump* issue 44 center color page (4th time)

This is the color page I drew to commemorate the launch of the anime. The whole Tamakoma gang is together. The caption over it in the first proof was, "Nobody can stop them!! They'll keep going forever!!" It was a little underwhelming and Jean Baptiste, who made the caption in the first place, wasn't too keen about it either, so it was rejected. It's still somewhat memorable though. I was happy I could draw Usami riding Raijin-Maru.

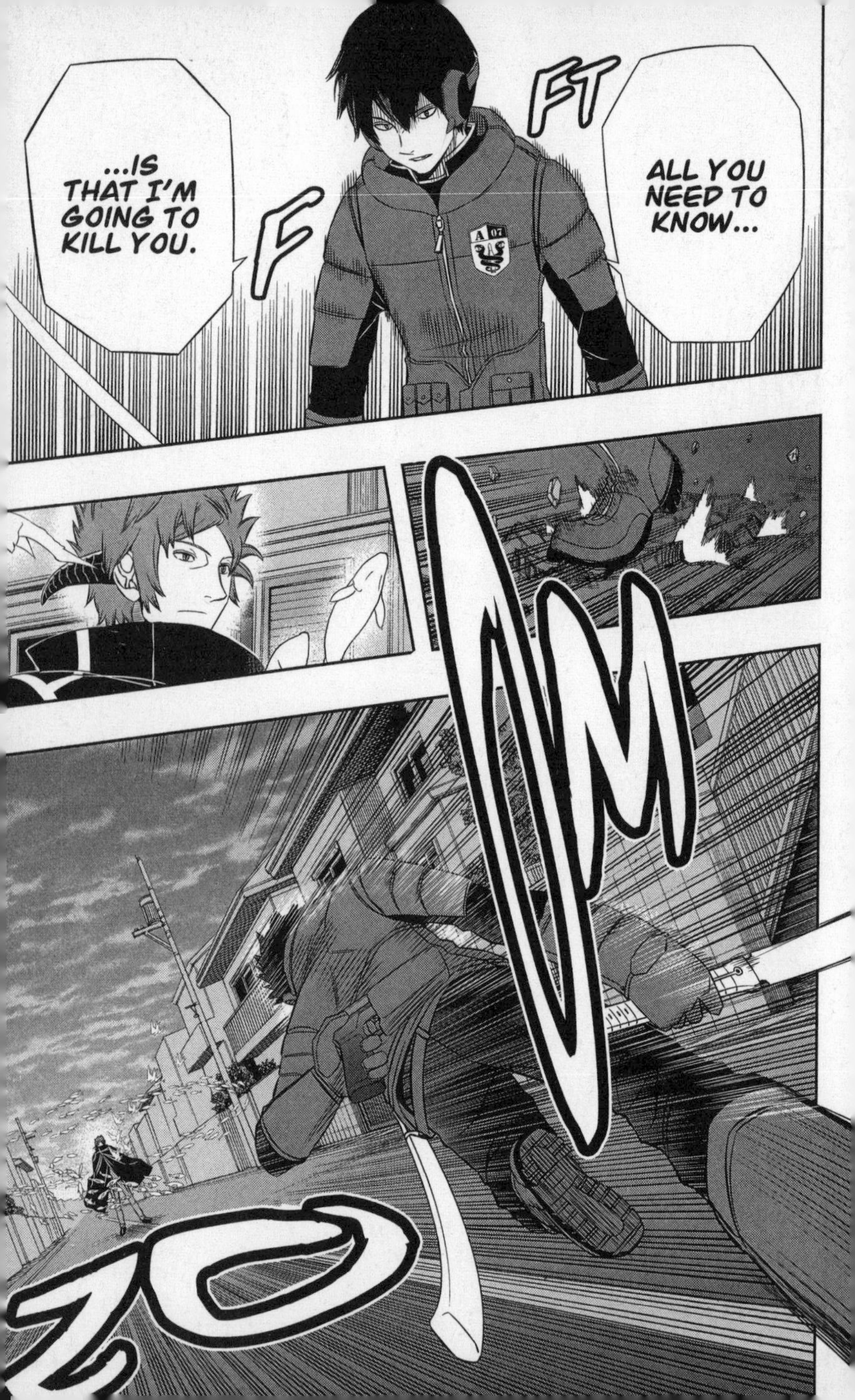
ALL YOU NEED TO KNOW...
FT
F
...IS THAT I'M GOING TO KILL YOU.

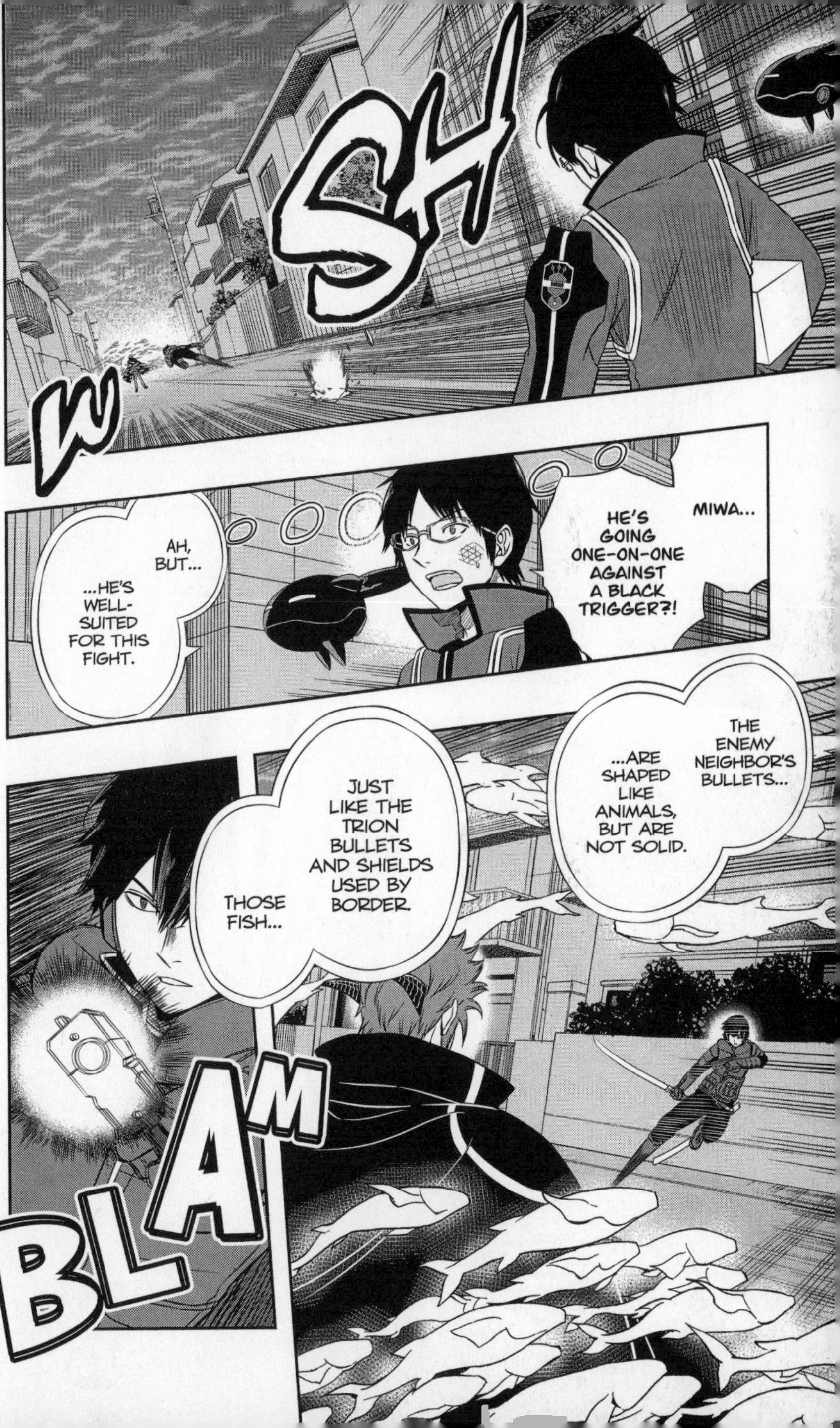
WSH
MIWA...
HE'S GOING ONE-ON-ONE AGAINST A BLACK TRIGGER?!
AH, BUT...
...HE'S WELL-SUITED FOR THIS FIGHT.
THE ENEMY NEIGHBOR'S BULLETS...
...ARE SHAPED LIKE ANIMALS, BUT ARE NOT SOLID.
JUST LIKE THE TRION BULLETS AND SHIELDS USED BY BORDER.
THOSE FISH...
BLAM

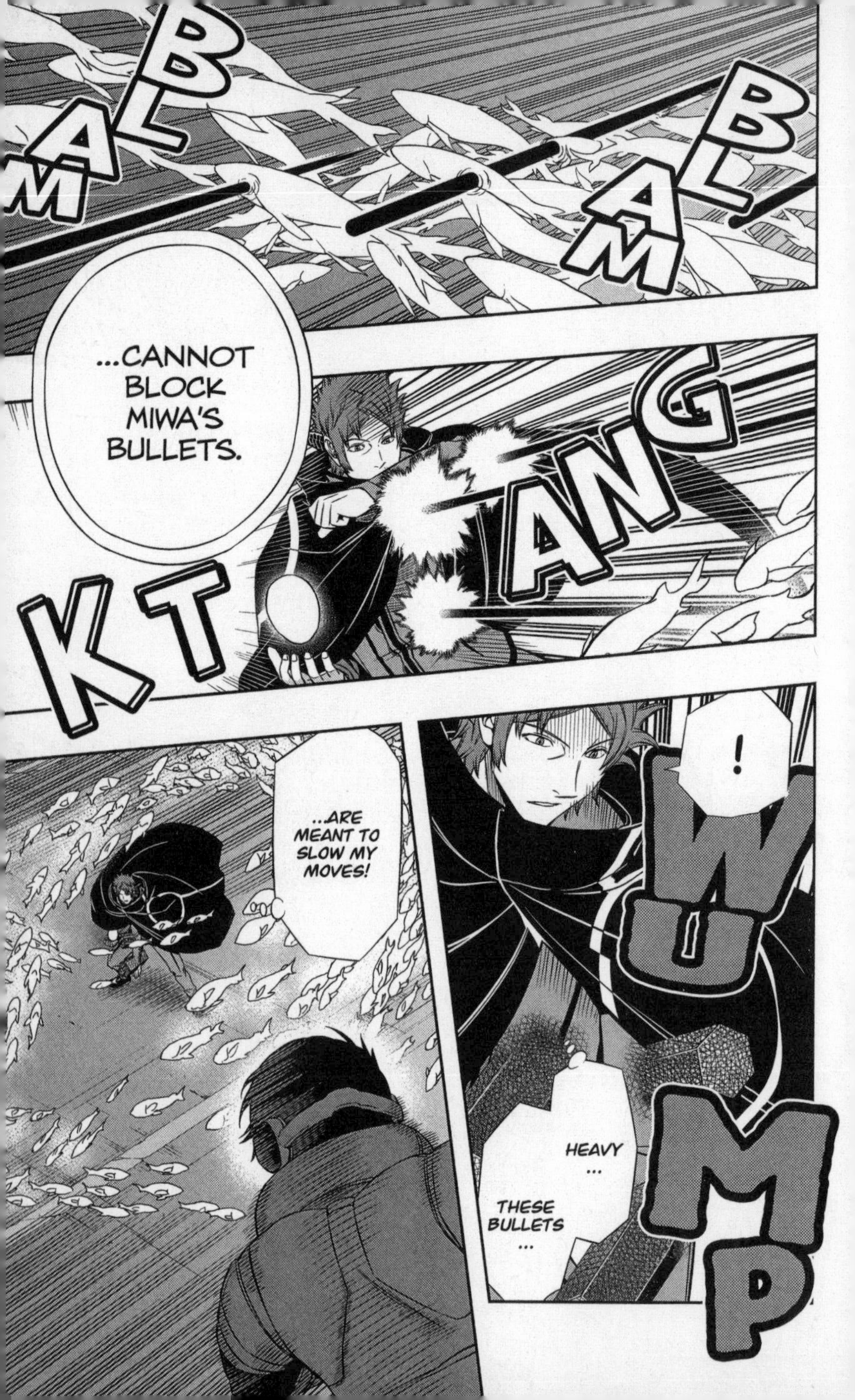
BLAM
BLAM
...CANNOT BLOCK MIWA'S BULLETS.
KTANG
!
WUMP
HEAVY ...
THESE BULLETS ...
...ARE MEANT TO SLOW MY MOVES!

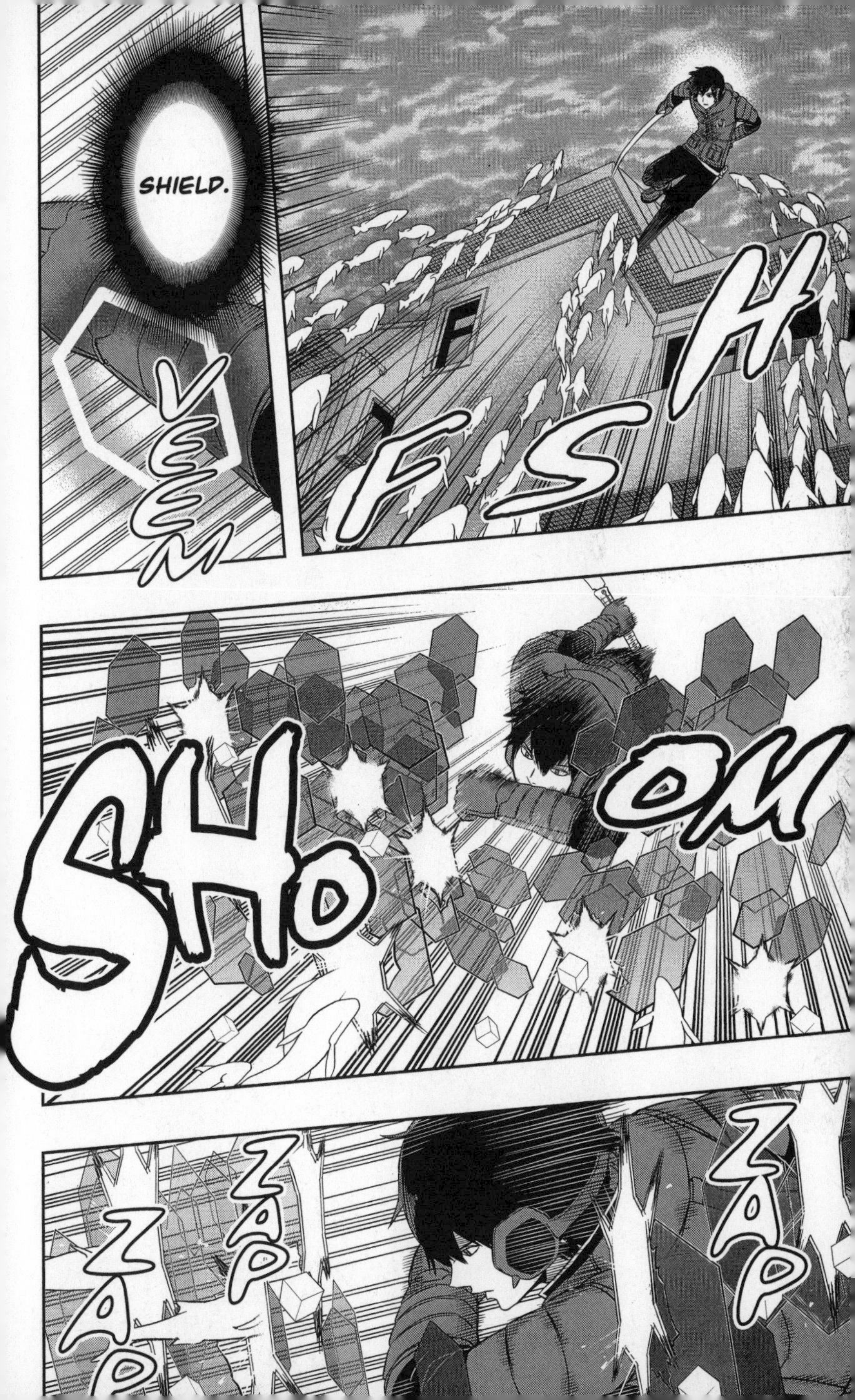
FSH
SHIELD.
VEEM
SHOOM
ZAP
ZAP
ZAP

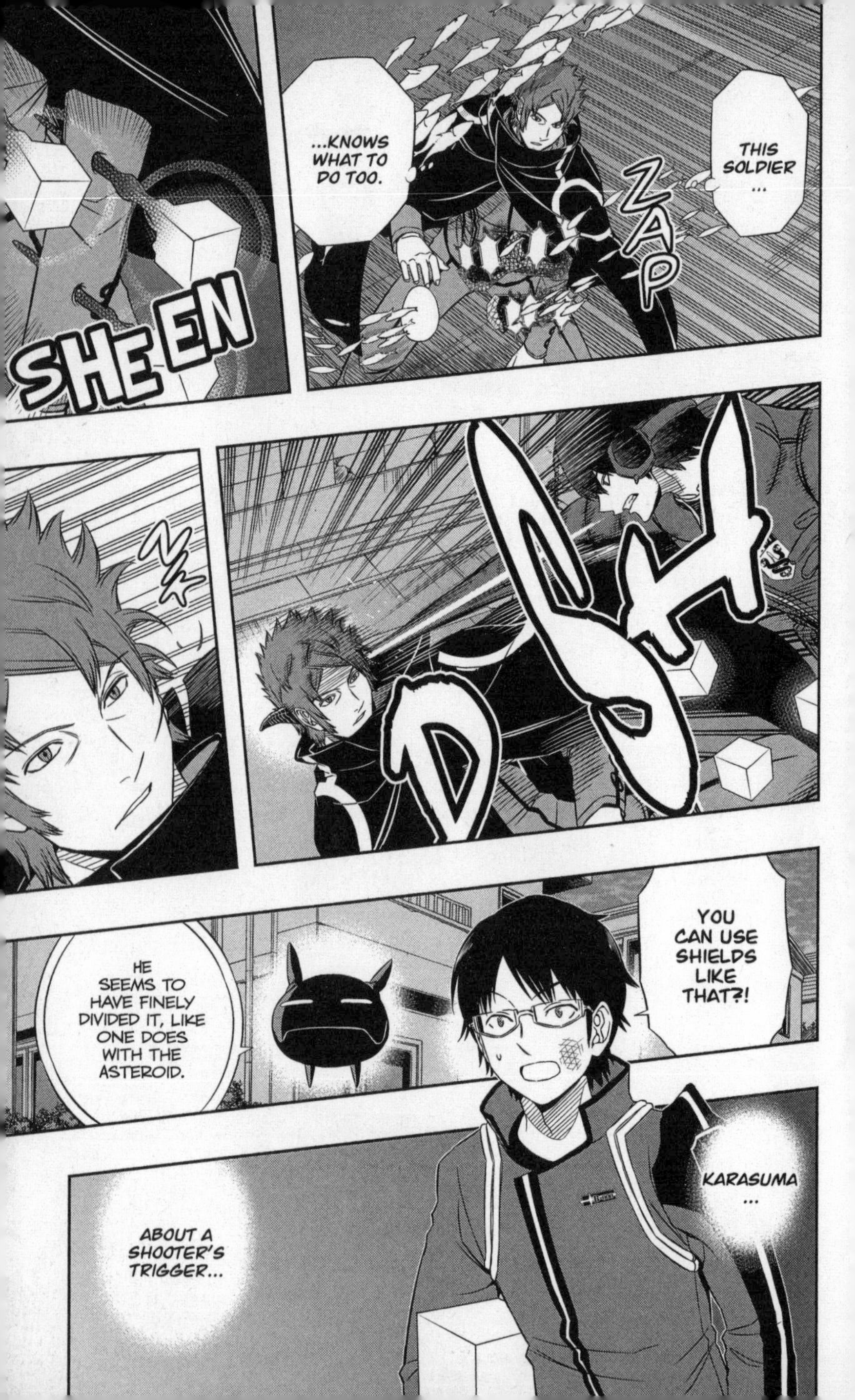
THIS SOLDIER ...
...KNOWS WHAT TO DO TOO.
ZAP
SHEEN
YOU CAN USE SHIELDS LIKE THAT?!
HE SEEMS TO HAVE FINELY DIVIDED IT, LIKE ONE DOES WITH THE ASTEROID.
KARASUMA ...
ABOUT A SHOOTER'S TRIGGER...

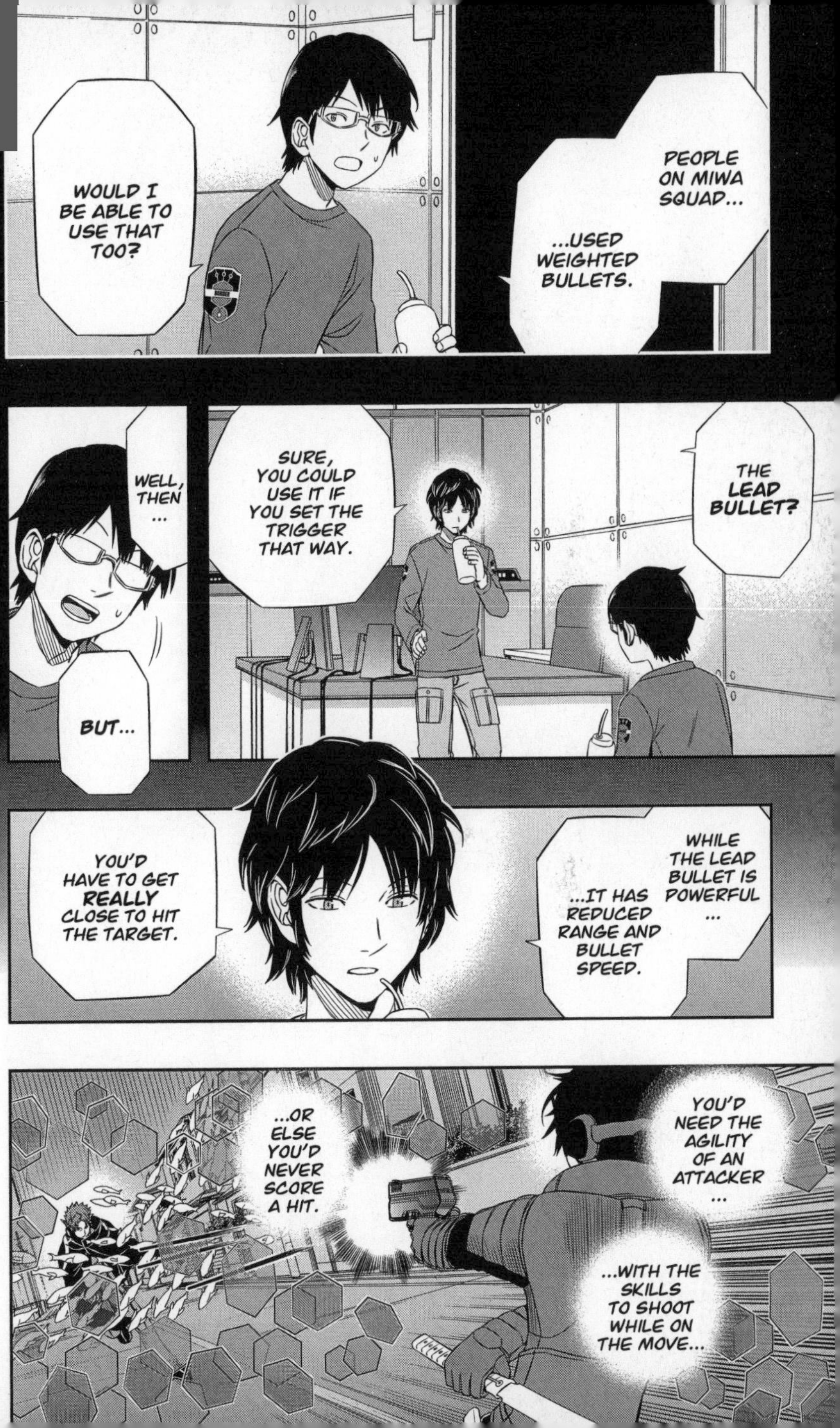
PEOPLE ON MIWA SQUAD...
...USED WEIGHTED BULLETS.
WOULD I BE ABLE TO USE THAT TOO?
THE LEAD BULLET?
SURE, YOU COULD USE IT IF YOU SET THE TRIGGER THAT WAY.
WELL, THEN ...
BUT...
WHILE THE LEAD BULLET IS POWERFUL ...
...IT HAS REDUCED RANGE AND BULLET SPEED.
YOU'D HAVE TO GET REALLY CLOSE TO HIT THE TARGET.
YOU'D NEED THE AGILITY OF AN ATTACKER ...
...WITH THE SKILLS TO SHOOT WHILE ON THE MOVE...
...OR ELSE YOU'D NEVER SCORE A HIT.

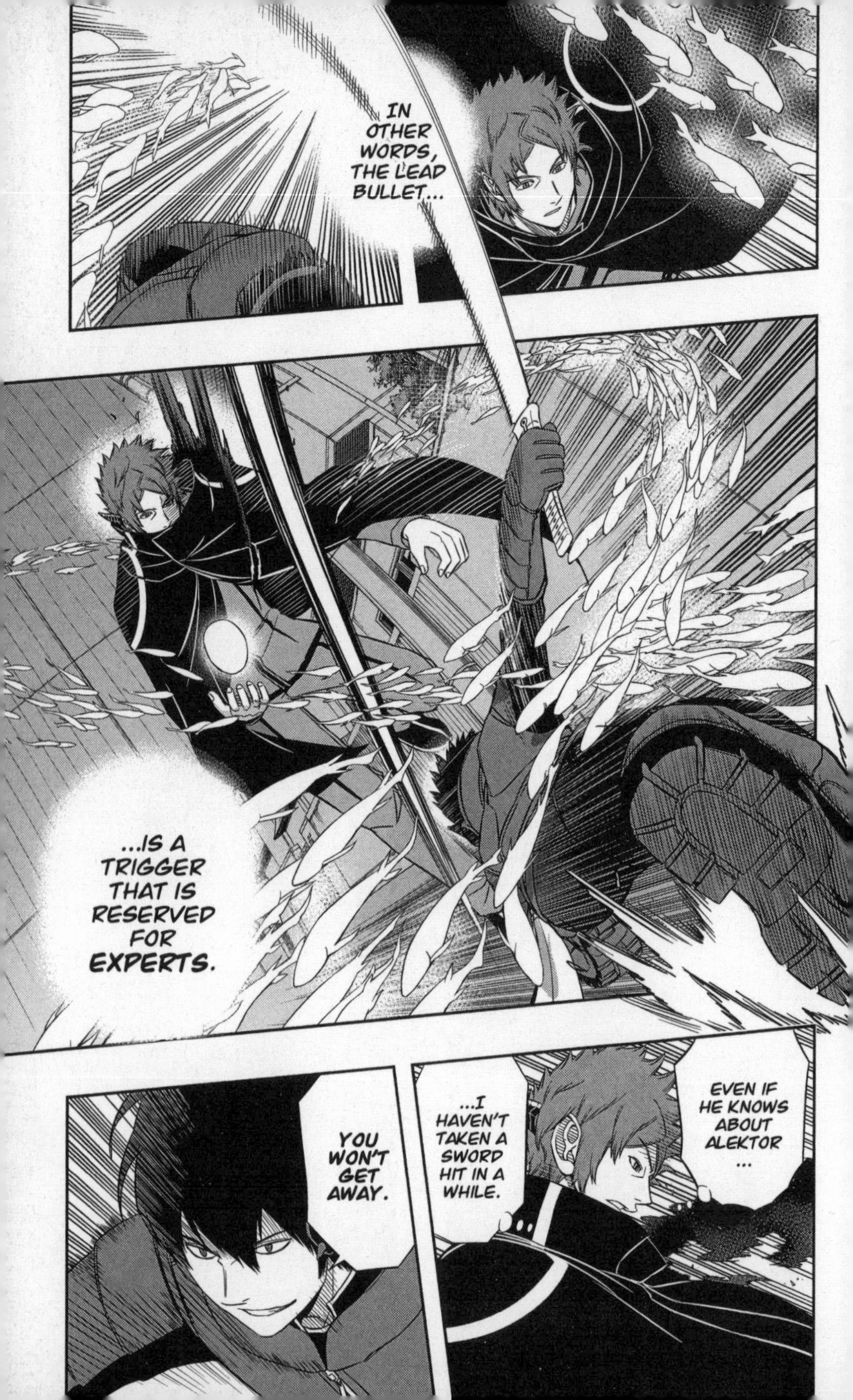
IN OTHER WORDS, THE LEAD BULLET...
...IS A TRIGGER THAT IS RESERVED FOR EXPERTS.
EVEN IF HE KNOWS ABOUT ALEKTOR ...
...I HAVEN'T TAKEN A SWORD HIT IN A WHILE.
YOU WON'T GET AWAY.

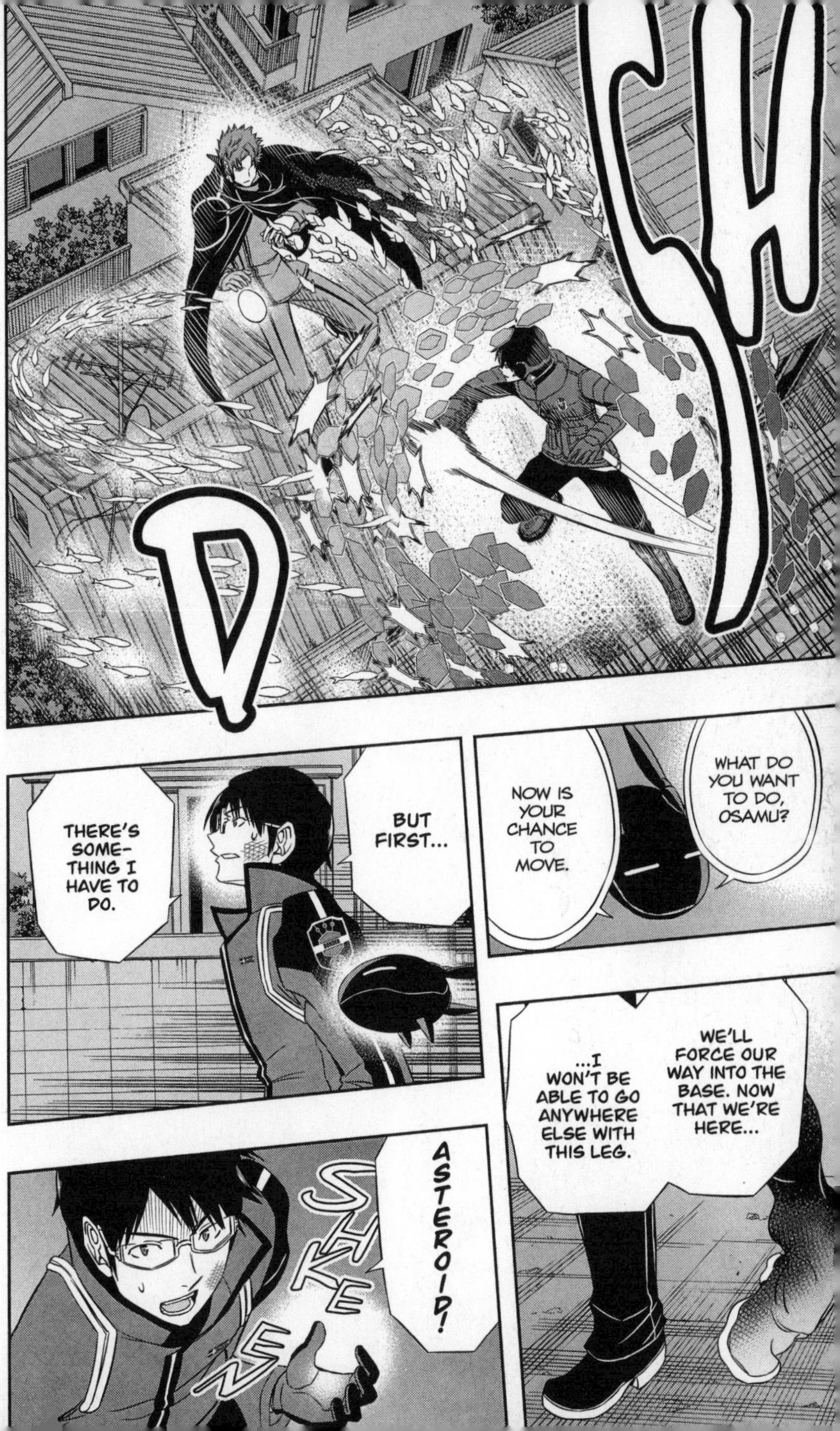
DSH
WHAT DO YOU WANT TO DO, OSAMU?
NOW IS YOUR CHANCE TO MOVE.
BUT FIRST...
THERE'S SOME-THING I HAVE TO DO.
WE'LL FORCE OUR WAY INTO THE BASE. NOW THAT WE'RE HERE...
...I WON'T BE ABLE TO GO ANYWHERE ELSE WITH THIS LEG.
ASTEROID!
SHKEEN

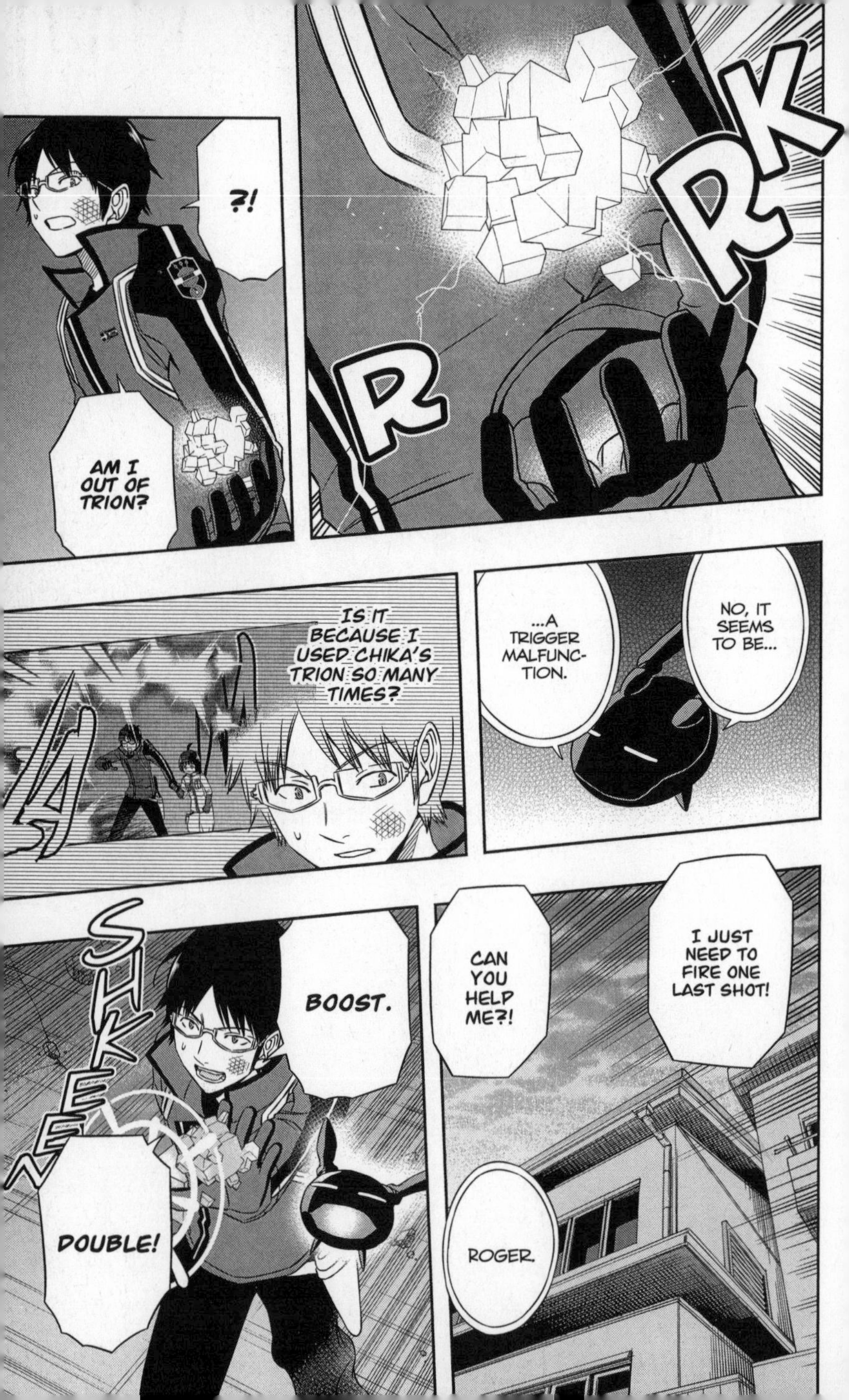
RK
R
?!
AM I OUT OF TRION?
NO, IT SEEMS TO BE...
...A TRIGGER MALFUNCTION.
IS IT BECAUSE I USED CHIKA'S TRION SO MANY TIMES?
I JUST NEED TO FIRE ONE LAST SHOT!
CAN YOU HELP ME?!
ROGER.
BOOST.
SHKEEN
DOUBLE!

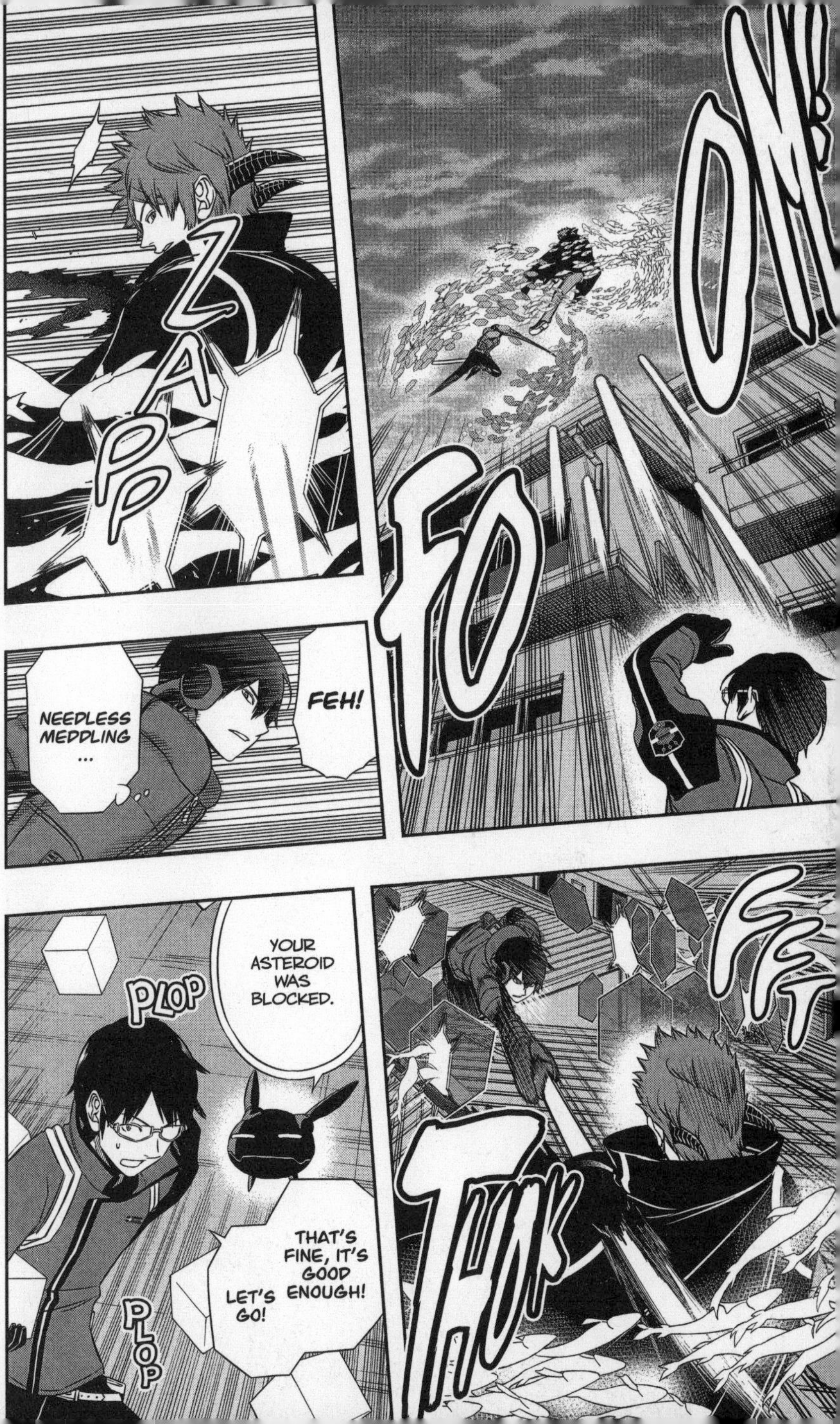
FOOM!
ZAPP
FEH!
NEEDLESS MEDDLING ...
THOK
YOUR ASTEROID WAS BLOCKED.
PLOP
THAT'S FINE, IT'S GOOD ENOUGH!
LET'S GO!
PLOP

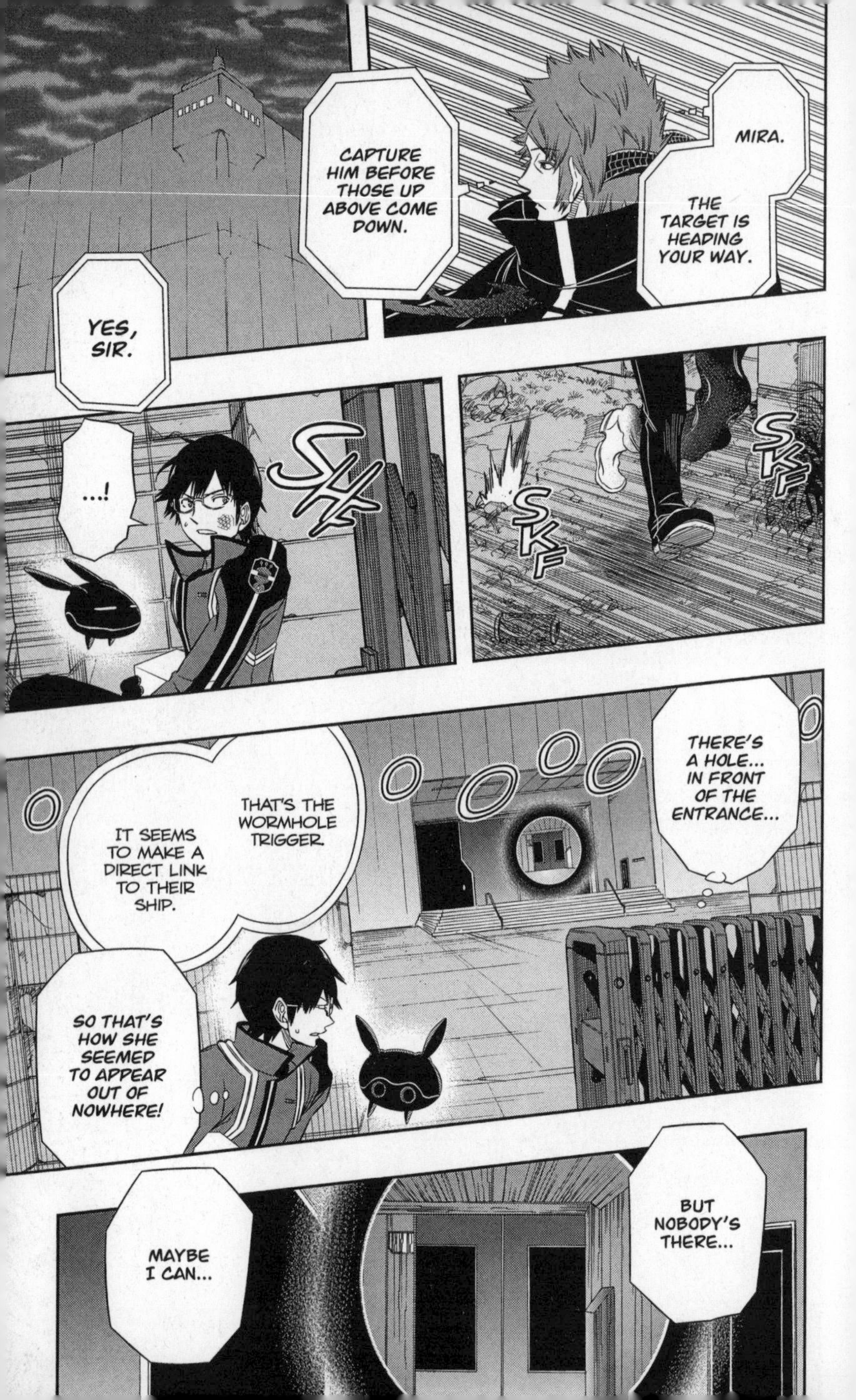
MIRA.
THE TARGET IS HEADING YOUR WAY.
CAPTURE HIM BEFORE THOSE UP ABOVE COME DOWN.
YES, SIR.
SKF
SKF
SH
...!
THERE'S A HOLE... IN FRONT OF THE ENTRANCE...
THAT'S THE WORMHOLE TRIGGER.
IT SEEMS TO MAKE A DIRECT LINK TO THEIR SHIP.
SO THAT'S HOW SHE SEEMED TO APPEAR OUT OF NOWHERE!
BUT NOBODY'S THERE...
MAYBE I CAN...

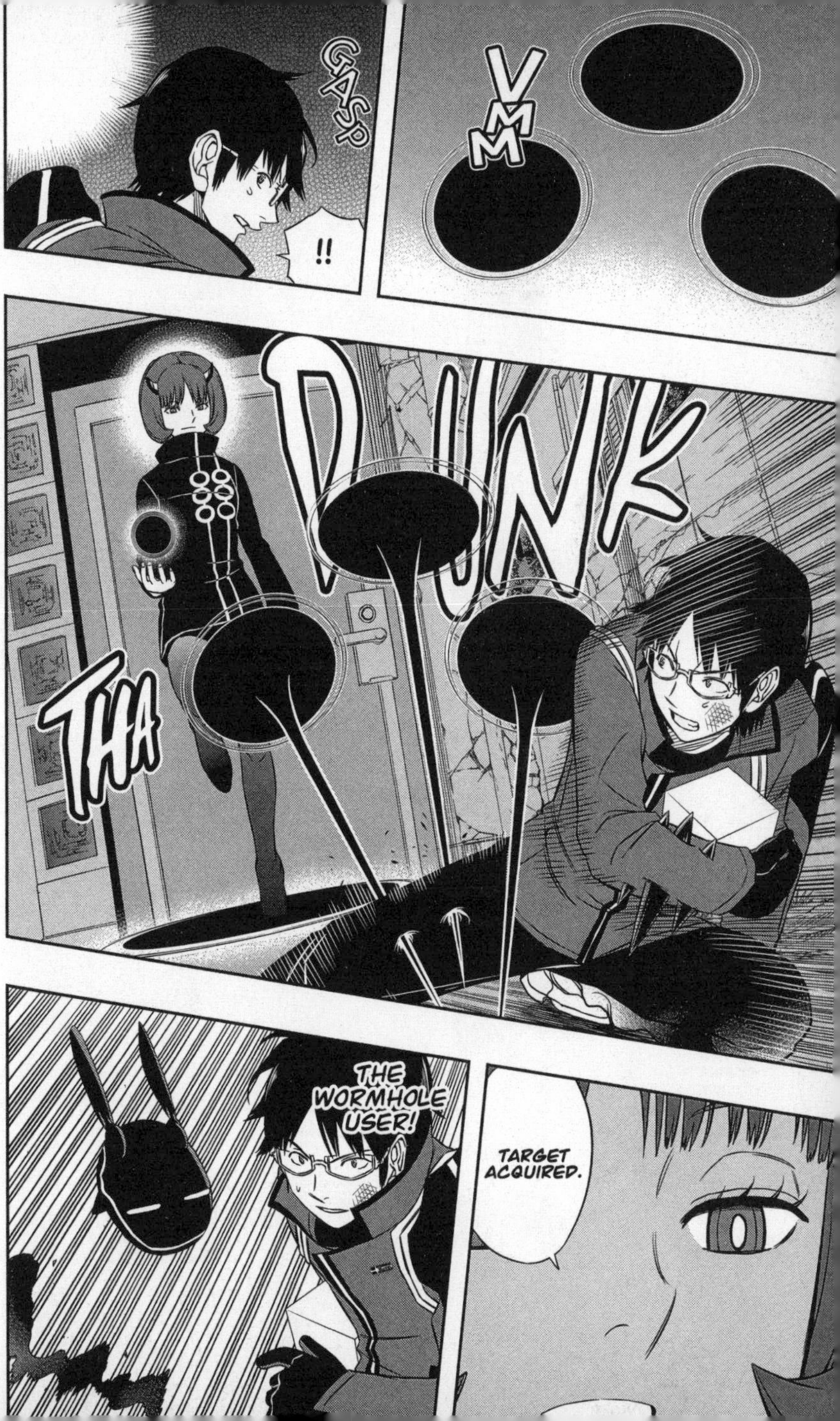
VMM
GASP
!!
DUNK
THA
TARGET ACQUIRED.
THE WORMHOLE USER!

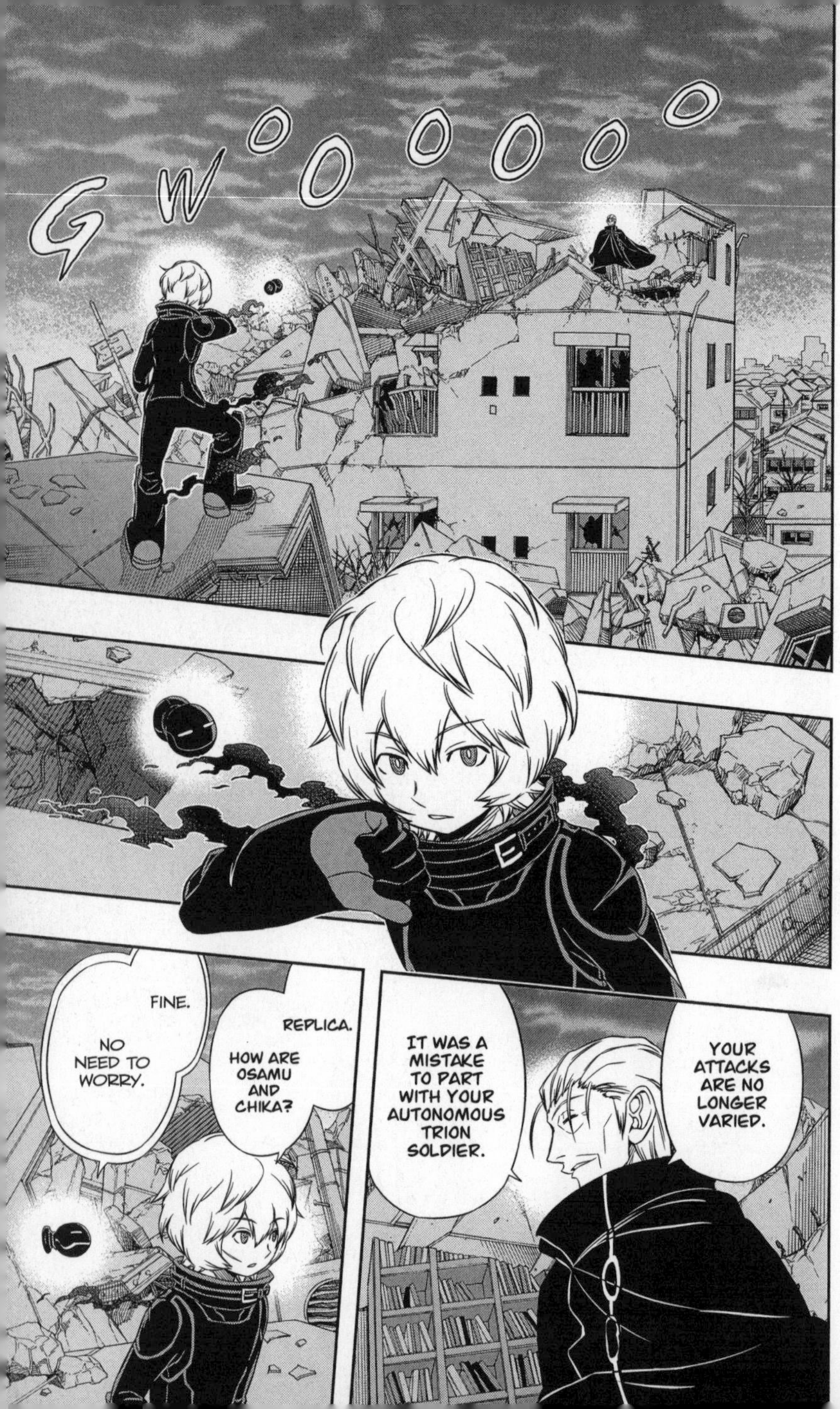
GWOOOOOO
YOUR ATTACKS ARE NO LONGER VARIED.
IT WAS A MISTAKE TO PART WITH YOUR AUTONOMOUS TRION SOLDIER.
REPLICA.
HOW ARE OSAMU AND CHIKA?
FINE.
NO NEED TO WORRY.

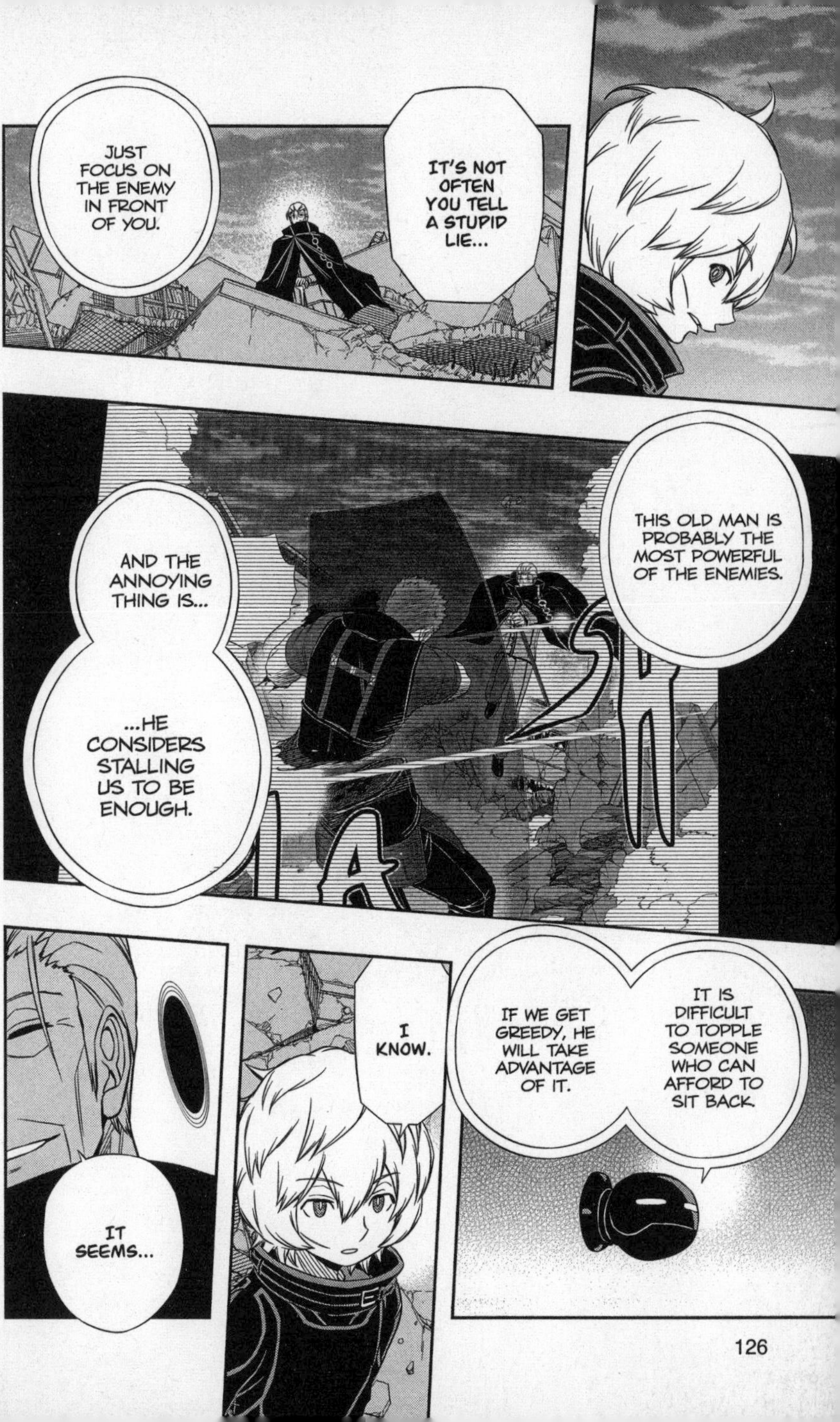
IT'S NOT OFTEN YOU TELL A STUPID LIE...
JUST FOCUS ON THE ENEMY IN FRONT OF YOU.
THIS OLD MAN IS PROBABLY THE MOST POWERFUL OF THE ENEMIES.
AND THE ANNOYING THING IS...
...HE CONSIDERS STALLING US TO BE ENOUGH.
IT IS DIFFICULT TO TOPPLE SOMEONE WHO CAN AFFORD TO SIT BACK.
IF WE GET GREEDY, HE WILL TAKE ADVANTAGE OF IT.
I KNOW.
IT SEEMS...

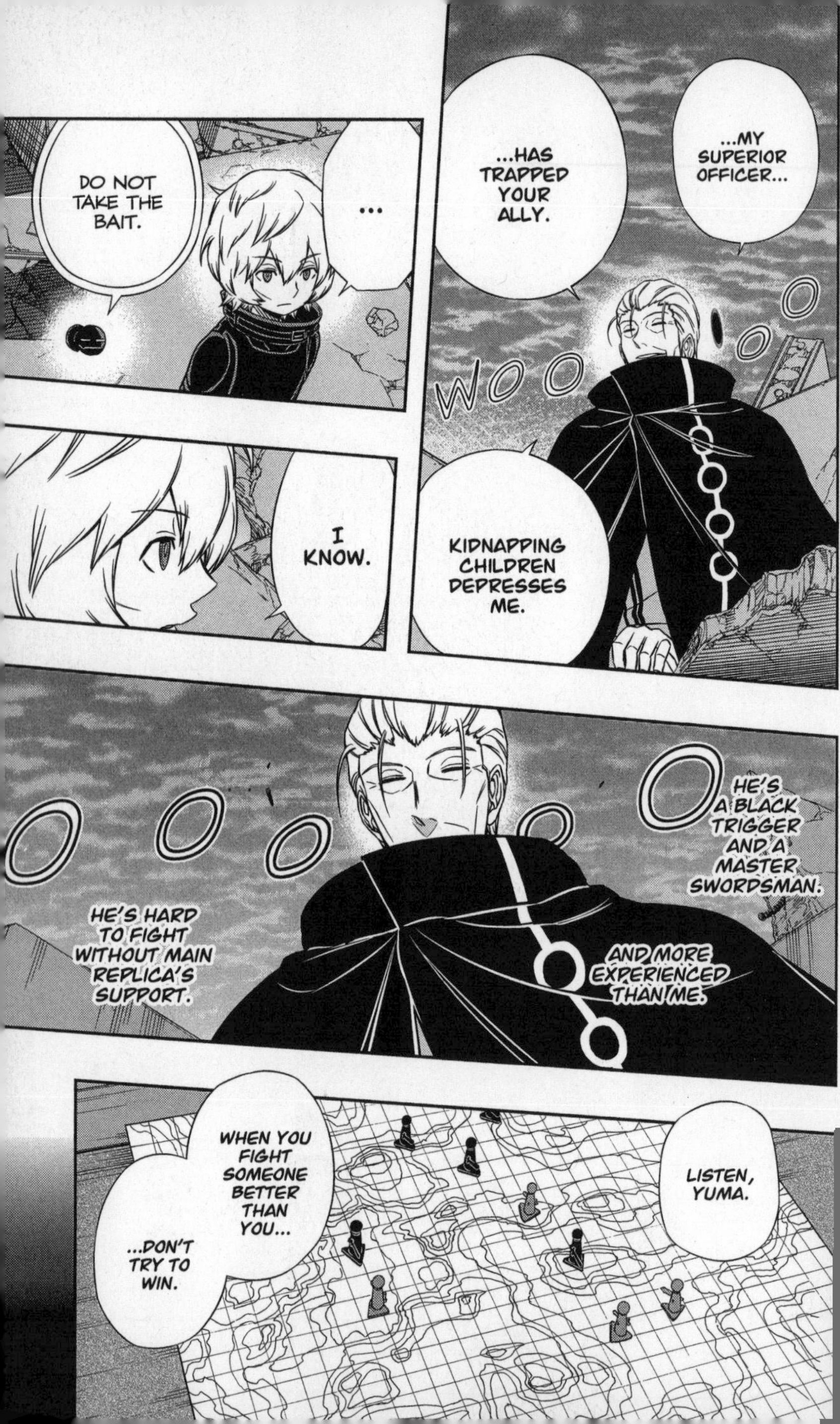
...MY SUPERIOR OFFICER...
...HAS TRAPPED YOUR ALLY.
WOOO
KIDNAPPING CHILDREN DEPRESSES ME.
...
DO NOT TAKE THE BAIT.
I KNOW.
HE'S A BLACK TRIGGER AND A MASTER SWORDSMAN.
AND MORE EXPERIENCED THAN ME.
HE'S HARD TO FIGHT WITHOUT MAIN REPLICA'S SUPPORT.
LISTEN, YUMA.
WHEN YOU FIGHT SOMEONE BETTER THAN YOU...
...DON'T TRY TO WIN.

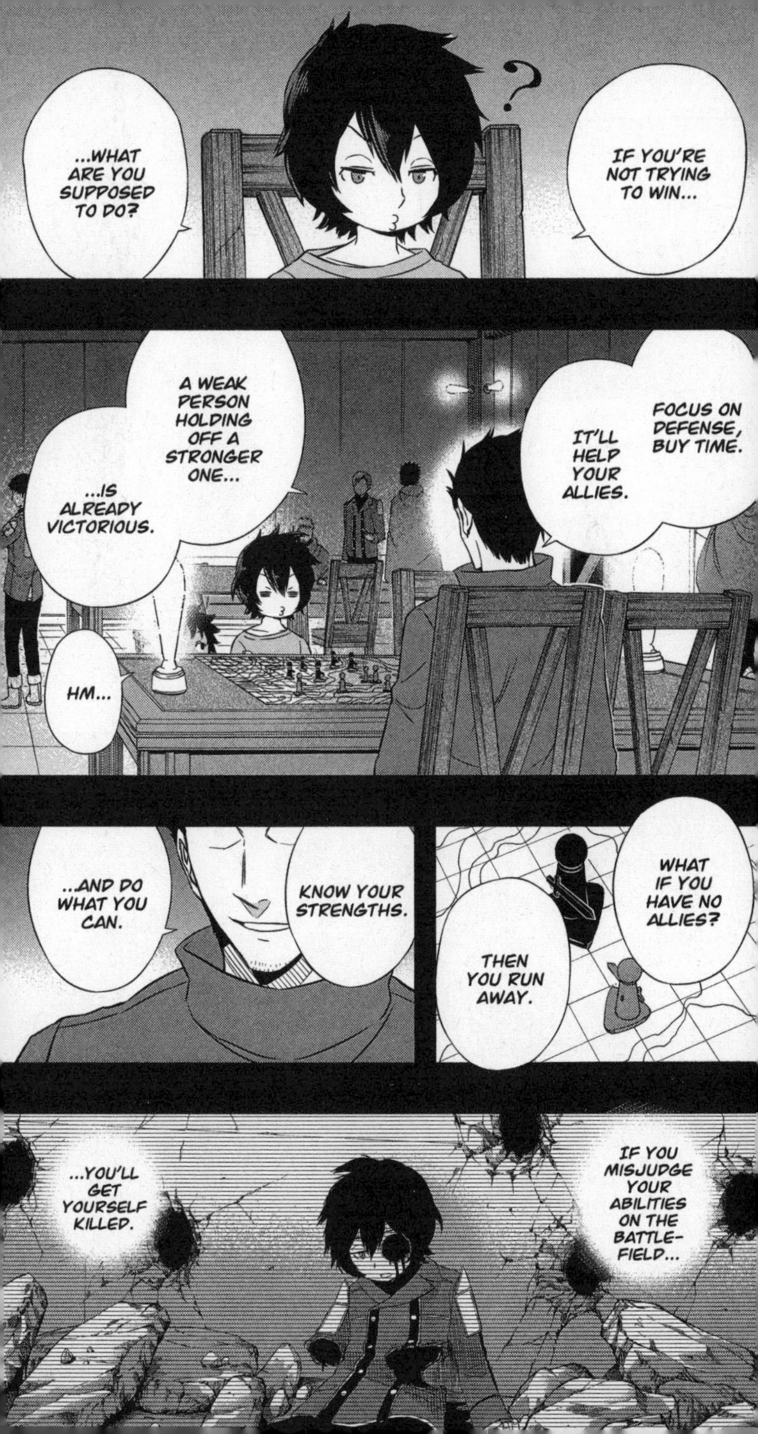
IF YOU'RE NOT TRYING TO WIN...
...WHAT ARE YOU SUPPOSED TO DO?
FOCUS ON DEFENSE, BUY TIME.
IT'LL HELP YOUR ALLIES.
A WEAK PERSON HOLDING OFF A STRONGER ONE...
...IS ALREADY VICTORIOUS.
HM...
WHAT IF YOU HAVE NO ALLIES?
THEN YOU RUN AWAY.
KNOW YOUR STRENGTHS.
...AND DO WHAT YOU CAN.
IF YOU MISJUDGE YOUR ABILITIES ON THE BATTLEFIELD...
...YOU'LL GET YOURSELF KILLED.

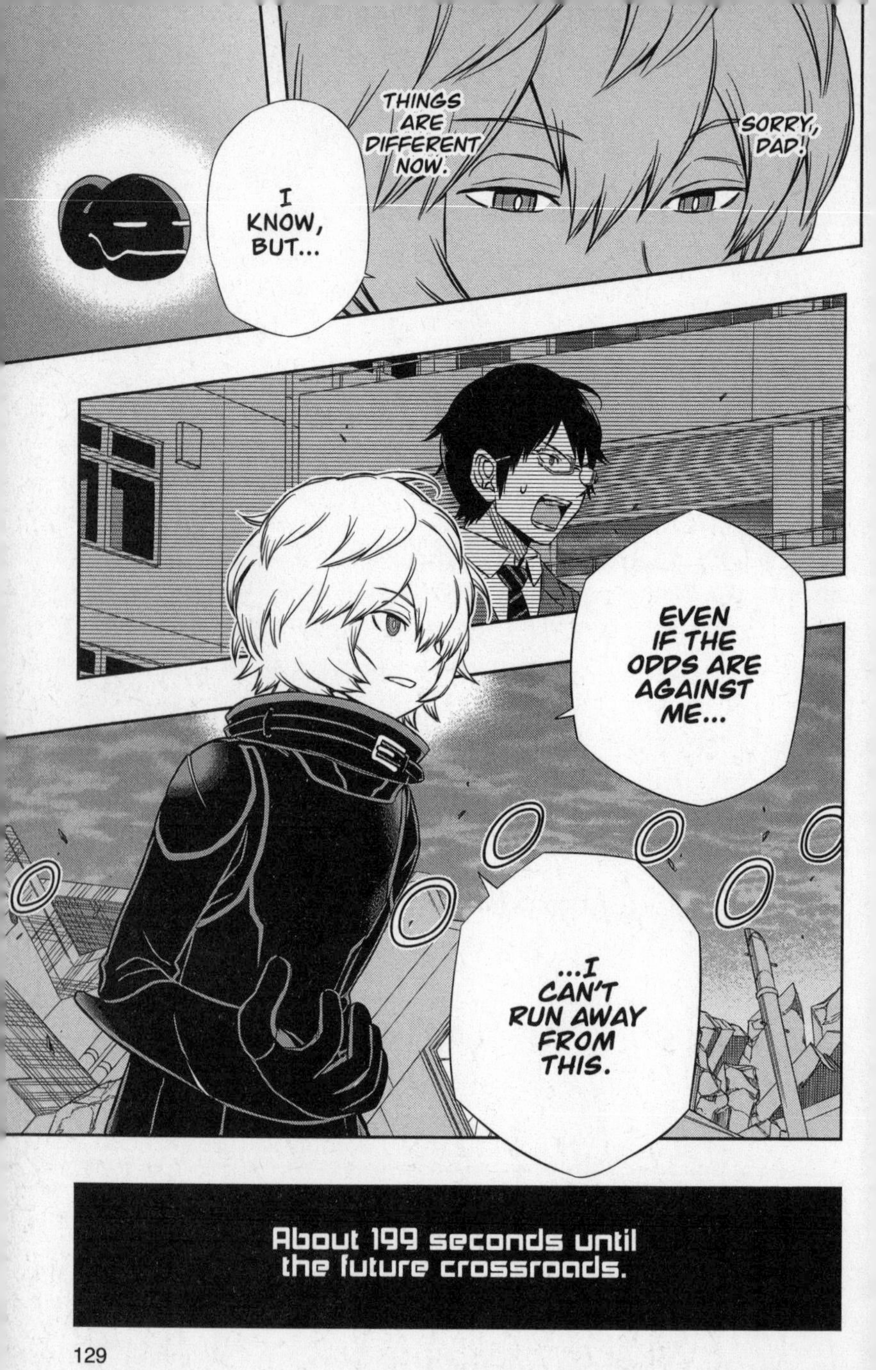
SORRY, DAD!
THINGS ARE DIFFERENT NOW.
I KNOW, BUT...
EVEN IF THE ODDS ARE AGAINST ME...
...I CAN'T RUN AWAY FROM THIS.

About 199 seconds until the future crossroads.

■ PR Assistant

Sakurako Taketomi (15)
B-Rank #18
Ebina Squad Operator

One of the PR characters for the Weekly Jump ad pages. She was a character I was going to introduce during the Rank Wars, but then I redesigned and submitted her for this role instead. She's an announcer with a Trigger that allows her to do a play-by-play anywhere. Thinking back, I probably didn't need to make this many variations of her facial expressions.

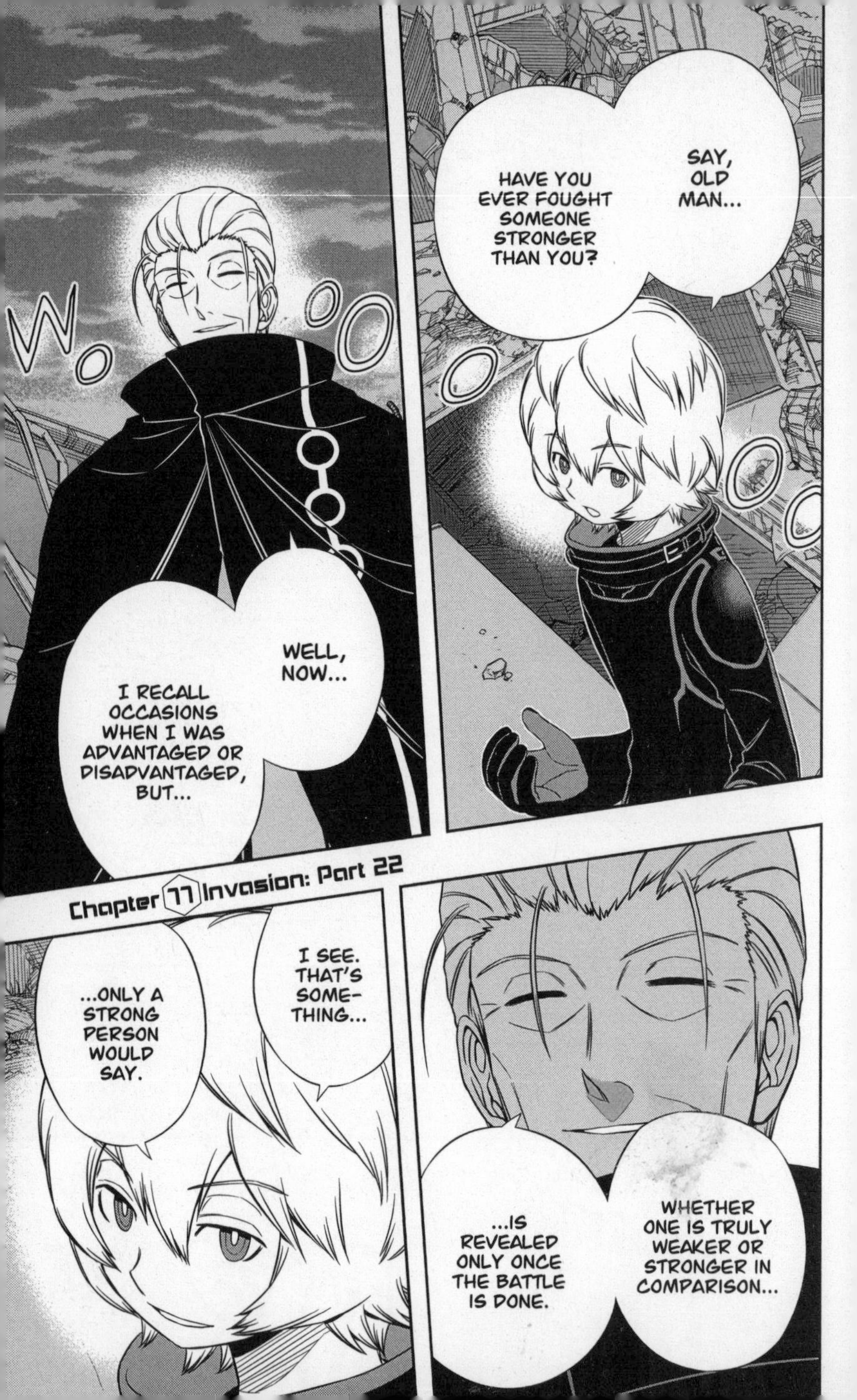
SAY, OLD MAN...
HAVE YOU EVER FOUGHT SOMEONE STRONGER THAN YOU?
WOOOO
WELL, NOW...
I RECALL OCCASIONS WHEN I WAS ADVANTAGED OR DISADVANTAGED, BUT...
Chapter 77 Invasion: Part 22
WHETHER ONE IS TRULY WEAKER OR STRONGER IN COMPARISON...
...IS REVEALED ONLY ONCE THE BATTLE IS DONE.
I SEE. THAT'S SOME-THING...
...ONLY A STRONG PERSON WOULD SAY.

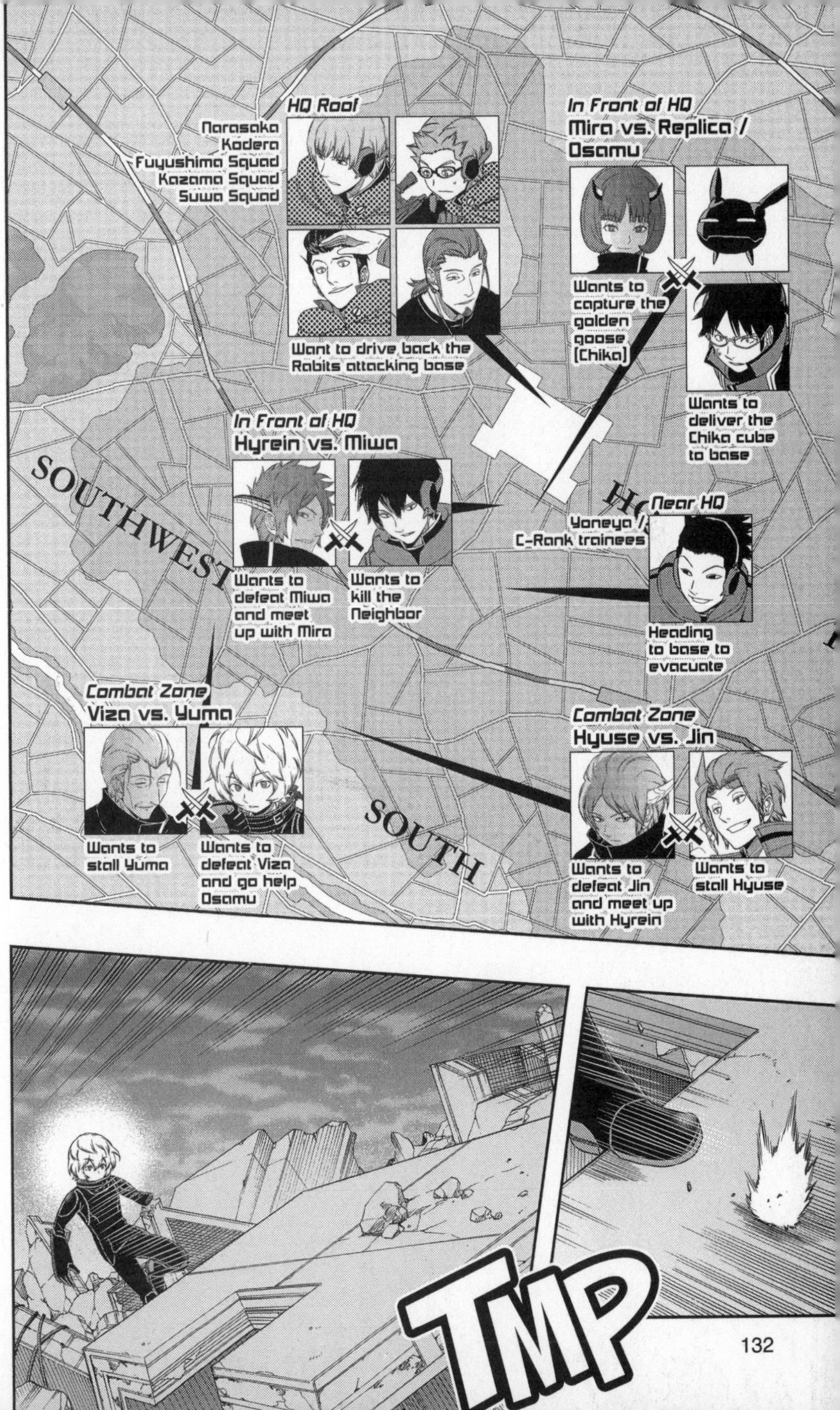
In Front of HQ
Mira vs. Replica / Osamu
Wants to capture the golden goose (Chika)
Wants to deliver the Chika cube to base
HQ Roof
Narasaka
Kodera
Fuyushima Squad
Kazama Squad
Suwa Squad
Want to drive back the Rabits attacking base
Near HQ
Yoneya / C-Rank trainees
Heading to base to evacuate
In Front of HQ
Hyrein vs. Miwa
Wants to kill the Neighbor
Wants to defeat Miwa and meet up with Mira
SOUTHWEST
Combat Zone
Hyuse vs. Jin
Wants to stall Hyuse
Wants to defeat Jin and meet up with Hyrein
SOUTH
Combat Zone
Viza vs. Yuma
Wants to defeat Viza and go help Osamu
Wants to stall Yuma
TMP

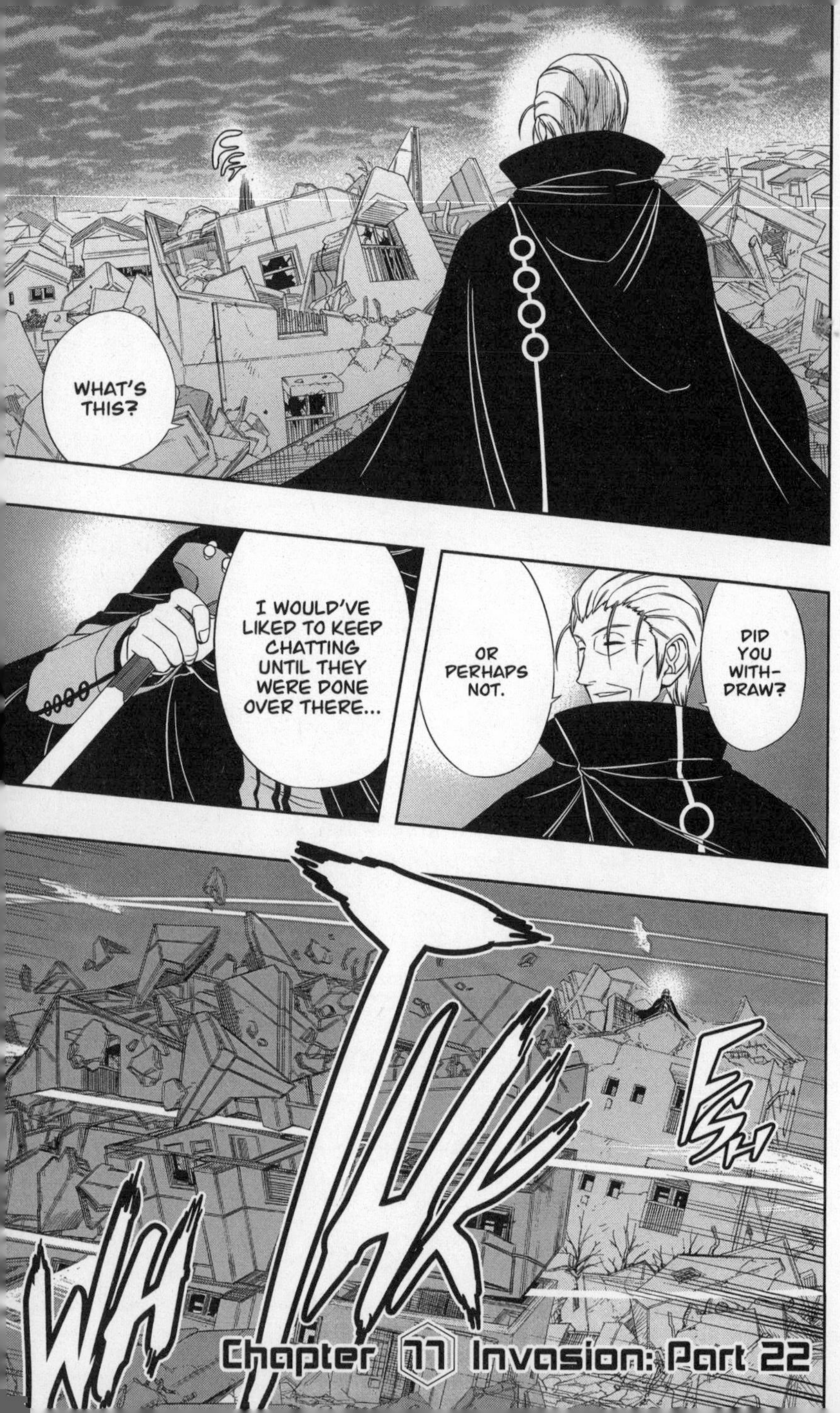
WHAT'S THIS?
DID YOU WITH-DRAW?
OR PERHAPS NOT.
I WOULD'VE LIKED TO KEEP CHATTING UNTIL THEY WERE DONE OVER THERE...
WHAK
Chapter 77 Invasion: Part 22

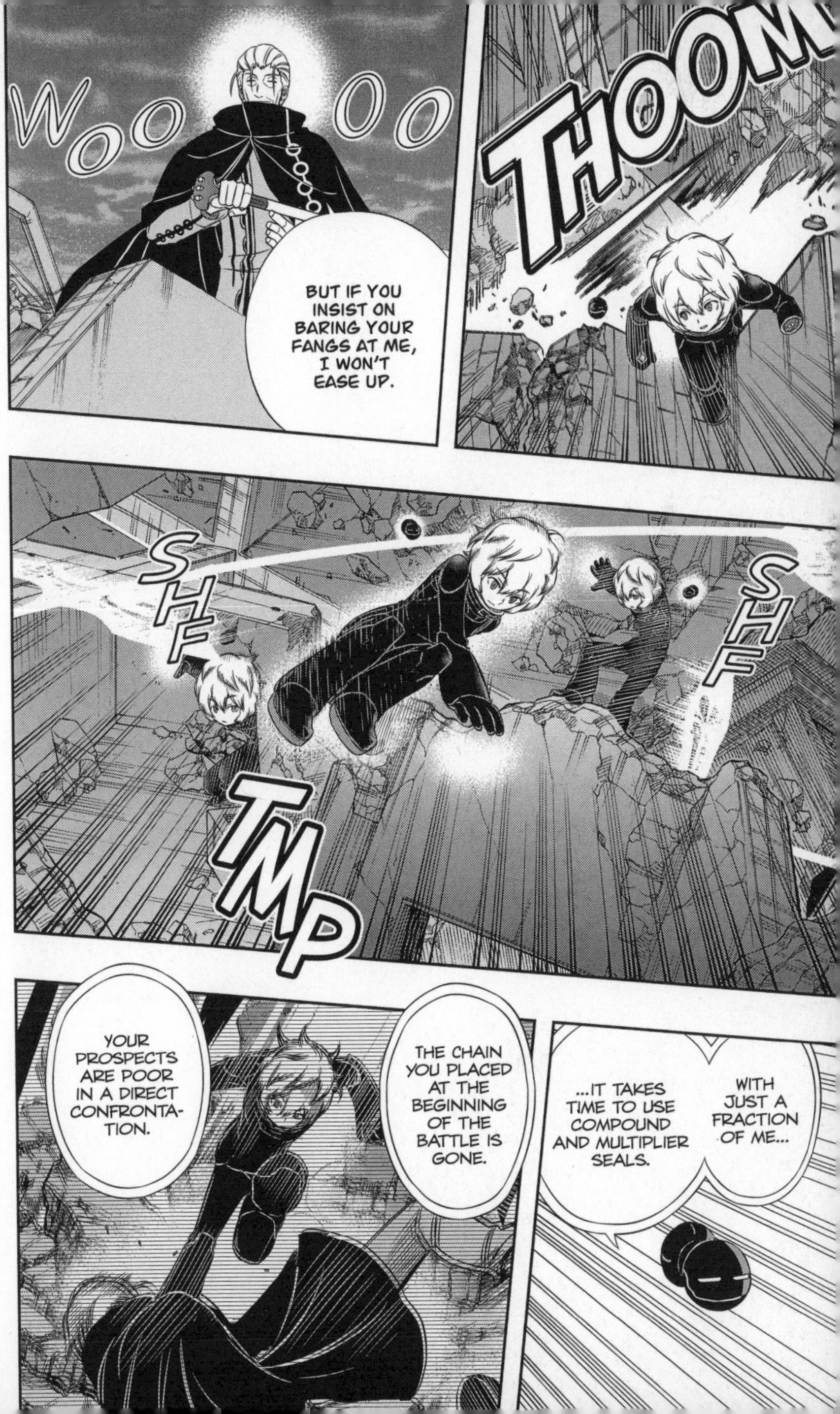
THOOM
WOOOOO
BUT IF YOU INSIST ON BARING YOUR FANGS AT ME, I WON'T EASE UP.
SHF
SHF
TMP
WITH JUST A FRACTION OF ME...
...IT TAKES TIME TO USE COMPOUND AND MULTIPLIER SEALS.
THE CHAIN YOU PLACED AT THE BEGINNING OF THE BATTLE IS GONE.
YOUR PROSPECTS ARE POOR IN A DIRECT CONFRONTATION.

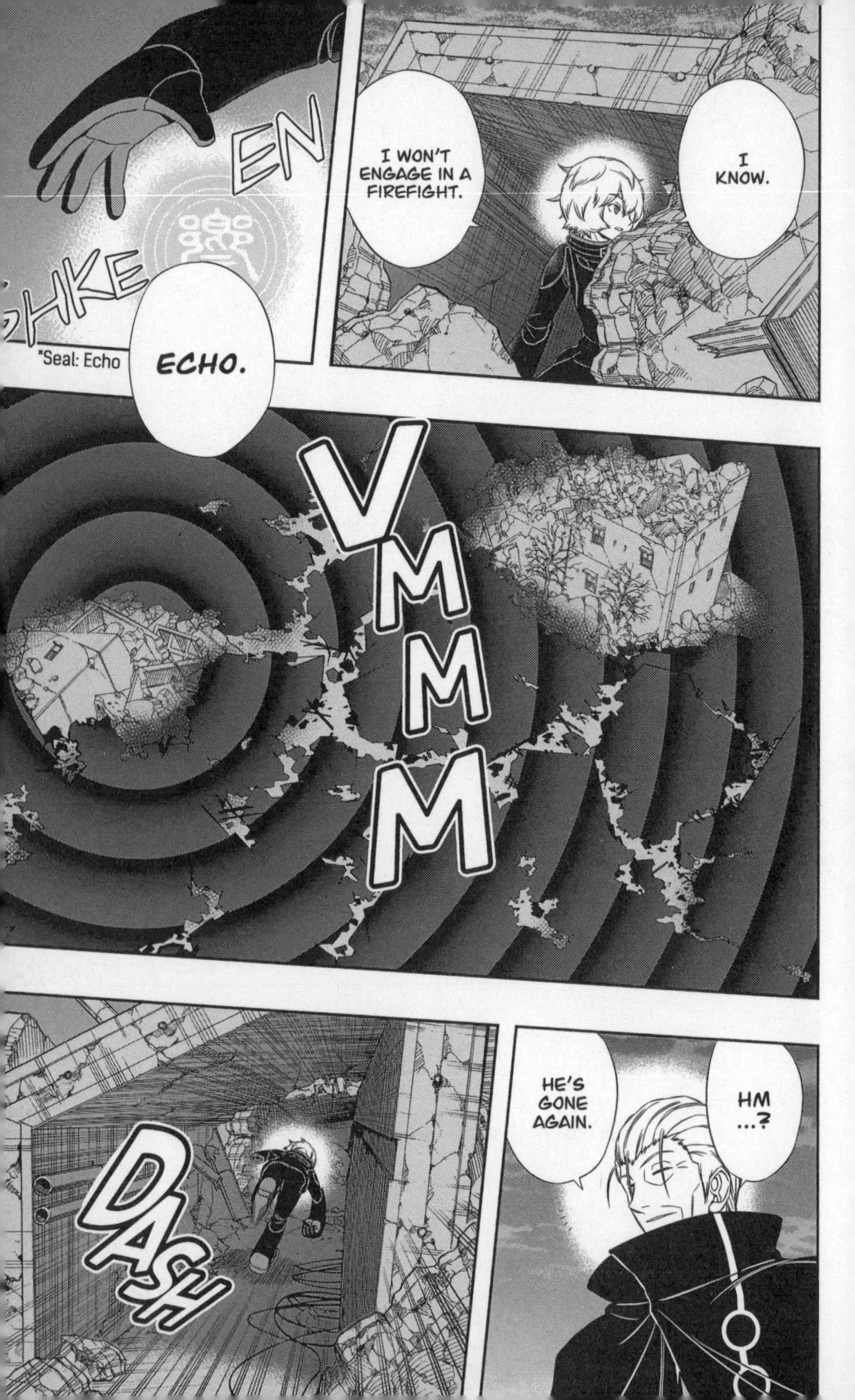
I KNOW.
I WON'T ENGAGE IN A FIREFIGHT.
EN
HKE
ECHO.
*Seal: Echo
VMMMM
HM ...?
HE'S GONE AGAIN.
DASH

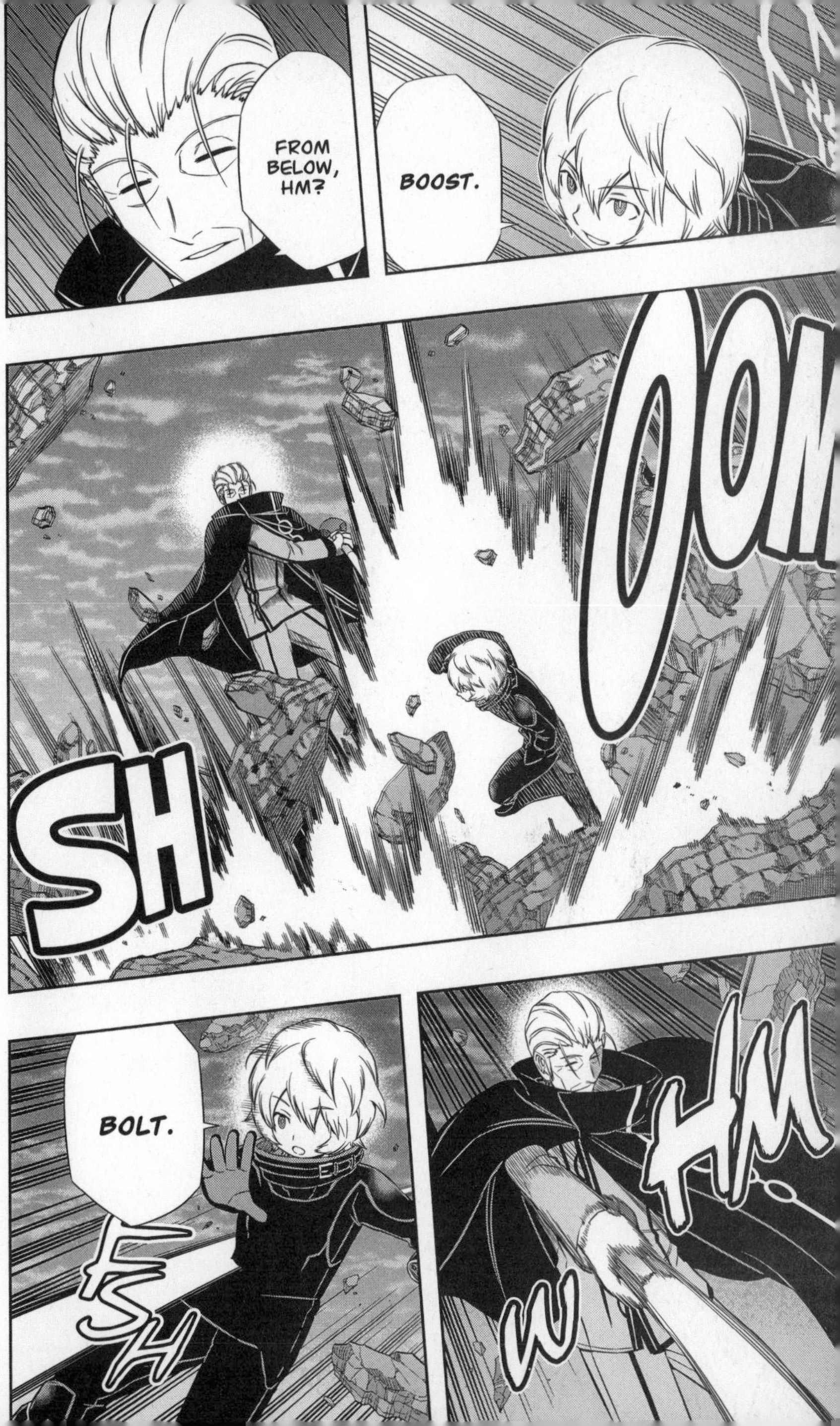
BOOST.
FROM BELOW, HM?
OOM
SH
HM
W
BOLT.
FSH

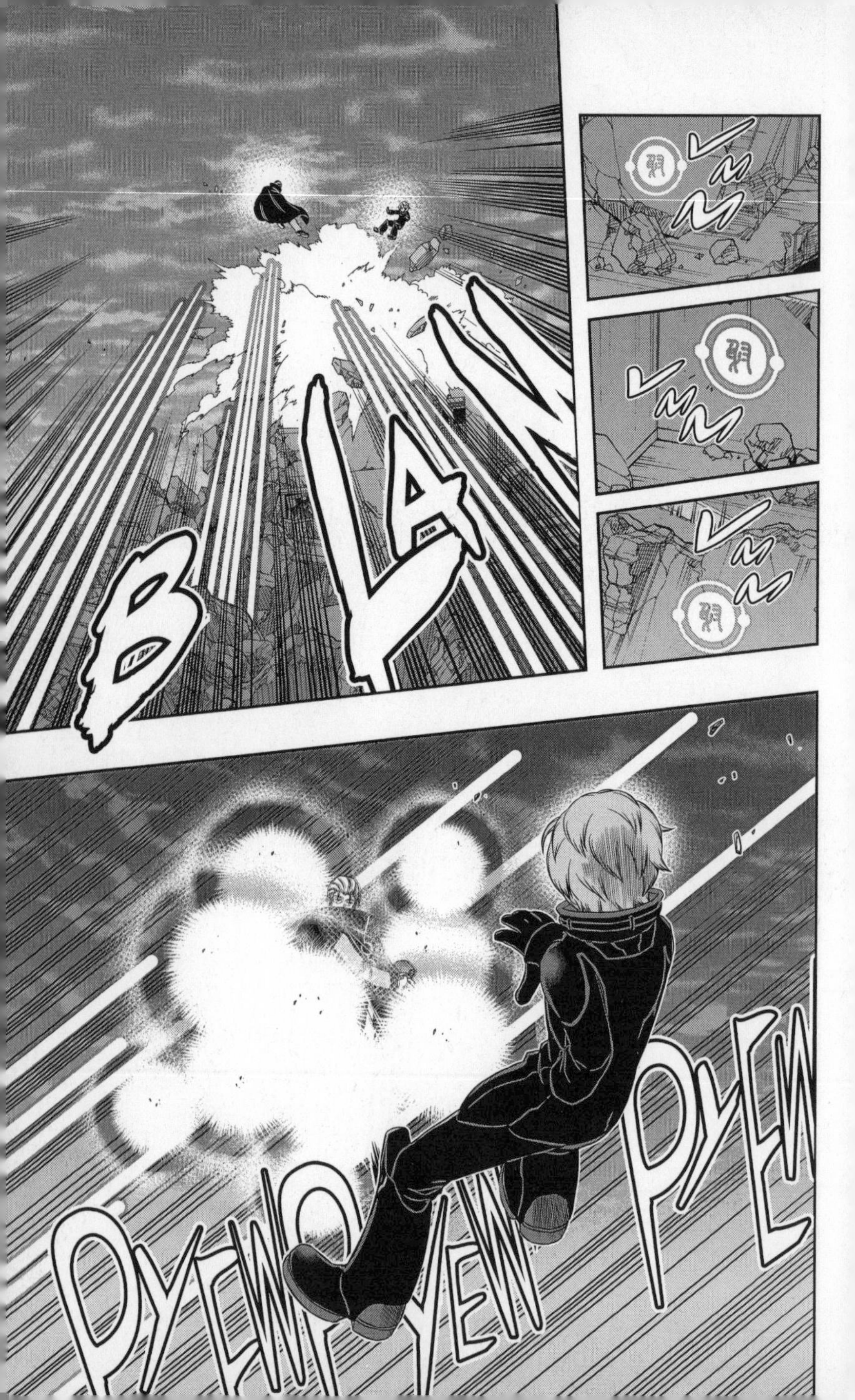
VMMM
VMMM
VMMM
BLAM
PYEW PYEW PYEW

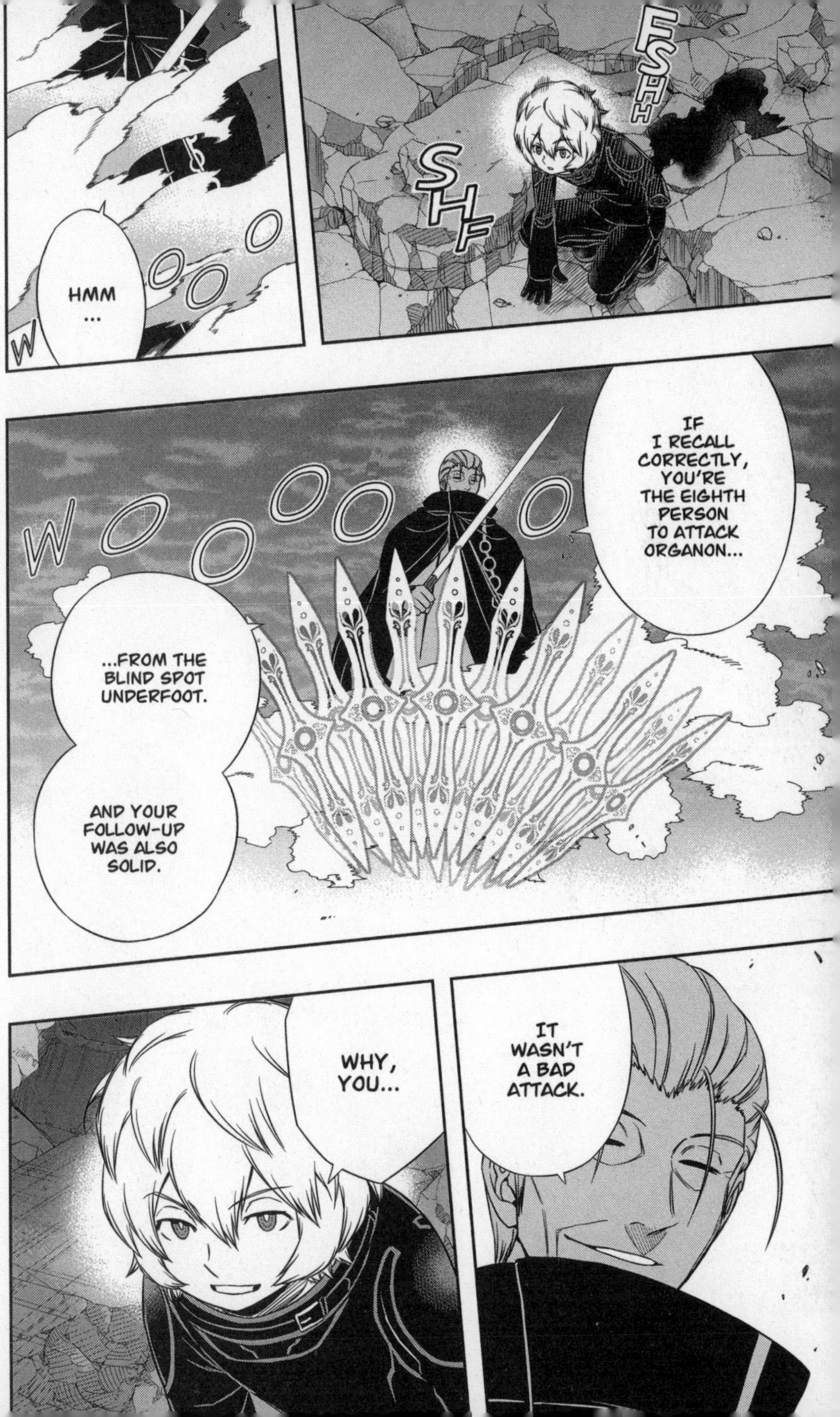
FSHH
SHF
HMM...
WOOOO
IF I RECALL CORRECTLY, YOU'RE THE EIGHTH PERSON TO ATTACK ORGANON...
...FROM THE BLIND SPOT UNDERFOOT.
AND YOUR FOLLOW-UP WAS ALSO SOLID.
WOOOOOO
IT WASN'T A BAD ATTACK.
WHY, YOU...

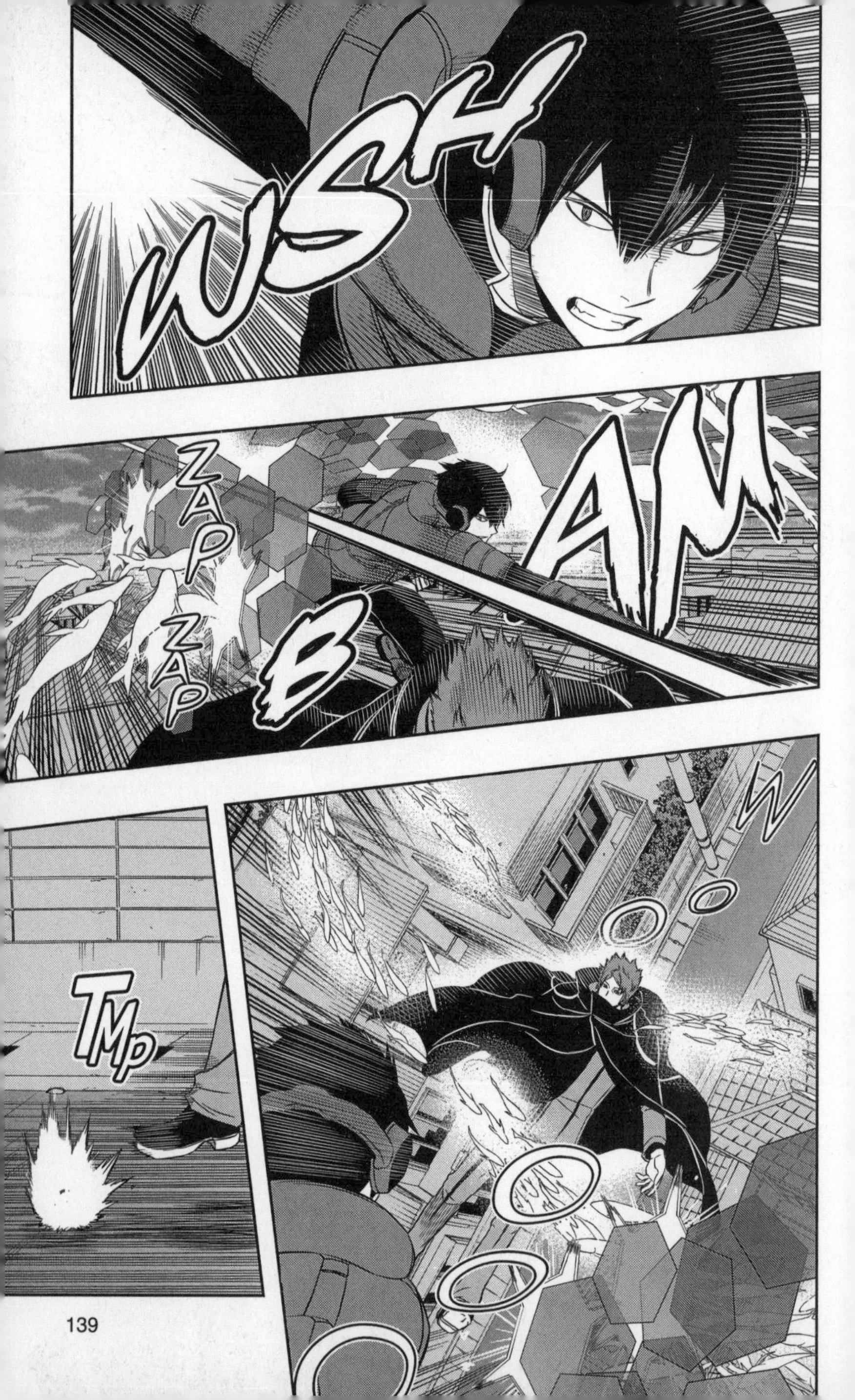
WSH
BAM
ZAP ZAP
ZAP ZAP
WOOO
TMP

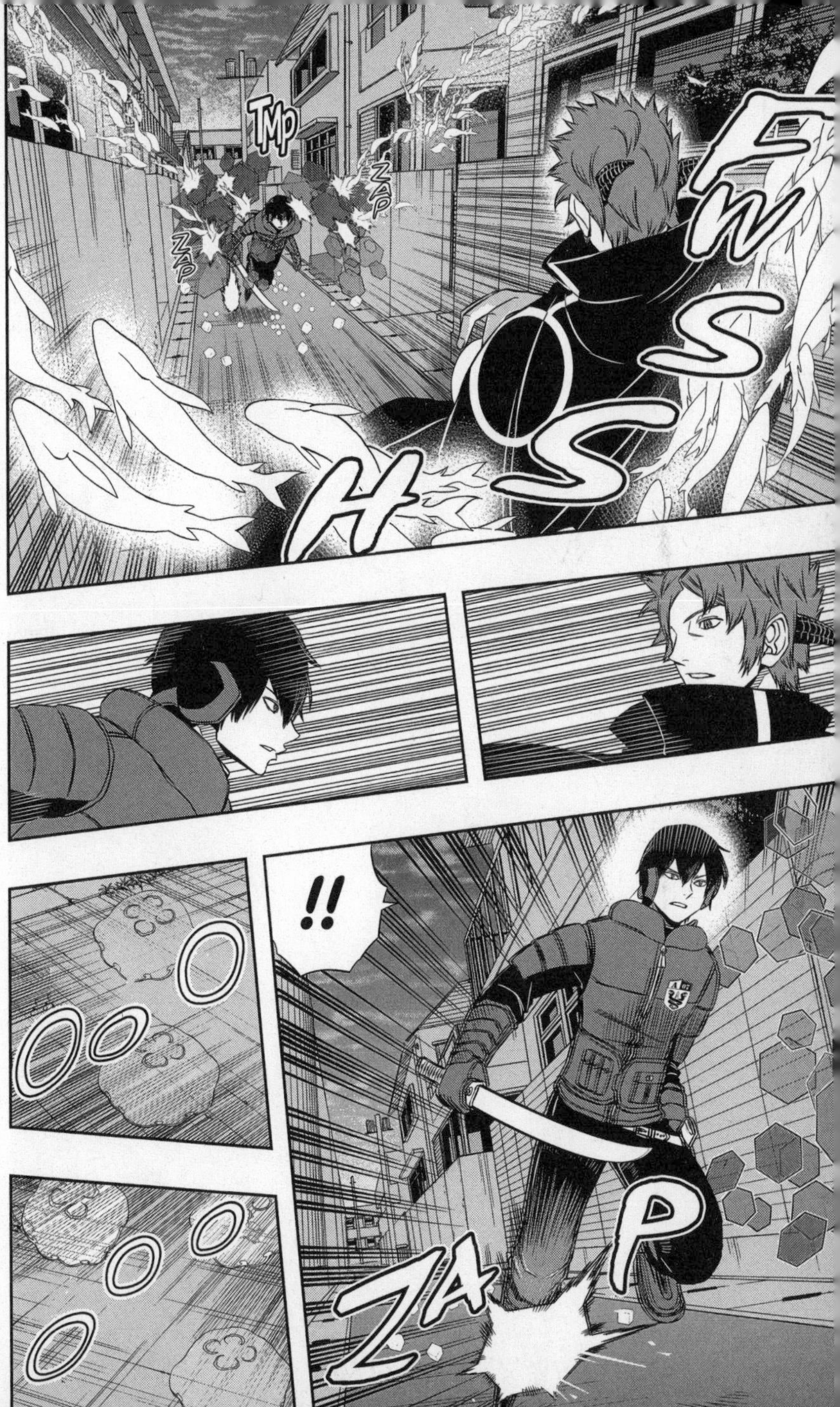
FWSSH
TMP
ZAP
ZAP
!!
ZAP
OOO
OOOO

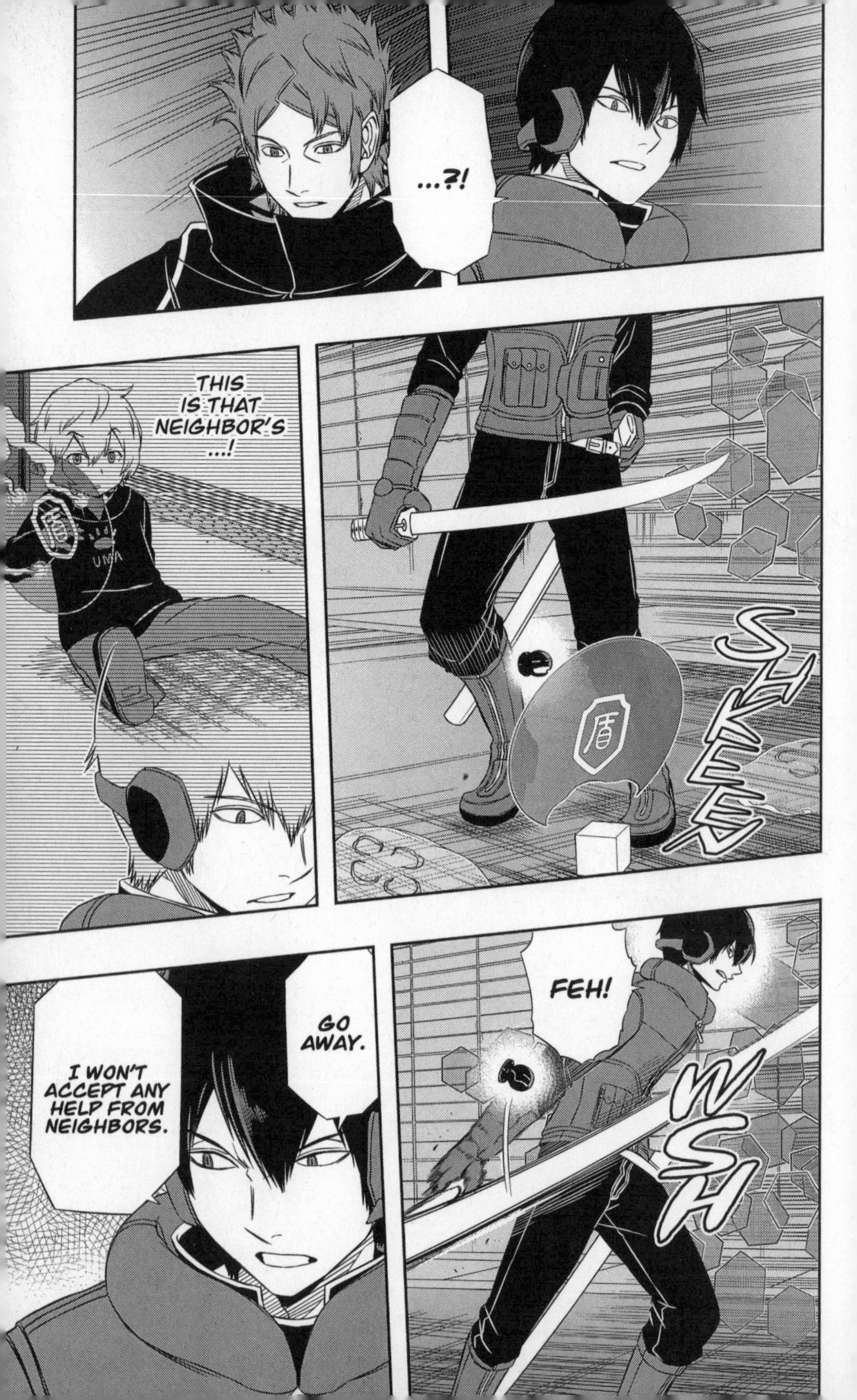

...?!
SHKEEN
THIS IS THAT NEIGHBOR'S ...!
FEH!
WSH
GO AWAY.
I WON'T ACCEPT ANY HELP FROM NEIGHBORS.

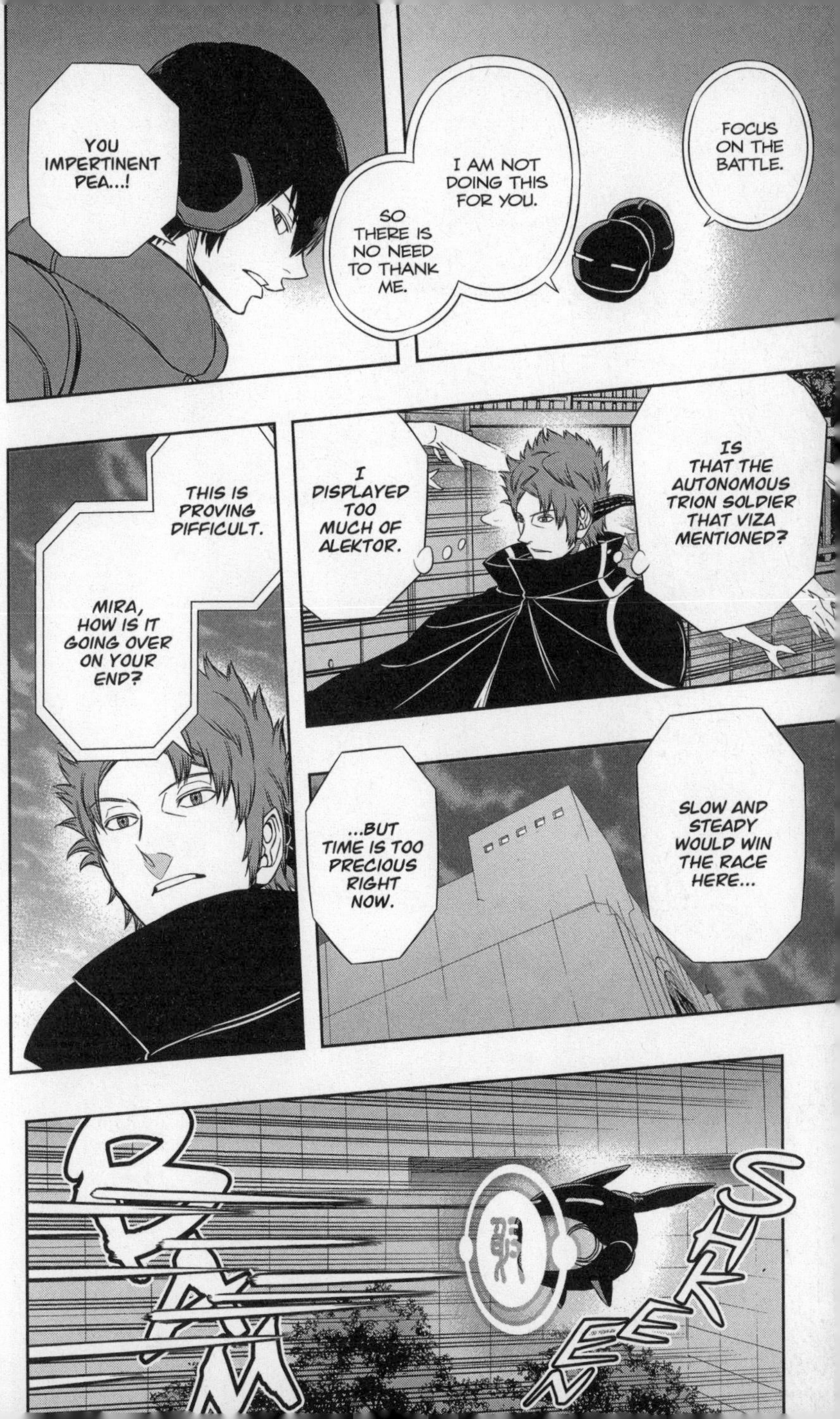
FOCUS ON THE BATTLE.
I AM NOT DOING THIS FOR YOU.
SO THERE IS NO NEED TO THANK ME.
YOU IMPERTINENT PEA...!
IS THAT THE AUTONOMOUS TRION SOLDIER THAT VIZA MENTIONED?
I DISPLAYED TOO MUCH OF ALEKTOR.
SLOW AND STEADY WOULD WIN THE RACE HERE...
...BUT TIME IS TOO PRECIOUS RIGHT NOW.
THIS IS PROVING DIFFICULT.
MIRA, HOW IS IT GOING OVER ON YOUR END?
SHKEEN
BAM

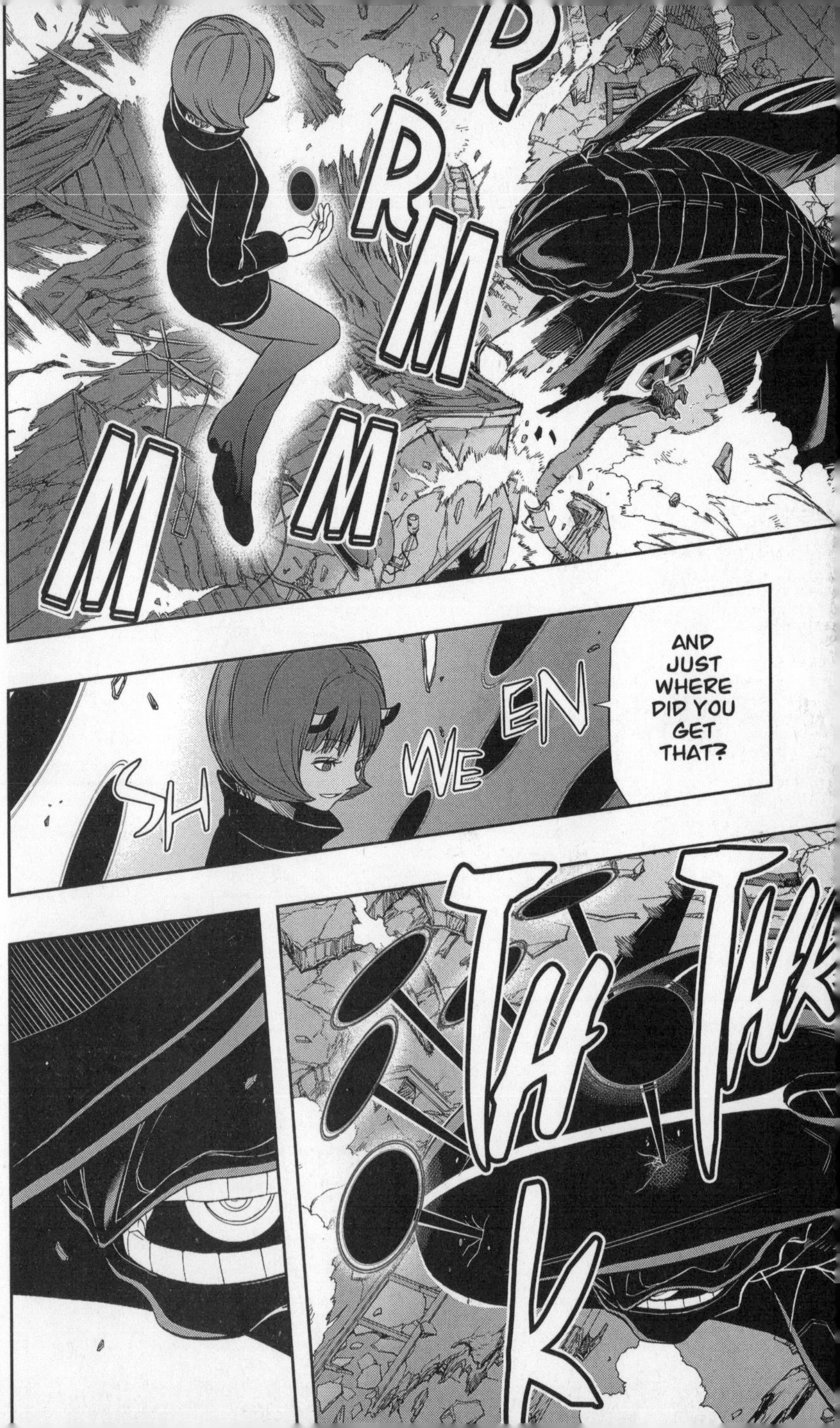
RRMMM
AND JUST WHERE DID YOU GET THAT?
SHWEEN
THK THK

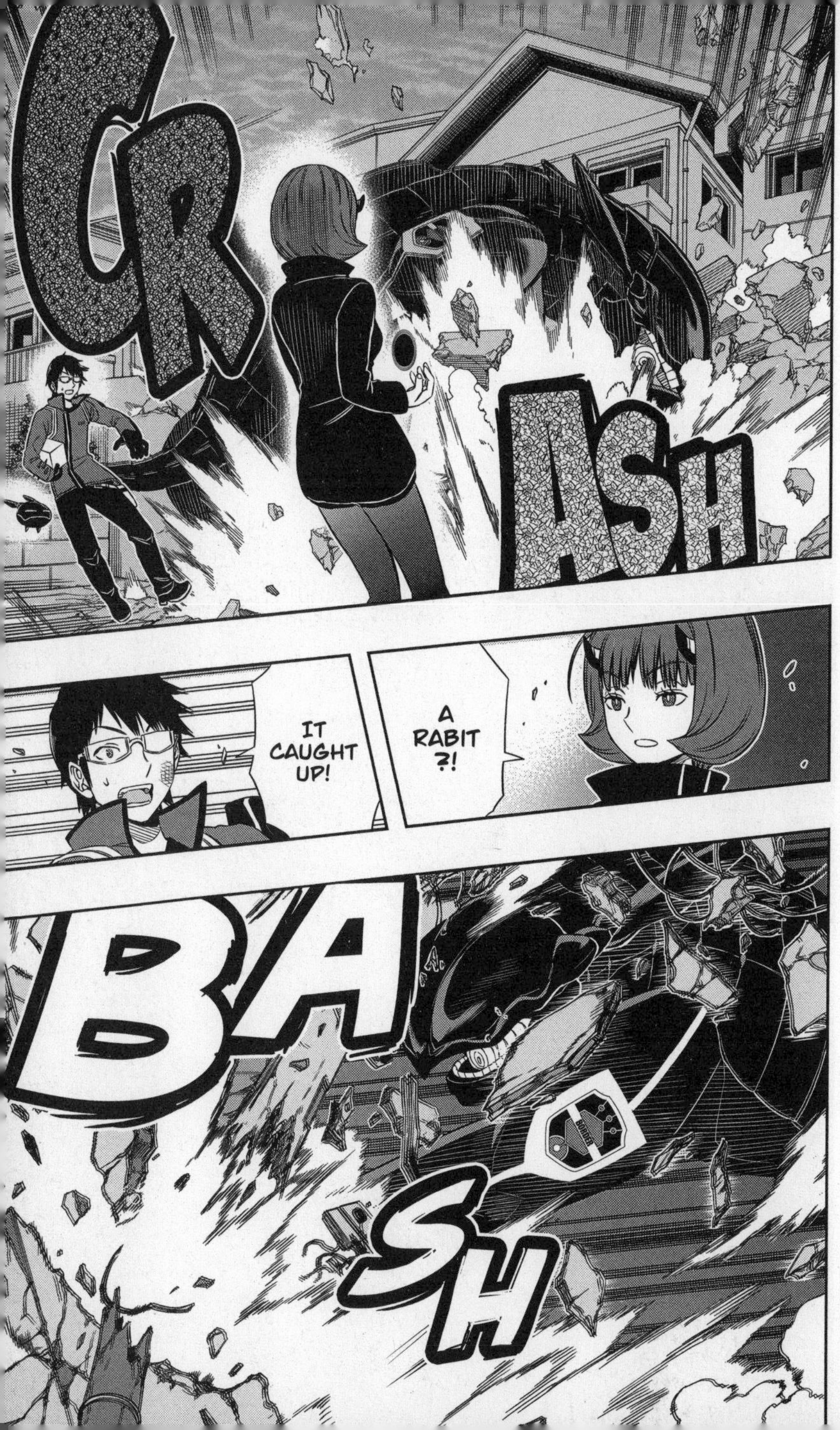
CR
ASH
A RABIT ?!
IT CAUGHT UP!
BA
SH

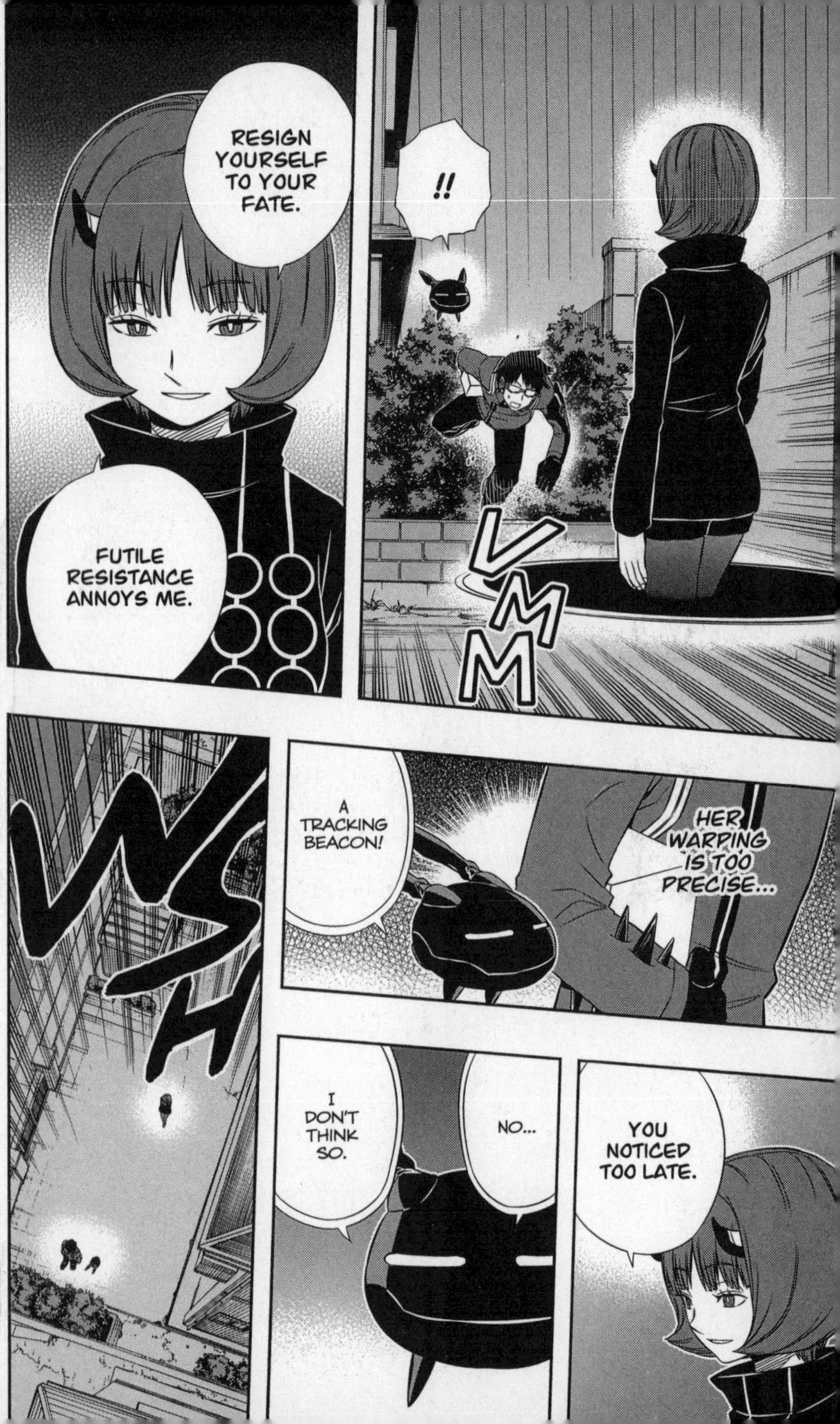
!!
VMM
RESIGN YOURSELF TO YOUR FATE.
FUTILE RESISTANCE ANNOYS ME.
HER WARPING IS TOO PRECISE...
A TRACKING BEACON!
YOU NOTICED TOO LATE.
NO...
I DON'T THINK SO.
WSH

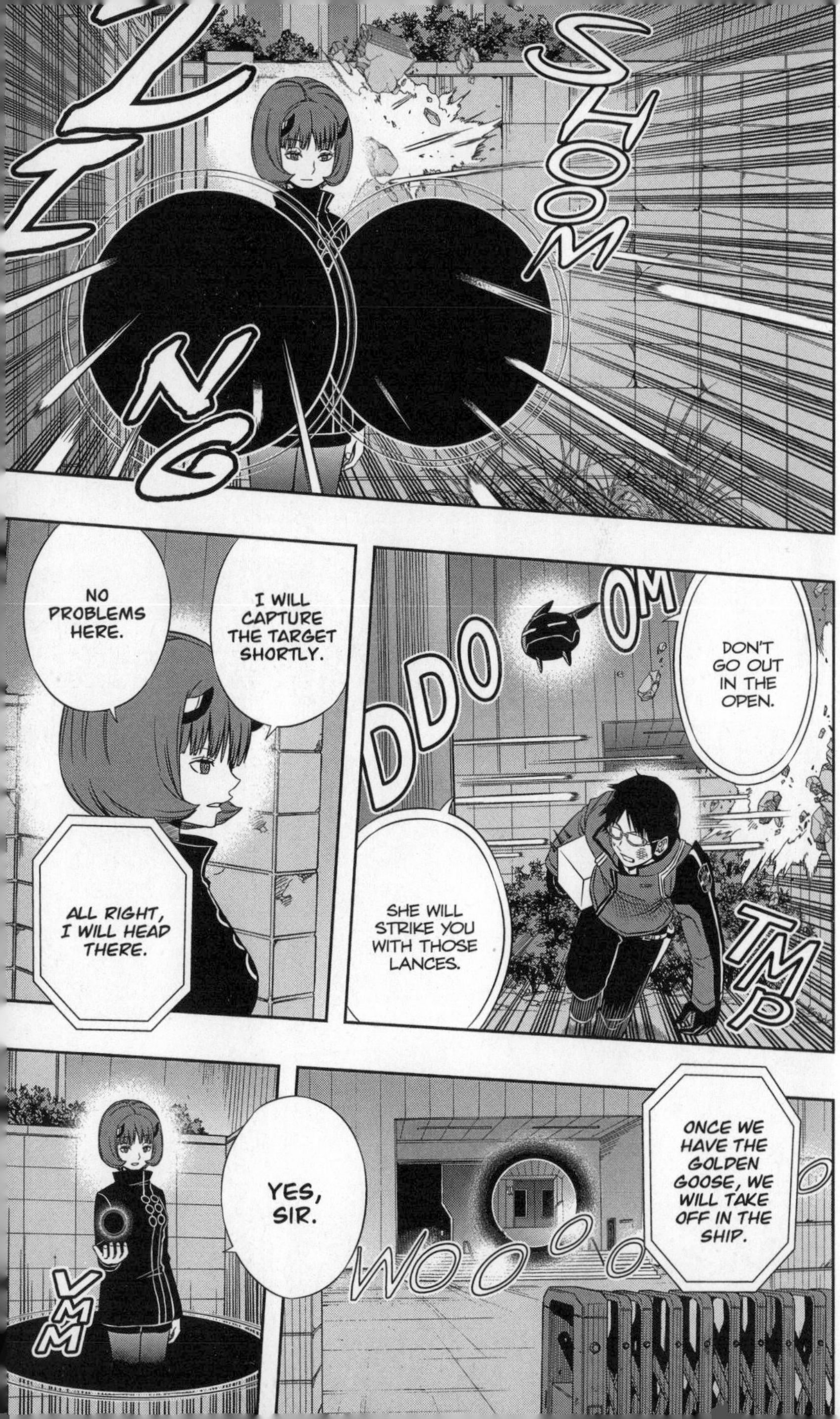
SHOOM
ZING
DON'T GO OUT IN THE OPEN.
DDOOM
SHE WILL STRIKE YOU WITH THOSE LANCES.
TMP
I WILL CAPTURE THE TARGET SHORTLY.
NO PROBLEMS HERE.
ALL RIGHT, I WILL HEAD THERE.
ONCE WE HAVE THE GOLDEN GOOSE, WE WILL TAKE OFF IN THE SHIP.
WOOOOOO
YES, SIR.
VMM

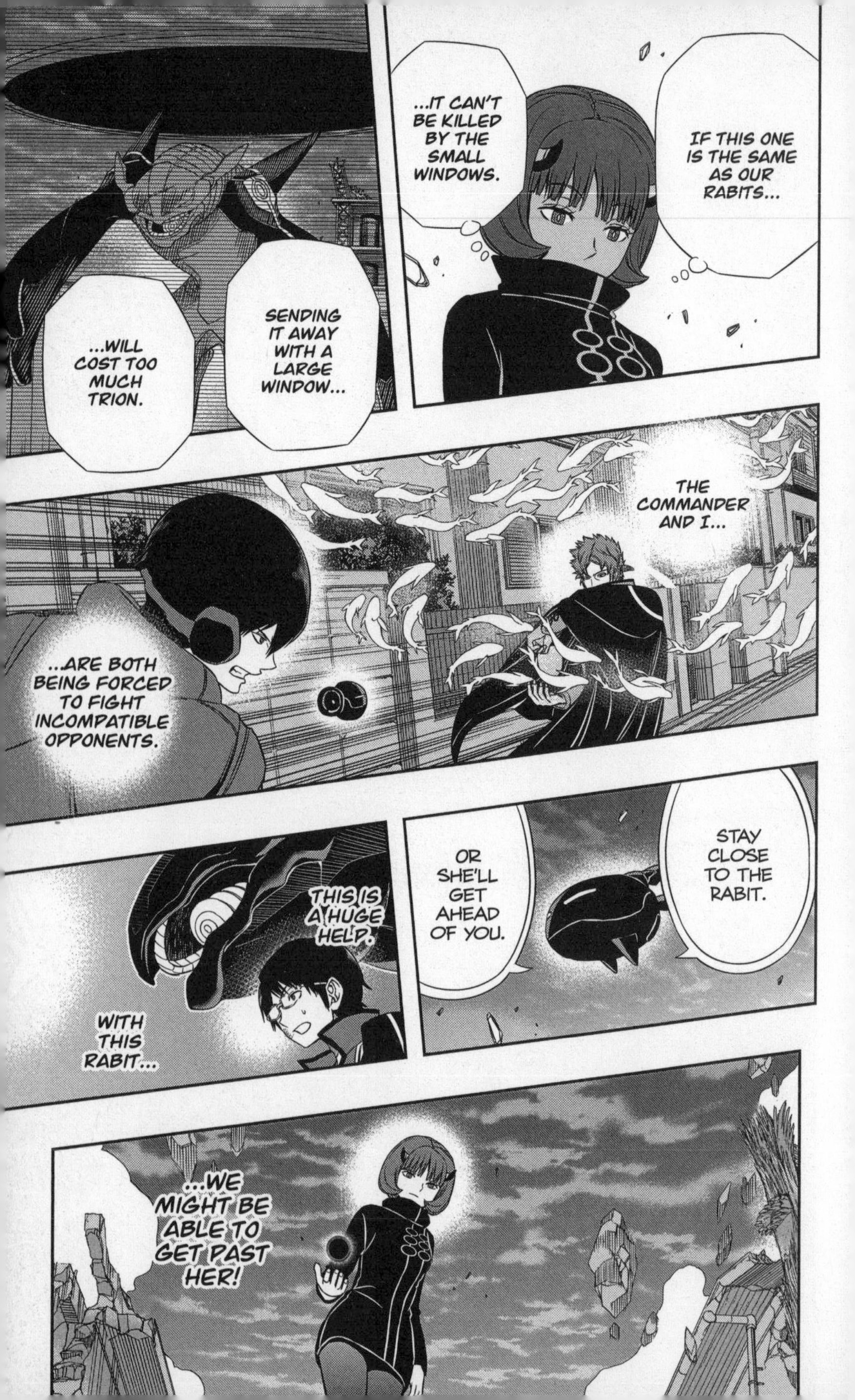
IF THIS ONE IS THE SAME AS OUR RABITS...
...IT CAN'T BE KILLED BY THE SMALL WINDOWS.
SENDING IT AWAY WITH A LARGE WINDOW...
...WILL COST TOO MUCH TRION.
THE COMMANDER AND I...
...ARE BOTH BEING FORCED TO FIGHT INCOMPATIBLE OPPONENTS.
STAY CLOSE TO THE RABIT.
OR SHE'LL GET AHEAD OF YOU.
THIS IS A HUGE HELP.
WITH THIS RABIT...
...WE MIGHT BE ABLE TO GET PAST HER!

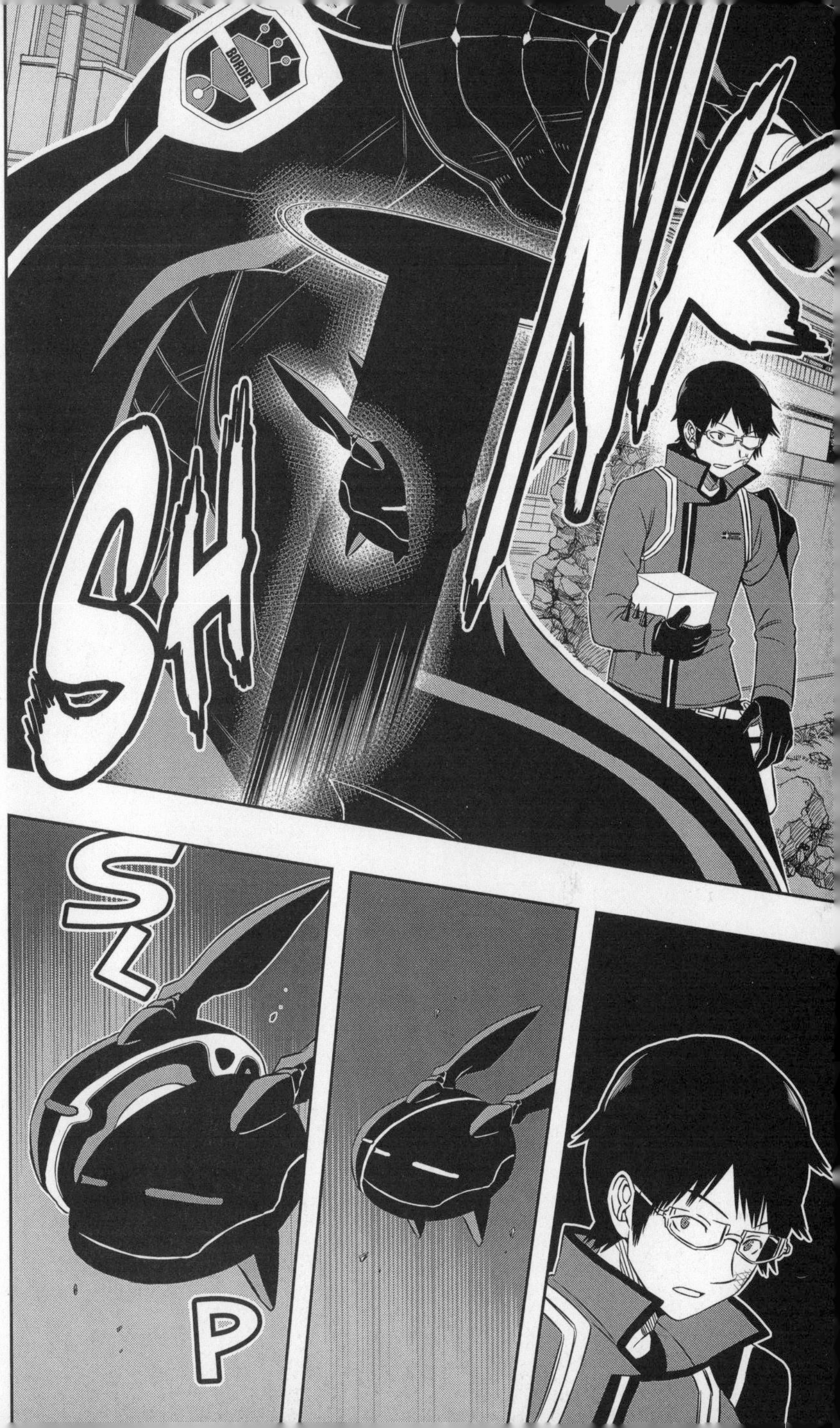
BORDER
SHNK
SLP

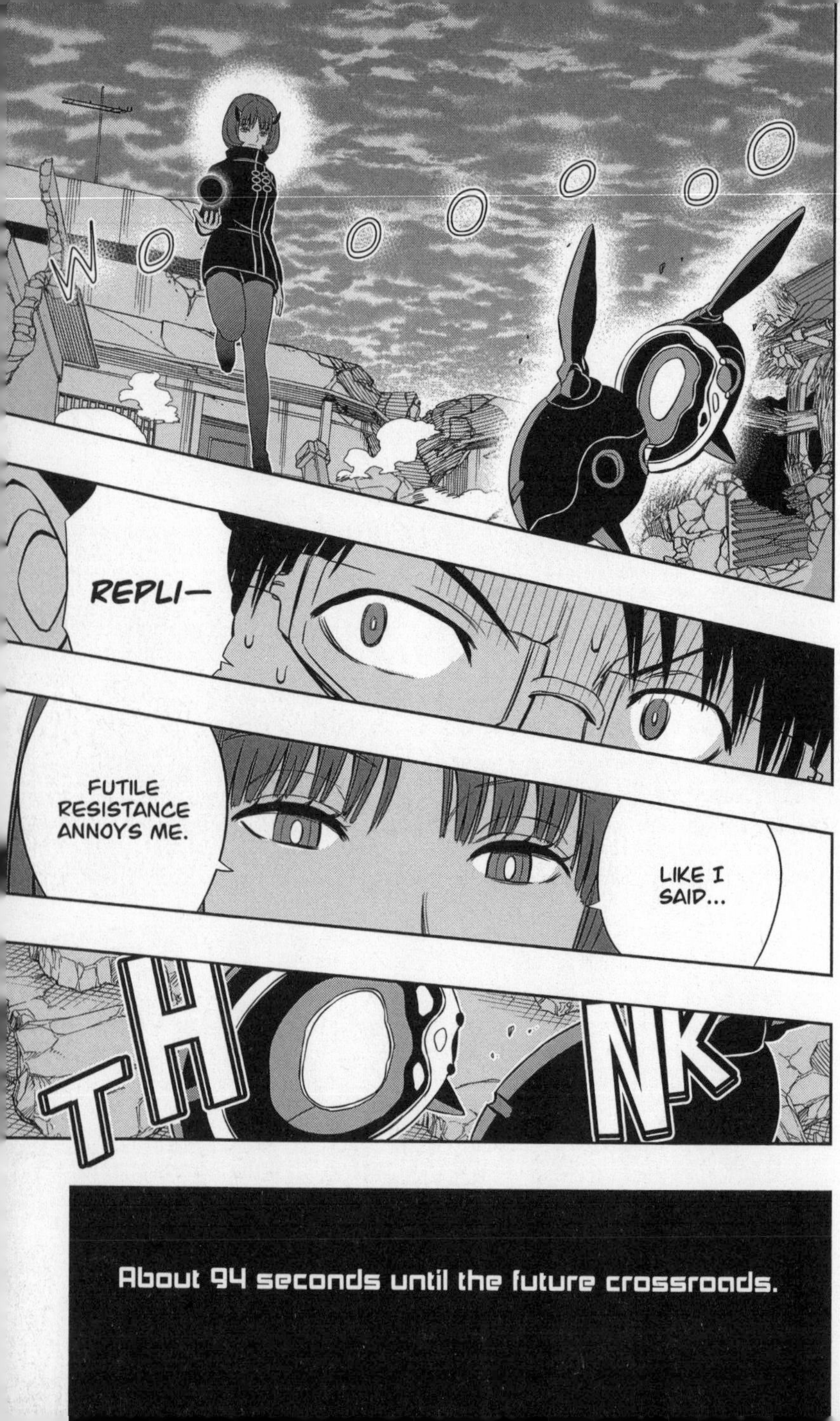
WOOOOOOO
REPLI—
LIKE I SAID...
FUTILE RESISTANCE ANNOYS ME.
THONK

About 94 seconds until the future crossroads.

■ PR Chief

Akira Jean-Baptiste Hattori

Media relations (magazine, website)

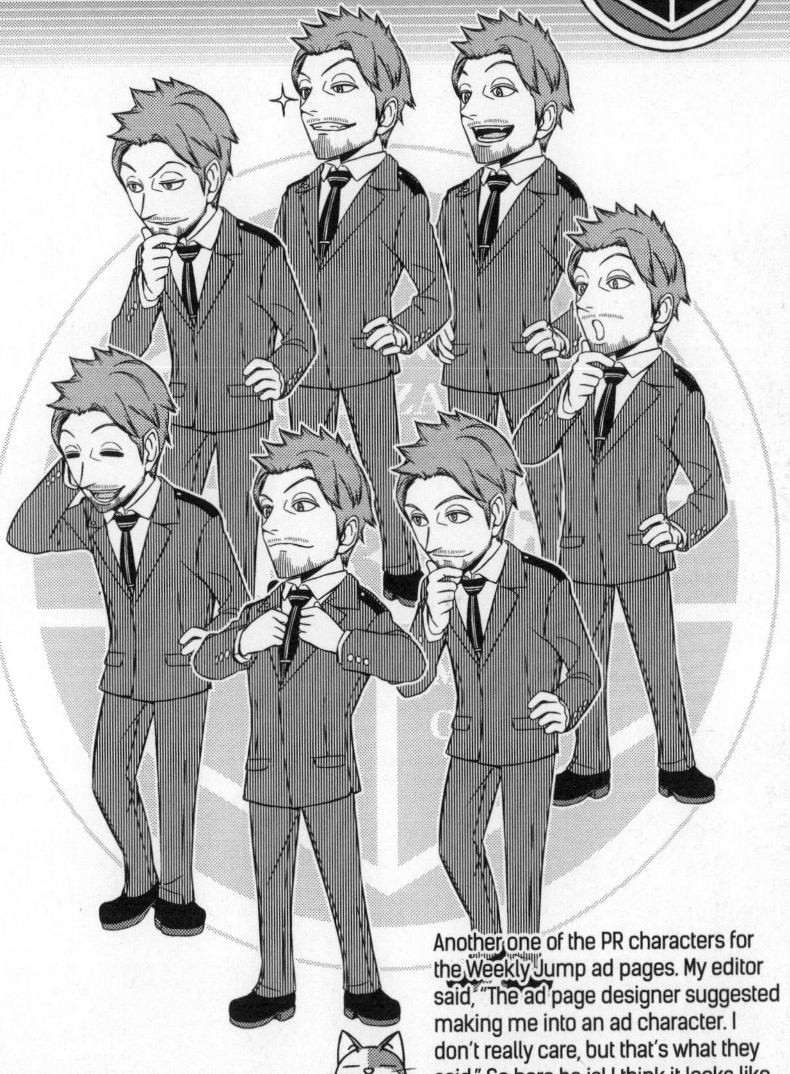

Another one of the PR characters for the Weekly Jump ad pages. My editor said, "The ad page designer suggested making me into an ad character. I don't really care, but that's what they said." So here he is! I think it looks like him. He was also really pleased.

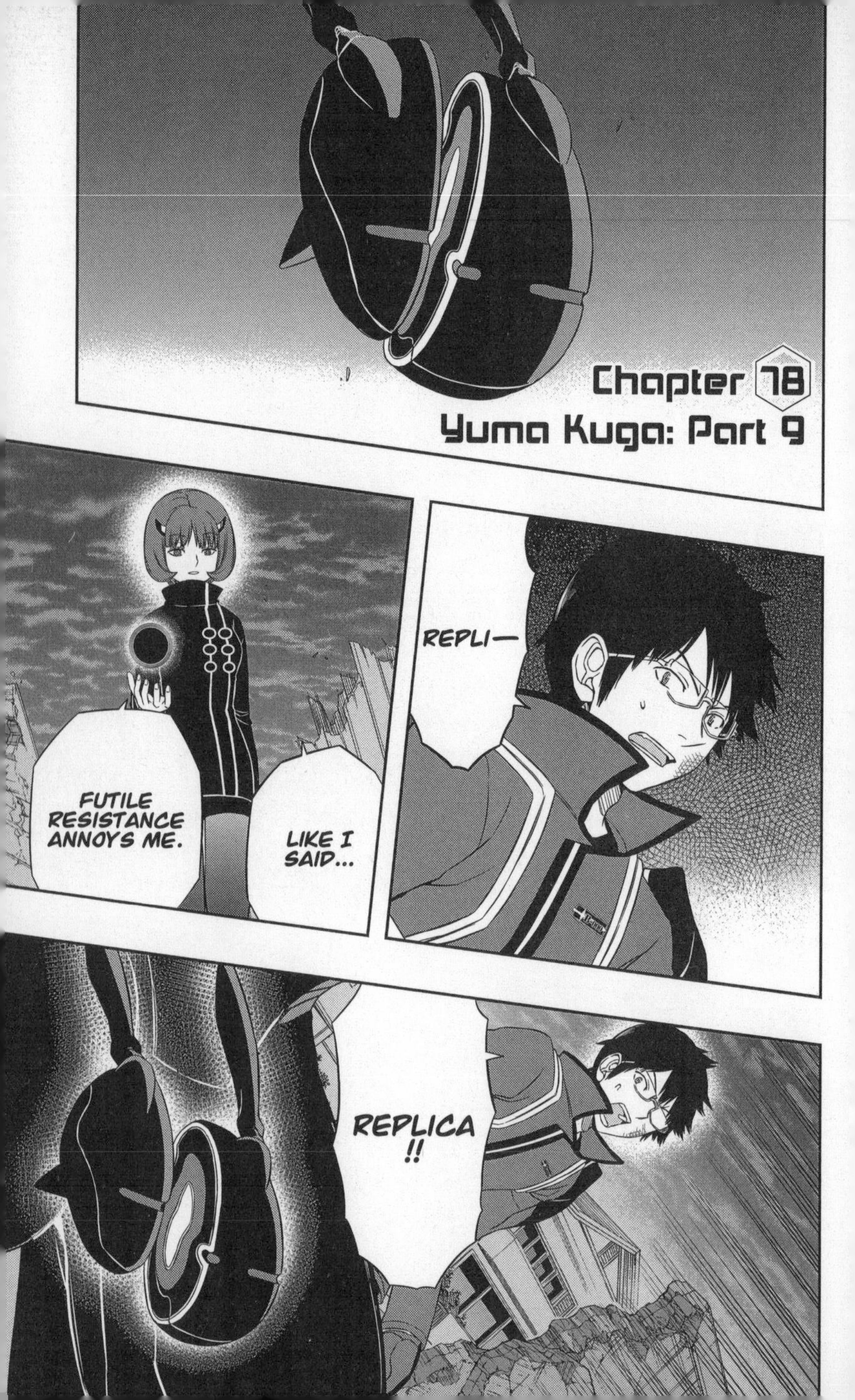
Chapter 78
Yuma Kuga: Part 9
REPLI—
LIKE I SAID...
FUTILE RESISTANCE ANNOYS ME.
REPLICA!!

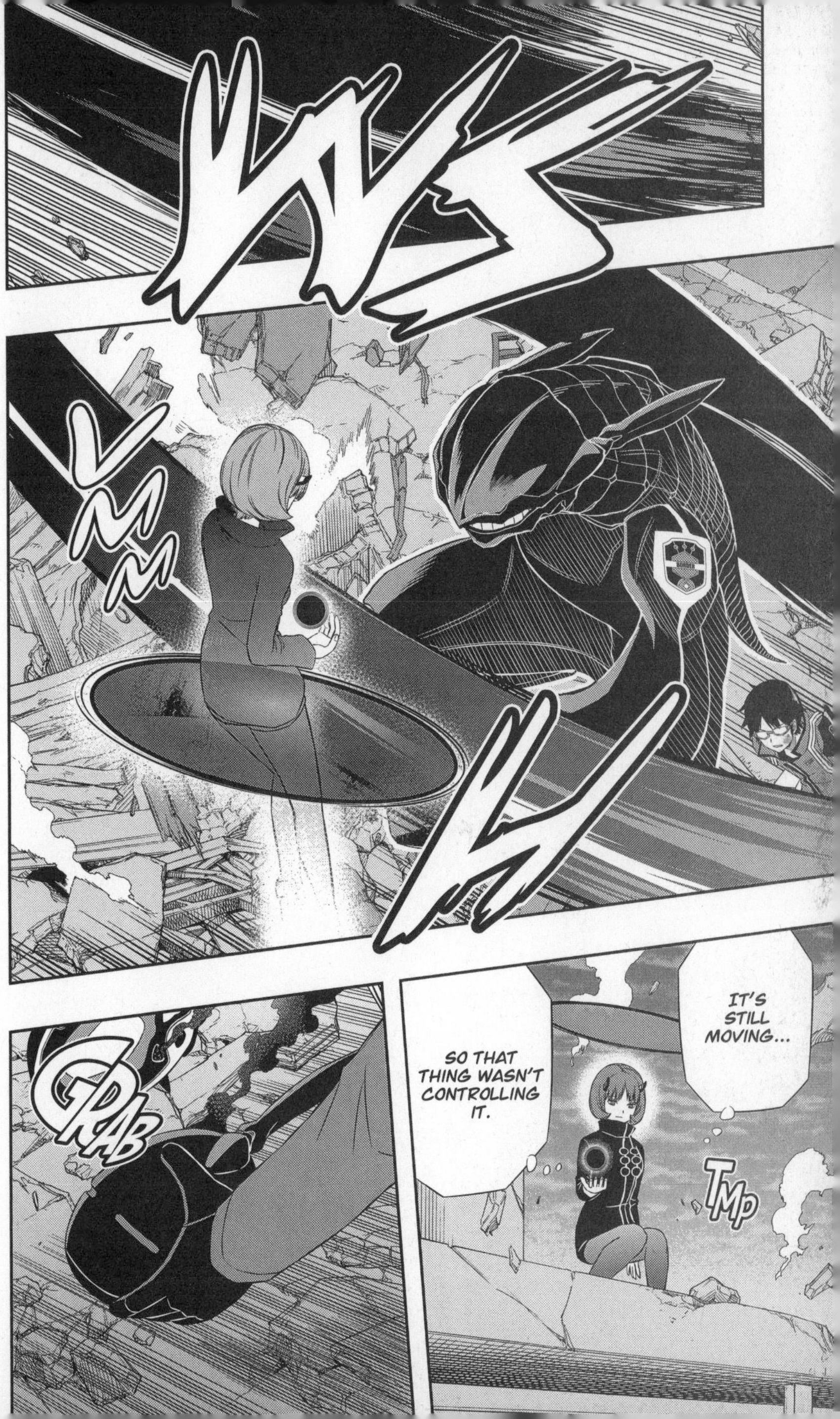
VMMM
IT'S STILL MOVING...
SO THAT THING WASN'T CONTROLLING IT.
TMP
GRAB

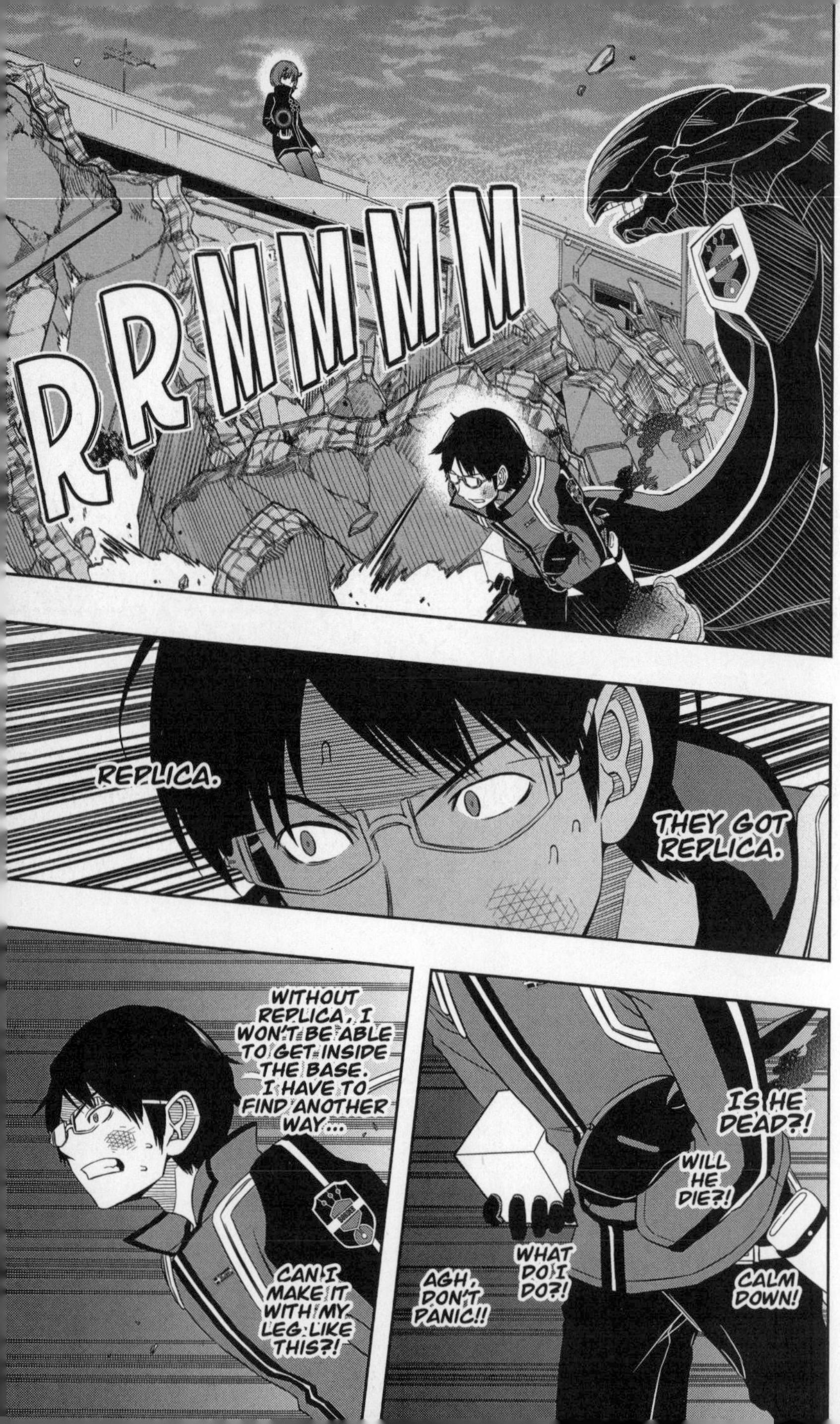
RRMMMMM
REPLICA.
THEY GOT REPLICA.
IS HE DEAD?!
WILL HE DIE?!
CALM DOWN!
WHAT DO I DO?!
AGH, DON'T PANIC!!
WITHOUT REPLICA, I WON'T BE ABLE TO GET INSIDE THE BASE. I HAVE TO FIND ANOTHER WAY...
CAN I MAKE IT WITH MY LEG LIKE THIS?!

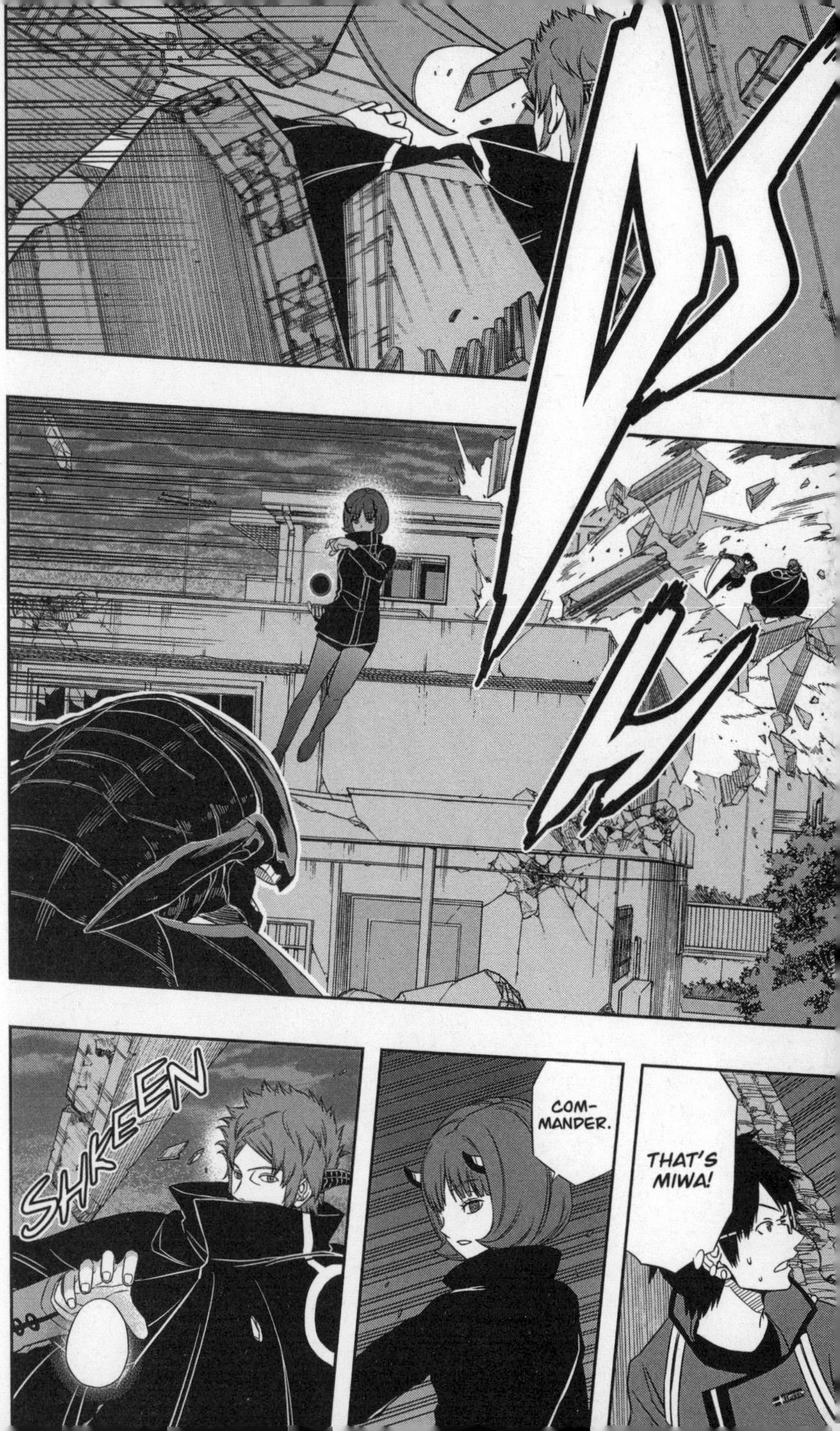
THAT'S MIWA!
COM-MANDER.
SHKEEN

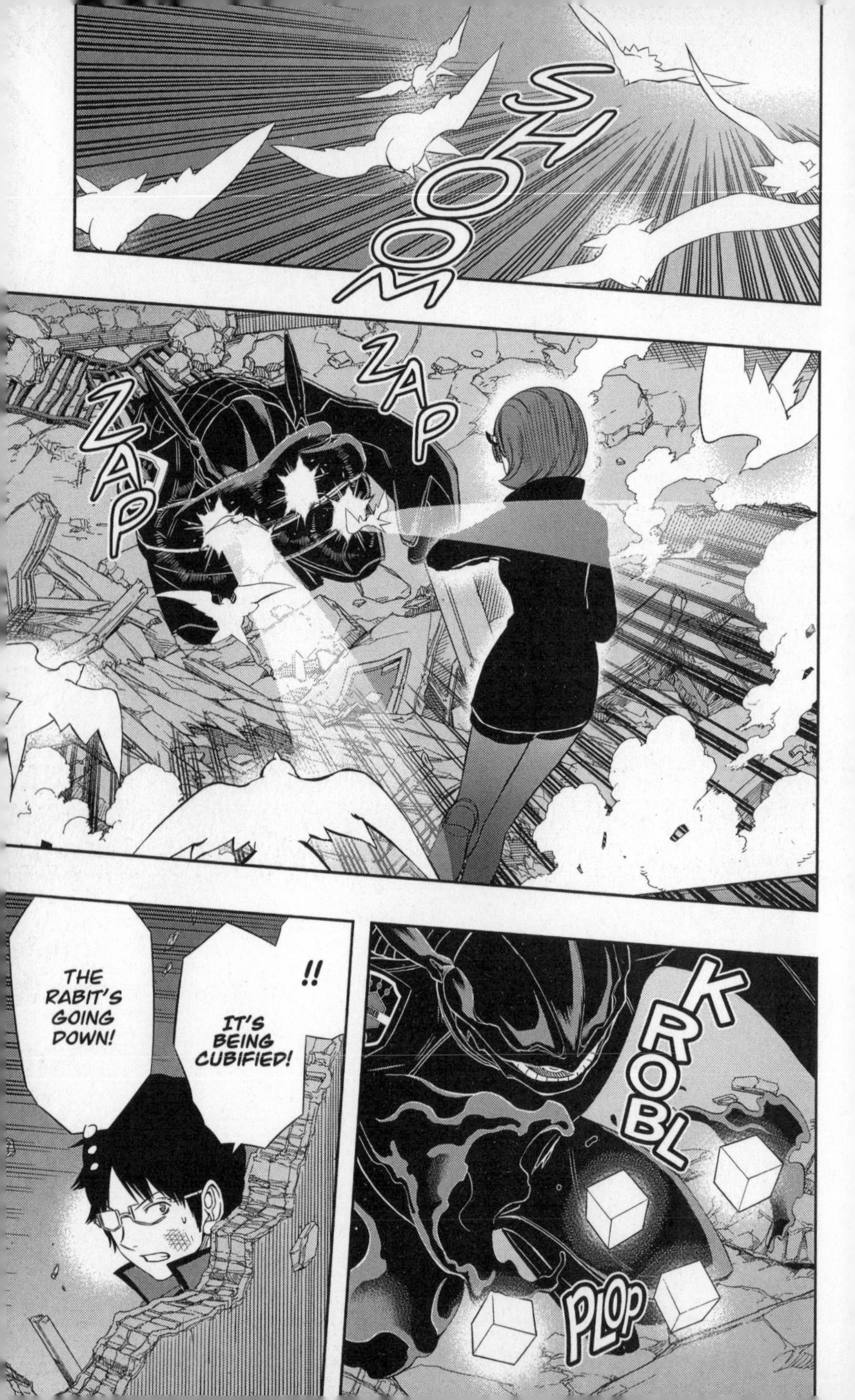
SHOOM
ZAP
ZAP
KROBL
PLOP
!!
IT'S BEING CUBIFIED!
THE RABIT'S GOING DOWN!

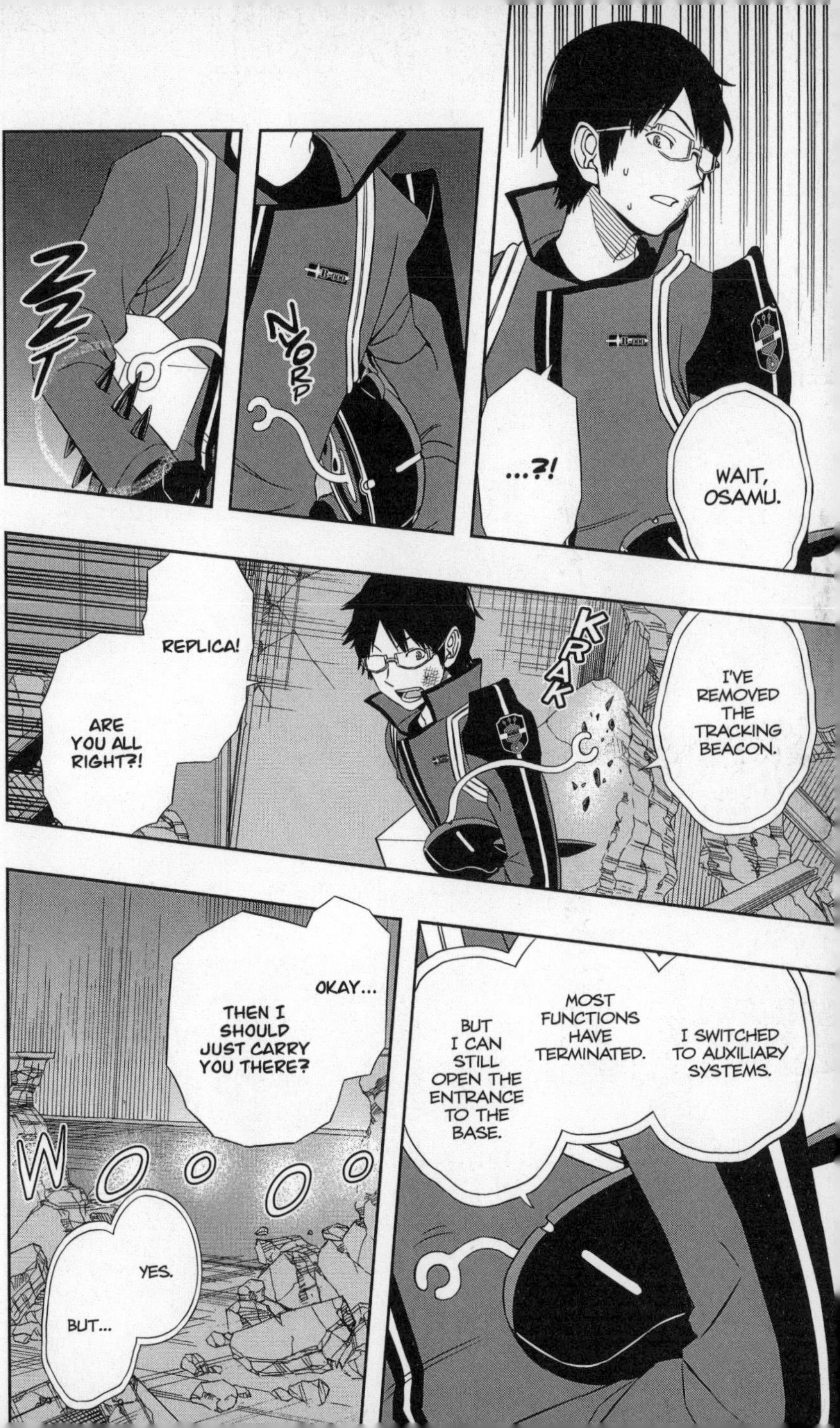
WAIT, OSAMU.
...?!
NYORP
ZZZT
I'VE REMOVED THE TRACKING BEACON.
KRAK
REPLICA!
ARE YOU ALL RIGHT?!
I SWITCHED TO AUXILIARY SYSTEMS.
MOST FUNCTIONS HAVE TERMINATED.
BUT I CAN STILL OPEN THE ENTRANCE TO THE BASE.
OKAY...
THEN I SHOULD JUST CARRY YOU THERE?
WOOOO
YES.
BUT...

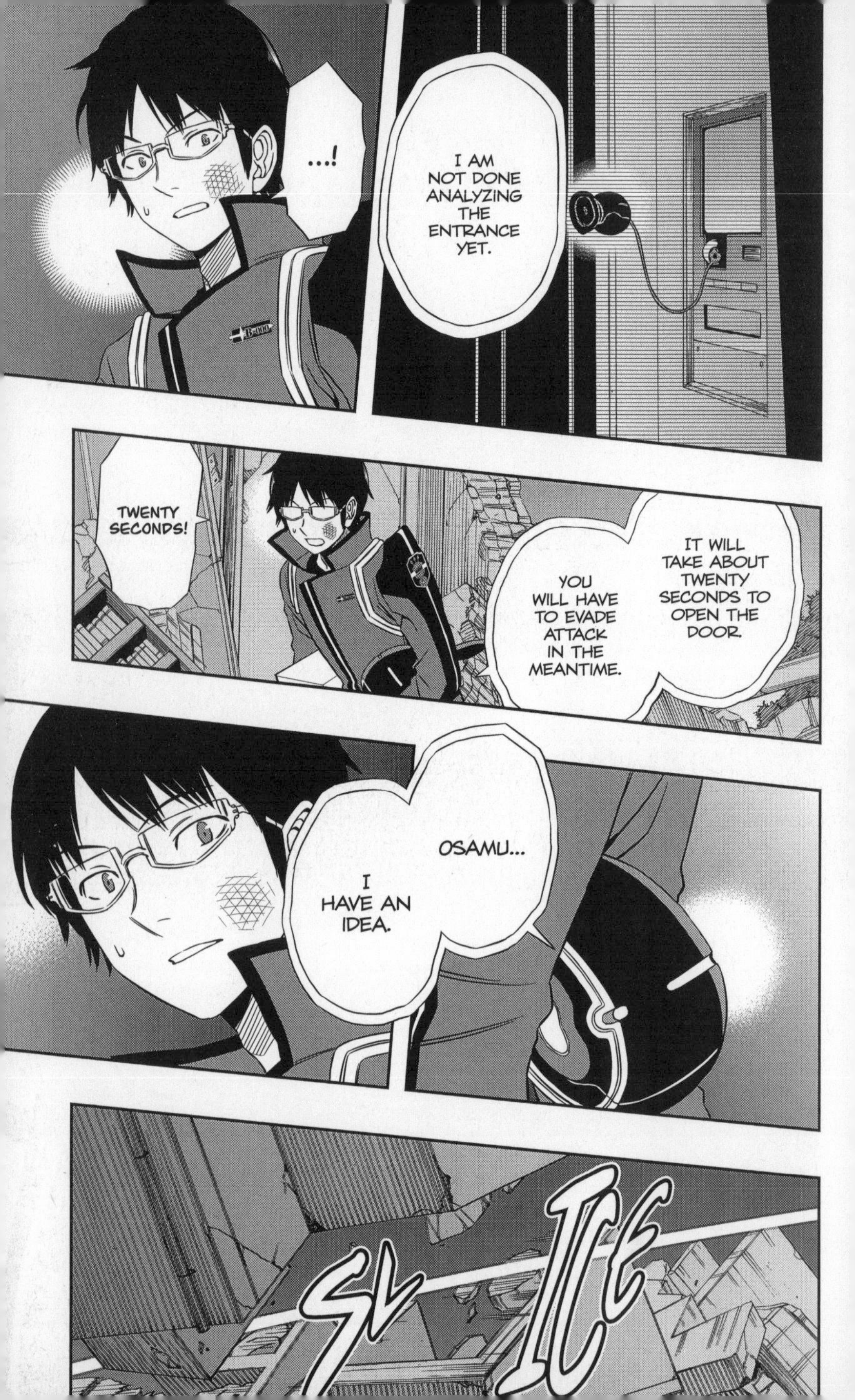
I AM NOT DONE ANALYZING THE ENTRANCE YET.
...!
IT WILL TAKE ABOUT TWENTY SECONDS TO OPEN THE DOOR.
YOU WILL HAVE TO EVADE ATTACK IN THE MEANTIME.
TWENTY SECONDS!
OSAMU...
I HAVE AN IDEA.
SLICE

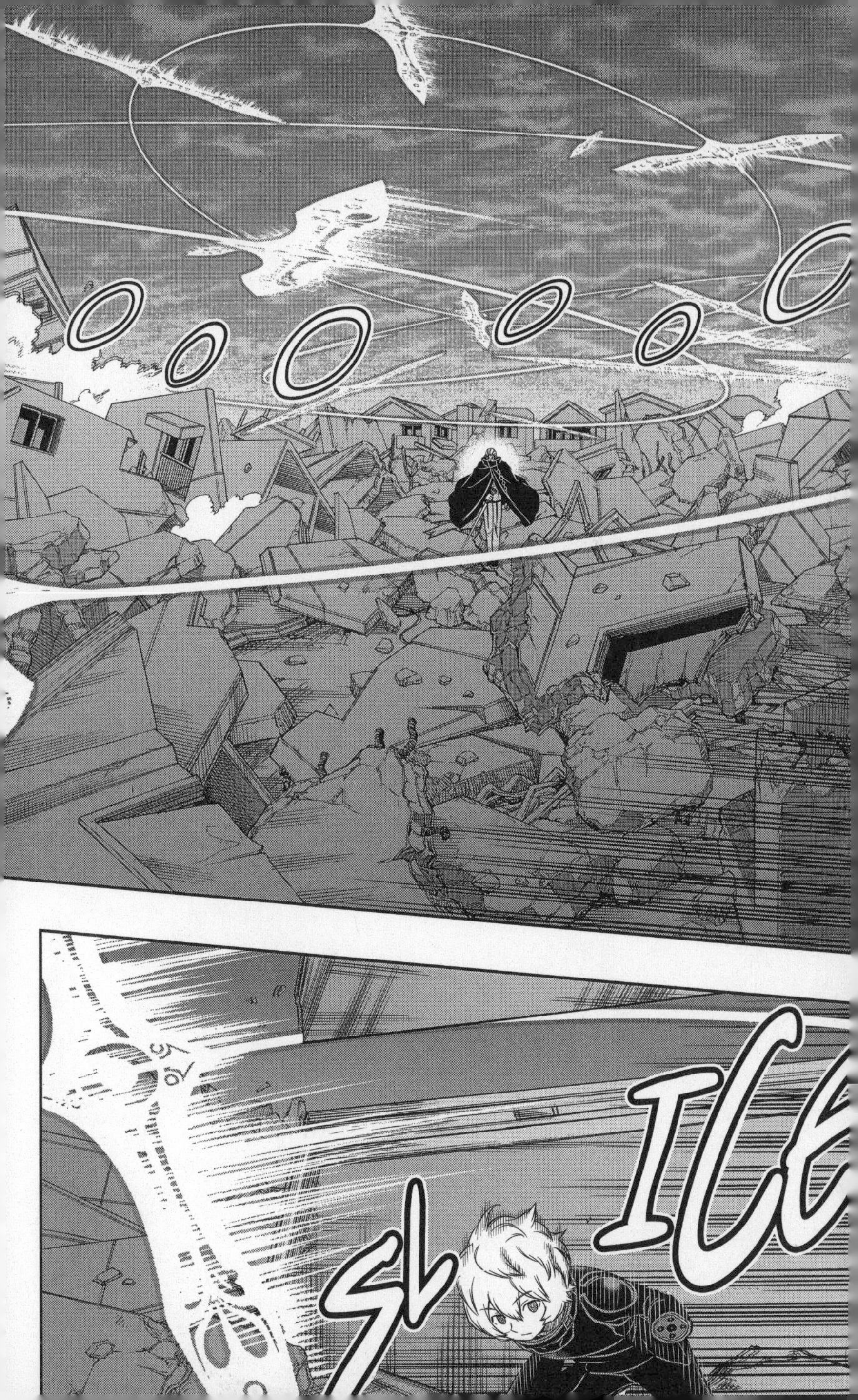
SL
ICE

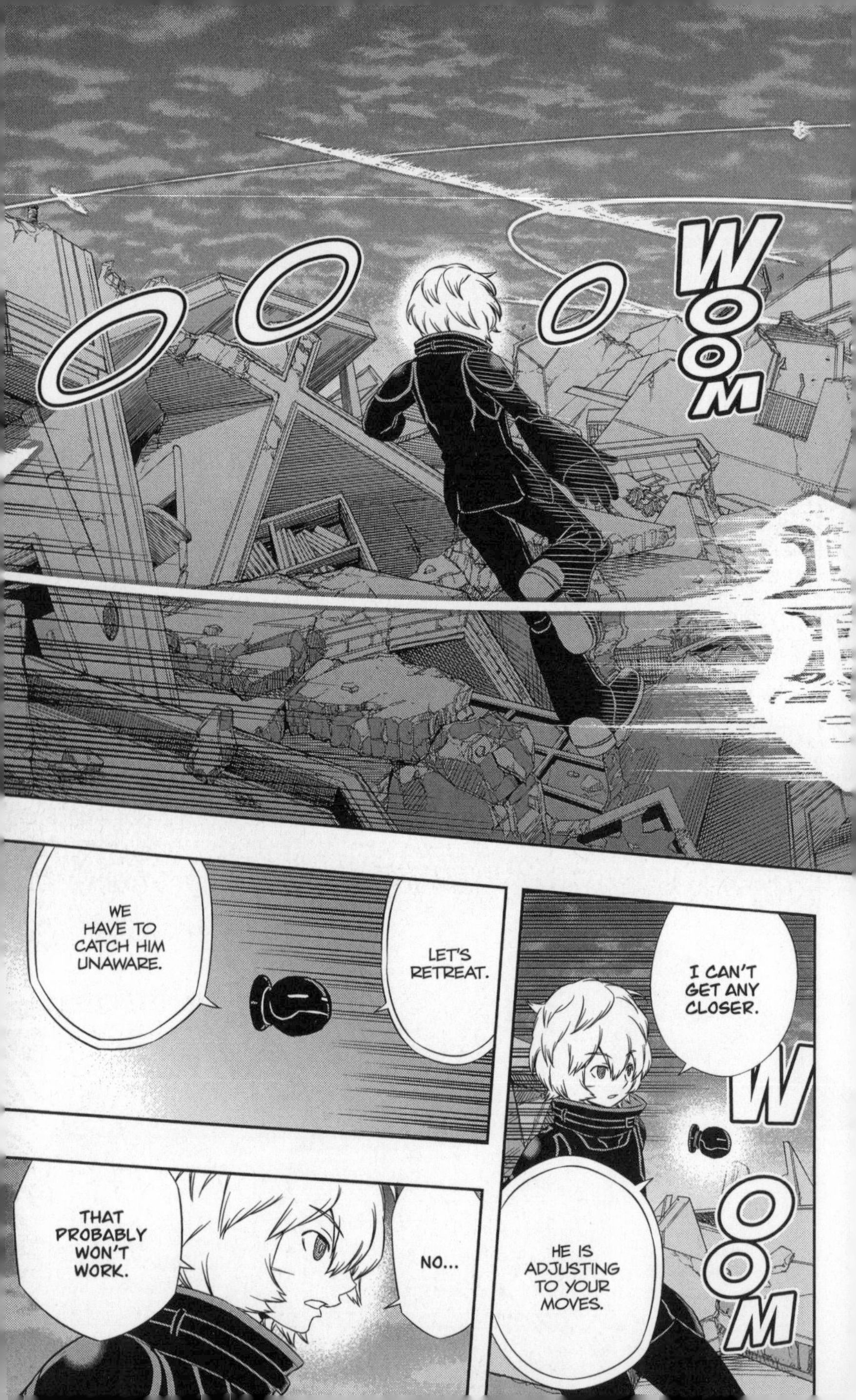
WOOOM
I CAN'T GET ANY CLOSER.
WOOM
HE IS ADJUSTING TO YOUR MOVES.
LET'S RETREAT.
WE HAVE TO CATCH HIM UNAWARE.
NO...
THAT PROBABLY WON'T WORK.

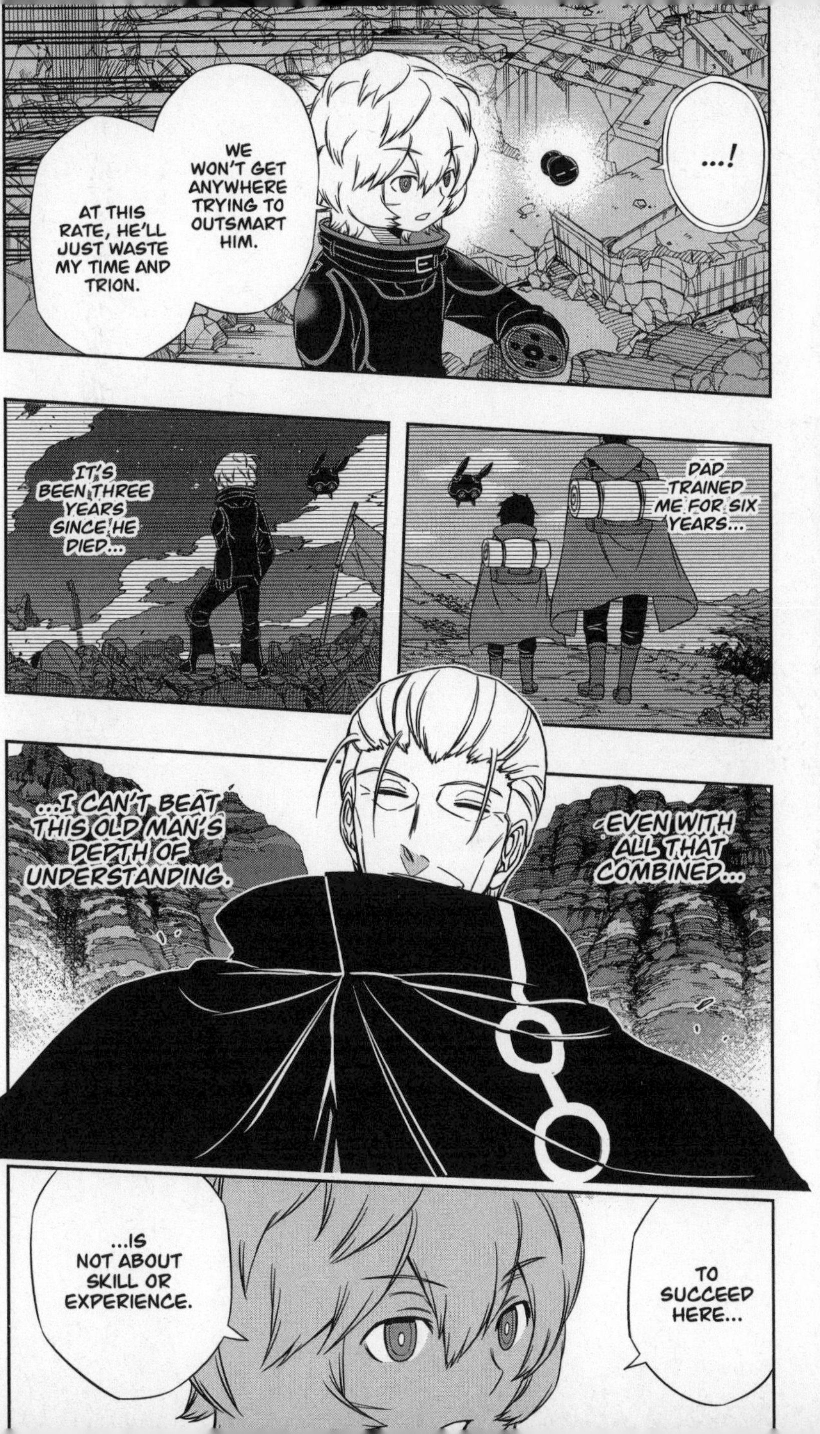
...!
WE WON'T GET ANYWHERE TRYING TO OUTSMART HIM.
AT THIS RATE, HE'LL JUST WASTE MY TIME AND TRION.
DAD TRAINED ME FOR SIX YEARS...
IT'S BEEN THREE YEARS SINCE HE DIED...
EVEN WITH ALL THAT COMBINED...
...I CAN'T BEAT THIS OLD MAN'S DEPTH OF UNDERSTANDING.
TO SUCCEED HERE...
...IS NOT ABOUT SKILL OR EXPERIENCE.

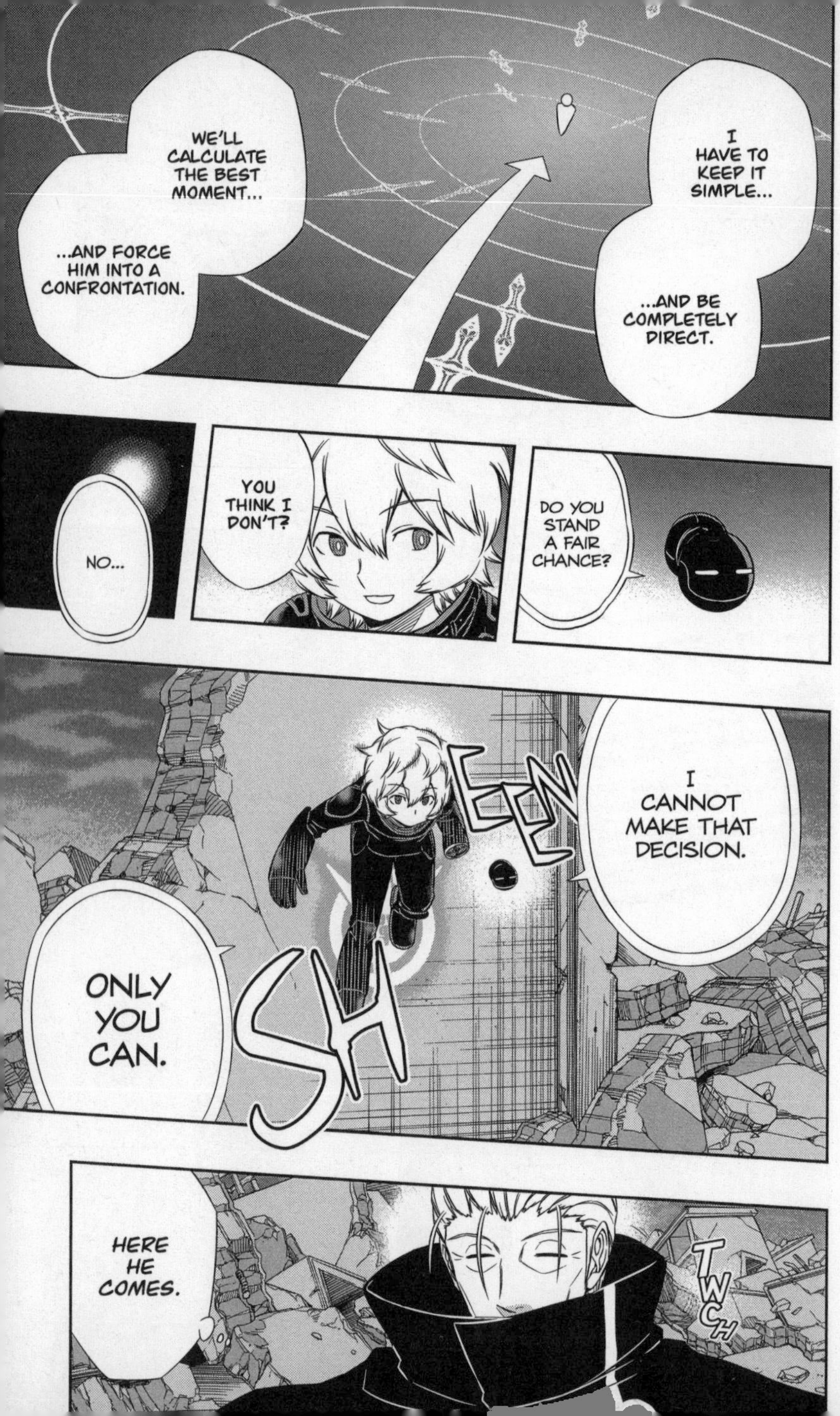
I HAVE TO KEEP IT SIMPLE...
...AND BE COMPLETELY DIRECT.
WE'LL CALCULATE THE BEST MOMENT...
...AND FORCE HIM INTO A CONFRONTATION.
DO YOU STAND A FAIR CHANCE?
YOU THINK I DON'T?
NO...
I CANNOT MAKE THAT DECISION.
SHEEEN
ONLY YOU CAN.
TWCH
HERE HE COMES.

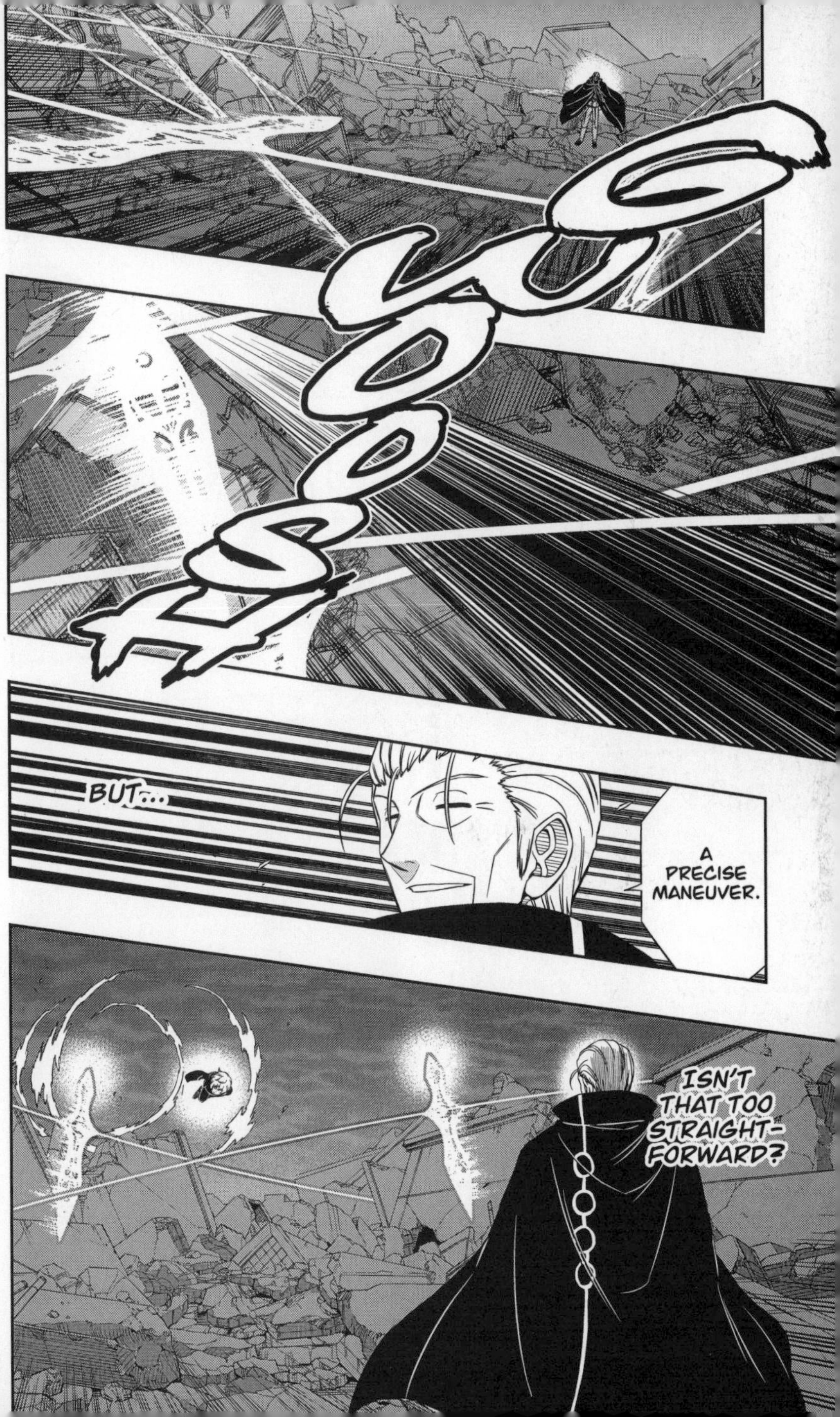
GOOOSH
A PRECISE MANEUVER.
BUT...
ISN'T THAT TOO STRAIGHT-FORWARD?

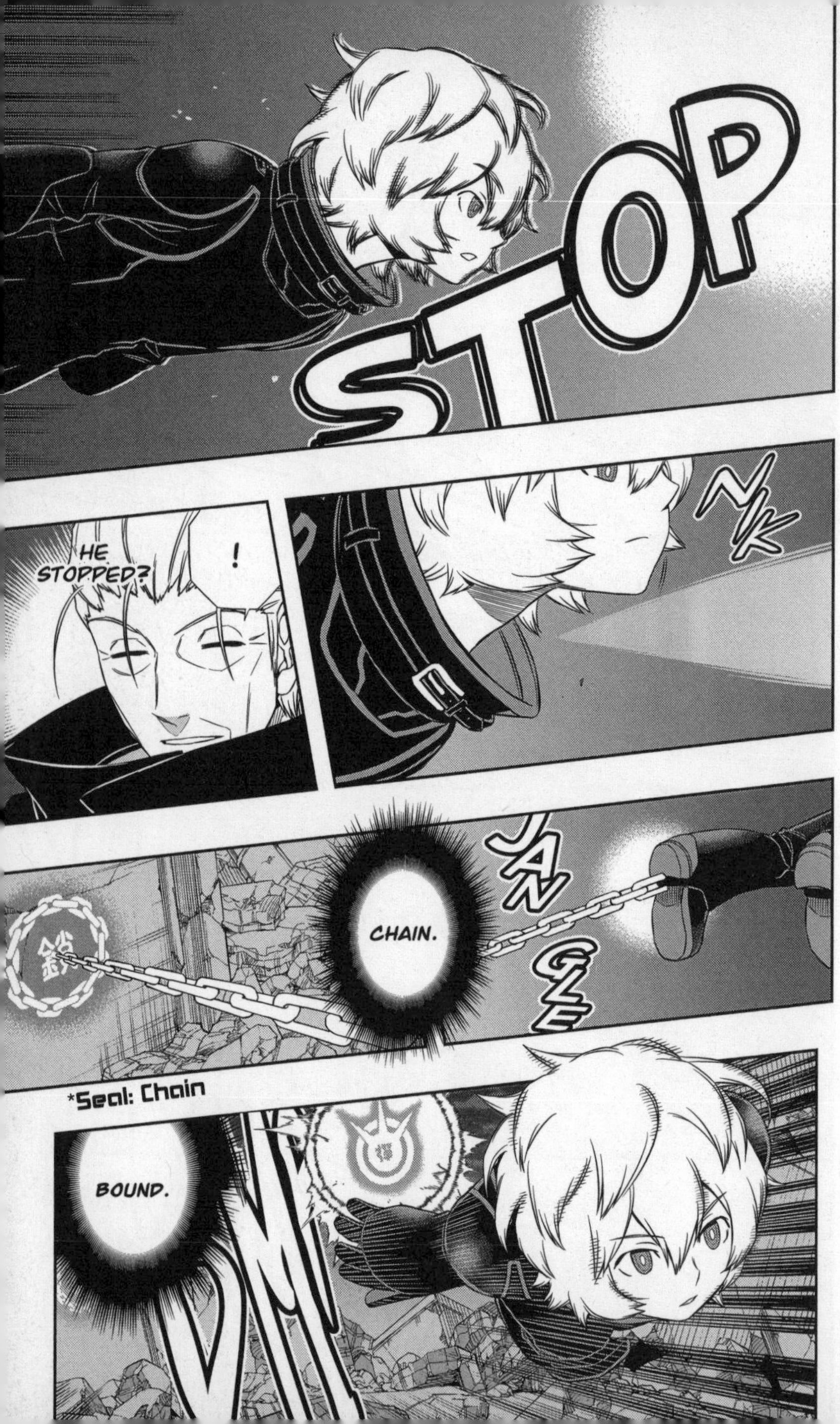
STOP
NK
!
HE STOPPED?
JANGLE
CHAIN.
*Seal: Chain
BOUND.

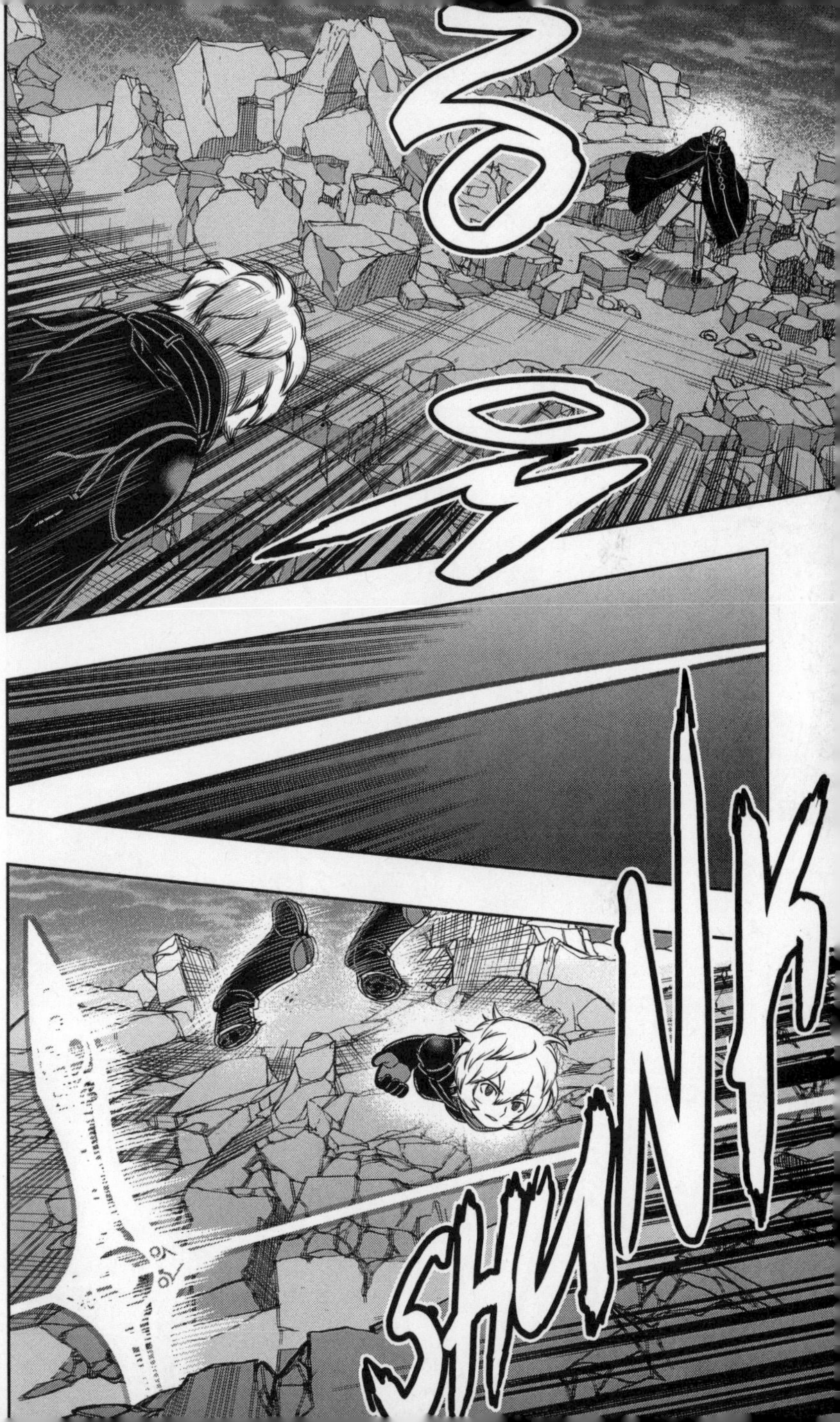
SHUNK

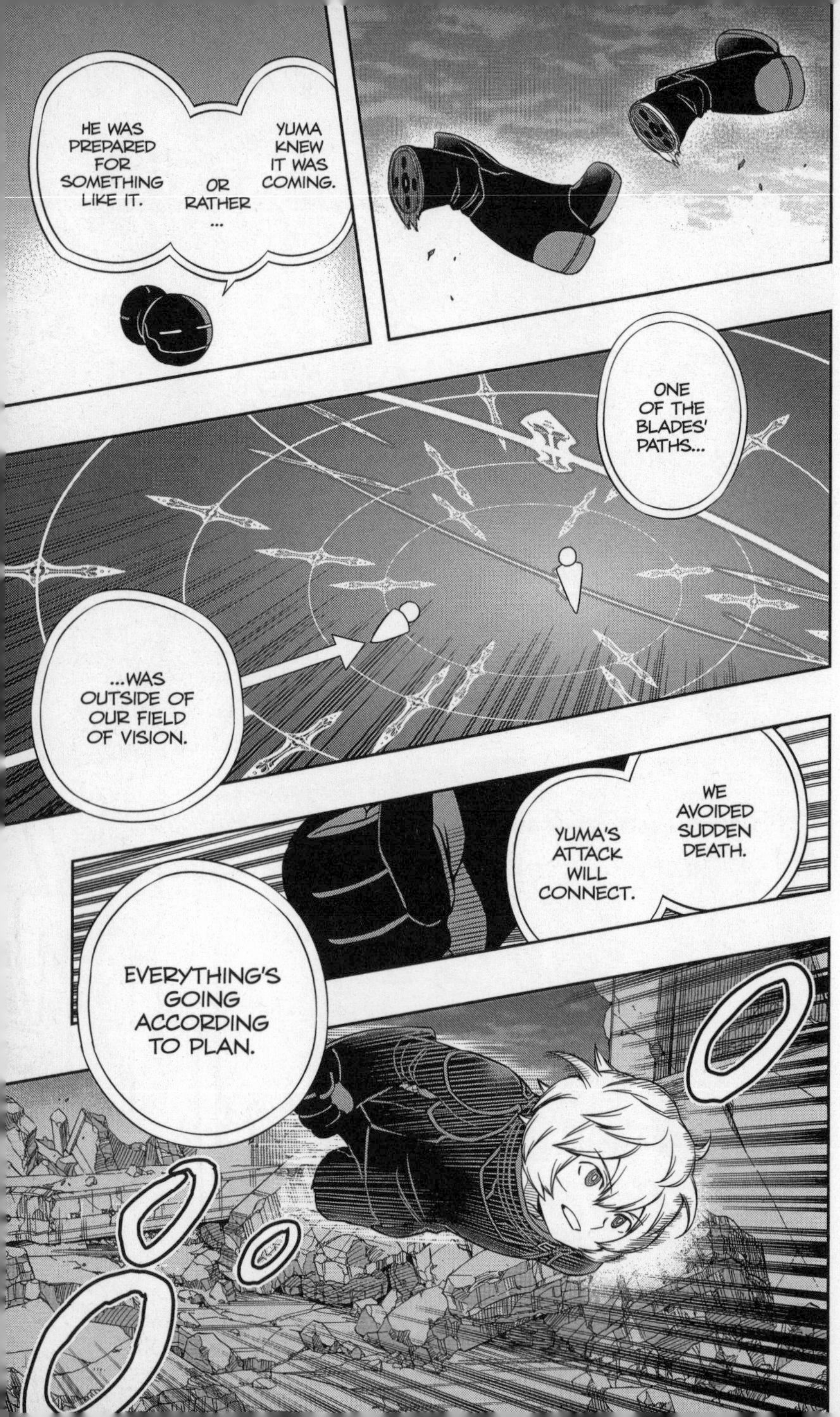
YUMA KNEW IT WAS COMING.
OR RATHER...
HE WAS PREPARED FOR SOMETHING LIKE IT.
ONE OF THE BLADES' PATHS...
...WAS OUTSIDE OF OUR FIELD OF VISION.
WE AVOIDED SUDDEN DEATH.
YUMA'S ATTACK WILL CONNECT.
EVERYTHING'S GOING ACCORDING TO PLAN.

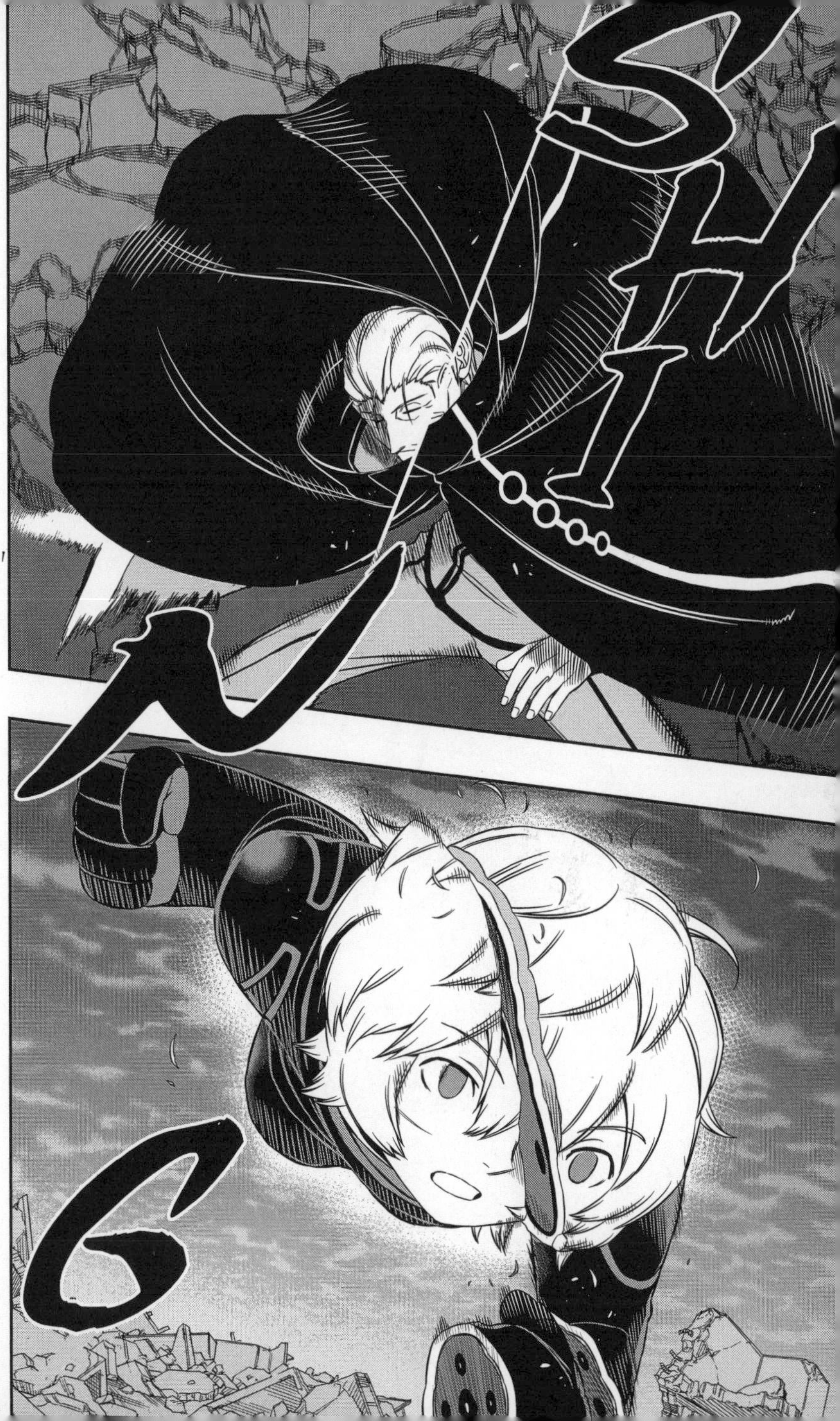
SHING

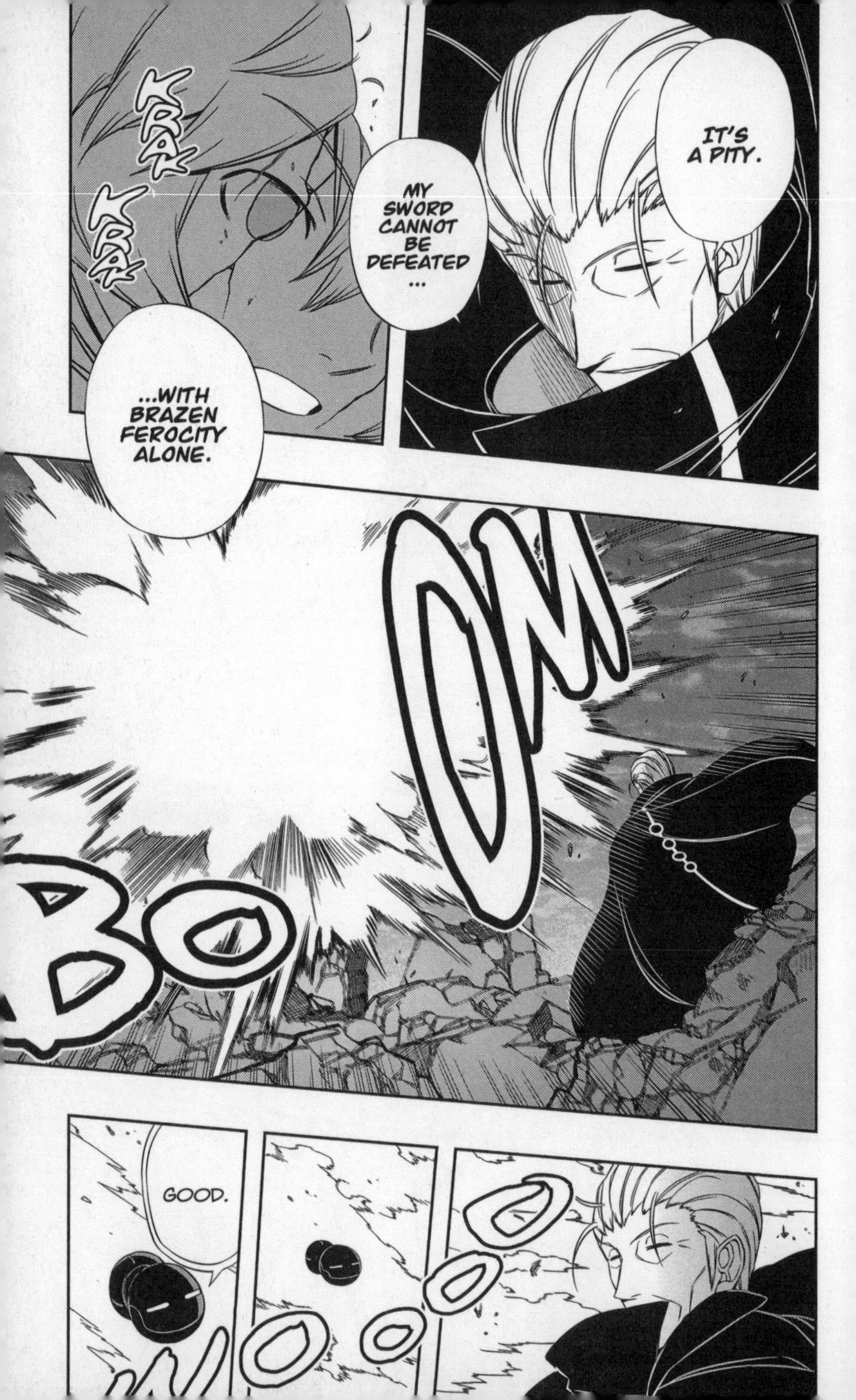
IT'S A PITY.
MY SWORD CANNOT BE DEFEATED...
...WITH BRAZEN FEROCITY ALONE.
KRAK KRAK
BOOM
GOOD.

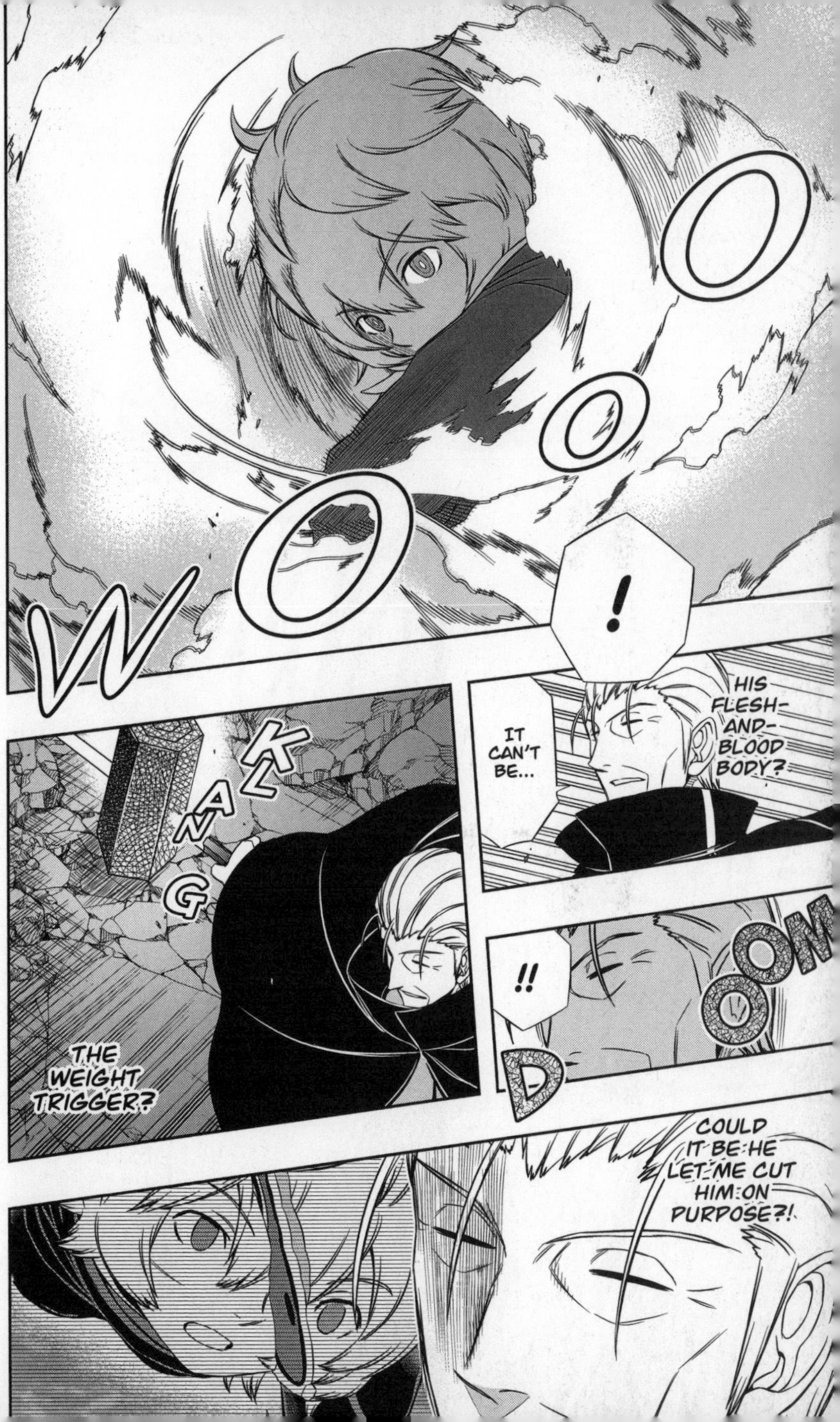
WOOOO
!
HIS FLESH-AND-BLOOD BODY?
IT CAN'T BE...
!!
DOOOM
KLANG
THE WEIGHT TRIGGER?
COULD IT BE HE LET ME CUT HIM ON PURPOSE?!

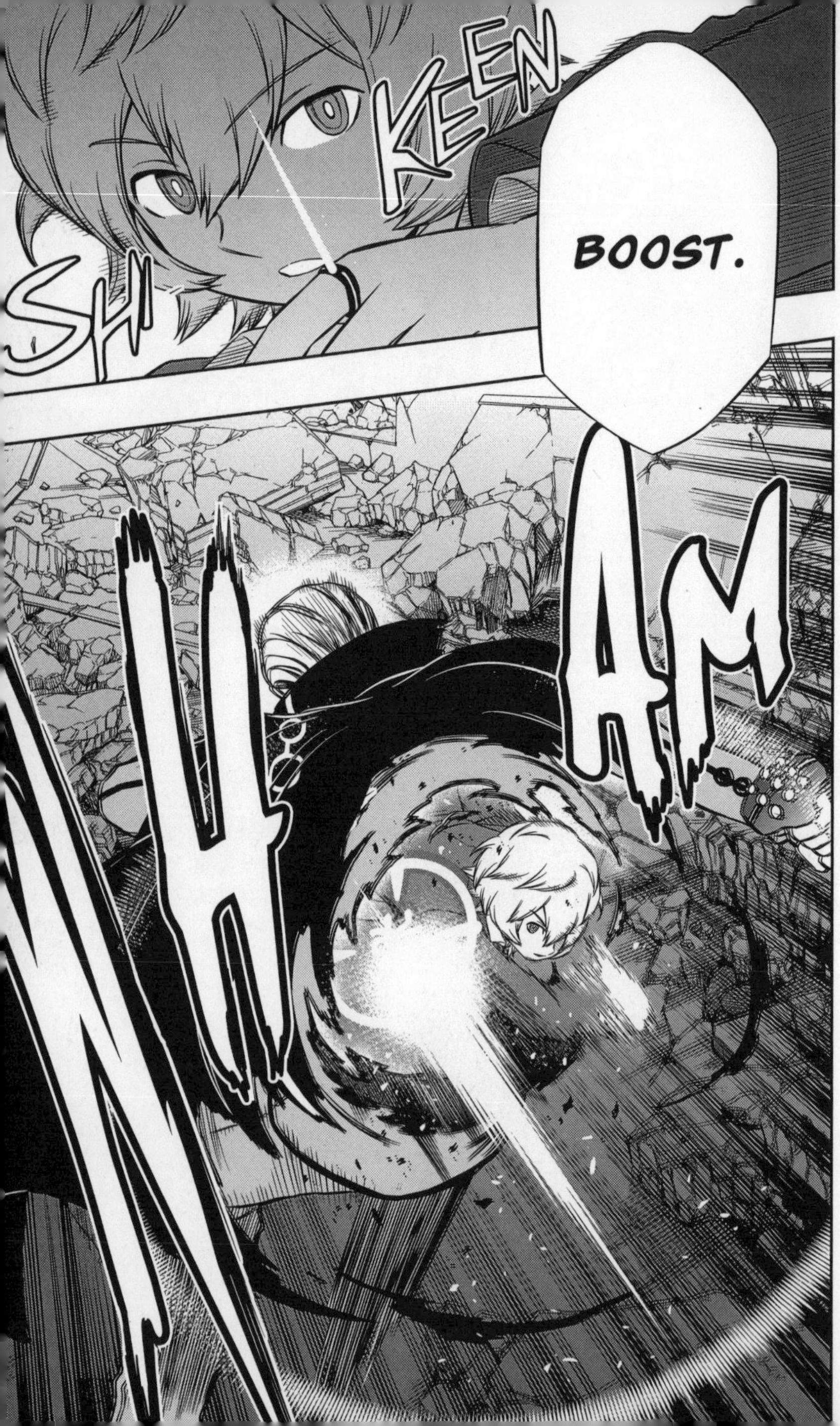
BOOST.
SHI
KEEN
WHAM

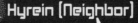

Hyrein (Neighbor)

- ■ 29 years old
- ■ From Aftokrator
- ■ Height: 5'11"
- ■ Trigger: Alektor (Egg Crown)
- ■ Likes: Distinguished personnel, diversions and fragmenting armies, family, peaceful living

The boss of Aftokrator. He has a Black Trigger that is, pretty much a huge cheat like how Viza's is but kind of different. He's the prudent type who worked really hard to research Meeden long before chapter three. He favors tactics that divide the enemy. Considering that his plan is solely focused on the C-Rank trainees, he seems more like a civil servant than a military officer. Maybe that's why he was compatible with Alektor.

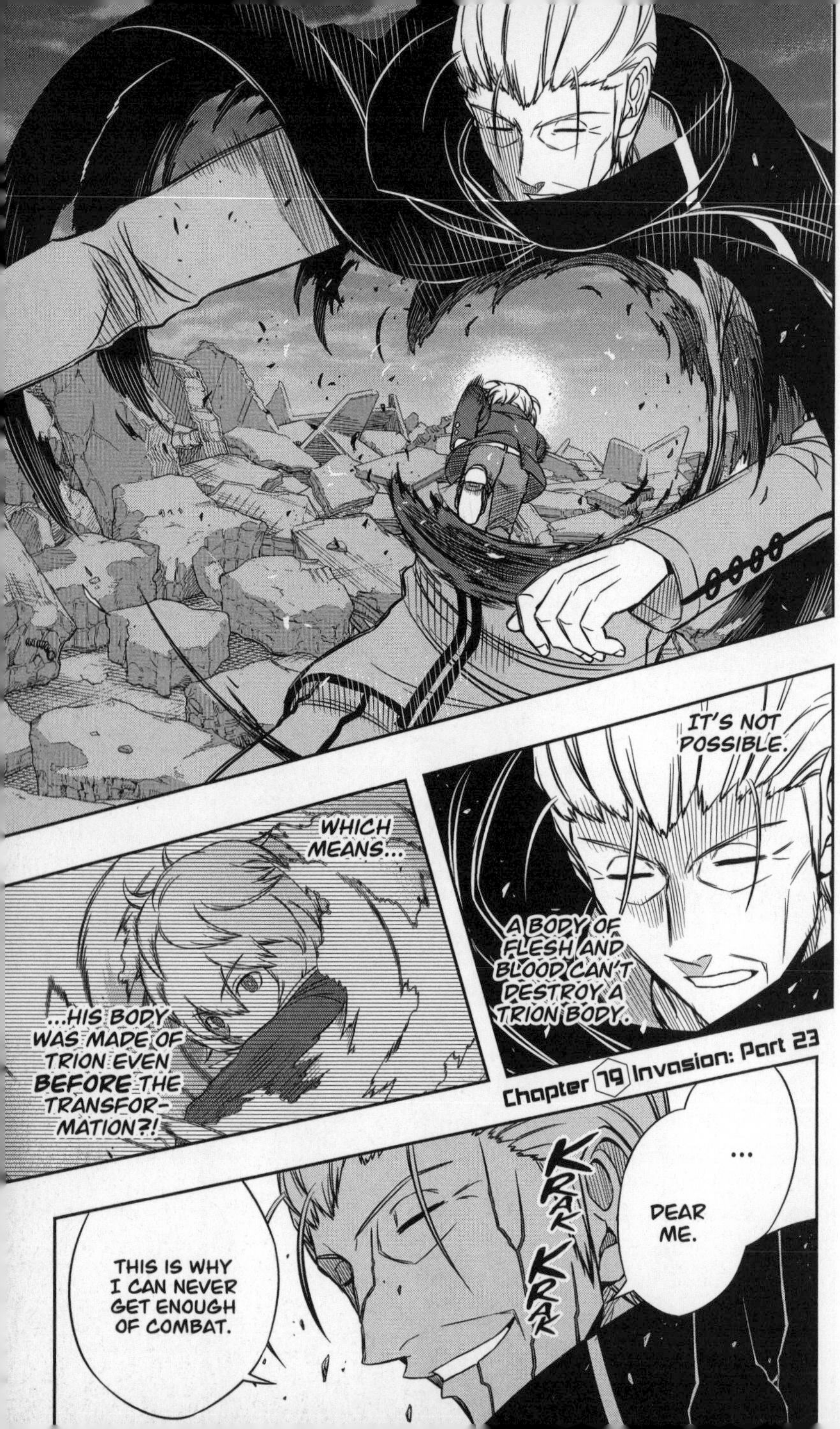
IT'S NOT POSSIBLE.
A BODY OF FLESH AND BLOOD CAN'T DESTROY A TRION BODY.
WHICH MEANS...
...HIS BODY WAS MADE OF TRION EVEN BEFORE THE TRANSFOR-MATION?!
Chapter 19 Invasion: Part 23
...
DEAR ME.
KRAK KRAK
THIS IS WHY I CAN NEVER GET ENOUGH OF COMBAT.

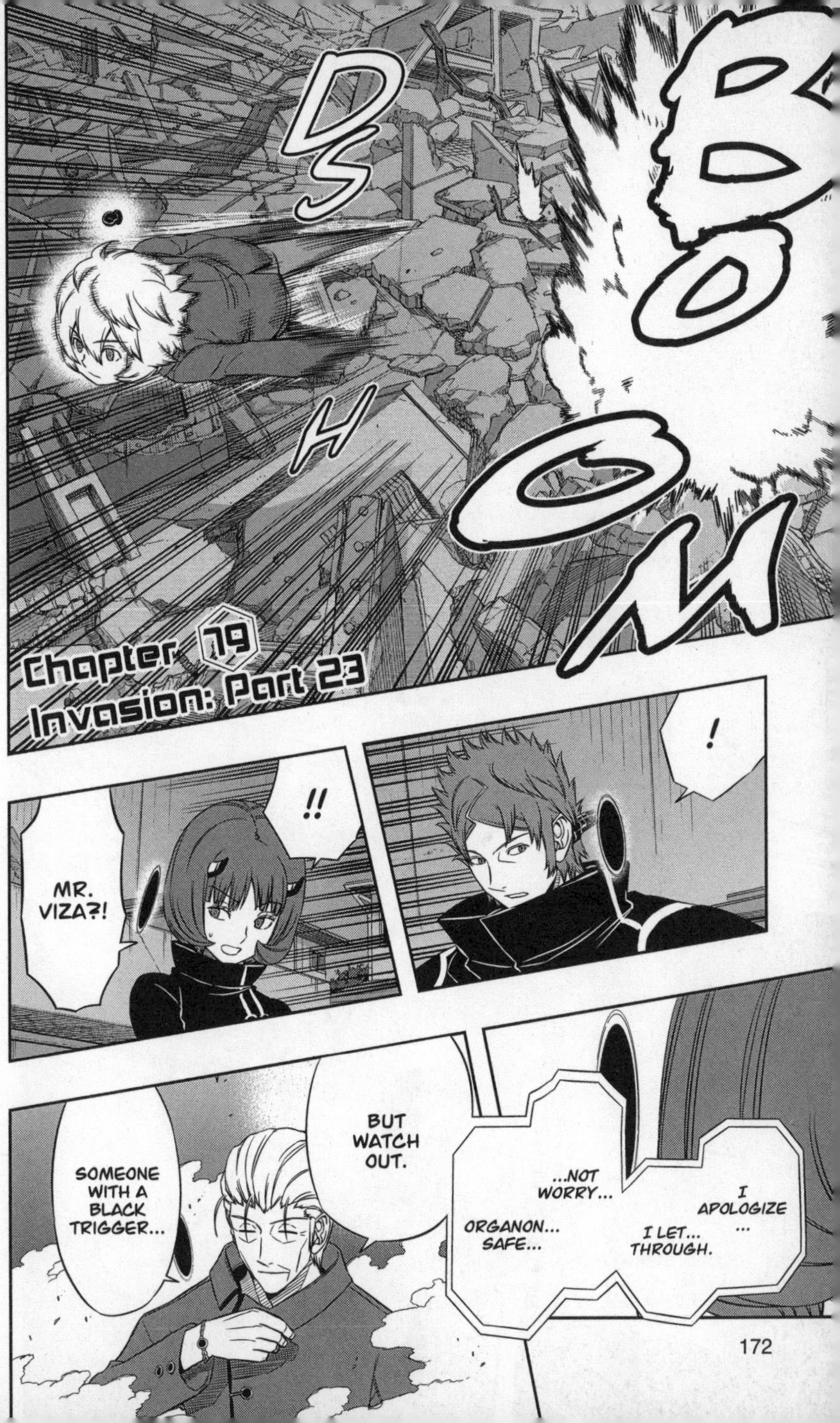
BOOM
DSH
Chapter 79
Invasion: Part 23
!
!!
MR. VIZA?!
I APOLOGIZE ... I LET... THROUGH.
...NOT WORRY... ORGANON... SAFE...
BUT WATCH OUT.
SOMEONE WITH A BLACK TRIGGER...

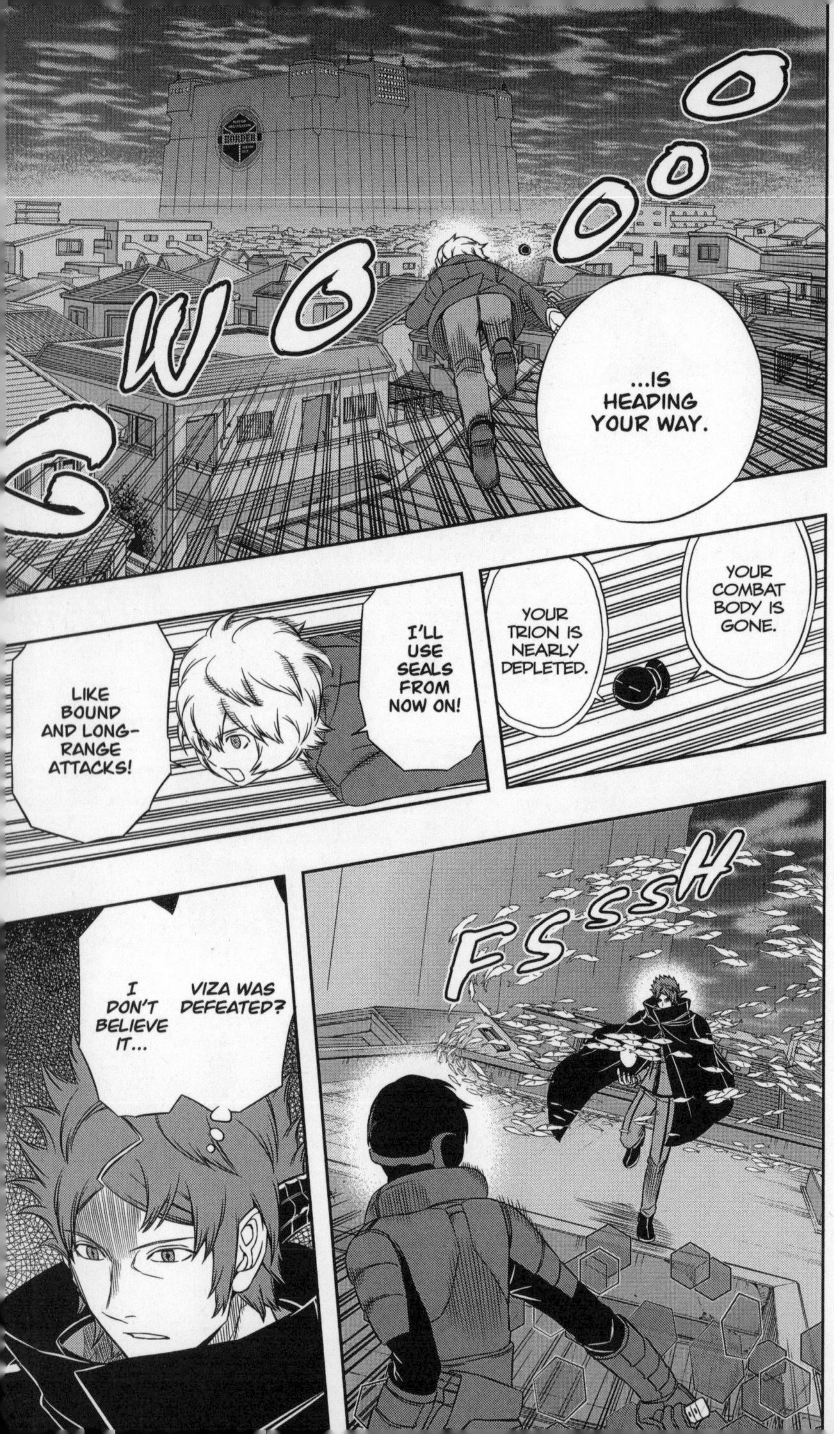
GWOOOOO
...IS HEADING YOUR WAY.
YOUR COMBAT BODY IS GONE.
YOUR TRION IS NEARLY DEPLETED.
I'LL USE SEALS FROM NOW ON!
LIKE BOUND AND LONG-RANGE ATTACKS!
FSSSH
VIZA WAS DEFEATED?
I DON'T BELIEVE IT...

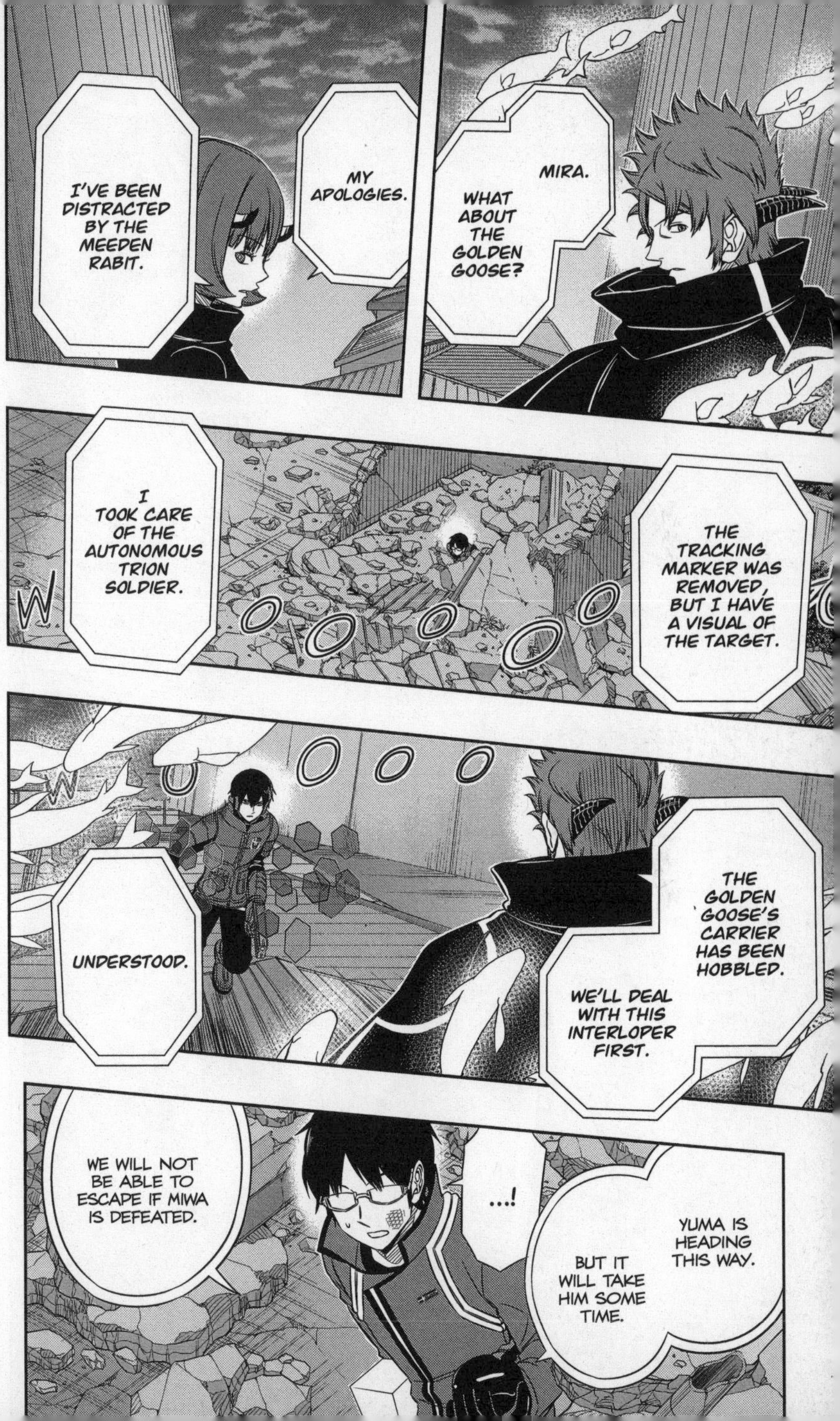
MIRA.
WHAT ABOUT THE GOLDEN GOOSE?
MY APOLOGIES.
I'VE BEEN DISTRACTED BY THE MEEDEN RABIT.
THE TRACKING MARKER WAS REMOVED, BUT I HAVE A VISUAL OF THE TARGET.
I TOOK CARE OF THE AUTONOMOUS TRION SOLDIER.
THE GOLDEN GOOSE'S CARRIER HAS BEEN HOBBLED.
WE'LL DEAL WITH THIS INTERLOPER FIRST.
UNDERSTOOD.
YUMA IS HEADING THIS WAY.
BUT IT WILL TAKE HIM SOME TIME.
...!
WE WILL NOT BE ABLE TO ESCAPE IF MIWA IS DEFEATED.

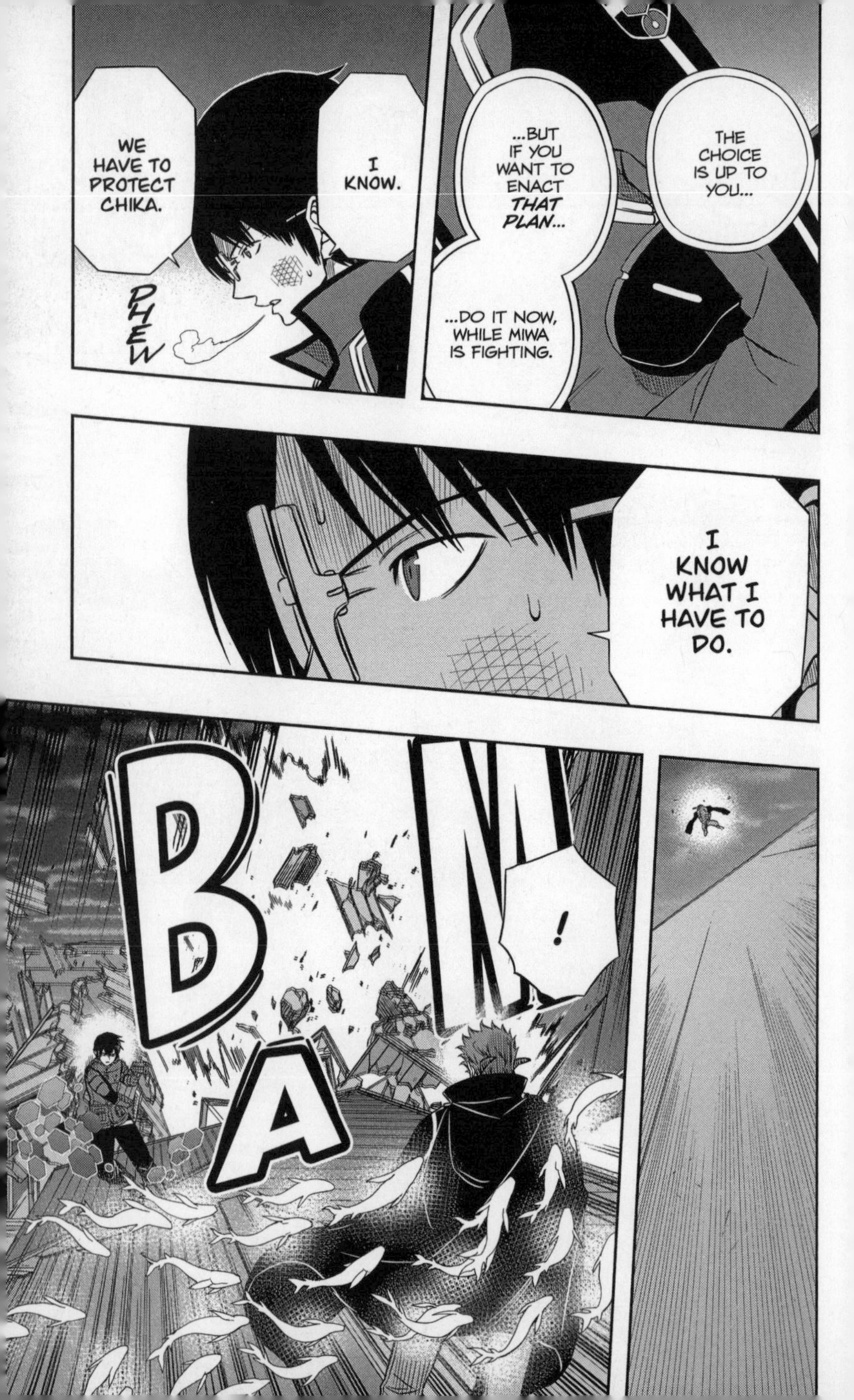
THE CHOICE IS UP TO YOU...
...BUT IF YOU WANT TO ENACT *THAT PLAN*...
...DO IT NOW, WHILE MIWA IS FIGHTING.
I KNOW.
WE HAVE TO PROTECT CHIKA.
PHEW
I KNOW WHAT I HAVE TO DO.
!
BAM

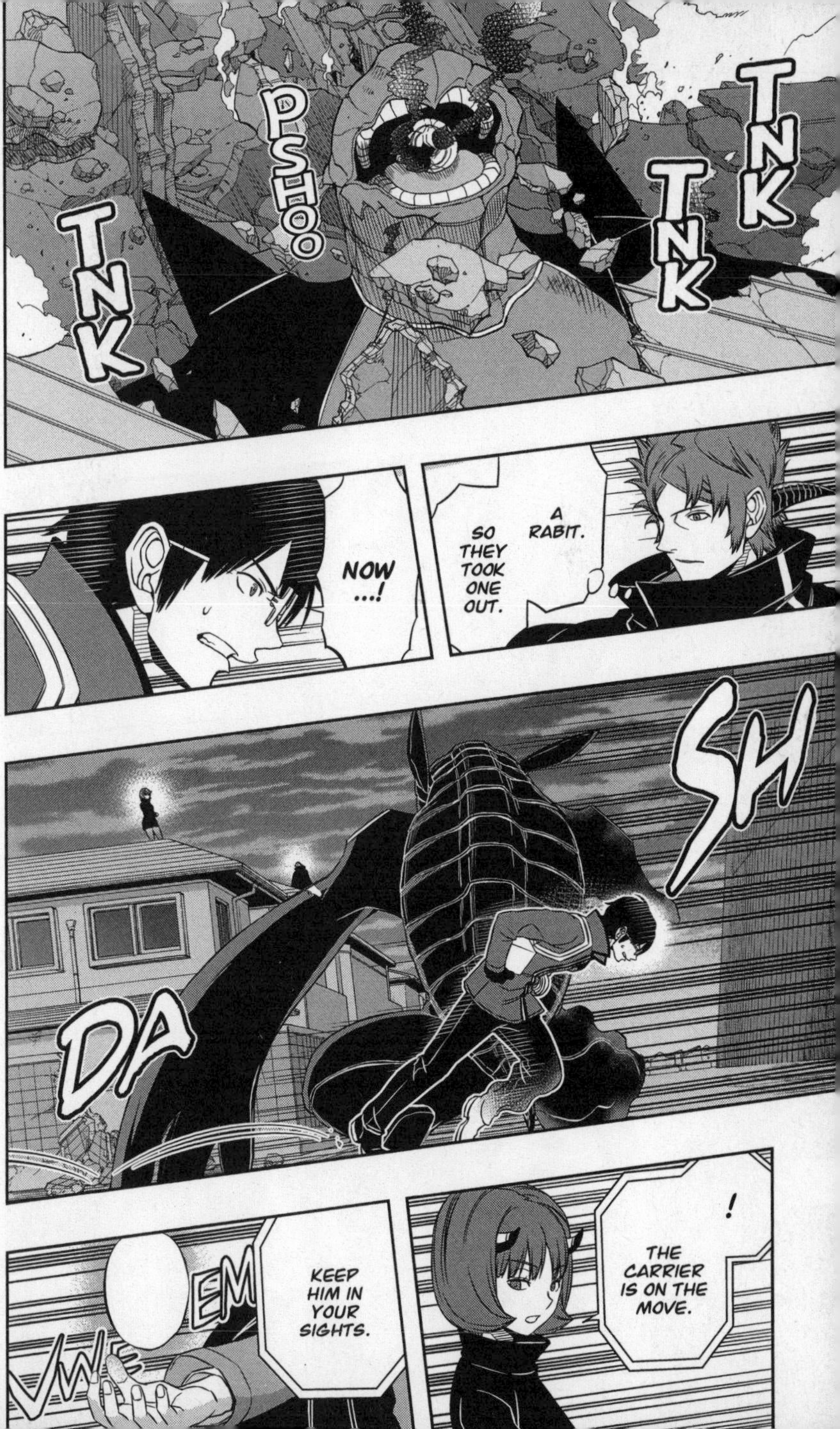
TNK
TNK
PSHOO
TNK
A RABIT.
SO THEY TOOK ONE OUT.
NOW ...!
SH
DA
!
THE CARRIER IS ON THE MOVE.
KEEP HIM IN YOUR SIGHTS.
VWEEM

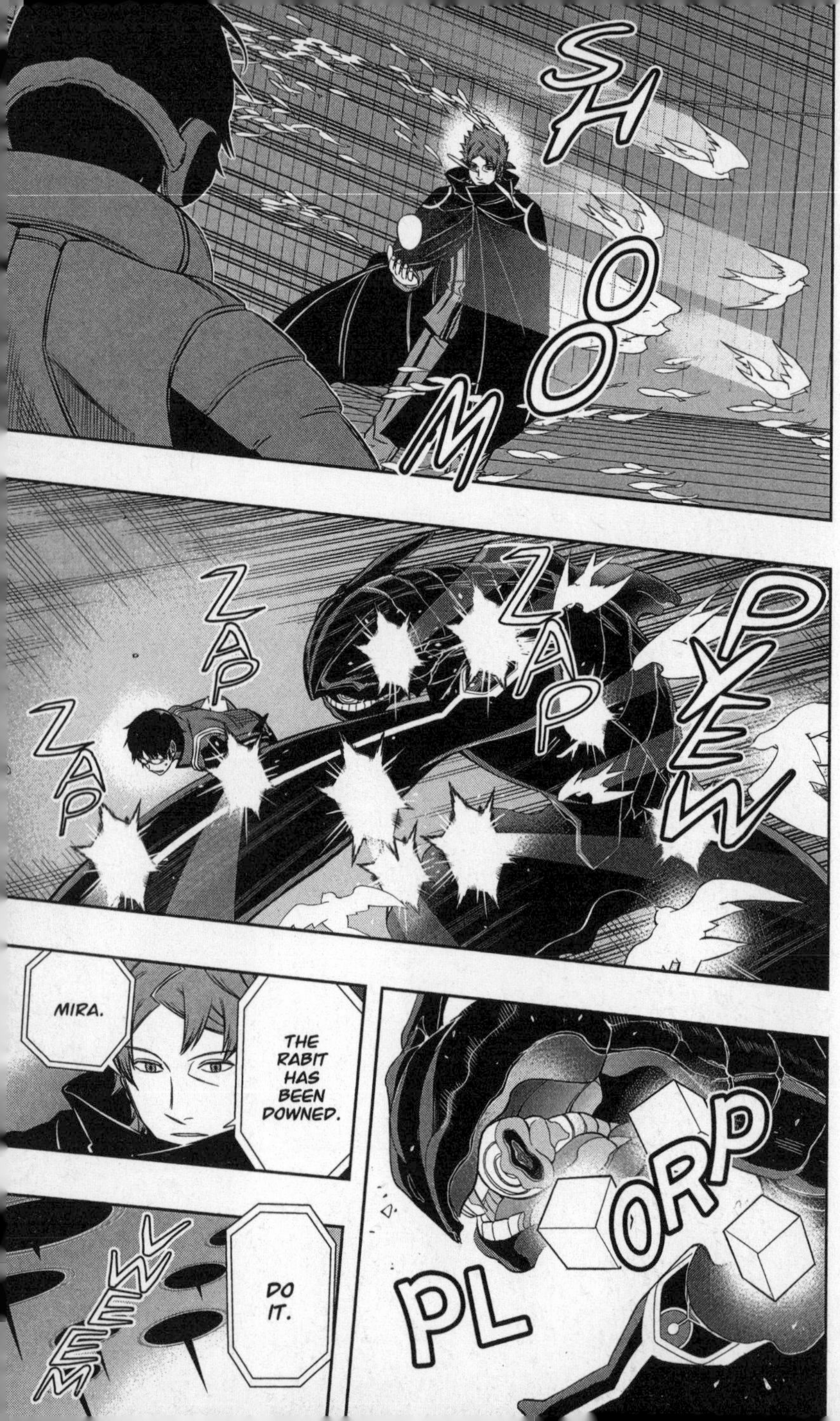
SHOOOM
PYEW
ZAP
ZAP
ZAP
PLORP
MIRA.
THE RABIT HAS BEEN DOWNED.
DO IT.
VWEEM

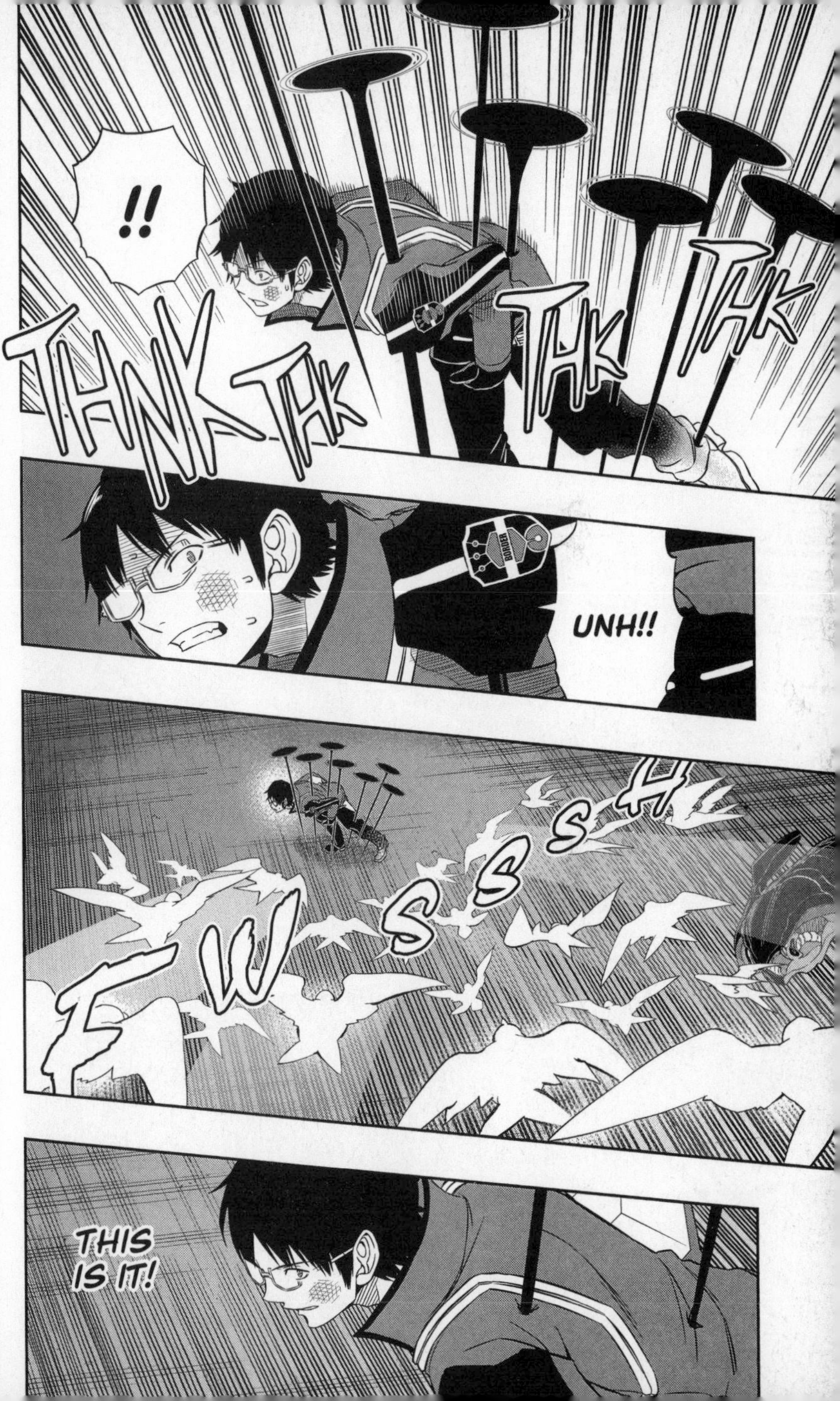
THK
THK
!!
THK
THNK
UNH!!
FWSSSH
THIS IS IT!

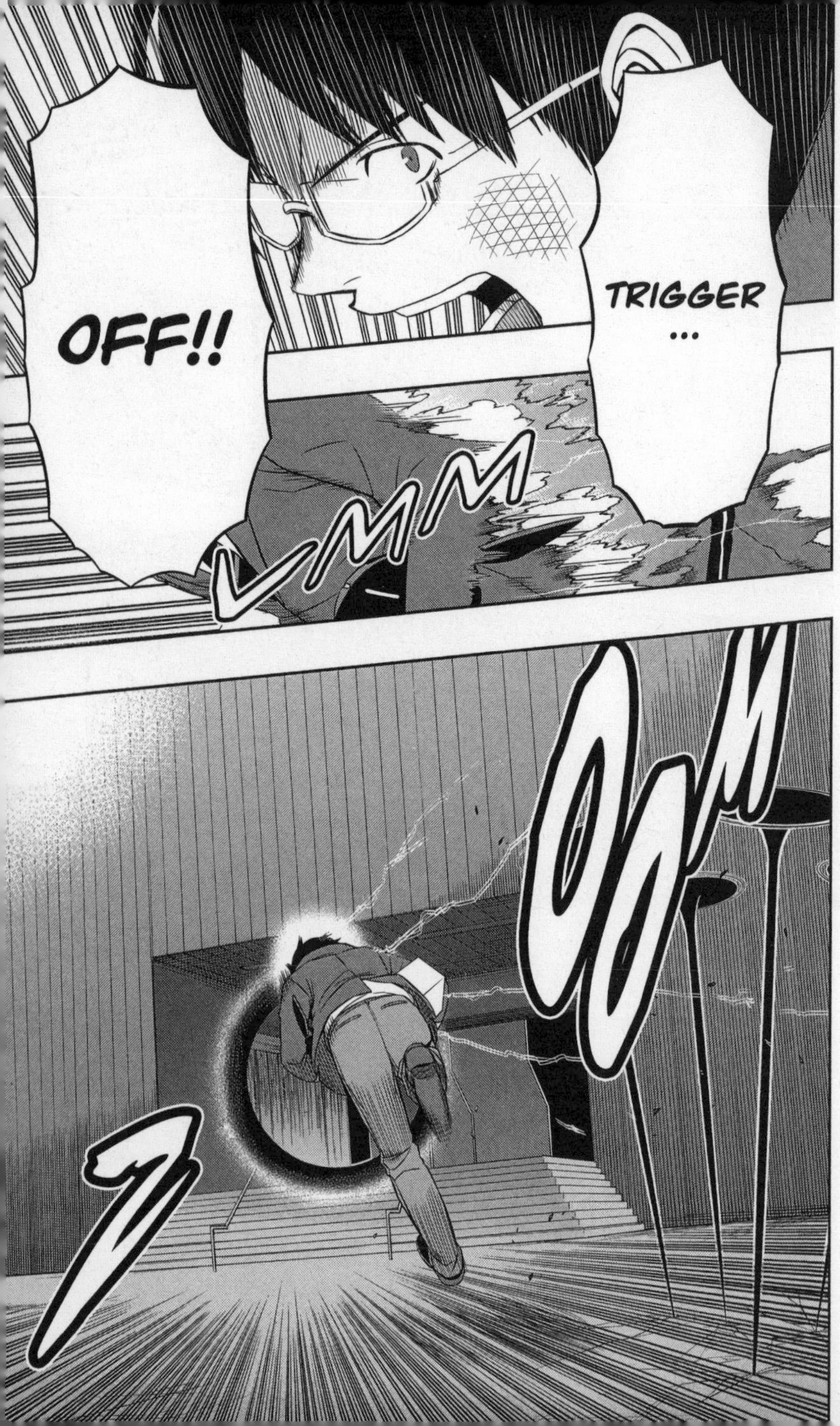
TRIGGER ...
OFF!!
VMMM
ZOOM

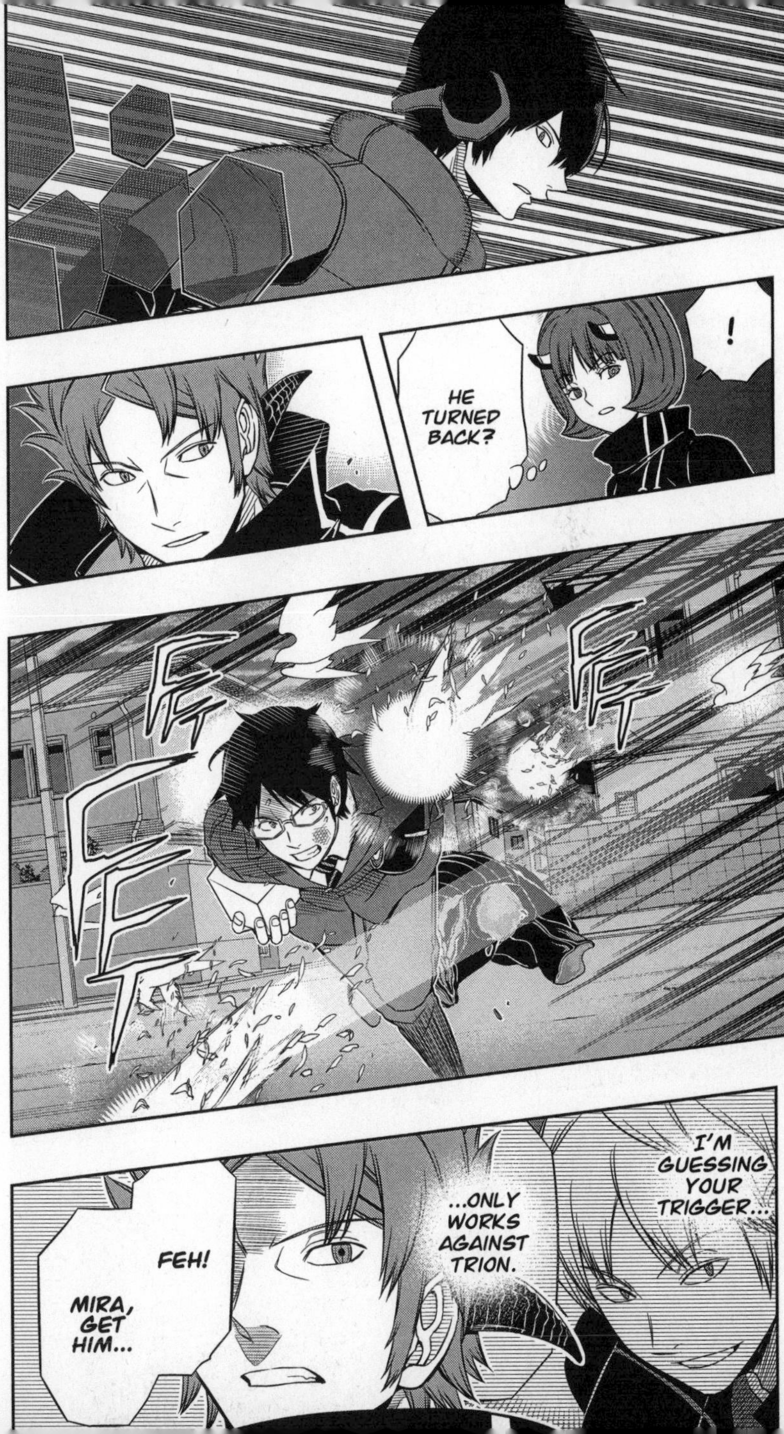
!
HE TURNED BACK?
FFT
FFT
FFT
I'M GUESSING YOUR TRIGGER...
...ONLY WORKS AGAINST TRION.
FEH!
MIRA, GET HIM...

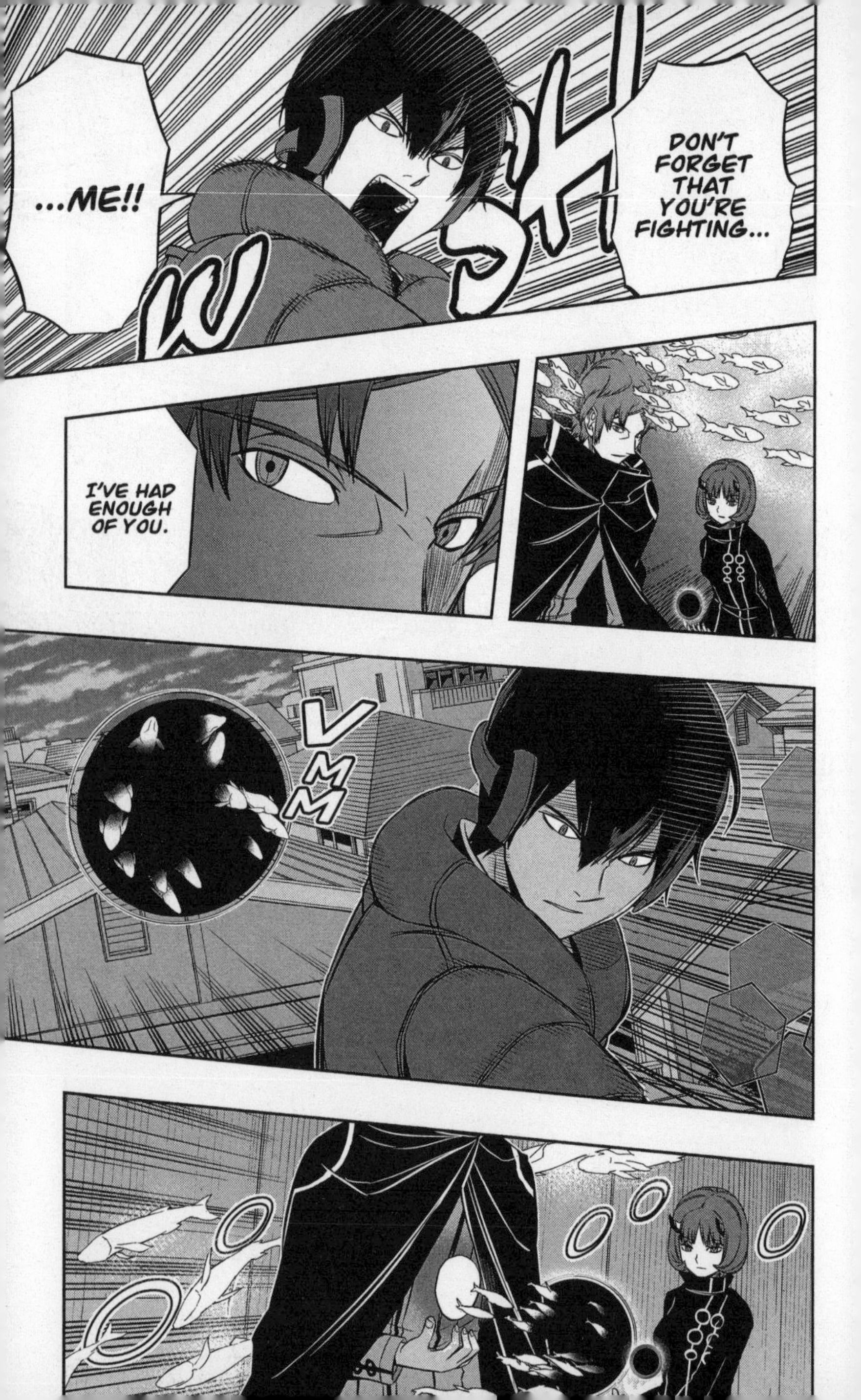
DON'T FORGET THAT YOU'RE FIGHTING...
...ME!!
I'VE HAD ENOUGH OF YOU.
VMM

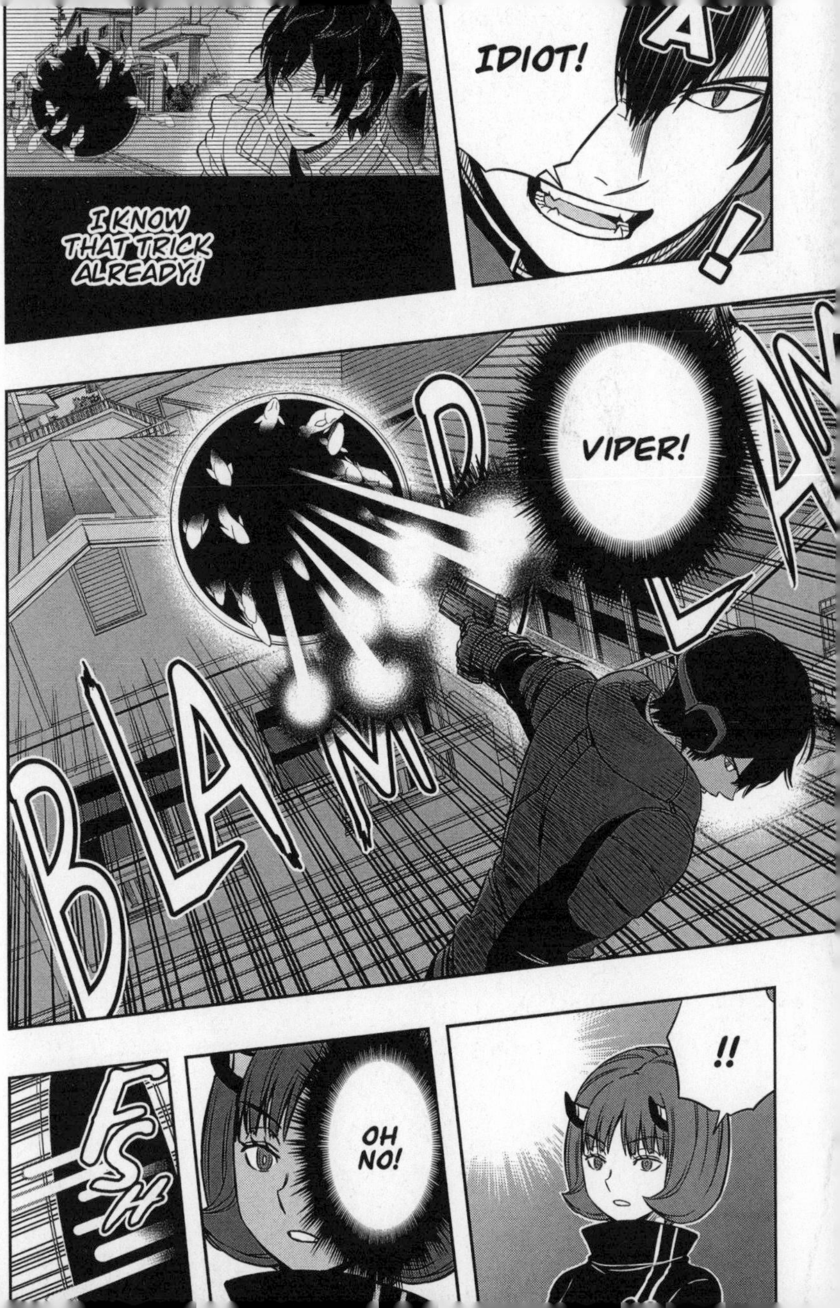
IDIOT!
!
I KNOW THAT TRICK ALREADY!
VIPER!
BLAM
!!
OH NO!
FSH

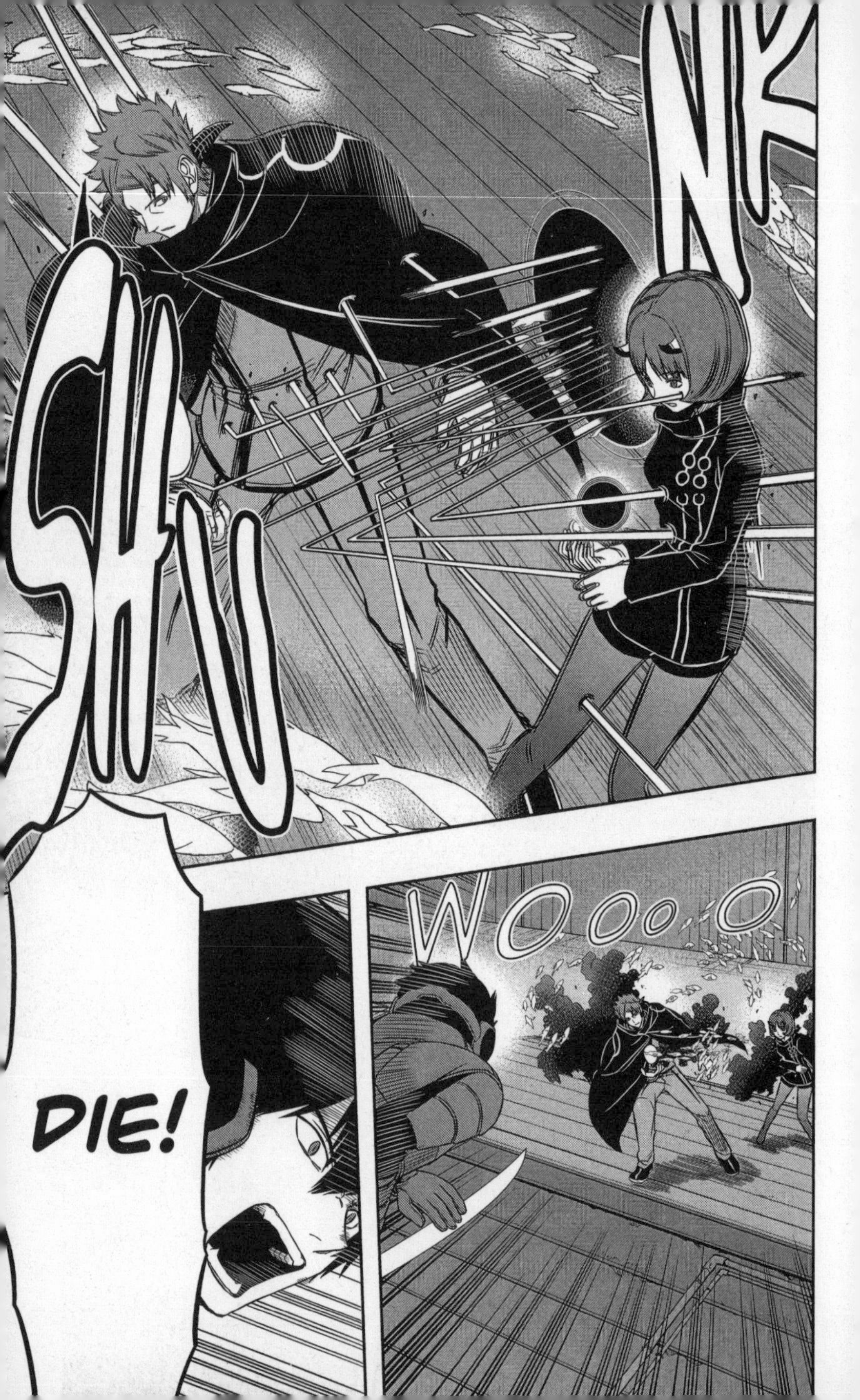
SHU
WOOOO
DIE!

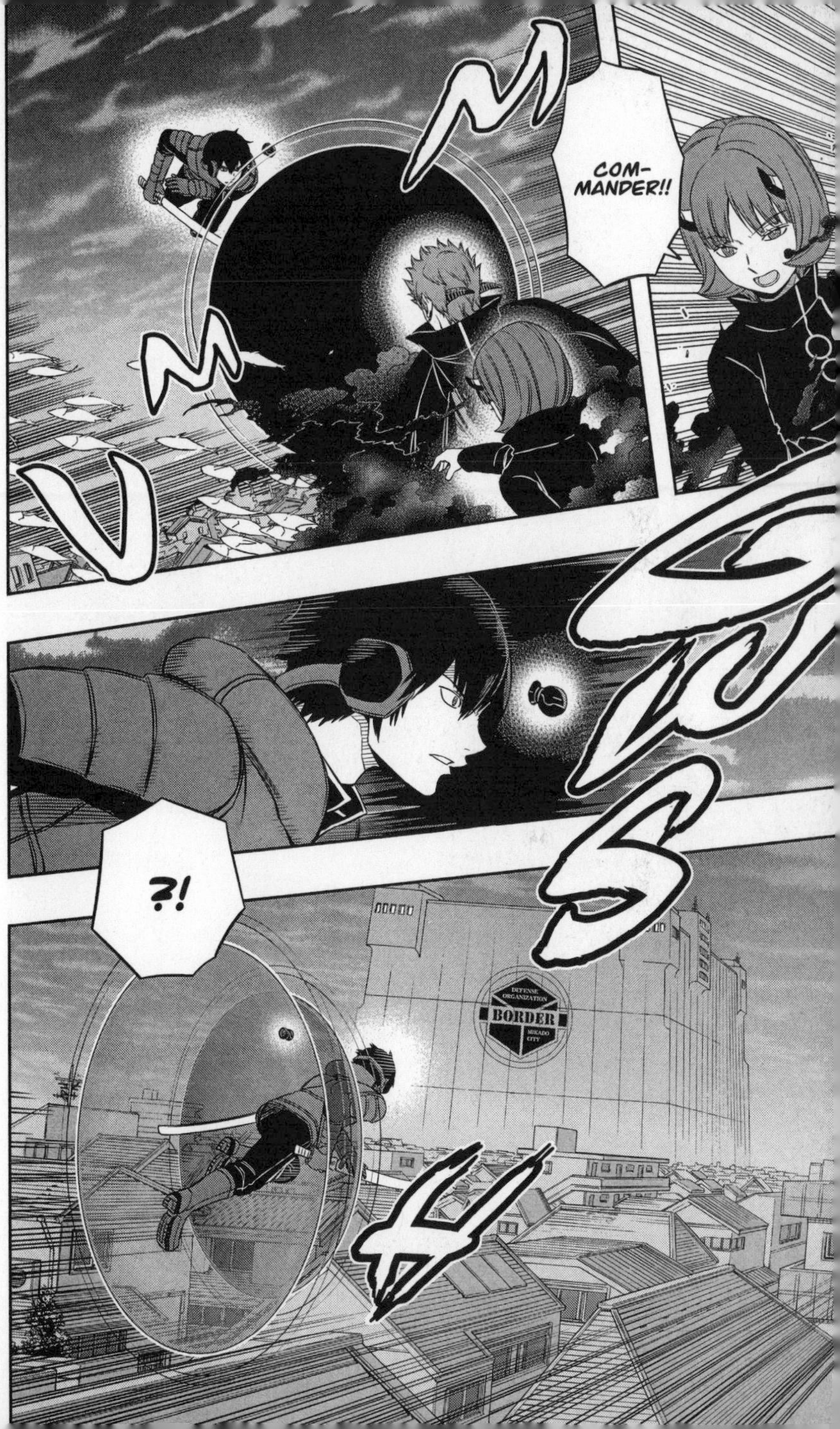
COM-MANDER!!
VMM
?!
DEFENSE ORGANIZATION
BORDER
MIKADO CITY

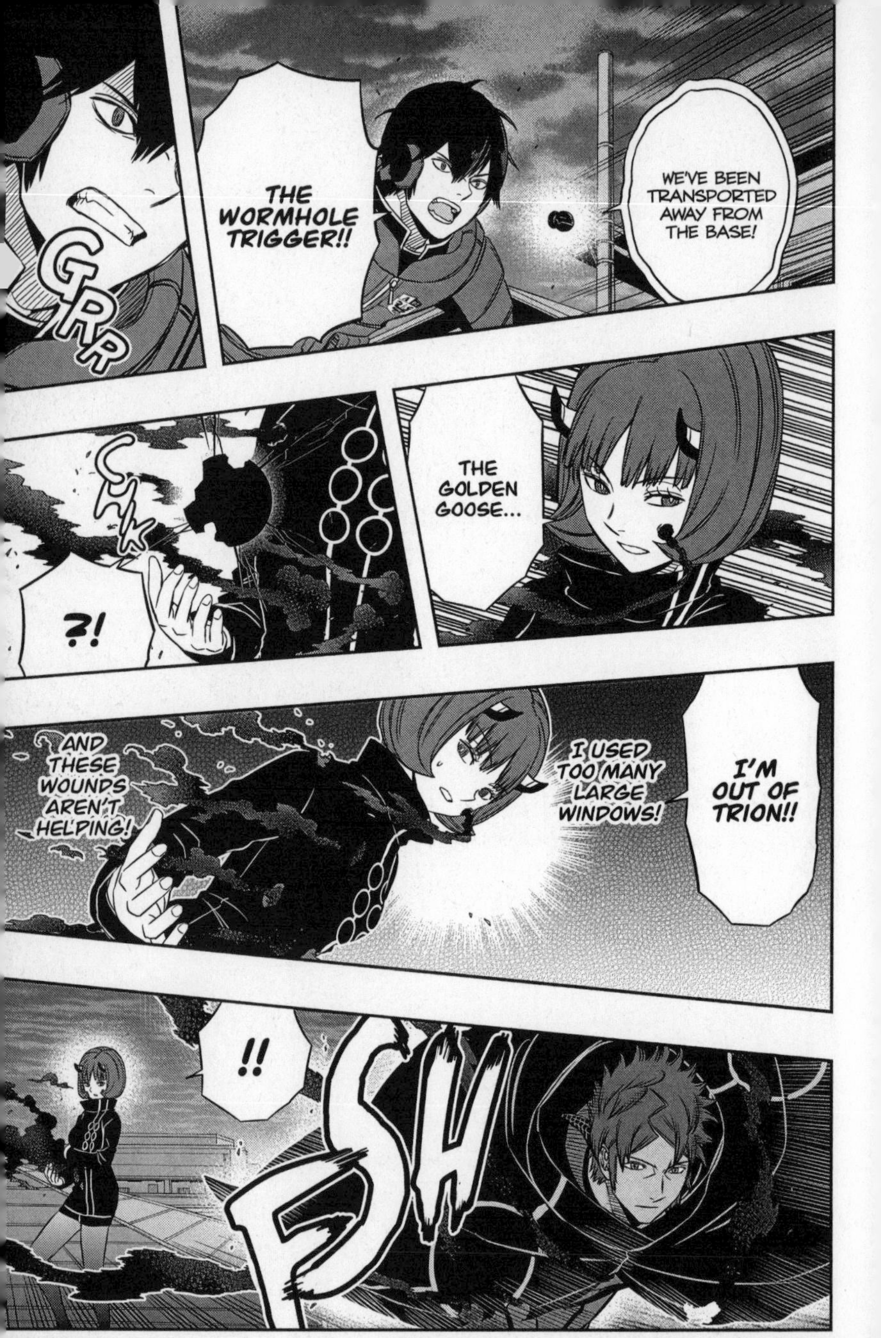
WE'VE BEEN TRANSPORTED AWAY FROM THE BASE!
THE WORMHOLE TRIGGER!!
GRR
THE GOLDEN GOOSE...
CHK
?!
I'M OUT OF TRION!!
I USED TOO MANY LARGE WINDOWS!
AND THESE WOUNDS AREN'T HELPING!
FSH
!!

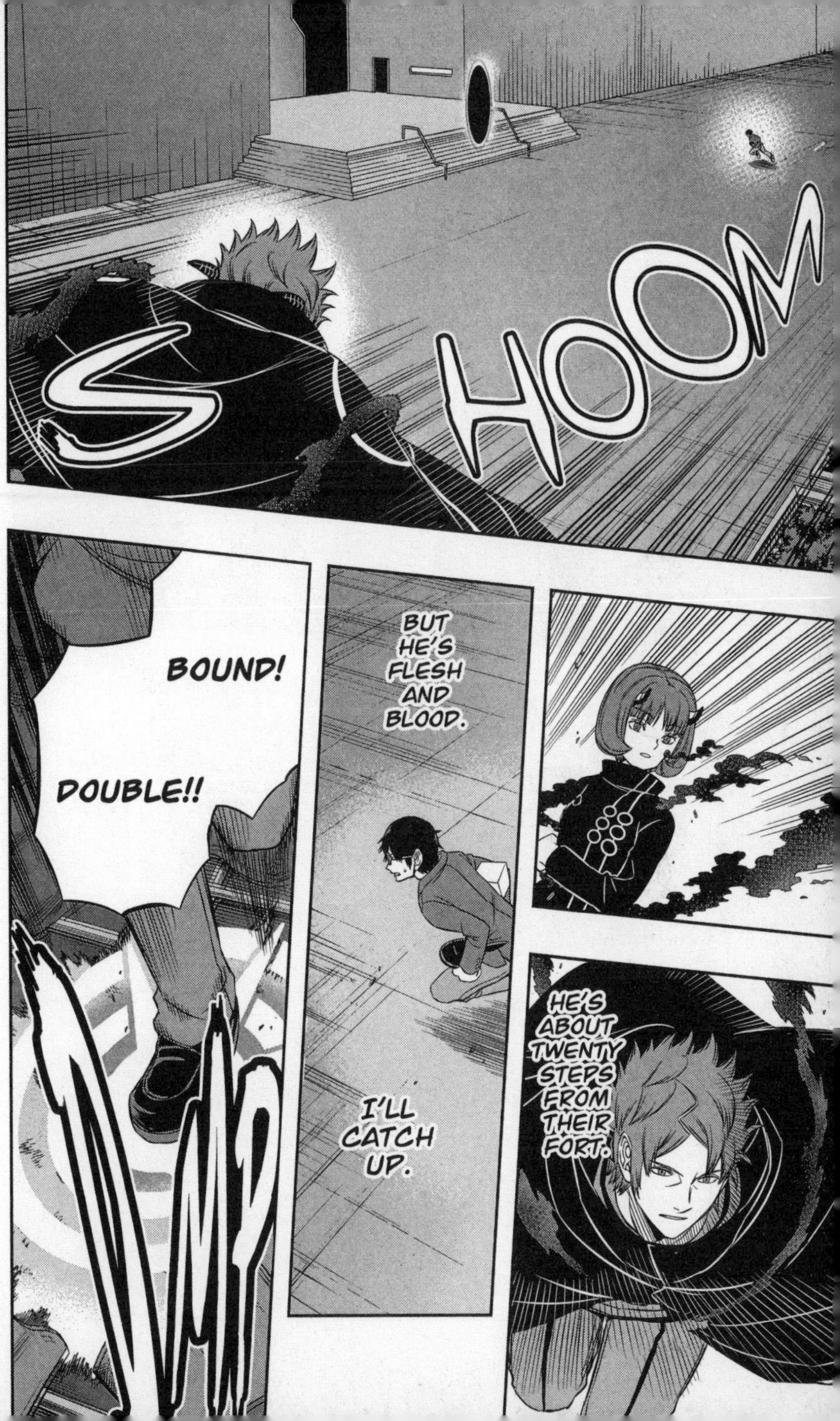
SHOOM
HE'S ABOUT TWENTY STEPS FROM THEIR FORT.
BUT HE'S FLESH AND BLOOD.
I'LL CATCH UP.
BOUND!
DOUBLE!!

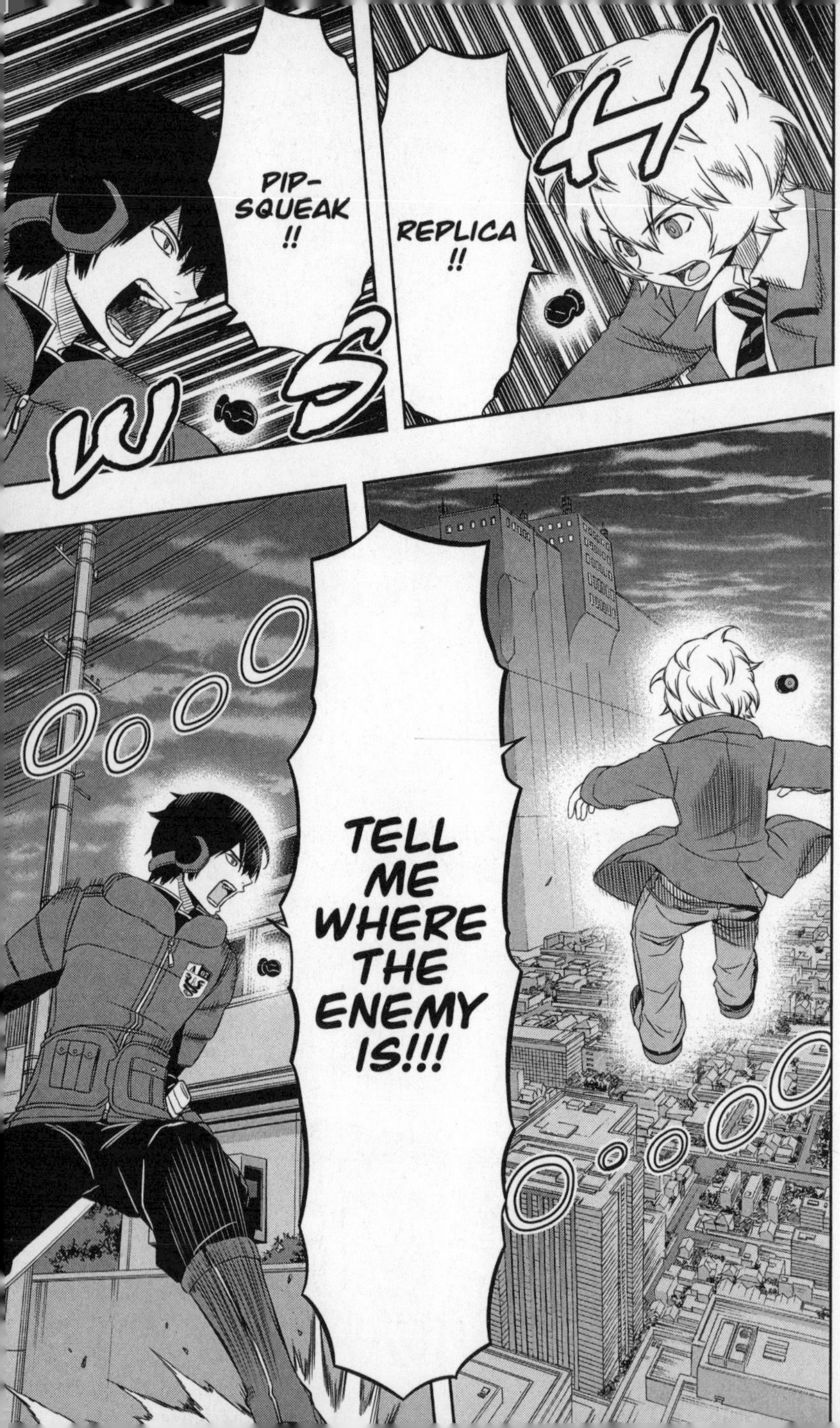
REPLICA !!
PIP-SQUEAK !!
TELL ME WHERE THE ENEMY IS!!!

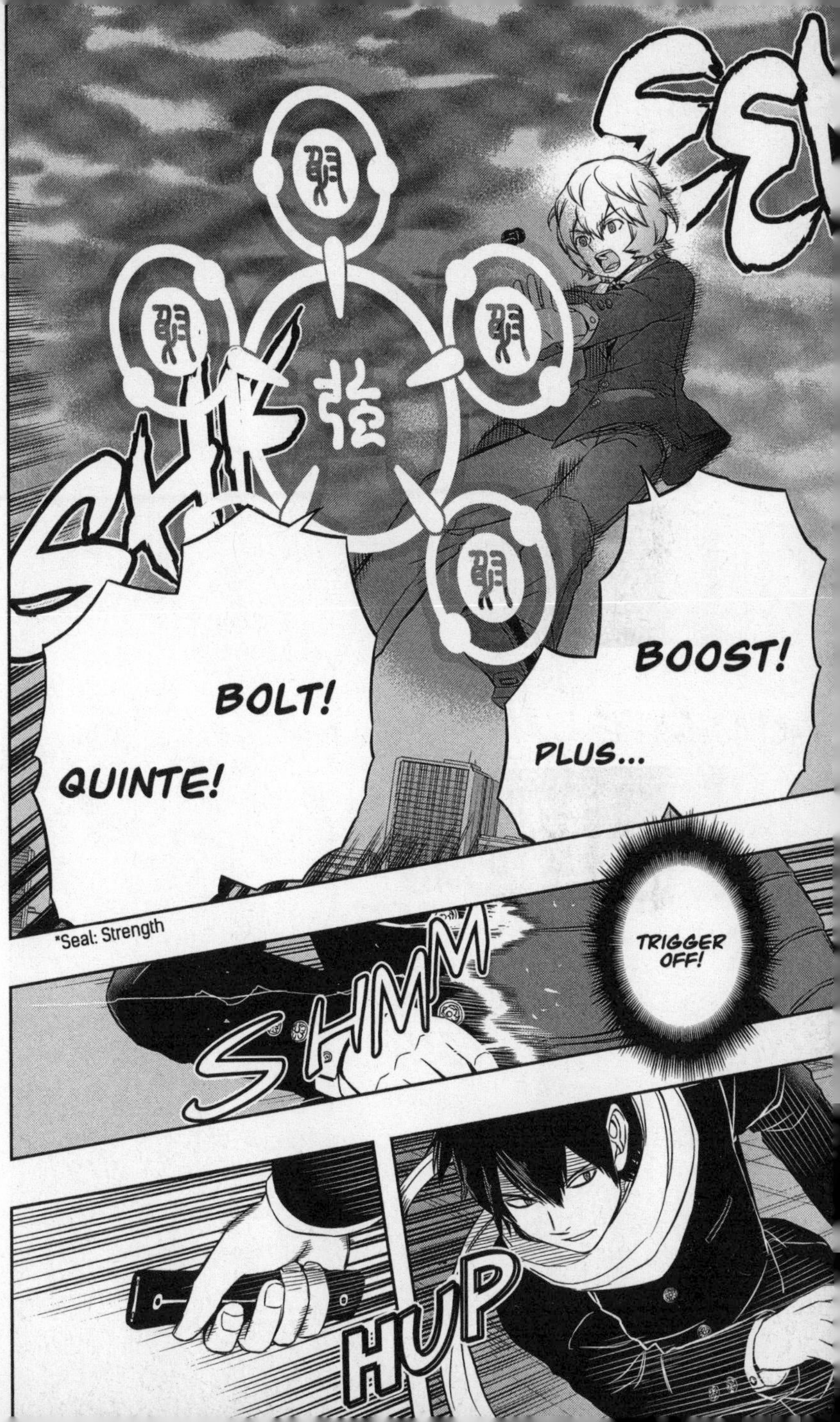
BOOST!
PLUS...
BOLT!
QUINTE!
SHK
*Seal: Strength
TRIGGER OFF!
SHMM
HUP

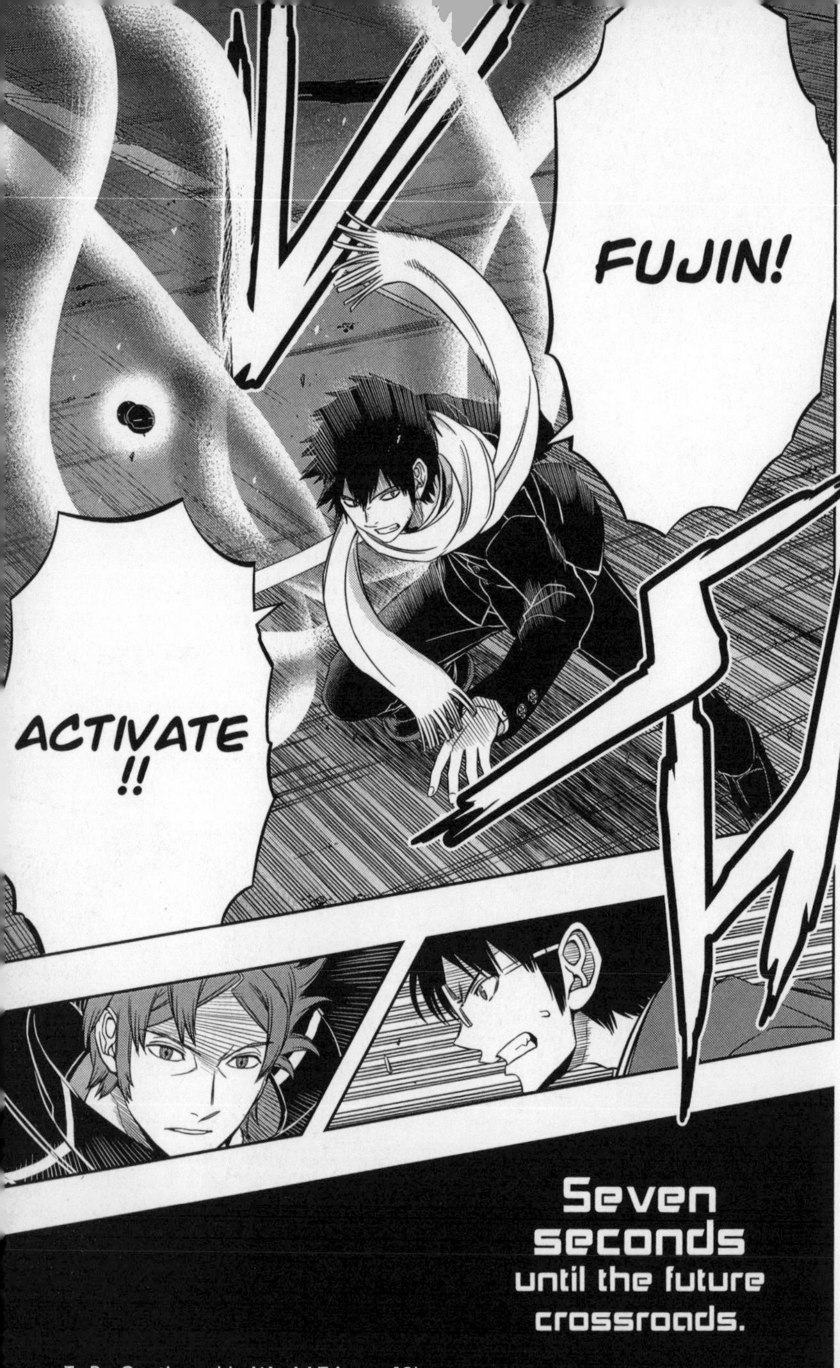
FUJIN!
ACTIVATE !!
Seven seconds until the future crossroads.

To Be Continued In **World Trigger** 10!

WORLD TRIGGER

Bonus Character Pages

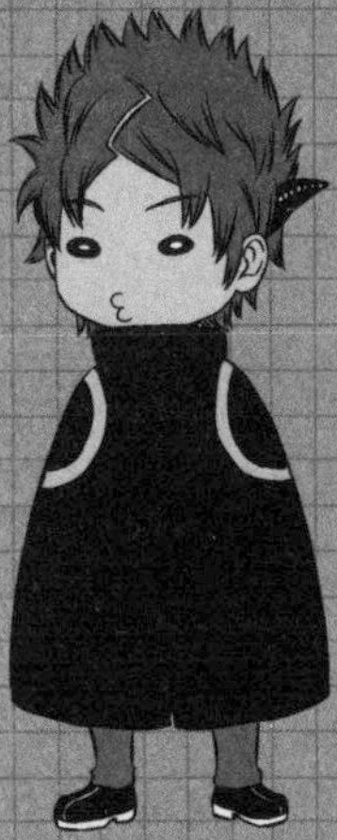

HYREIN

Mr. Discovery Channel

A natural entertainer who let the doves(?) fly loose the minute he landed. He can control over fifty different species of animal bullets. His favorite ones are the frog and giant tortoise, but they never actually hit an opponent. His horns lie flat on his head, meaning they don't go out sideways like Hyuse's, so he can't sleep on his back, but he can sleep on his side. Why didn't I do that for Hyuse's horns? My design inspiration for him was a dragon.

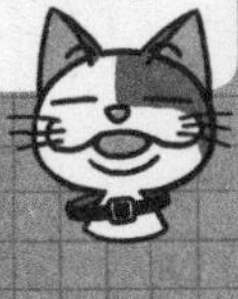

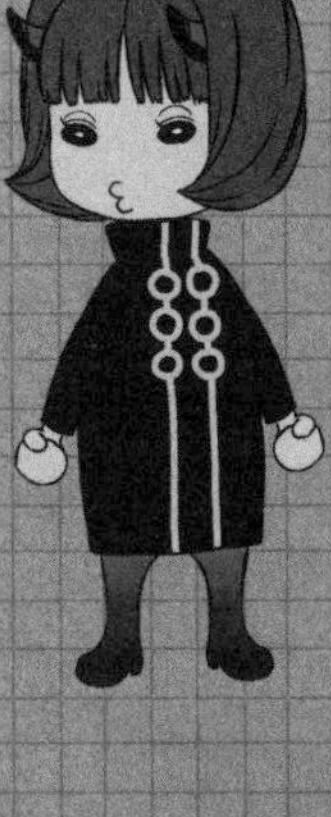

MIRA

Sadistic Wormhole Woman

She's not someone you'd want as your enemy. Her wormholes and thorny smile terrify all of Aftokrator. Just saying, "The wormhole woman is coming," will make even a whining child go silent with fear. She's annoyed about her reputation though. She is supposed to have a political marriage with either Hyrein or Ranbanein, and they're probably both terrified at the thought of it. My design inspiration for her was the devil.

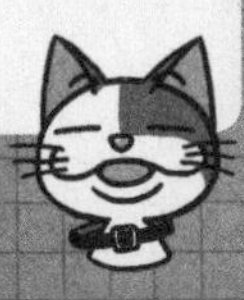

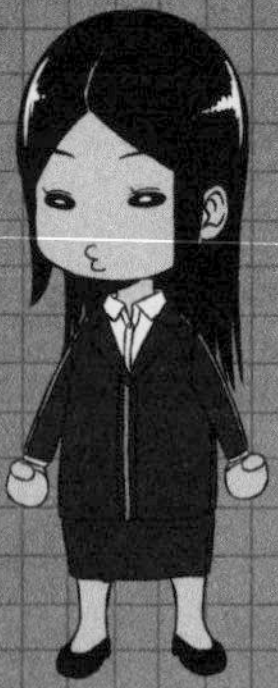

TSUKIMI

Too Good for You

She has been in the series since chapter two (voice only) and it took 70 weeks until her face was revealed. She's oblivious to cockroaches, but she hates all bugs so it doesn't matter. Women who are too good for you tend to care only for the talented train-wreck guys. She set the record by improving both Tachikawa and Miwa's performance by 20 percent through a Spartan training regimen.
Too good for your standard C-cup.

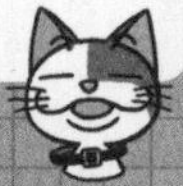

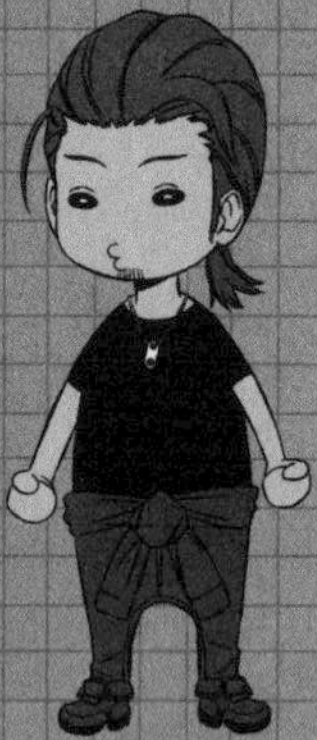

CAPTAIN FUYUSHIMA

Winter T-shirt [Techie]

Showed up only in name in chapter 25 but was smart enough to lie low and wait for 50 more chapters. With his long hair, weird inventions and squatting in combat zones—he was earning his intellectual points but ruined it all with an ugly T-shirt. He joined Border as an engineer, but was later scouted by an operator named Risa Maki. He's a 29-year-old who can't say no to a high school girl.

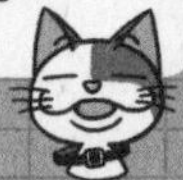

MINI REPLICAS

If You See One, There's Thirty

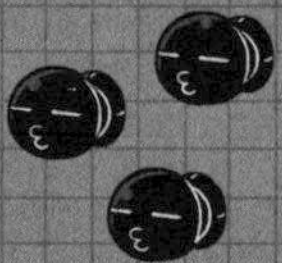

Pipsqueaks that budded off from the rice cooker. They're very handy, easy to draw, and very knowledgeable about Neighbors. Such capable characters! Replica can create as many minis as his Trion reserves can support, making him a surprise key player in the Invasion arc. Yuma's dad sure did build something super convenient. Amazing!

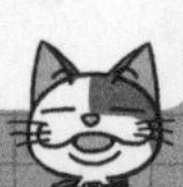

YOU'RE READING THE WRONG WAY!

World Trigger reads from right to left, starting in the upper-right corner. Japanese is read from right to left, meaning that action, sound effects, and word-balloon order are completely reversed from the English order.

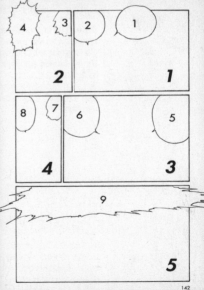